The National Disability Insurance Scheme

Mhairi Cowden · Claire McCullagh
Editors

The National Disability Insurance Scheme

An Australian Public Policy Experiment

palgrave
macmillan

Editors
Mhairi Cowden
Nous Group
Perth, WA, Australia

Claire McCullagh
Nous Group
Perth, WA, Australia

ISBN 978-981-16-2243-4 ISBN 978-981-16-2244-1 (eBook)
https://doi.org/10.1007/978-981-16-2244-1

This Palgrave Macmillan imprint is published by the registered company Springer Nature Singapore Pte Ltd.
The registered company address is: 152 Beach Road, #21-01/04 Gateway East, Singapore 189721, Singapore

This book is dedicated to people with disability in Australia, for whom the National Disability Insurance Scheme represents both hope and frustration.

Foreword—The Hon. Bill Shorten MP

There are many things Australia, a young democracy, does better than the rest of the world. Often these things go without remark as it is just not in our nature to crow about them.

The immediate aftermath of the recent US election gave me pause to consider just how superior, for instance, our electoral system is in Australia: The way we combine compulsory voting for a full account of the electorate with a truly professional and independent national counting system in the Australian Electoral Commission.

Many of the national schemes Australia does so well are hard-won creations of Labour governments. They have been brought about through vision and perseverance and only constant vigilance ensures their continued existence.

I would count among these our targeted social security system, Medicare and Superannuation.

And, of course, the National Disability Insurance Scheme.

When I became Parliamentary Secretary for Disabilities in 2007, I realised that the fundamental problem confronting people with disability, their carers and loved ones was not their impairment but a lack of money and power. I thought I'd seen disadvantage in my union life but nothing prepared me for the institutionalised, second class, life-in-exile that was the daily reality for so many Australians with disability. So my aim became to create the best scheme in the world.

German political economist Max Weber memorably described politics as 'the slow boring of hard boards'. Bringing about the NDIS required disparate disability groups to unite behind one banner. While I campaigned within Labour and within Government, a vital parallel campaign was waged by grassroots groups like Every Australian Counts. We obtained a Productivity Commission review into the possibility, need and feasibility of a national scheme which, when it reported back in 2011, was ultimately positive. Prime Minister Julia Gillard committed to it and the rest is history.

Bringing an Australian NDIS into being has been one of the abiding passions of my life and one of the most satisfying achievements as a Parliamentarian.

I am gratified to be asked to provide this Foreword and commend Mhairi Cowden and Claire McCullagh on this scholarly yet practical analysis of the NDIS. It is the first of its kind and importantly it includes voices of disability advocates and the stories of people with disability themselves.

The NDIS was founded on two philosophies. One that people with disability—one in five of us—should be treated as an equal part of our broad Australian community, and not as something separate and apart from that. And, two: that the scheme would cover any supports that were reasonable and necessary to those ends. This was broad enough that the national scheme could evolve to suit the needs of the Australian disability community as it was rolled out nationally and bedded down as part of the furniture of our civic life.

It was my hope that the rollout and evolution of the NDIS might be overseen by successive Labour governments which could adapt the scheme in real time as shortcomings and unforeseen consequences became apparent. In the effort to constantly improve the Scheme there would be no finish line.

Unfortunately, by 2013 Labour was out of power and has been since. We must count our blessings that eight years of national Coalition rule, while damaging to the NDIS, has not proved fatal to the Scheme. It is unfortunate however that the early stewardship of this social democratic scheme has been left to a succession of neo-liberal governments which are ill-suited to that purpose and strangers to the Scheme's founding vision. So as issues have arisen—whether it be the absence of a proactive watchdog to monitor and sanction provider abuse and neglect, or the closure of good programs due to a lack of funding—they have not been addressed and have been left to worsen. The Coalition's latent resentment of the cost of the NDIS has also seen billions of dollars taken out of the Scheme. The kindest description you can give the Coalition's administration of the Scheme would be "minimalist".

All this has meant our current focus must be defending the scheme when this should be a time of improvement and evolution. Future horizons include better coordination with states, better assistance for Australians with psychosocial disability and harmonising the Scheme for people over 65.

Fortunately, much of what the scheme achieves is unassailable. It has brought disability into mainstream view. It has removed the ability of political leaders to ignore disability issues or confine them to a policy ghetto. But most importantly it has moved hundreds of thousands of lives out of quiet desperation, and brought them comfort and agency.

Thirteen years ago as Parliamentary Secretary for Disability I had high hopes for the NDIS. It has delivered much. As the following pages will make clear. There is more to do. As the following pages will also make clear. But I still have those high hopes today.

Victoria, Australia
December 2020

Bill Shorten

Acknowledgements

Like most major undertakings this book would not have been possible without the help of many different people. The idea to write a book on the National Disability Insurance Scheme (NDIS) came about when we were both working at the Department of the Premier and Cabinet in Western Australia. We noticed that, apart from the Productivity Commission's original 2011 report describing the vision for the scheme, there was no text that public policy professionals or researchers could use when seeking to understand what the NDIS was all about. We somewhat naively thought that we could fill this gap.

We would like to thank Palgrave Macmillan who backed us right from the beginning, offering us the time and support we needed to complete this project. We would also like to thank the many authors—representing the best minds currently working on the NDIS—who have generously written chapters for this book. We are grateful for their excellent contributions and think you will agree that the collective force of their analysis provides a rich overview of the many facets of the NDIS.

We would also like to thank two young up and coming women who assisted with getting the book to where it is now. To Jennifer Tran who provided some of the most comprehensive literature reviews we have seen, and to Kit Muirhead who applied her excellent editing and referencing skills to the text.

Since the initial germ of an idea for this book, a lot has happened in our lives: New jobs, the arrival of a baby and a global pandemic to name some examples. These competing priorities have not always made writing a book easy, but it has been a joy working together on this joint endeavour. Finally we would like to thank each other—for making writing a book together a fun adventure and for a friendship full of challenging and pushing ourselves further.

Contents

Part II

Notes on Contributors

Jody Barney is a Birri-Gubba/Urangan woman from Queensland. After 13 years as a business owner of Deaf Indigenous Community Consultancy, Jody now works primarily as a consultant and trainer in Indigenous affairs. Jody contribution to the sector includes numerous board appointments, chairing an all Indigenous-led sub fund Koondee Woonga-gat Toor-tong in Victoria, as well as national representation on the Disability Royal Commission First Nations Strategic Advisory Group and Women with Disability Australia. Jody is also the first Deaf Atlantic Fellow for Atlantic Fellow for Social Equity Australia and the first Deaf Aboriginal woman to receive international invitation representing the needs of Deaf Aboriginal woman and girls at the Deaf Native Gatherings global.

Professor Christine Bigby is the Director of the Living with Disability Research Centre, La Trobe University. She is well known nationally and internationally for her research on the social inclusion of adults with intellectual disability. The primary focus of her work is on policy issues, program effectiveness and frontline practice that supports quality of life outcomes for people with intellectual disability.

Associate Professor Dr. Gemma Carey is the Research Director at the Centre for Social Impact, UNSW. She is a public policy and health researcher and has been examining the implementation of the NDIS since 2014.

Dr. Mhairi Cowden is a public policy professional and social policy researcher. Dr. Cowden has worked for the Department of the Premier and Cabinet in Western Australia advising on community services issues including the transition to the NDIS. She is currently a Director at Nous Group, a management consulting firm. Her previous publications include 'Children's Rights: From Philosophy to Public Policy' published with Palgrave MacMillan. She holds a PhD from the Australian National University examining the philosophy and public policy implications of children's rights.

Dr. Ash Evans is an actuary and Principal at Taylor Fry, an analytics and actuarial consulting firm. He provides advice to government departments and organisations across Australia in the fields of disability, health and accident compensation. Ash provided actuarial advice to the Western Australian NDIS, which joined the nationally delivered NDIS in April 2018.

Alan Greenfield is an actuary and co-founder of Taylor Fry, an analytics and actuarial consulting firm. He has over 30 years' experience and was the Scheme Actuary to the Western Australian NDIS, which joined the nationally delivered NDIS in April 2018. In 2015, he was awarded Actuary of the Year by the Actuaries Institute for his contribution in developing the investment approach to public policymaking.

Dr. David Henderson is a Research Fellow at the Living with Disability Research Centre, La Trobe University. He is a historian whose interests include oral history and the history of intellectual disability in modern Australia.

Samantha Jenkinson is a long-term advocate for disability rights with numerous roles throughout her career in community grassroots organisations, government departments and with national organisations. Through the campaign and formation of the NDIS, Samantha has represented people with disability on campaign steering groups, expert policy groups, and state and national advisory groups. Samantha is a social worker and person with a disability. She was Executive Director of People with Disabilities WA from 2014 to 2020.

Penny Knight is Managing Director of BaxterLawley, an Australia management advisory service and a Senior Research Fellow at the University of Western Australia. She is also Director of Not-for-Profit organisations caring for people with disabilities and the elderly. She has over 25 years experience in improving organisation performance using evidenced-based strategy.

Eleanor Malbon is a Research Director at the Centre for Social Impact, UNSW. She is a public policy researcher and her MPhil focuses on the implementation of the NDIS.

Claire McCullagh is a consultant and public policy professional. She is currently a Director at Nous Group—a management consulting firm—where she specialises in public policy, strategy and organisational performance. Prior to this, she worked as a public servant for the Western Australian Government including policy roles at the Department of the Premier and Cabinet, the Mental Health Commission and the Disability Services Commission. She holds a Master of Public Policy from the University of Oxford, and a Bachelor of Arts (Honours) majoring in Philosophy from the University of Western Australia.

Dr. Sue Olney is a Research Fellow (Public Policy) in the Melbourne Disability Institute and an Honorary Senior Fellow in the Melbourne School of Government at the University of Melbourne, and a Visiting Fellow in the Public Service Research Group at UNSW Canberra. She is on the editorial board of the Australian Journal of Public Administration and is co-director of the social policy discussion platform Power to Persuade.

Dr. Geoffrey Smith is a Consultant Psychiatrist, has extensive experience both as a clinician and senior executive in the WA health system, including Director of Mental Health Services, Chief Medical Adviser in Strategic Planning and Evaluation and Medical Director of the Western Australian Centre for Mental Health Policy Research. He is currently Senior Psychiatrist, Research and Strategy with the Western Australian Office of the Chief Psychiatrist and Clinical Associate Professor in the School of Psychiatry and Clinical Neurosciences at the University of Western Australia.

Ian Thompson has 25 years of experience in Australian health care and human services at Commonwealth and State and Territory Government levels and as a consultant. His expertise spans operational management of hospital, community health and mental health services through to participation in national health reform and strategic policy development and management of national health programs. As Deputy Director General of ACT Health, he managed Canberra Hospital and the associated community and mental health services.

Jennifer Tran is a management consultant with experience in the education, health and human services sectors. Her projects have had a strong focus on improving outcomes for children and young people across Western Australia. She has a Bachelor of Arts in Political Science, International Relations and Business Law from the University of Western Australia.

Dr. Ilan Wiesel is a senior lecturer at the School of Geography, University of Melbourne. His research is focused on social and economic inequalities in cities, with a particular interest in the social inclusion and exclusion of people with intellectual disability.

Adjunct Associate Professor Theresa Williams is a Clinical Psychologist with extensive experience as a senior executive in policy and planning within WA Health. She was inaugural Director of the WA Centre for Mental Health Policy Research and is currently the Director of Research and Strategy, Western Australian Office of the Chief Psychiatrist and Adjunct Associate Professor at the University of Western Australia.

Sarah Wood is a former public servant working to ensure to ensure the actuarial and analytics advice provided by consulting firm Taylor Fry is clearly communicated and policy relevant. Prior to joining Taylor Fry, she held policy roles at the New Zealand Treasury and Ministry of Justice. She has a Bachelor of Arts in Economics.

List of Figures

List of Tables

Part I

CHAPTER 1

Introduction

Mhairi Cowden and Claire McCullagh

Consider what you did today in order to be here reading this book. Maybe your day started with getting out of bed, making yourself a coffee and getting dressed. Maybe you took care of a few jobs around the house, then got on a bus or train to go to work. Or maybe you drove yourself to a café, library or the park. Perhaps you went to the gym, or the shops or the movies. Or took your kids to school. Or went on a date. Or caught up with a friend. A complicated mix of people, infrastructure, services and supports worked together to make this day happen for you, but perhaps you didn't think too much about them—they just happened.

Maybe you had a different kind of normal day. Your morning might have involved assistance to get out of bed, wash and dress. Leaving the house could have required planning and negotiating with several service providers. Maybe you went to work, school, the shops, the movies or the park, with support in the form of assistive technology. Perhaps you also drew on family, friends, trusted carers and strangers to support you throughout the day. Like everyone else, your day is also made possible by a mix of services and supports working together, but making them work

M. Cowden (✉) · C. McCullagh
Nous Group, Perth, WA, Australia

M. Cowden and C. McCullagh (eds.), *The National Disability Insurance Scheme*, https://doi.org/10.1007/978-981-16-2244-1_1

for you has often involved extra cost, time and, in some cases, hassle and frustration for you, your family and carers.

While this second kind of day is often hidden from mainstream narratives, it will be familiar to many of the 1 in 5 people living with disability in Australia. According to the Australian Institute of Health and Welfare (AIHW), disability is best understood as a continuum from having no impairment or limitation to the complete loss of functioning or ability to complete a task. Disability can be the result of genetic disorders, illnesses, accidents, ageing or a combination of these factors (AIHW 2019).

Everyday structural and financial barriers have prevented many people with disability from enjoying routine and active participation in their communities. Participation has historically been a costly exercise, with people often given little choice over what support they get, when it arrives and who provides it. Government or not-for-profit funding has often been available, but has come with a contract, an expiry date or a long list of prerequisites and conditions. Communities have come a long way in their social attitude to disability, but many still view disability as a terrible personal affliction: something to be 'fixed', rather than the product of a society designed with a very narrow view of what a 'normal' life looks like. For some people with disability, as well as their families and carers, these extra barriers have made everyday life a constant battle: a painful and distressing experience, which is unreasonably and prohibitively expensive. For most, the risk and cost associated with significant disability is not something that can be adequately prepared for (Productivity Commission 2011, 1–2).

In 2009, hundreds of voices from across Australia contributed to consultations as part of development of a National Disability Strategy. This strategy was the first time that all governments in Australia committed to a national approach to improving the lives of people with disability, their families and carers. A consistent message heard throughout consultations was that people with disability simply want the same opportunities as everyone else. One contributor wrote: "ideally, we want to live in a dignified and simplified society where we have the confidence and self-esteem to speak our mind and have the opportunities that everyone has" (Commonwealth of Australia 2009, iv). Another wrote: "we can put men on the moon, we can go to war but we cannot fulfil basic needs enabling our disabled community to live with human dignity" (Commonwealth of Australia 2009, 21). Many contributors spoke of a constant struggle to obtain what the rest of the community would consider to be an ordinary life. They did not want special treatment—they just want the barriers removed so they could get on with living (Commonwealth of Australia, iv).

Introducing the National Disability Insurance Scheme

The National Disability Insurance Scheme (known commonly as the NDIS) was introduced as a radical new way of funding disability services in Australia. It commenced on 1 July 2013 through launch (later known as trial) sites in specific geographic areas, with transition to a full scheme beginning in 2016. The NDIS responded to a disability support system described by the Productivity Commission as "underfunded, unfair, fragmented, and inefficient" (2011, 1–2); and by former Australian Prime Minister the Hon. Julia Gillard MP as "…a system that reacts to crisis. A system that metes out support rationed by arbitrary budget allocations, not real human needs" (Gillard 2012).

Rather than introducing incremental improvements, the NDIS would roll back and almost entirely replace the previous disability support system provided under the former National Disability Agreement. The vision for the NDIS was that it would fundamentally change the way that disability services are funded in Australia. It was intended to address the inadequacy and inequity of Australia's disability system, giving people with disability opportunities to the same choice, control and certainty that many other Australians enjoy. Challenging traditional views of paternalism, the NDIS had ambitions to radically transform the way disability services were provided by enshrining in legislation the right of the individual with disability to choose and govern their lives and the services they receive. This would represent a structural shift in power, providing participants with a degree of control over their funding that many would never have experienced before.

At the time of its introduction, it was estimated that the NDIS would cost an additional $6.5 billion per year—more than double the funding previously provided for disability services in Australia. It was predicted that many participants in the scheme would receive substantially more government funding for their disability supports, with many receiving funded support for the first time (Productivity Commission 2011, 1–3).

The sheer scale and ambition of the NDIS should be pause for thought. It is a rare moment in politics and policymaking that an idea as revolutionary, ambitious and expensive as the NDIS makes it into its implementation phase. This is particularly astonishing for an initiative that makes explicit, as part of its aims, moving funding control away from the government and into the hands of people with disability, their families and carers. Not surprising, then, that the NDIS has been described by many as the biggest social shift in Australia since Medicare.

At the time of writing, the NDIS had just finished a rapid period of transition to become operational in all geographic regions of Australia. The world is also in the midst of an unprecedented COVID-19 global pandemic, which has left many people with disability, especially vulnerable, and others with a new appreciation of what it feels like to be locked inside and shut out of their own communities.

It is therefore timely to pause and reflect upon the ambition and goals of the NDIS, and the negotiations and compromises struck to make its introduction possible. Lessons learned from early days of the scheme have the potential to change the way other social services are delivered in Australia. Reflections may also offer some insight for the introduction of similar schemes internationally, as countries across the world look for ways to improve social and economic opportunities for people with disability and their families.

What Is This Book About?

While the NDIS has been the subject of wide publication in both academic and grey literature, most writing about the scheme has been so far narrow in scope and addressed only specific aspects of the scheme, such as its legal implications, financial risks or its relevance to service providers. Nowhere has there yet been a comprehensive summary and analysis of the scheme through both a scholarly and a practical public policy lens.

This book will be a key text for scholars and public policy professionals wishing to understand exactly what the NDIS was intended to achieve, how it was designed, and lessons learned through its introduction and roll-out. The book will also consider how the NDIS has intersected with particular cohorts and sectors, and some of the challenges that have arisen in its roll-out across Australia so far. It also includes a collection of personal stories from participants and families in the NDIS, to provide readers with an understanding of how the scheme is playing out for people in practice. The book will identify key insights for moral philosophy, public policy and social services and consider the future of the scheme and the implications of lessons learned for social policy reforms elsewhere in Australia, or internationally.

This book is written in three parts. **Part I** comprises chapters (including this introduction) that together provide a general overview of the history and design of the NDIS. We do not attempt to describe the scheme as it has been interpreted across the various policies, procedures and operating guidelines that have been introduced by the National Disability Insurance Agency (NDIA) since commencement of the scheme, as the rapidly evolving nature of these documents would render such analysis quickly outdated. Instead, we cover the history, aims, design principles and philosophy of the scheme as it was first laid out by the Productivity Commission, and the major practical considerations and changes that have happened as part of the scheme's introduction from 2013.

Chapter 2 examines the history of disability services in Australia. It tracks how perceptions of disability have changed across time, and describes key historic influences on Australia's disability system in the lead up to the NDIS. Chapter 2 focuses particularly on disability rights, the personalisation of social services and the rise of accident compensation schemes in Australia and New Zealand in the years leading up to the NDIS. It also considers how these historical influences have together shaped the design of the NDIS.

Each state and territory began the NDIS journey from different starting points. Chapter 3 presents an overview of the service landscape prior to the roll out of the NDIS. It outlines the prevalence of disability in Australia, the different service delivery histories and evidence regarding outcomes for people with disability. This information provides important scene setting to the enormity of the challenge in rolling out the NDIS to achieve the goal of equality of access set out by the original scheme design.

In Chapter 4, we seek to describe what the NDIS actually is, covering its original design as articulated by the Productivity Commission in its 2011 Report entitled Disability Care and Support. This chapter also comments on how the scheme changed when it was put into practice by highlighting variations between the Commission's original blueprint for the NDIS what was written into its legislation and agreements around the NDIS launch date.

Chapter 5 provides an overview of the initial phase of the NDIS roll out—known as the launch or trial phase. It summarises the different approaches to trialling the NDIS that were taken for each state and territory, and the initial lessons from the NDIS trial evaluations and reports. This period is characterised by continual negotiations between the Commonwealth Government and State and Territory Governments, a fast pace of roll out and variable outcomes experienced by NDIS participants.[1]

Chapter 6 outlines the various agreements that were reached with each between the Commonwealth and each State and Territory Government for transition, and discusses a selection of transition challenges and lessons learned.

Chapter 7 will close out Part I of the book by examining the philosophical principles relating to theories of rights that have guided the design and implementation of the NDIS.

Part II of the book will examine how the NDIS has interacted with specific cohorts and sectors so far. It presents a selection of commentaries and arguments about the scheme from authors who are experts in their fields as both academics and practitioners. Authors have been asked to explain how the NDIS has been introduced in relation to a particular cohort or sector, and draw out lessons learned so far from the introduction and roll out of the scheme.

In Chapter 8, Gemma Carey and Eleanor Malbon reflect on the collective challenges of implementing the NDIS to date. They examine the interplay of politics and implementation, along with 'path dependency', whereby new policies fall into old traps and legacies of former initiatives. Carey and Malbon argue that dismantling old systems has been a major barrier to implementation of the scheme, and an interrelated challenge has been balancing short-term, often politically driven, goals and the longer-term vision of the scheme. Their chapter explores how these tensions have played out during the implementation of the NDIS and their implications for the future of the scheme.

In Chapter 9, Theresa Williams and Geoff Smith argue that the late additional of mental health to the NDIS has contributed to an ongoing debate about whether and how to make the NDIS work for people with disability arising from mental illness (psychosocial disability). Their chapter draws suggestions from the mental health sector about how

[1] We use 'Commonwealth Government' to refer to the legal entity that is the national government of Australia, established by the Constitution.

the NDIS could be made more suitable and effective for people with psychosocial disability.

In Chapter 10, Ian Thompson discusses the potential benefits and challenges associated with the NDIS and the health care systems to date. Drawing on academic literature and 25 years experience in operational management of hospital and community health services, Thompson argues that long-standing tensions between the cultures of the health and disability sectors have proved challenging for implementation. He contends that a lack of attention to these existing interface challenges and how to overcome them has been a key shortcoming in the NDIS roll out.

The housing needs of NDIS participants, and the adequacy of provisions both within the scheme and beyond it in meeting these needs, are in Chapter 11. In this chapter, Ilan Weisel argues that the success of the NDIS in fulfilling its principles relating to the rights of people with disability depends on the adequacy of participants' housing. Yet, housing options for people with disability in both the private market and the social housing system are extremely constrained, and the NDIS itself was not designed to address the housing needs of most of its participants. Weisel therefore recommends that it is time to review and expand the housing responsibilities of the NDIS beyond the funding of Specialist Disability Accommodation (SDA).

Chapter 12, written by Mhairi Cowden, considers the treatment of children by and within the NDIS. In this chapter, Cowden argues that the NDIS's emphasis on choice and control rights assumes a level of capacity that many young children do not yet possess, and that there is a need for greater guidance about the exercise of choice and control by parents and guardians of children with disability.

In Chapter 13, Jody Barney examines the experiences of Indigenous people in the NDIS, many of whom live in regional and remote areas of Australia where there are limited services. Her chapter describes some of the stories of when things have, and have not, worked well for Indigenous people accessing the NDIS.

In Chapter 14, Christine Bigby argues that a more nuanced understanding of people with severe and profound intellectual disability and what the exercise of the right for choice and control looks like for them is integral if the NDIS is to properly accommodate them in the scheme.

In Chapter 15, Sue Olney examines a key aspect of the original NDIS Productivity Commission design—employment for people with disability—and discusses the challenges in realising this aspect of the scheme.

Chapter 16 spends time explaining and exploring an aspect of the scheme that many know little about: the role of actuaries in forecasting scheme costs and guiding the build of NDIS individual packages. In this chapter, Alan Greenfield, Ash Evans and Sarah Wood draw on actuarial experience to explain how actuarial insights can strengthen the operation of the NDIS.

In Chapter 17, Penny Knight describes the critical role of not-for-profits in delivery of the NDIS. She challenges four key assumptions argued to have underpinned the scheme design: that the NDIS operates like a market, that not-for-profits are inefficient, that human need can be defined as a package of transactions and that the NDIS is or can be the whole system for people with disability. Knight argues for more focus on understanding the whole person, their family and community, providing the best information and keeping the pressure on government entities as a way forward.

In Chapter 18, Samantha Jenkinson looks at the campaign, development and ongoing improvement of the NDIS from the perspective of people with disability and advocates with disability. She argues that the NDIS has the promise of a fundamental power shift in the way disability support is done, but will take conscious work to keep the shift moving in the right direction, from those within the scheme as decision-makers, and those advocating. Jenkinson concludes that advocacy and peer-led organisations will be critical to continuous feedback and improvement of the NDIS at policy and practice levels.

Part III of this book includes a collection of personal stories from people with disability who have accessed NDIS services. Bigby and Henderson have collated personal stories of people with severe and profound intellectual disability. Jenkinson has provided editorial assistance for a further five personal stories representing different disabilities, experiences and all told in their own words.

The final chapter of this book, written by Cowden and McCullagh, draws together insights from Parts I, II and III. It includes a discussion about the key challenges for the NDIS and finishes with a reflection on the opportunities and hope for the NDIS in future.

How to Read This Book

There are many ways to introduce you to the NDIS and there are many aspects of this complex scheme. One way to read this book is from cover to cover. If you do this you will (hopefully) come away with an understanding of the scheme from its origins, theoretical concepts, policy design and current operation. You may, however, be more interested in one aspect of the scheme than another. In this case, the book has been designed for you to dip in and out, with each chapter written as a standalone piece.

The most important chapter for many will be Chapter 4: What Is the NDIS? In this chapter, we attempt to systematically take you through the design of the scheme, its component parts and how it is intended to work. Reading this chapter will give you a basic understanding of the NDIS, with more detail about the scheme's design and component parts are pulled apart, analysed and expanded upon in subsequent chapters.

As much as we have attempted to capture the key aspects of the scheme, there will inevitably be nuances, issues and areas which we have not been able to address. We hope to be able to build on what we have created here through future editions of this book. The NDIS is growing and evolving. This public policy experiment is far from over, and the story of the NDIS is only in its infancy. We hope this book begins to capture the ambition and hope that the NDIS represents to many Australians.

References

Australian Institute of Health and Welfare. 2019. Disability. https://www.aihw.gov.au/reports-data/health-conditions-disability-deaths/disability.

Commonwealth of Australia. 2009. Shut Out: The Experience of People with Disabilities and Their Families in Australia. Department of Social Services. https://www.dss.gov.au/sites/default/files/documents/05_2012/nds_report.pdf.

Gillard, J. 2012. House of Representatives: National Disability Insurance Scheme Bill 2012, Second Reading Speech. PM Transcripts: Transcripts from the Prime Ministers of Australia. https://pmtranscripts.pmc.gov.au/release/transcript-18932.

Productivity Commission. 2011. Disability Care and Support: Productivity Commission Inquiry Report, Overview and Recommendations. Canberra: Commonwealth of Australia. https://www.pc.gov.au/inquiries/completed/disability-support/report/disability-support-overview-booklet.pdf.

CHAPTER 2

The History of Disability Services in Australia

Mhairi Cowden and Claire McCullagh

Introduction

Throughout history, people with disability have been treated differently to the rest of society. Before the twenty-first century, they were routinely dehumanised, institutionalised and often subjected to prison-like conditions away from the public gaze. People with disability have been stereotyped and systematically marginalised from debates about policy direction across a wide range of areas relevant to their lives.

The way disability services are provided in Australia today has clearly changed a lot over the past century. While some people with disability still live in institutions, the disability rights movement has fundamentally changed the way disability is conceptualised, leading to a shift in perceived collective obligations towards those who have disability.

Yet the decline of institutions is just the beginning of a long history of influential reforms and persistent challenges which have paved the way to the National Disability Insurance Scheme (NDIS). Before the NDIS, many people with disability found themselves excluded from society: shut out from buildings, homes, schools, businesses and socially (Commonwealth 2009a, vi). Support for people with disability varied significantly

M. Cowden (✉) · C. McCullagh
Nous Group, Perth, WA, Australia

M. Cowden and C. McCullagh (eds.), *The National Disability Insurance Scheme*, https://doi.org/10.1007/978-981-16-2244-1_2

across Australia, depending on the nature of the disability, how it was obtained and the postcode of the affected individual. Dominant narratives still conceptualised disability as a personal tragedy, requiring cure or care by allied health professionals, arguably privileging the voices of professionals to exercise paternalistic power in making decisions about the lives of people with disability (Thill 2014, 4–5) and reinforcing an enduring paradigm that people with disability are routinely 'spoken about, rather than listened to as experts' (Newell 2006, 280). Responding to these critiques and listening to the voices and experiences of people with disability has been a key call to action for the NDIS.

This chapter examines the history of disability services in Australia. It charts how perceptions of disability have changed across time, and how services for people with disability have changed with them. It describes a number of key historic influences on Australia's disability system in the lead up to the NDIS, including the disability rights movement—which sought to challenge traditional perceptions of people with disability and re-design society as an inclusive place for everyone—the personalisation of social services, and the rise of accident compensation schemes in Australia and New Zealand in the years leading up to the NDIS. It considers how these historical influences have together shaped the design of the NDIS.

The Historic Institutionalisation of People with Disability

The institutionalisation of people with disability was a common practice in Australia throughout the nineteenth and early twentieth century. Large institutions housing sometimes hundreds of people with different types of disability were common in most states, supported by government funding, charitable donations and private contributions from family members. This included establishments with names like the Destitute Asylum, founded in 1856 in Adelaide for those unable to work due to age, infirmity or disability; the "Idiot Ward" in Melbourne, established in 1887 as an attachment to the Key Asylum; and the Fremantle Lunatic Asylum and Invalid Depot, opened in 1865 as the permanent home for many Western Australians with mental illness and intellectual disability.

Institutions frequently operated as prison-like environments. It was common for inhabitants (sometimes referred to as "inmates") to be almost completely segregated from the general population, with limited freedom to move around and almost no contact with their families.

Inmates at the South Australian (SA) Destitute Asylum, for example, were required to wear a uniform, to rise, eat and retire at set times, and to remain on the premises for all but one afternoon a week. For children living at the Asylum, parents could visit for just two hours a month (Geyer 2014).

Confining people with disability to institutions was at the time considered the best way to protect them from themselves and to safeguard society. There were fears that if allowed to mingle with the general public, people with disability, especially intellectual disability, would descend into lives of 'vagrancy, crime and drunkenness' (Hayes and Hayes 1982, 143). Incarceration was therefore seen as a way to protect people with disability as well as to 'safeguard the future of humans' (Hayes and Hayes 1982, 143).

Prior to Australia's federation in 1901, almost all support for people with disability came from an individual's family or from donations from churches and charities. State and local governments played a very small role, predominantly by operating or funding disability institutions like the 'Destitute Asylum'. The notion that people with disability were entitled to funding or support did not yet exist; they were viewed as objects of pity, dependent on the goodwill and charity of others and unable to control or make decisions about how to live their own lives. Regardless of what the individual wanted, they were to be kept separate from society in the interests of themselves and society as a whole.

Federation and the Australian Welfare State

The turn of the century saw the role of government in disability services increase across Australia. Shortly after federation, Australia took steps to establish itself as a welfare state by becoming one of the first countries in the world to introduce a nationwide government-funded income support system for social protection. The newly formed Commonwealth Government of Australia became involved in providing disability support for the first time with the introduction of the Invalid Pension (known today as the Disability Support Pension) in 1908. The Pension did not replace existing state, territory and local government-funded services such as disability institutions, but instead operated alongside these (Dixon and Hyde 2000).

Both First and Second World Wars led to a rapid increase in the number of people with disability in Australia. To cope with increasing demand for support, the Commonwealth Government began to consider alternative forms of care to asylums and institutions. The Commonwealth Rehabilitation Service (CRS) was established in 1941 as the first government-funded rehabilitation program in Australia. This happened as part of a broader increase in government-funded welfare across the nation that saw the introduction of a child endowment in 1941, a widows' pension in 1942, a wife's allowance in 1943 and unemployment, sickness and special benefits in 1945.

Another important shift during this time was the expansion of the role of volunteer and charity organisations. Following the First and Second World Wars, there was significant expansion of the number of sheltered workshops and accommodation services run by volunteer and charity organisations across Australia (Australian Human Rights Commission 2016). There was also a rapid increase in the formation of associations of, and for, people with disability, often set up with and by people with disability and their families, independent or only partly reliant upon government contributions. These organisations tended to focus on improving quality of living for select groups of individuals, as well as searching for medical "cures" and rehabilitation opportunities (Hurst 2003, 572). This included the establishment of the Western Australian (WA) and New South Wales (NSW) Civilian Maimed and Limbless Associations in 1949 and 1954 (Lever 1985, 10); the NSW and Victorian Paraplegic and Quadriplegic Associations in 1961 and 1962 respectively; and the Australian Quadriplegics Association of NSW in 1967 (Jones 1992, 2).

With additional government and organisational supports available, more and more people with disability were able to live outside of institutional settings. However, their experience was far from an integrated and liberated one. Separate schools, transportation and infrastructure were still default practice. While now more often physically located within communities, people with disability still found themselves frequently excluded from many mainstream services and social circles, and limited in the choices they could make about how to live their lives.

The International Disability Rights Movement

Through the 1950s and 1960s, Australia's Commonwealth and State Governments increasingly provided funding through disability organisations for accommodation, employment and other support services.

However, the real shift in the way disability services were provided in Australia came as part of the international disability rights movement.

Disability activism as a broader social movement gained momentum during the mid-twentieth century. In the UK, people with disability (some of whom still lived inside of institutions) came together to define disability on their own terms, from their direct experiences. They began to conceptualise their experiences of institutionalisation, segregation and disposition as being a problem for society, not just for them as individuals (Hurst 2003, 573). Separate transport and schools for people with disability were viewed as a symbol of 'otherness' from society and the rest of humanity (Hurst 2003, 573).

In the USA, groups of people with disability came together to fight for their right to live independently and make choices about their lives. They demanded more accessible educational institutions and public infrastructure, arguing from the view that people with physical disability deserved access to the whole world, not just some parts of it (Fleischer and Zames 2011, 33–48). This independent living movement in the USA took the experience of the black and women's civil rights movements as similar examples, advocating that individuals with disability had the same right to exercise control over their lives as everyone else, and demanding that governments and public institutions bear some of the responsibility for ensuring these rights were upheld (Hurst 2003, 572).

While many of the disability advocacy groups fighting for disability rights during this time operated in isolation until the late 1970s, they shared a common commitment to universal freedoms and rights for people with disability. These groups departed from the view that disability was merely a personal affliction, to be treated or cured. They understood 'disability' as the outcome of environmental barriers, put in place by a society which unwittingly excluded individuals with disability by organising itself only with those without disability in mind. This represented a departure from the so-called medical model of disability, which considered 'disability' as a health condition and an "abnormality" to be dealt with by medical professionals, and began to establish a social model of disability as an interaction between people living with impairments and an environment filled with physical, attitudinal, communication and social barriers which (sometimes without meaning to) discriminated unfairly against them (Hurst 2003, 573). This shift carried with it the implication that it is the environment and social attitudes that should change, not individuals with disability.

Another significant step came with the United Nations proclamation of 1981 as the 'International Year of Disabled Persons'. In that year, people with disability and advocates from across the world came together with the United Nations General Assembly (UNGA) to produce the World Programme of Action Concerning Disabled Persons. This Programme asserted the equal rights for people with mental, physical or sensory impairments. The Programme was accepted by all UNGA member states (Hurst 2003, 573), setting the stage for action across the world to better uphold equal rights and opportunities for people with disability. To implement the World Program of Action Concerning Disabled Persons the United Nations proclaimed a Decade of Disabled Persons that ran from 1983 to 1992. Among the major outcomes of the Decade of Disabled Persons was the adoption in 1993, by the General Assembly, of the Standard Rules on the Equalisation of Opportunities for Persons with Disabilities.

From the 1970s through to the 1990s, Australia introduced a range of initiatives to more actively recognise and support equal rights and opportunities of people with disability. In 1974, the Commonwealth established the *Handicapped Persons Assistance Act*, which provided funding for a limited range of service types to support those with disability. In 1986, it introduced the *Disability Services Act*, which provided a much more comprehensive framework for the funding and provision of disability support services across Australia. In 1991, it announced the Disability Reform Package, changing income support payments to encourage better workforce integration of people with disability. In 1991, the first Commonwealth State Disability Agreement was signed, to reduce the amount of duplication and complexity in disability funding and service arrangements. The agreement gave the Commonwealth responsibility for income support and employment services, and the states and territories responsibility for accommodation and other support services. In 1992, the *Disability Discrimination Act* was introduced, which aimed to eliminate discrimination against people with disability; ensure equality before the law and promote acceptance of the fundamental rights of people with disability.

In 2007, the United Nations adopted and opened for signature the Convention on the Rights of Persons with Disabilities (UN CRPD). The UN CRPD, ratified by Australia in 2008, took to a new level the movement away from viewing persons with disability as "objects" of charity, medical treatment and social protectionism, towards viewing persons with disability as "subjects" with rights, who are capable of making decisions about their own lives based on their free and informed consent as well as being active members of society. It specifically called on state parties to ensure persons with disability have access to social and economic goods on an equal basis to the rest of society, including the right to live independently, to be included in the community, and access to the community support services necessary for living, inclusion and the prevention of isolation from the community (UNGA, 2007).

The Personalisation of Social Services

Personalisation has been a key driver of historic changes to Australia's disability system in recent years and has shaped the design of the NDIS. In its widest sense, personalisation—or self-directed care—is where an individual is directly involved in the delivery of the services they have chosen (Williams and Dickinson 2015, 151). There is a spectrum of personalisation. On the 'shallow' end personalisation is just a user-friendly interface with existing services, on the 'deep' end individuals can directly commission, co-design and co-produce services (Leadbeater 2004).

Self-directed care is now closely associated with providing individual budgets to people for their care (known as individualised funding). For example, individual budgets emerged in the health system in the UK in the 1990s, with the introduction of individual budgets for adults with disability receiving direct payment entitlements (Williams and Dickinson 2015, 150). Under this arrangement, direct payments could be used to contract private or not-for-profit agencies to provide services or to directly hire staff. They could not be used to purchase public sector services (Oliver and Sapey 1999, 175).

In Australia, personalisation and individual budgets have emerged across the health and human services sector. Throughout the 1980s and 1990s, small-scale personalisation and self-directed funding projects for people with disability were set up in multiple states (Gadsby 2013, 11). In 2010, the Commonwealth Government introduced consumer directed care for older people, with the intention of promoting greater choice and control, and more flexible and responsive services in the aged care system. There are also examples of individualised budgets and personalised care in the community mental health sector, such as WA's Individualised Community Living Strategy (ICLS) Program, which was established in

2011 to provide community-based support for those on their mental health recovery journey.

By introducing self-directed care and individual budgets, it has been argued that personalisation has been partly driven by a desire to achieve inclusion and uphold human rights (Dickinson and Williams 2015). Personalisation has also been positioned as a radical, user-led programme of reform (Glasby and Littlechild 2009) and as part of a suite of initiatives with the potential to 'turn the welfare state upside down' (Glasby et al. 2013, 3). The personalisation of social service funding and market-based provision has also been identified as trends closely linked to a move away from collective social welfare provision in favour of markets, where the individual can purchase components of their care (Carey et al. 2018, 2).

The principles of individual rights and empowerment and fiscal management may sit in tension with each other (Needham and Glasby 2015). As such, some have argued that personalisation is simply an extension of the New Public Management philosophy designed to increase market reach and force individual responsibility. Others say it has become symbolic of a neo-liberal agenda to dismantle the welfare state and has potential to lessen government responsibility for providing welfare support (Ferguson 2007, 401; Williams and Dickinson 2015). This tension is between the benefits of tailored service provision to the individual and empowering people in the services they receive and on the other hand the perceived benefits of governments playing a strong role in decisions about individual welfare and public trust in institutions. Williams and Dickinson (2016, 150) ask whether 'strengthening the personal inevitably weakens the social, and if so, if this is a price worth paying in the quest for more effective welfare arrangements'.

Accident Compensation Schemes in Australia

The history of Australia's disability support system requires consideration of the various accident compensation schemes that have existed since the beginning of the twentieth century. These schemes have long been a source of funding and support to people who acquire disability as the result of accidental injury. Major reforms to the way these schemes operated across Australia and New Zealand have also fundamentally shaped Australia's disability sector and have been critical influences in the design of the NDIS.

Workplace and Motor Vehicle Accident Compensation

Workplace injury insurance schemes were first introduced in Australia as statutory schemes (i.e. written into legislation) at the start of the twentieth century. Prior to this, injured workers could only claim compensation in the form of civil damages by suing their employer through the courts, typically by claiming employer negligence. Workers rarely succeeded in winning compensation in this way due to what has been called the 'unholy trinity' of legal defences available to employers, who could argue that an employee's injury was due in some part to their own negligence (contributory negligence); was caused by the negligence of a fellow employee (common employment); or that the employee was assumed to have known the risk implied in his or her job (voluntary assumption of risk) (Fleming 1987; Haller 1988).

The introduction of workplace injury legislation in Australia in the early 1900s saw states begin to treat work injuries as an inevitable cost of running a business. This new legislation typically stood alongside existing common law arrangements (e.g. for cases involving negligence) prescribing the amounts of compensation that employers should pay if an employee suffered an injury arising out of and in the course of employment. Statutes were typically based on 'no-fault' principles, meaning that employer fault did not have to be established for compensation to be awarded, provided employees could prove that their injuries were work-related. The first state to introduce workers' compensation legislation was SA in 1900, followed by WA in 1902, Queensland in 1905, Tasmania in 1910, Victoria in 1914, the Northern Territory (NT) in 1920, NSW in 1926 and the Australian Capital Territory (ACT) in 1951. The Commonwealth's first *Officers' Compensation Act* was also passed in 1908, covering certain Commonwealth Government employees, and the *Seamen's Compensation Act* was passed in 1911 (Industry Commission 1994, F3).

While initially limited in their coverage, these early workers' compensation schemes were broadened over the years through a combination of legislative change, judicial interpretation and administrative decisions to include injuries 'arising out of *or* in the course of employment', rather than merely injury 'arising out of *and* in the course of employment'. Benefits became more substantial and were offered for longer periods of time, and purchase of insurance by employers over time became compulsory in most jurisdictions (Industry Commission 1994, F3).

In the 1930s and 1940s, Australian jurisdictions also began introducing Compulsory Third Party (CTP) insurance as a requirement to legally operate a motor vehicle. Before this, getting compensation for a motor accident injury was only possible through the common law system, but was difficult as many vehicle operators could not afford, or would be left destitute by paying, the compensation they owed (Minogue 1978, 8). These problems provided motivation for governments to require vehicle owners and operators to purchase personal injury insurance against third party liability for damages and establish legislative frameworks specifying motor vehicle compensation eligibility and benefit entitlements. The first Australian jurisdiction to introduce CTP insurance legislation was Tasmania in 1935, followed by SA and Queensland in 1936; Victoria in 1939 (commencing 1941), NSW in 1942, WA in 1943, ACT in 1948 and the NT in 1949. These schemes were initially established as common law schemes, with court judgements made by a judge, not a jury (except in Victoria and NSW) (Fronsko and Woodroffe 2017, 3).

Up until the 1970s, both workers compensation and CTP insurance schemes were mostly privately underwritten and managed.[1] This meant that, rather than a government statutory authority being the sole provider of insurance, private companies could be responsible for setting prices, banking premiums and paying and managing claims. In some jurisdictions, State Government Insurance Offices operated in competition with private insurers.

The Woodhouse Reports (1967 and 1974)

The 1970s saw sweeping changes to Australia's accident insurance schemes. Existing schemes faced criticisms for being costly and inefficient, and because they were not leading to good outcomes for individuals and communities. Key issues included:

[1] WA's CTP scheme became publicly underwritten in 1949, when the Motor Vehicle Insurance Trust was established to administer the Motor Vehicle (Third Party Insurance) Act 1943 (WA). Workers' Compensation in Queensland and the Commonwealth commenced with public underwriting without private sector participation (Fronsko and Woodroffe 2017, 4: 61).

- Escalating costs and dipping premium affordability (Industry Commission 1994, F3.2, Fronsko and Woodroffe 2017, 4:12–14); and concerns that 'unfettered discounting' among workplace insurers was generating insufficient reserves to fully cover the long-term cost of claims (Industry Commission 1994, F3.2).
- Delays in claims processing, due to delays in the common law processes in the case of CTP claims, and inefficient underwriting arrangements leading to long backlogs of claims in the case of workers (Fronsko and Woodroffe 2017, 4: 12–15).
- Growing dissatisfaction with a perceived focus by insurers on compensation over rehabilitation and good outcomes for individuals, including concerns that lump sum payments (then a common feature of compensation) were a disincentive to the rehabilitation of the injured party (Byrne 1980; Cooney 1984).
- In the absence of a negligent party who could be found at fault, compensation was usually not available under CTP.

After facing similar challenges to Australia throughout the 1960s in relation to both its workplace and motor vehicle insurance schemes, the New Zealand Government established a Royal Commission to consider all forms of compensation resulting from accident, chaired by Sir Owen Woodhouse. The Commission's final report found New Zealand's accident compensation system to be inadequate, capricious and fragmented, failing to compensate large numbers of accident victims and involving huge administrative costs and lengthy delays (Woodhouse 1967). Five guiding principles were put forward as central to any modern injury compensation system:

1. Community responsibility. As economies depend on a productive workforce, accident compensation (including physical and economic rehabilitation) should be considered a community rather than an individual responsibility (Woodhouse 1967, 20).
2. Comprehensive entitlements. Accidents should be compensated, regardless of the causes which gave rise to it. Entitlements should not be concentrated upon a single type of accident to the exclusion of others (Woodhouse 1967, 21).

3. Complete rehabilitation. Accident compensation schemes must be deliberately organised around the complete recovery of injured individuals. Every injured worker should be encouraged to recover the maximum degree of bodily health and vocational utility in a minimum of time (Woodhouse 1967, 39–40).
4. Real compensation. Compensation should be based on a realistic assessment of total loss, both physical and economic. This should include income losses and recognition of permanent bodily impairment as a loss in itself (Woodhouse 1967, 20).
5. Administrative efficiency. This principle reflects that the scheme must balance "the ideal with the practical" and "pass the economic test" (Woodhouse 1967, 21).

The 1967 Woodhouse Report led to the creation of New Zealand's *Accident Compensation Act 1972*, which provided 'no fault' compensation for personal injury covering all injuries to employees and motor vehicle injuries. This was amended in 1973 to include those not covered by the 1972 Act, including students, people not working, and visitors to New Zealand. In 1974, the New Zealand Government established the Accident Compensation Corporation (ACC) to manage its compensation programs (ACC 2018).[2]

In 1974, Woodhouse was also commissioned to produce a more comprehensive compensation scheme for Australia, covering both injury and disability more generally. The Report of the National Committee of Inquiry into Compensation and Rehabilitation in Australia was completed later that year. It recommended a general accident scheme that would provide for compensation for all accidents, regardless of cause (Woodhouse and Meares 1974). The Whitlam Government had intended to introduce the proposed scheme, but the dismissal of the Government in 1975 meant that this never happened (Industry Commission 1994, F3.1).

Accident Compensation Reforms in the 1980s

While Commonwealth-led action was put on hold by the events of 1975, the 1980s nevertheless saw significant changes to accident compensation

[2] While there have been multiple statutory reconstructions, administrative changes and variations to New Zealand's Accident Compensations Scheme, it still exists to this day.

schemes across Australian states and territories. The Victorian, Tasmanian, NT and NSW Governments all introduced new CTP schemes focused providing long-term benefits for people who sustain severe injury[3] (Walsh and Johnson 2013, 328). NSW, Victoria and SA transitioned to publicly underwritten workplace compensation schemes in the 1980s, grounded in the Woodhouse model. Most other states conducted major reviews of both their workers compensation and/or motor vehicle injury schemes, resulting in restrictions to common law provisions (Walsh and Johnson 2013, 328).

The accident compensation schemes of the 1980s were different to those before them. They focused far more on rehabilitation and prevention, typically as a statutory requirement, and each was governed by an independent statutory authority (Industry Commission 1994, F3.2). For many, legislative changes sought to mitigate financial risks to governments by outlining specific requirements for scheme monitoring, reporting and actuarial analysis,[4] including Victoria's *Accident Compensation Act 1985*, SA's *Workers Rehabilitation and Compensation Act 1986* and the NT's *Return to Work Act 1986*.

The 'Insurance Crisis' and Long-Term Care

Accident compensation underwent further reform at the start of the twenty-first century, when the rising cost of public liability and professional indemnity insurance[5] led to the collapse of HIH—Australia's second largest insurance company—and a so-called insurance crisis. In 2002, Commonwealth, State and Territory Governments commissioned the Negligence Review Panel, chaired by the Hon Justice David Ipp (the Ipp Review) to recommend changes to personal injury laws which would reduce the numbers of litigated claims and size of court awarded compensation payments to injured claimants (Ipp et al. 2002). From the Ipp

[3] Repealed in NSW in 1989 following a change of government.

[4] Actuarial analysis is a type of risk assessment used to ensure sufficient funds exist to pay required liabilities.

[5] Public liability insurance protects a business if a customer, supplier or member of the public is injured or sustains property damage as a result of negligent business activities. Professional Indemnity insurance protects professionals against claims of negligence or breach of duty made by a client as a result of receiving professional advice or services from a business.

Review, an Insurance Ministers Council (IMC) was established to review jurisdictional legislation, eventually resulting in changes that restricted common law damage claims.

During the early 2000s, there also arose a national interest in meeting the needs of people with lifelong disability resulting from major accident. In 2003, the Heads of Treasury Insurance Issues Working Group (a sub-group of the IMC) commissioned two reports on the feasibility and options for a new national model focusing specifically on long-term care and support for people with a major disability (PricewaterhouseCoopers 2004, 2005). Following finalisation of these reports, states were invited by the IMC to continue working on this model. NSW was the first jurisdiction to do so, introducing its Lifetime Care and Support Scheme (LCSS) in 2006 to cover the future care and support needs of people severely injured in motor accidents. The LCSS, unlike many before it, was a scheme that sought to balance the desire to provide people with choice and control over their supports with the need to achieve sustainability and contain costs within the system. Other states would eventually go on to introduce similar models for workers and motor vehicle compensation as part of their NDIS negotiations (Walsh and Johnson 2013, 329).

Underfunded, Unfair, Fragmented and Inefficient: Australia's Disability System in the Twenty-First Century

By the start of the twenty-first century, Australia had come a long way from the routine segregation and institutionalisation of people with disability. Yet Australia's disability system, and outcomes for those who relied on it, was far from ideal. Under Commonwealth State Disability Agreements (in place until 2009) Commonwealth funding allocations for disability supports were based on the previous years' funding, adjusted for indexation, rather than an estimate of the underlying support needs of people with disability. Under these arrangements, many people were not getting enough services or were getting no services at all (NSW Government 2010, 8). Existing support for catastrophic injury, even after substantial reform, was inconsistent depending on the type of accident, its location and exact circumstances (and as of 2005) only about half of those who were injured catastrophically had access to some form of insurance—usually CTP motor vehicle cover (PricewaterhouseCooper 2005, 2).

In 2006, the NSW Government responded to this unequal and unsustainable system with Stronger Together: a 10-year plan to provide more services in more flexible ways to better support people with disability living in NSW. Like many of Australia's accident insurance schemes before it, Stronger Together was built upon a bottom-up supply and demand model, which compared the current supply of disability support to a best estimate of the underlying population need. It included a substantial increase in the NSW disability funding, as well as restructuring in the way support was delivered, with greater focus on early intervention, community support and personal budgets (NSW Government 2010).

In 2008, national interest in a long-term disability scheme was reinvigorated. The then Parliamentary Secretary for Disabilities Bill Shorten established a Disability Investment Group (DIG) with both public and private sector representation. He asked the group to explore innovative funding ideas from the private sector that will help people with disability and their families to access greater support for the future (Commonwealth of Australia 2009b, 1). In April of 2008, the then Prime Minister the Hon. Kevin Rudd MP held the '2020 Summit' in Canberra to discuss critical policy areas for Australia's future. At the Summit, Bruce Bonyhady (a DIG member, who went on to serve as Chair of the NDIA Board) and Helen Sykes put forward a proposal for a lifetime care and support scheme for people with disability. Bonyhady and Sykes (2008, 2) argued that the time was right for reform of the disability sector, away from a current crisis-driven welfare system to a planned and fully-funded NDIS. The idea was supported at the Summit and the Final Summit Report recommended an NDIS be established for the families of children with brain injury from birth and other non-insurable injuries (Commonwealth of Australia 2008, 175). The Commonwealth Government responded to the Summit Report in April 2009, committing to consider development of an NDIS. It also promised to develop the first-ever National Disability Strategy, through the Council of Australian Governments (COAG), as the central mechanism through which Australia would implement its obligations under the UN CRPD.

The drafting of Australia's first National Disability Strategy was supported by a broad consultation process, culminating in the 2009 publication of a confronting report entitled Shut Out: The Experiences of People with Disabilities and their Families in Australia (Shut Out Report). The Shut Out Report concluded that Australia's disability system was "broken and broke", leaving people with disability far from the full social, economic and cultural participation idealised by the UN CRPD. It declared that chronic underfunding had led to a crisis-driven system, struggling against a "vast tide of unmet need" which presented people with disability with multiple barriers to meaningful participation (Commonwealth of Australia 2009a, 3–4). The Report also highlighted that there were continued widespread misconceptions and stereotypes about disabilities, leaving people with disability feeling marginalised and devaluated (Commonwealth of Australia 2009a, 11–12).

Submissions to Shut Out argued that programs and services were built around organisation and system needs rather than the needs of individuals. They told stories of people forced to play the tragedy card and paint the worst picture possible in order to get services. Submissions also noted the lack of portability of funding across jurisdictions, with different systems and different funding meaning people could receive services in one state, move to another, and then not receive them anymore (Commonwealth of Australia 2009a, 20). Submissions noted a constant struggle for resources and support, with people with disability reporting themselves 'exhausted and worn out with constant battles, haunted by an ever-present fear that even a limited service would be withdrawn' (Commonwealth of Australia 2009a, 19).

The system characterised by the Shut Out Report was irretrievably broken. While increased funding would be welcomed, this was also considered insufficient because issues regarding service access, quality and one-sized fits all approaches would persist. Instead, many people called for a fundamental change of the system that would place the emphasis on people themselves (Commonwealth of Australia 2009a, 22). The Shut Out Report noted calls for individualised flexible funding packages that people could spend how they saw fit and a 'move away from a welfare model of service provision to a person-centred approach that sees services not as charity but as a social investment in realising the potential of people with disabilities' (Commonwealth of Australia 2009a, 5). The Report showed that people were calling for a lifetime care and support scheme.

Bringing It All Together: Rights, Insurance and the Proposal for the NDIS

In September of 2009, the DIG submitted its report The Way Forward: A New Disability Policy Framework for Australia to Government. It recommended a feasibility study be conducted into an NDIS for Australia (Commonwealth of Australia 2009b, 1). The Productivity Commission was subsequently requested to conduct an inquiry into a national disability long-term care and support scheme. The Report of this Inquiry, released in 2011, echoed the conclusions of the Shut Out Report, finding Australia's disability system to be underfunded, unfair, fragmented and inefficient, giving people with disability and their families little choice or certainty of access to appropriate supports (Productivity Commission 2011, 1:2). It emphasised that Australia's disability system was increasingly unsustainable and unstable, with funding shortages leading to crisis-driven investments displacing early intervention and leading to even more families falling into crisis (Productivity Commission 2011, 1:5). The Commission's final report ultimately recommended that an NDIS be introduced to provide insurance cover for all Australians in the event of disability (Productivity Commission 2011, 1:2). It also recommended that a separate no-fault National Injury Insurance Scheme, driven by individual State and Territory Governments, be established (Productivity Commission 2011, 1:3).

The NDIS described by the Productivity Commission (outlined in greater detail in Chapter 4) combined influences from Australia's disability sector with elements of its existing accident compensation schemes. It built upon Australia's commitment to protect the rights of people with disability, as articulated in the UN CRPD, recognising the rights of people with disability to autonomy, choice and to the full and equal enjoyment of social and economic opportunities (Productivity Commission 2011, 1:99–103, 151). It reflected the growing influence of personalisation within social services, describing a service model which would provide participants with individualised funding and support packages, tailored to their unique goals and needs (Productivity Commission 2011, 1:344–375). Similar to contemporary accident compensation schemes, the NDIS described was to be overseen by an independent statutory authority—the National Disability Insurance Agency (NDIA)—and grounded in supply and demand modelling (Productivity Commission 2011, 1:2–3, 2:747–788). The scheme design also drew on Woodhouse's guiding principles for modern injury compensation systems, seeking to balance the provision of comprehensive, long-term entitlements, focused on rehabilitation, with governance, monitoring, reporting and actuarial analysis mechanisms to control scheme costs and ensure sustainability (Productivity Commission 2011, 1:305–342, 401–470, 2:563–604).

Conclusion

The NDIS is sometimes lauded as a piece of public policy that happened quickly, from the point of the idea being first officially floated to when it was legislated in Parliament. However, what the experiences of people with disability outlined in the Shut Out Report showed was that it was a long journey to get this far. The scheme has emerged as a public policy idea throughout a period of change for disability services, the rise of the disability rights movement, the increasing role of non-government providers, the introduction of new approaches to social policy such as personalisation and individual budgets, and accident compensation distribution and reform.

This chapter has sought to provide a summarised history of relevant changes and trends that paved the way to an NDIS. It is intended to provide an understanding where the NDIS has come from—context which will be essential to understanding the way the scheme has been designed and what it is hoped to achieve for people with disability.

References

Accident Compensation Corporation (ACC) (New Zealand). 2018. Our History. ACC Website. https://www.acc.co.nz/about-us/who-we-are/our-history/#1900--new-zealand-leads-the-way-in-workers-compensation

Australian Human Rights Commission. 2016. Disability Rights: Facilitating the Empowerment of People with Disability.https://humanrights.gov.au/our work/education/publications/disability-rights-facilitating-empowerment-people-disability.

Australian Human Rights Commission. 2013. Timeline: 20 Years, 20 Stories Celebrating 20 Years of the Disability Discrimination Act. https://www.humanrights.gov.au/twentystories/timeline.html.

Bonyhady, Bruce, and Helen Sykes. 2008. 'Disability Reform: From Crisis Welfare to a Planned Insurance Model': Submission to Australia 2020 Summit. Parliament of Australia. https://parlinfo.aph.gov.au/parlInfo/search/display/display.w3p;query=Id:%22library/jrnart/275951l%22.

Byrne, D.E. 1980. Workers Rehabilitation and Compensation Board for South Australia—The Key to Rapid Rehabilitation and Equitable Compensation for Those Injured at Work. Tripartite Committee on the Rehabilitation and Compensation of Persons Injured at Work. http://library.safework.sa.gov.au/attachments/3443/A%20Workers%20Rehabilitation%20and%20Compensation%20Board%20for%20South%20Australia%20-%20Byrne%20Report%201980.pdf.

Carey, Gemma, Eleanor Malbon, Sue Olney, and Daniel Reeders. 2018. The Personalisation Agenda: The Case of the Australian National Disability Insurance Scheme. *International Review of Sociology* 28 (1) (January): 20–34.

Commonwealth of Australia. 2008. Australia 2020 Summit Final Report. Department of the Prime Minister and Cabinet. https://apo.org.au/node/15061.

Commonwealth of Australia. 2009a. Shut Out: The Experience of People with Disabilities and their Families in Australia. https://www.dss.gov.au/sites/default/files/documents/05_2012/nds_report.pdf.

Commonwealth of Australia. 2009b. The Way Forward: A NEW Disability Policy Framework for Australia. Disability Investment Group. https://www.dss.gov.au/sites/default/files/documents/05_2012/dig_report_19oct09.pdf.

Cooney, B.C. 1984. Committee of Enquiry into the Victorian Workers' Compensation. Government Printer.

Dixon, John, and Mark Hyde. 2000. A Global Perspective on Social Security Programmes for Disabled People. *Disability and Society* 15: 709–730.

Ferguson, Iain. 2007. Increasing User Choice or Privatizing Risk? The Antinomies or Personalization. *British Journal of Social Work* 37: 387–403.

Find and Connect. 2018. The Home for Incurables (1879–1981). https://www.findandconnect.gov.au/guide/sa/SE01203.

Fleischer, Dorris, and Frieda Zames. 2011. *The Disability Rights Movement: From Charity to Confrontation*. Philadelphia: Temple University Press.

Fleming, John G. 1987. *The Law of Torts*, 7th ed. Sydney, NSW: Law Book Co.

Fronsko, Dr Andrew, and Alan Woodroffe. 2017. Public vs. Private Underwriting and Administration of Personal Injury Statutory Insurance Schemes: Actuaries Institute Injury and Disability Schemes Seminar 12–14 November 2017. Injury and Disability Schemes. https://www.actuaries.asn.au/Library/Events/%20InjuryDisabilitySchemesSeminar/2017/PublicVsPrivatePaper.pdf.

Gadsby, Erica Wirrman. 2013. Personal Budgets and Health: A Review of the Evidence. Centre for Health Studies, University of Kent. https://pdfs.semanticscholar.org/4e17/992ef37a79514f15d8db3f6e48cd732fb4c7.pdf.

Geyer, Mary-Louise. 2014. Destitute Asylum. Adeladia. http://adelaidia.sa.gov.au/places/destitute-asylum.

Glasby, Jon, and Rosemary Littlechild. 2009. *Direct Payments and Personal Budgets: Putting Personalisation into Practice*. Bristol: Policy Press.

Glasby, Jon, Robin Millerand, and Jennifer Lynch. 2013. Turning the Welfare State Upside Down? Developing a New Adult Social Care Offer: Health Services Management Centre Policy Paper. Centre for Welfare Reform. https://www.centreforwelfarereform.org/library/turning-the-welfare-state-upside-down.html.

Haller, John. 1988. Industrial Accidents—Worker Compensation Laws and the Medical Response. *Western Journal of Medicine* 148: 341–348.

Hayes, Susan, and Robert Hayes. 1982. *Mental Retardation: Law, Policy and Administration*. Sydney: Law Book Co.

Hurst, Rachel. 2003. The International Disability Rights Movement and the ICF. *Disability and Rehabilitation* 25: 572–576.

Industry Commission, Commonwealth of Australia. 1994. Workers' Compensation in Australia: Report No. 36. Australian Government Publishing Service. https://www.pc.gov.au/inquiries/completed/workers-comp/36worker.pdf.

Ipp, David Andrew, Peter Cane, Don Sheldon, and Ian Macintosh. 2002. Final Report of the Review of the Law of Negligence. Commonwealth of Australia. https://treasury.gov.au/sites/default/files/2019-03/R2002-001_Law_Neg_Final.pdf.

Jones, A. 1992. AQA…the Beginning of Something Big. Quad Wrangle, Official Journal of the Australian Quadriplegic Association.

Leadbeater, Charles. 2004. *Personalisation Through Participation: A New Script for Public Services*. London: Demos.

Lever, I. 1985. Thirty Years of Self-Help. *Community Quarterly* 5: 8–13.

Minogue John (The Honourable Sir John Q.C.). 1978, The Board of Inquiry into Motor Vehicle Accident Compensation in Victoria. Government Printer. https://www.parliament.vic.gov.au/papers/govpub/VPARL1978-79No24.pdf.

Needham, Catherine, and Jon Glasby. 2015. Personalisation–Love It or Hate It? *Journal of Integrated Care* 23: 268–276.

Newell, Cristopher. 2006. Disability, Bioethics and Rejected Knowledge. *The Journal of Medicine and Philosophy: A Forum for Bioethics and Philosophy of Medicine* 31: 269–283.

NSW Government. 2010. Stronger Together: A New Direction for Disability Services in NSW 2006–2016. The Second Phase: 2011–2016. NSW Government. https://www.facs.nsw.gov.au/__data/assets/pdf_file/0010/236359/Stronger-Together.pdf.

Oliver, Michael, and Bob Sapey. 1999. *Social Work with Disabled People*. Basingstoke: Macmillan.

Perkins, Daniel, Lucy Nelms, and Paul Smyth. 2004. Beyond Neo-liberalism: The Social Investment State? Social Policy Working Paper No. 3. http://library.bsl.org.au/jspui/bitstream/1/570/1/beyond_neoliberalism_social_investment_state.pdf.

PricewaterhouseCoopers. 2004. Long Term Care Scheme, Design, Funding and Service Delivery Options. PricewaterhouseCoopers.

PricewaterhouseCoopers. 2005. Long Term Care: Actuarial Analysis on Long Term Care for the Catastrophically Injured. PricewaterhouseCoopers.

Productivity Commission. 2011. Disability Care and Support: Productivity Commission Inquiry Report, Commonwealth of Australia. https://www.pc.gov.au/inquiries/completed/disability-support/report

Thill, Cate. 2014. Listening for Policy Change: How the Voices of Disabled People Shaped Australia's National Disability Insurance Scheme. *Disability and Society* 30: 15–28.

Todd, Stephen. 2016. *The Law of Torts in New Zealand*, 7th ed. Thomson Reuters: Wellington.

United Nations General Assembly (UNGA). 2007. Convention on the Rights of Persons with Disabilities: resolution / Adopted by the General Assembly, 24 January 2007, A/RES/61/106. RefWorld. https://www.refworld.org/docid/45f973632.html.

Walsh, John, and Sarah Johnson. 2013. Development and Principles of the National Disability Insurance Scheme. *The Australian Economic Review* 46: 327–337.

Williams, Iestyn, and Helen Dickinson. 2015. Going It Alone or Playing to the Crowd? A Critique of Individual Budgets and the Personalisation of Health Care in the English National Health Service. *Australian Journal of Public Administration* 75: 149–158.

Williams, Iestyn, and Helen Dickinson. 2016. Going It Alone or Playing to the Crowd? A Critique of Individual Budgets and the Personalisation of Health Care in the English National Health Service. *Australian Journal of Public Administration* 75: 149–158. https://doi.org/10.1111/1467-8500.12155.

Woodhouse, Arthur Owen, and Meares, Charles Leycester Devenish. 1974. Report of the National Committee of Inquiry on Compensation and Rehabilitation in Australia: National Rehabilitation and Compensation Scheme Committee of Inquiry. Australian Government Publishing Service. https://catalogue.nla.gov.au/Record/142091.

Woodhouse, Owen. 1967. Royal Commission of Inquiry into Compensation for Personal Injury in New Zealand Compensation for Personal Injury in New Zealand: Report of the Royal Commission of Inquiry. Government Printer. https://www.worldcat.org/title/compensation-for-personal-injury-in-new-zealand-report-of-the-royal-commission-of-inquiry/oclc/858813182.

CHAPTER 3

Australia Before the National Disability Insurance Scheme

Mhairi Cowden, Claire McCullagh, and Jennifer Tran

Introduction

As its name suggests, the National Disability Insurance Scheme (NDIS) set out to introduce a national approach to the delivery of disability supports services across Australia. However, the roll out of the scheme across the country has been far from uniform. This is largely unsurprising as each state and territory has a different number of people with disability, with different characteristics, and a different history of service delivery. Each state and territory thus transitioned to the NDIS from different starting points.

This chapter presents an overview of the prevalence of disability in Australia, and the service landscape which existed in each state and territory of Australia prior to NDIS roll out. While Chapter 2 gave an overview of disability history generally, and discussed key influences on the NDIS design, this chapter considers the context and readiness of each jurisdiction for the NDIS. It covers the size of the disability service market in each state and territory, and its relative experience with individualised

M. Cowden (✉) · C. McCullagh · J. Tran
Nous Group, Perth, WA, Australia

M. Cowden and C. McCullagh (eds.), *The National Disability Insurance Scheme*, https://doi.org/10.1007/978-981-16-2244-1_3

funding approaches: whereby personalised budgets are allocated to, or against, individuals, rather than 'block funding' being provided to organisations. This chapter provides important scene setting to the enormity of the challenge in rolling out the NDIS and achieving equal access in a system where disability prevalence rates, service coverage and care quality has historically varied.

The Prevalence of Disability in Australia

Disability prevalence refers to the proportion of the population who experience disability: defined by the Australian Bureau of Statistics (ABS) as any limitation, restriction or impairment which restricts everyday activities and has lasted, or is likely to last, for at least six months (ABS 2019). Measuring disability prevalence is not an exact science; rates can be affected by a range of factors including general life expectancy, the survival rate for specific health conditions and the broader demographic characteristics of a population. In addition, disability prevalence in Australia is generally self-reported, and therefore can be influenced by changing societal attitudes towards disability, government policy or how the questions are asked in the survey (AIHW 2020).

At the time of writing this book, 17.7% of Australians—4.4 million people—reported to experience disability (ABS 2019). Rates are similar for males (17.6%) and females (17.8%). Nearly one in three (32%) people with disability (1.4 million people; 5.8% of the Australian population) have severe or profound disability, meaning they sometimes or always need help with day-to-day activities related to self-care, mobility or communication (AIHW 2020).

The reported overall proportion of people with disability in Australia has decreased slightly over the last decade (17.7% in 2018, 18.3% in 2015 and 18.5% in 2012) (ABS 2019). However, there has been an increase in disability prevalence rates in Australians over the age of 65, which has been linked to the ageing population. In addition, there has been a significant increase in the measured prevalence of Autism Spectrum Disorder (ASD). In 2018, there were 205,200 Australians with autism, a 25.1% increase from the 164,000 with the condition in 2015. The significant increase is likely due to an increased number of diagnoses due to a change in the diagnostic tool (ABS 2019). This demonstrates that our understanding of disability continues to change.

Table 3.1 People with disability by state or territory of usual residence 2018

State or territory	*Number of people reported having disability*	*Percentage of state or Territory population*
New South Wales	1,346,200	16.9
Victoria	1,098,200	17.0
Queensland	938,100	19.1
Western Australia	411,500	16.4
South Australia	332,500	19.4
Northern Territory	20,700	11.5
Tasmania	140,100	26.8
Australian Capital Territory	80,000	19.4

Source ABS (2019)

Prevalence of disability differs across the states and territories in Australia, as showed in Table 3.1 (ABS 2019).

A number of reasons could explain the differing prevalence of disability across the Australian states and territories. The most likely explanation is the different age structures across jurisdictions. Disability prevalence is more likely to be higher among older Australians, and therefore states with an older population are more likely to have a higher prevalence of disability overall. Immigration and migration within Australia due to economic trends are also likely to influence the broader demographic profile of different states and territories. The variation of diagnostic teams for disabilities such as Autism across different states and territories may also contribute to the difference in prevalence statistics. For example, while some states and territories require an Autism Spectrum Disorder diagnosis to be made through a multidisciplinary assessment team, other states have less stringent criteria (Whitehouse et al. 2017, 2). This may lead to higher or lower levels of reported disability.

Whatever the factors that may influence these differences, the prevalence of people with disability is not uniform across all Australian jurisdictions and this poses challenges for the implementation of any nationalised disability system.

Indigenous People

Although data on disability among Indigenous people is limited, the Australian Institute of Health and Welfare estimated that Indigenous people are twice as likely as non-Indigenous people to have severe or profound disability (AIHW 2015, 81). Furthermore, the ABS found in 2009 that 14.2% of Indigenous children aged 0–14 had a disability compared with 6.6% of non-Indigenous children of the same age (ABS 2009).

The Australian Law Reform Commission has identified that there are several explanations of the higher prevalence of disability among Indigenous people:

> disability may be attributable to socio-economic disadvantage and exposure to high-risk factors such as poor nutrition and substance abuse. There may also be cultural reasons, for example, as 'disability' is not a concept that is recognised among some Aboriginal and Torres Strait Islander communities. Where it is understood, it may be dismissed as insignificant or irrelevant to their identity, leading to Aboriginal and Torres Strait Islander people not identifying themselves as people with disability. Further, often the impact of past removal from family and community deters Aboriginal and Torres Strait Islander people from seeking government assistance. (Australian Law Reform Commission 2013, 300)

This particularly impacts the Northern Territory (NT), which has the highest proportion of Indigenous people in comparison with other states and territories (ABS 2016a).

People from Culturally and Linguistically Diverse Backgrounds

The literature identifies that people from culturally and linguistically diverse (CaLD) backgrounds may face some distinct difficulties in relation to stereotypes and stigma as well as cultural concepts of disability; the role of family; language and accessibility barriers; access to income support payments; and lack of willingness to engage with complaint mechanisms or broader court or dispute resolution processes (Australian Law Reform Commission 2013, 303).

Difficulty in accessing interpreters or information in community languages also appears to be a significant issue for CaLD people with disability in terms of their engagement with service providers and government agencies (Australian Law Reform Commission 2013, 304). This may be of greatest influence in states and territories with a higher relative proportion of the population born overseas, including Victoria, NSW and Western Australia (ABS 2016b).

People in Rural, Remote and Regional Areas

Research shows that disability tends to be more prevalent in rural, remote and regional areas of Australia compared to urban areas (Australian Law Reform Commission 2013, 315). In 2015, the ABS reported that 535,600 people with disability lived in outer regional and remote areas of Australia (22.3% of all people in outer regional and remote areas) (ABS 2015). It has been noted that people with disability living outside of major cities are significantly less likely to access disability support services than those living within major cities. This relates to the lack of services in these areas, transport challenges, and issues with the capability and capacity of the disability support workforce in these areas (Australian Law Reform Commission 2013, 316). This is particularly significant for the disability system in the NT, given that 40.4% of its population live in remote or very remote areas (NT Department of Treasury and Finance, n.d.).

The Service Delivery Landscape Before the NDIS

Before the NDIS, Australia's disability service delivery varied significantly across jurisdictions. This pre-scheme system has been described as a 'lottery', where people with similar levels of functionality received vastly different levels of support, depending on where they lived (Productivity Commission 2011, 1:6).

This next section summarises the size of the disability service market in each state and territory prior to the introduction of the NDIS. It also describes the relative experience each jurisdiction already had in individualised funding approaches—a central design feature of the NDIS to come.

NSW

Prior to the introduction of the NDIS, there were 602 agencies[1] managing 5,999 service type outlets[2] across NSW. Most of these agencies were funded by the state government (88.4%), with the remaining being

[1] Organisations delivering one or more service types, under the former National Disability Agreement (NDA) which, prior to the NDIS, outlined government responsibilities in relation to disability care and support.

[2] Service type outlets deliver a particular service type—such as advocacy, accommodation support or respite care—at or from a discrete location.

funded by the Commonwealth Government (11.6%) (AIHW 2014, 12–14). Most service type outlets were in the non-government sector, with about 77.3% being income tax exempt charities (AIHW 2014, 15). The accommodation support service type outlets included 21 large residential facilities or institutions (which provided 24-hour residential support in a setting of more than 20 beds) (AIHW 2014, 13).

At this time, NSW's disability system was funded predominantly through block-funded arrangements: where funding is allocated by the government to service provider organisations for the delivery of a specific service, or set of services. Block funding typically could only be used to fund specific services, and block-funded services could not be easily tailored to the needs of individual users (NSW Government 2018, 18).

A small amount of individualised funding was available to people with disability through programmes and pilots that aimed at increasing user choice and autonomy (Fisher et al. 2010). Under these programmes, funding was either held by a service provider, who would provide or buy services on behalf of a person with disability, or be held by the person and/or their family to purchase services from an open market (Fisher et al. 2010, 16). Examples of individualised funding initiatives being trialled in NSW prior to the introduction of the NDIS include:

- The Attendant Care Program (ACP): this program allowed funding to be held by an individual or intermediary, which could be used to directly purchase personal care services,[3] to support people with physical disability to live and participate in their community.
- Extended Family Support Program: this program provided up to $50,000 for families of children with a disability, who were at risk of relinquishing their child into supported care. The aim was to put in place 'whatever it takes' to keep the child in the care of their family, and help parents to regain a sense of control and capacity to manage necessary care routines.
- Community Participation Program: funding for this program was held and managed by a financial intermediary, and could be used to purchase support on a person's behalf to enable them to pursue skills

[3] Personal or attendant care services are provided to assist a person to manage their essential and regular personal care needs. Generally attendant care services are provided to assist people with activities such as grooming, bathing, feeding, dressing, toileting and other personal or hygiene needs.

and training for employment, leisure and recreation. Funding could also be used to help people with disability participate in a range of skill development activities.
- Family Assistance Fund: this fund provided small amounts of discretionary funding to families to help them address needs unable to be met through standard services, other funding sources or which would otherwise be unaffordable to address. The fund aimed to increase the capacity of families to provide ongoing care for their children and young people at home (Fisher et al. 2010, 17).

Through these programs, the NSW Government began building an evidence base for how individualised disability funding could be further developed and implemented across the state (Fisher et al. 2010, 17). The NSW Government had a stated aim to give all people the option of individualised funding by 2014 (Purcal et al. 2014, 95).

Victoria

Prior to the introduction of the NDIS, there were 564 agencies managing 2,868 service type outlets across Victoria. Most of these agencies were funded by the state government (79.9%), with the remaining being funded by the Commonwealth Government (21.1%) (AIHW 2014, 12–14). Most service type outlets were in the non-government sector, with about 50% being income tax exempt charities (AIHW 2014, 15). The accommodation support service type outlets included three large residential facilities (AIHW 2014, 13).

Victoria had more extensive experience than NSW with individualised funding arrangements prior to the introduction of the NDIS. The Productivity Commission (2011, 1:396) identified in the Disability Care and Support reports that Victoria, prior to the NDIS, was "a rapidly developing [system]" and that "Australia can benefit from [its] experiences'. Similarly, the Victorian Auditor-General noted in its Individualised Funding for Disability Services reports that "Victoria is a leader in Australia in reforming disability services" (Victorian Auditor-General 2011, vii).

Individualised funding was introduced in Victoria the early 1990s with flexible funding packages. These packages allowed a person with disability to be allocated individual funding via their preferred service providers. Packages were primarily for personal or attendant care services, although they progressed over time to encompass a broader range of services. In 2008, several funding and support packages were combined by the Victorian Government into a single Individual Support Package that funded people's disability-related goals and needs. The Individual Support Package had three elements:

1. Self-directed planning: participants could plan the support they needed, with help if required. Parents or guardians could develop plans on behalf of their children.
2. Self-directed funding: participants could direct use of their funds in line with their preferences or in response to changes in their circumstances.
3. Self-directed support: services were tailored to individual participant needs, to help them achieve their goals (Victorian Auditor-General 2011, 2).

Individual Support Package funds could be applied in three ways: directly to a person or their nominated representative to purchase supports in line with their plan; through a state-wide financial intermediary service which would hold funding on a person's behalf and pay bills on their request; or through direct funding to a registered service provider through a service agreement. This last application was usually used when all or most of a participant's supports were purchased from a single provider (Victorian Auditor-General 2011, 3).

Queensland

Prior to the introduction of the NDIS, there were 376 agencies managing 3,138 service type outlets across Queensland. Most of these agencies were funded by the state government (84.8%), with the remaining being funded by the Commonwealth Government (15.2%) (AIHW 2014, 12–14). Most service type outlets were in the non-government sector, with about 57.5% being income tax exempt charities (AIHW 2014, 15). The accommodation support service type outlets included 13 large residential facilities or institutions (AIHW 2014, 13).

A mixture of funding approaches was used in Queensland prior to the introduction of the NDIS. This included block funding, individualised funding and hybrid funding which combined the two. Individualised funding was allocated either to a service provider for an agreed type of service for individuals, or to an individual as a direct payment to spend in an open market or use to employ support staff. However, legislation in Queensland specified that the government could only provide funds to incorporated non-government organisations (Fisher et al. 2010, 19). To receive funds directly, individuals needed to incorporate (i.e. set themselves up as an organisation) and meet the requirements of a service provider. As a result, only about 10% of people with disability received direct funding, most of whom had a physical rather than intellectual disability. It is likely to have been more difficult for people with intellectual disability to meet the legal requirements for incorporation (Fisher et al. 2010, 19).

Queensland piloted a hybrid funding model that combined some block funding for service providers to deliver shared accommodation support, with individual funding provided to people for their individual care and community access needs. This model sought to protect the viability of disability service providers, while also ensuring control and portability for people with disability (Fisher et al. 2010, 20).

WA

Before the NDIS in WA, there were 177 agencies managing 1,362 service type outlets across WA. Most of these agencies were funded by the state government (85.5%), with the remaining being funded by the Commonwealth Government (14.5%) (AIHW 2014, 12–14). Most service type outlets were in the non-government sector, with about 53.8% being income tax exempt charities (AIHW 2014, 15). The accommodation support service type outlets included five large residential facilities or institutions (AIHW 2014, 13).

Prior to the introduction of the NDIS, WA was one of the more experienced jurisdictions in terms of individual funding arrangements. In its Disability Care and Support report, the Productivity Commission stated that WA "already has a well-developed system" (2011, 1:396). The WA Disability Services Commission (2012) has also suggested that WA "has been at the forefront of disability services reform well before the introduction of the [NDIS]".

In 1988, WA became the first Australian state to extensively use individual funding packages (Purcal et al. 2014, 97). Initially, some people and families could hold and manage their allocated funds directly.

However, accountability, administrative and reporting requirements grew over time, as did the allocated funding amount and complexity (Fisher et al. 2010, 23). Consequently, this option was withdrawn in 2003, though people and families who had commenced previously with this option could continue to use it. People could instead select a service provider or a government-employed Local Area Coordinator who would provide brokerage, planning and coordination for people with disability to manage their funds (Laragy et al. 2015, 284). By 2008, nobody was self-managing funds and all funding was held and managed by service providers or Local Area Coordinators on peoples' behalf (Laragy et al. 2015, 286).

Most individualised funding packages during this time were allocated through a centralised mechanism that independently assessed and prioritised funding applications annually, known as the Combined Application Process (CAP). CAP funding was provided to applicants whose need was considered most urgent and critical by a central, independent board, relative to other applicants in that round. The CAP budget available each year was capped, with funding provided to applicants in order of priority until the budget was exhausted (WA Disability Services Commission 2014). By 2012, over 80% of WA Government disability funding was allocated as individual funding packages through CAP to people with disability and their families. The remaining funding was allocated as block funding to service providers for therapy, respite and episodic support services (Laragy et al. 2015, 286).

Before the NDIS was agreed, the WA Government had begun to respond to the need for reform highlighted in reports such as the Productivity Commission's 2011 Disability Care and Support. In February 2012, the former WA Disability Services Commission (the Commission) initiated a three-year trial of a program entitled 'My Way' in four geographical areas across WA—the Lower South West, Cockburn-Kwinana, Perth Hills and the Goldfields (Disability Services Commission 2012, 2). 'My Way' built on the strengths of WA's Local Area Coordination program, using a decentralised model for determining the appropriate funding level required for each person with disability based on an assessment of what supports would be reasonable and necessary. 'My Way' was intended to replace CAP over time as the mechanism for allocating individual disability funding. It differed from CAP and sought to be better aligned with the NDIS model proposed by the Productivity Commission in the following ways:

- 'My Way' was not solely geared to meeting urgent and critical need. The focus was instead on support which was reasonable and necessary for individuals. This meant that individuals would be able to access funding earlier, and ideally, would be able to purchase necessary supports before finding themselves in crisis.
- The 'My Way' process was based on person-centred planning. An individual with disability would have a My Way Coordinator who would work with them and their family to plan for how they would like their life to be and determine strategies for achieving that. The focus was on the individual's plan, goals and outcomes, not the funding.
- Decision-making regarding funding occurred locally, rather than being made by a panel in a centralised location (Disability Services Commission 2012, 6).

The 'My Way' model was initially adopted for the WA NDIS trial, which is discussed in Chapter 5 of this book.

South Australia

Prior to the introduction of the NDIS, there were 197 agencies managing 1,478 service type outlets across South Australia (SA). Most of these agencies were funded by the state government (82.4%), with the remaining funded by the Commonwealth Government (17.6%) (AIHW 2014, 12–14). Most service type outlets were in the government sector (65.8%), with only about 3.1% being income tax exempt charities (AIHW 2014, 15). The accommodation support service type outlets included eight large residential facilities or institutions (AIHW 2014, 13).

Prior to the introduction of the NDIS, the disability system in SA was largely welfare based and underpinned by government block funding to service providers (Government of SA 2017, 2). Individual funding packages were not uncommon for people with disability, though not across all types of service. Funding was dispensed via a brokerage model, involving contracts between government agencies and service providers to support people to expend individualised budgets for specific reasons and timeframes. Following assessment of their needs, each individual's funding package would be calculated and allocated to their preferred registered service providers for brokerage and service provision. Disability service providers would need to meet criteria and be registered by the Disability

Services Provider Panel before they could receive brokerage funding on an individual's behalf (Fisher 2010, 20). Though packages were portable between service providers, people could not self-manage their funds, or employ their own support workers. Packages also did not include all service types; for example, accommodation support was excluded (Purcal, Fisher and Laragy 2014, 96).

Tasmania

Before the NDIS, there were 116 agencies managing 334 service type outlets across Tasmania. Most of these agencies were funded by the state government (79.9%), with the remaining being funded by the Commonwealth Government (20.1%) (AIHW 2014, 12–14). Most service type outlets were in the government sector (75.7%), with about 18.9% being income tax exempt charities (AIHW 2014, 15). The accommodation support service type outlets included three large residential facilities or institutions (AIHW 2014, 13).

Prior to the introduction of the NDIS, block funding was the predominant funding type in Tasmania, although the government had begun to trial individualised funding. An initial pilot involved a person with disability entering into a contract with a non-government organisation, hiring their own staff and managing a support roster and paying an administration fee to the organisation. Although the pilot appeared to work well, it relied on the person or their support network's capacity to manage the complexities of employment relationships (Purcal et al. 2014, 96).

Northern Territory

Prior to the introduction of the NDIS, there were 48 agencies managing 222 service type outlets across the Northern Territory (NT). Most of these agencies were funded by the Territory Government (91.4%), with the remaining being funded by the Commonwealth Government (8.6%) (AIHW 2014, 12–14). Most service type outlets were in the non-government sector, with about 86.5% being income tax exempt charities (AIHW 2014, 15). There were no large residential facilities or institutions operating (AIHW 2014, 13).

Before the NDIS, the disability service system in the NT was small and struggled to meet the needs of people with disability. Rural and remote areas often had no service providers operating in the area, which presented challenges given that 40.4% of the NT population live in remote or very remote areas (NT Department of Treasury and Finance 2019). Before the NDIS, the NT did not have a robust block-funded system of services, as it was not possible to have single block-funded programs cover such remote and disparate locations. As a consequence, the NT relied on individual funding to 'fill the gaps in service provision' over and above universal health care, but in many cases, these gaps were not filled (Fisher et al. 2010, 18).

Individual Support Packages were introduced in the NT in 2000, supported by a system of Disability Case Coordinators and Case Managers. Disability Case Coordinators and Case Managers were responsible for undertaking needs assessments and developing individual support arrangements based on a budget and identification of a suitable service provider. A central panel met monthly to discuss applications, make decisions, prioritise and approve funds for eligible participants within the NT (Fisher et al. 2010, 18).

The NT Government preferred to hold formal funding agreements directly with service providers to ensure that funds were used for approved purposes (Fisher et al. 2010, 18). However, as a result of the shortage of disability service providers in the NT, in a little less than half of cases, the individual held the funding and arranged for a less formal contract with organisations or individuals who were not disability service providers (e.g. acquiring respite and accommodation support from neighbours) (Purcal et al. 2014, 10). In these cases, the NT Government had limited control over funding, and individuals were required to provide an acquittal form to substantiate the purchases they had made. Some officials were concerned about inadequate accountability under these arrangements (Fisher et al. 2010, 19).

Australian Capital Territory (ACT)

In the ACT, prior to the NDIS, there were 71 agencies managing 258 service type outlets across the ACT. Most of these agencies were funded by the Territory Government (93%), with the remaining being funded by the Commonwealth Government (7%) (AIHW 2014, 12–14). Most service type outlets were in the non-government sector, with about 60.5% being income tax exempt charities (AIHW 2014, 15). There were no large residential facilities or institutions operating (AIHW 2014, 13).

At this time, disability funding was primarily allocated through Individual Support Packages. Funding could be allocated in three ways: to an individual to choose and move between service providers; to the service provider of an individual's choice; or through individual grants to meet a one-off specific support requirement as a direct payment (Fisher et al. 2010, 15).

Individual Support Packages were based on individual need and were subject to guidelines on what the funding could and could not be used for. Funding decisions started from the principle that the people with disability and their families are in the best position to decide what support they need. Consequently, people with disability and their families were involved in the early stages in identifying, planning and designing a range of support to meet their needs (Fisher et al. 2010, 15).

Although people were able to change service providers, changing required a variation to an individual's contract. Choice between providers was also limited by the small size of the ACT disability services sector, with most people tending to remain with a single service provider (Fisher et al. 2010, 15).

Unmet Need Before the NDIS

Just as the service delivery landscape varied before the NDIS, so too did the level of interaction between people with disability with the service delivery system. Before the NDIS, there were clear differences in the amount of funding per service user with a disability, and in the breadth of service coverage across Australian states and territories. This is shown in Fig. 3.1.

In jurisdictions where service coverage is lower, the amount of spending per service user was generally higher. For example, in NSW in 2007–2008, although $34,400 was spent per service user, only 14.6% of the potential population accessed services. This reflects different approaches taken to manage trade-offs given a fixed budget, with jurisdictions either providing more supports to fewer people or less support to more people (Productivity Commission 2011, 1:137).

Prior to the NDIS, most service users were satisfied with the quality of formal services received. In 2012, 79.5% of Australians aged 15–64 with disability reported being satisfied with the quality of formal services received in the last six months (ABS 2012a). However, there was significant unmet need in every state and territory, with almost—if not more

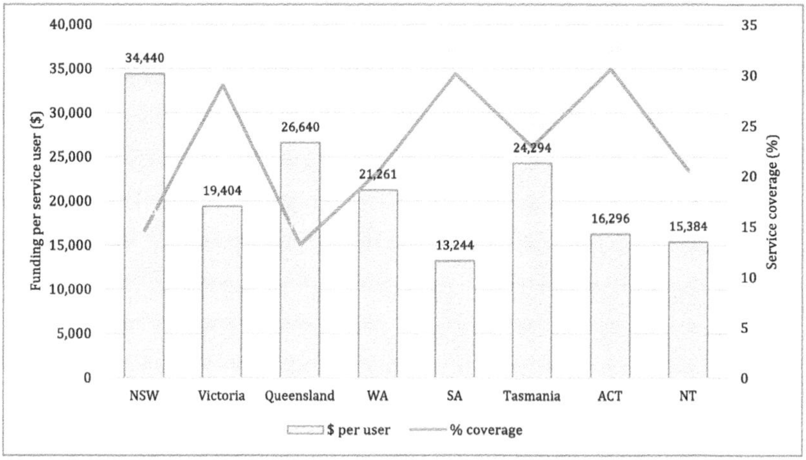

Fig. 3.1 Funding per service user and service coverage in 2007–2008 by state and territory (Productivity Commission 2011, 1:138)

than—half of people with disability reported having an unmet need for formal assistance. This is shown in Fig. 3.2 (ABS 2012b).

Conclusion

Each state and territory in Australia has differing prevalence of disability rates, different histories of delivery disability services and may experience different challenges to delivering disability services. The status of disability services across Australia prior to the introduction of the NDIS was not simple and set the stage for a challenging environment in which to introduce one of the biggest policy reforms in Australia's history.

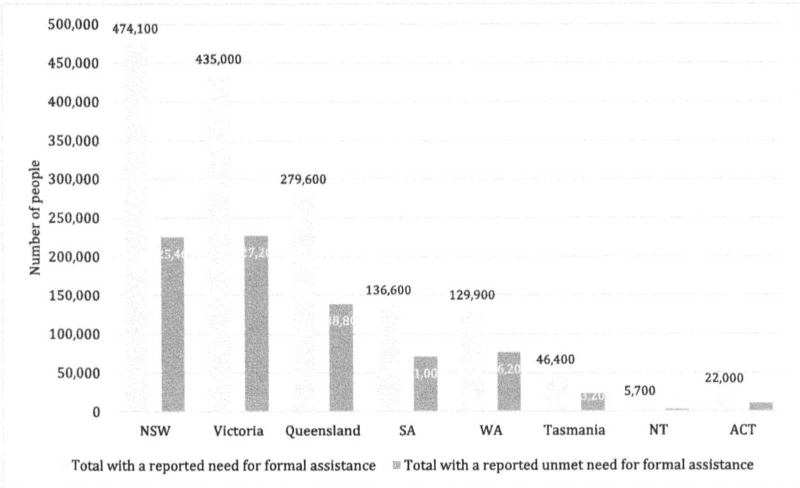

Fig. 3.2 Persons with disability with an unmet need for formal assistance in 2012 by state and territory (ABS 2012b)

References

Australian Institute of Health and Welfare (AIHW). 2014. Disability Support Services: Appendix 2012–13. Australian Government. https://www.aihw.gov.au/getmedia/14efafa1-871b-413f-ae7d-56c150eb1f76/17553-appendix.pdf.aspx.

AIHW. 2015. The Health and Welfare of Australia's Aboriginal and Torres Strait Islander Peoples 2015. Australian Government. https://www.aihw.gov.au/getmedia/584073f7-041e-4818-9419-39f5a060b1aa/18175.pdf.aspx?inline=true.

AIHW. 2020. People with Disability in Australia. https://www.aihw.gov.au/reports/disability/people-with-disability-in-australia/contents/people-with-disability/prevalence-of-disability.

Australian Bureau of Statistics (ABS). 2009. Profiles of Disability, Australia, 2009 (cat. no. 4429.0). AusStats. https://www.abs.gov.au/ausstats/abs@.nsf/Lookup/by%20Subject/4429.0~2009~Main%20Features~Home%20Page~1.

ABS. 2012a. Disability, Ageing and Carers, Australia: Additional Data Cubes, 2012 (cat. no. 4430.0.55.009). AusStats. https://www.abs.gov.au/ausstats/abs@.nsf/PrimaryMainFeatures/4430.0.55.009?OpenDocument.

ABS. 2012b. Unmet Need for Formal Assistance, 2012 (cat. no. 4433.0.55.007). AusStats. https://www.abs.gov.au/ausstats/abs@.nsf/mf/4433.0.55.007.

ABS. 2015. Disability, Ageing and Carers, Australia: Summary of Findings, 2015 (cat. no. 4430.0). AusStats. https://www.abs.gov.au/ausstats/abs@.nsf/Lookup/4430.0main+features202015.

ABS. 2016a. Estimates of Aboriginal and Torres Strait Islander Australians, June 2016 (cat. no. 3238.0.55.001). AusStats. https://www.abs.gov.au/ausstats/abs@.nsf/mf/3238.0.55.001.

ABS. 2016b. Census of Population and Housing: Reflecting Australia—Stories from the Census, 2016 (cat. no. 2071.0). AusStats. https://www.abs.gov.au/ausstats/abs@.nsf/mf/2071.0.

ABS. 2019. Disability, Ageing and Carers, Australia: Summary of Findings 2018 (cat. no. 4430.0). AusStats. https://www.abs.gov.au/ausstats/abs@.nsf/mf/4430.0.

Australian Law Reform Commission. 2013. Particular Disability Communities. Equality, Capacity and Disability in Commonwealth Laws 44. https://www.alrc.gov.au/publication/equality-capacity-and-disability-in-commonwealth-laws-ip-44/equality-capacity-and-disability-in-commonwealth-laws/particular-disability-communities/.

WA Disability Services Commission. 2012. The Introduction of My Way. WA Department of Communities Disability Services. Government of Western Australia (WA). http://www.disability.wa.gov.au/understanding-disability1/understanding-disability/history-of-disability-services/my-way--the-history/.

WA Disability Services Commission. 2014. Submission to the Community Development and Justice Committee Inquiry into Accommodation and Intensive Family Support Funding for People with Disabilities. Government of WA. https://www.parliament.wa.gov.au/Parliament/commit.nsf/luInquiryPublicSubmissions/1D85828034E4493448257C78002946C8/$file/20140102%20DSC%20Submission.pdf.

Fisher, Karen, Ryan Gleeson, Robyn Edwards, Christiane Purcal, Tomasz Sitek, Brooke Dinning, Carmel Laragy, Lel D'aegher, and Denise Thompson. 2010. Effectiveness of Individual Funding Approaches for Disability Support: Occasional Paper No. 29. Report to the Australian Government Department of Families, Housing, Community Services and Indigenous Affairs. Department of Social Services. https://www.dss.gov.au/sites/default/files/documents/05_2012/op29.pdf.

Government of South Australia. 2017. Productivity Commission Review of NDIS Costs: Submission from the South Australian Government. https://www.pc.gov.au/__data/assets/pdf_file/0016/217204/sub0203-ndis-costs.pdf.

Laragy, Carmel, Karen Fisher, Christiane Purcal, and Samantha Jenkinson. 2015. Australia's Individualised Disability Funding Packages: When Do They Provide Greater Choice and Opportunity? *Asian Social Work and Policy Review* 9: 282–292.

NSW Government. 2018. Inquiry into Implementation of the National Disability Insurance Scheme and the Provision of Disability Services in New South Wales, Submission no. 313. https://www.parliament.nsw.gov.au/lcdocs/submissions/62048/0313%20NSW%20Government%20ORIGINAL.pdf.

Northern Territory (NT) Department of Treasury and Finance. 2019. "Population." Northern Territory Economy. https://nteconomy.nt.gov.au/population.

Productivity Commission. 2011. Disability Care and Support. Commonwealth of Australia. https://www.pc.gov.au/inquiries/completed/disability-support/report

Purcal, Christiane, Karen Fisher, and Carmel Laragy. 2014. Analysing Choice in Australian Individual Funding Disability Policies. *Australian Journal of Public Administration* 33: 88–102.

Victorian Auditor-General. 2011. Individualised Funding for Disability Services. Melbourne. Parliament of Victoria. https://www.parliament.vic.gov.au/papers/govpub/VPARL2010-14No54.pdf.

Whitehouse, Prof Andrew, Dr Kiah Evans, Prof Valsamma Eapen, Prof Margo Prior and A/Prof John Wray. 2017. The Diagnostic Process for Children, Adolescents and Adults Referred for Assessment of Autism Spectrum Disorder in Australia: A National Guideline: Draft Version for Community Consultation. AutismCRC. https://www.autismcrc.com.au/sites/default/files/inline-files/Australian%20National%20Guideline%20for%20ASD%20Assessment%20-%20Draft%20Version%20for%20Community%20Consultation_0.pdf.

CHAPTER 4

What Is the NDIS?

Mhairi Cowden and Claire McCullagh

Introduction

The National Disability Insurance Scheme (NDIS) has been labelled one of the most important social policy reforms that Australia has seen in a century (Carey et al. 2018, 1). The scheme represents a revolutionary reform of the disability system in Australia, with its significance likened to the introduction of Australia's universal national healthcare system, Medicare (Thill 2014, 2). So much so that almost every media article, press conference by politician, or report begins by drawing this comparison. Time will tell whether the comparison is true. The NDIS is a large, complex piece of social policy, and there are many different moving parts still under development as it is trialled, rolled out, and regulations and practice are developed. However, the NDIS certainly has the potential to change the lives of hundreds of thousands of Australians with disability, their families and carers by improving their opportunities to work, participate in society and live out their goals.

In order to understand where the NDIS is now, it is important to first understand the original scheme design and underlying principles that were intended to drive its operation. This chapter provides an overview of

M. Cowden (✉) · C. McCullagh
Nous Group, Perth, WA, Australia

M. Cowden and C. McCullagh (eds.), *The National Disability Insurance Scheme*, https://doi.org/10.1007/978-981-16-2244-1_4

the NDIS as it was originally described by the Productivity Commission in its 2011 inquiry into a national disability long-term care and support scheme in Australia. It provides an interpretation of how the NDIS sought to introduce a new approach to disability care and support, based on insurance principles. It also comments on several headline changes made to the design of the scheme as it was written into intergovernmental launch agreements and legislated through the *National Disability Insurance Scheme Act* 2013 (the Act). Detailed descriptions of each bilateral agreement struck between the Commonwealth, State and Territory Governments for launch, transition and roll out are covered in Chapters Five and Six.

This chapter does not attempt to offer a comprehensive analysis of how the NDIS has been operationalised through the rules, policies and guidelines progressively introduced for, and following, the launch of the scheme on 1 July 2013. We recognise that these operational elements of the scheme have evolved constantly and rapidly since its introduction, and will continue to be updated regularly as the NDIS is further embedded across Australia. The final operational reality of the scheme, and the extent to which it embodies the Commission's vision in practice, could take many years to understand.

The Productivity Commission's Vision for the NDIS

In February 2010, the then Assistant Treasurer the Hon. Nick Sherry wrote to the Productivity Commission, requesting that it undertake an inquiry into a national disability long-term care and support scheme in Australia (Productivity Commission 2011, 1: IV). After examining a range of alternatives, the Productivity Commission (2011, 1:10) recommended that the Commonwealth Government and State and Territory Governments adopt a radically different approach to providing disability care and support in Australia, in the form of the NDIS. For disability resulting from an accident, the Productivity Commission (2011, 1:10, 1:88–89) recommended a separate no-fault insurance scheme—the National Injury Insurance Scheme (NIIS) to be legislated and administered by State and Territory Governments.

The NDIS was intended to largely replace the existing disability service system in Australia, described in Chapters 2 and 3.[1] It would represent an entirely new approach, functioning according to insurance principles and seeking to address the shortcomings of the previous system by improving outcomes for people and enhancing the overall sustainability of the system (Productivity Commission 2011, 1:2). The main components of the NDIS, and their difference from Australia's previous disability support system, are outlined below.

The Assurance of Lifetime Care and Support in the Event of Disability

One of the original goals of the NDIS was to provide all Australians with the assurance that if they were born with, or acquired a disability during their lifetime, they would receive adequate support regardless of who they were, where they lived, or how their disability came about (Productivity Commission 2011, 1:2). To achieve this, the NDIS was designed to benefit three cohorts of people—all Australians (tier one), a subset of people with disability (tier two) and a smaller subset of people with significant, permanent disability (tier three)—each in a different way.[2] Figure 4.1 shows the different mix of NDIS benefits accessible for each of these cohorts (Productivity Commission 2011, 1:158–160).

Tier One: All Australians

In a sense, all Australians[3]—whether they have a disability or not—were intended beneficiaries of the NDIS. The scheme was designed to provide everyone with the assurance that if they, or a member of their family, were to acquire a significant disability, they would be adequately supported for the rest of their life (Productivity Commission 2011, 1:10).

[1] The scheme would not replace the disability support pension, which would continue outside of the scheme.

[2] The language of 'tiers' is no longer used by governments to describe the different aspects of the scheme. The movement away from 'tiers' language was to avoid the assumption that the scheme was a hierarchy of supports with some aspects being 'better' or more desirable than others. We have chosen to use the language of tiers as we think it is a useful way to differentiate between different aspects of the scheme.

[3] The NDIS was intended to cover all residents of Australia who were either a citizen or permanent resident, New Zealand citizens who were Australian residents on 26 February 2001 and asylum seeks (Productivity Commission 2011, 1:64).

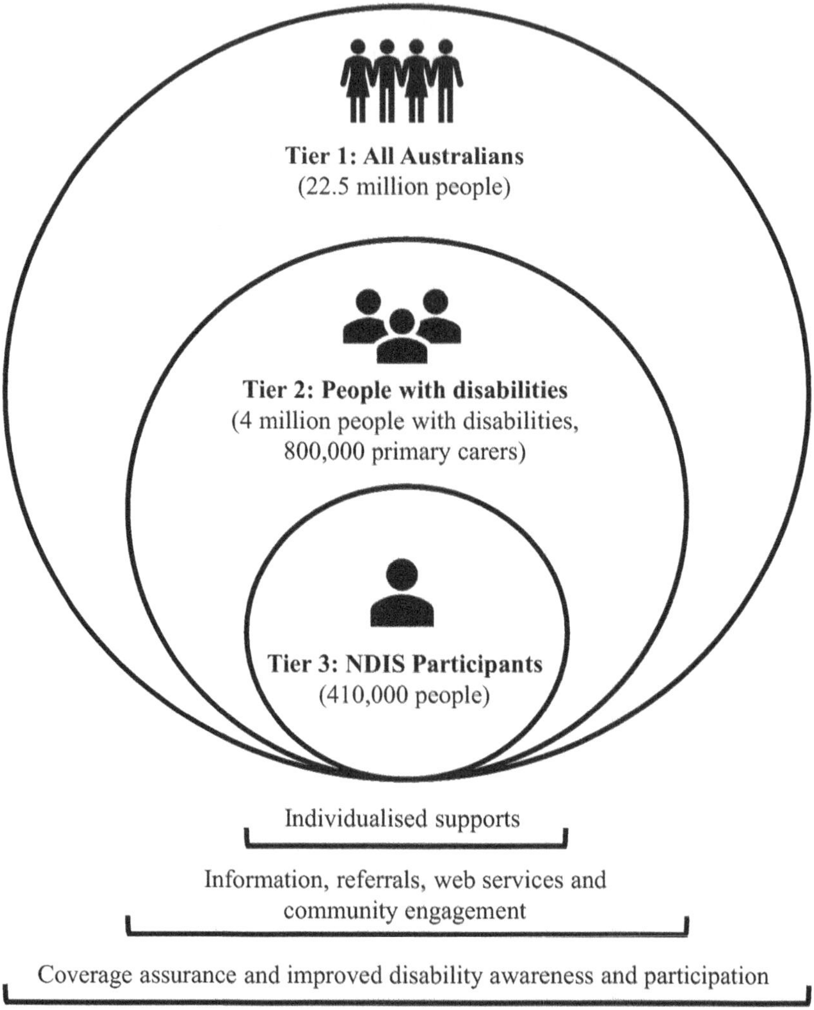

Fig. 4.1 NDIS and other supports available to different cohorts of people

The NDIS was also intended to help all Australians by creating a more inclusive society. It was designed to play a role in promoting opportunities for people with disability, raising awareness and drawing lessons from data and research to create fairer and more inclusive communities (Productivity Commission 2011, 1:12). The National Disability Strategy, discussed in Chapter 2, would also contribute to this goal by creating and supporting inclusive and accessible communities (policy area 1), learning and skill development opportunities for people with disability (policy area 5) and the health and wellbeing of people with disability (policy area six) (Productivity Commission 2011, 1:203; Commonwealth of Australia 2011).

Tier Two: A Subset of People Who Have, or Are Directly Affected by, Disability

At the time of the 2011 Productivity Commission Report (2011, 1:15), there were estimated to be four million people with some form of disability in Australia, and around 800,000 people acting as their primary carers. The NDIS was designed to support this cohort of people—tier two—by providing information and referrals to relevant services outside of the NDIS, such as mainstream health, employment, housing, child protection and education services (Productivity Commission 2011, 1:12). It was also supposed to support tier two individuals by working to strengthen the voluntary links which existed between the community and people with disability, for example, by helping link people with disability to local community groups (Productivity Commission 2011, 1:13). As with tier one, the National Disability Strategy was expected to play a role for this tier two population (Productivity Commission 2011, 1:2011).

Tier Three: A Smaller Subset of People with Significant, Permanent Disability

The final tier of the NDIS is the one that has received the most attention, as it involves the largest amount of funding, administration, innovation and complexity. The tier three cohort was to be individuals whose disability needs were the greatest, including people whose primary disability resulted from a mental health condition (psychosocial disability) (Productivity Commission 2011, 1:26). The tier three cohort would include:

- Those people whose disability was permanent, or likely to be permanent[4]; significantly reduced their functioning in terms of self-care, communication, mobility and/or self-management; and who required ongoing support. This cohort was originally estimated to include around 330,000 people (2011, 1:13–14).
- An early intervention group estimated to include around 80,000 people, for whom good evidence suggested that intervention would safely improve outcomes for them in a cost-effective way. This would include where an intervention could improve functioning over time (e.g. for an acquired brain injury) or delay a decline in functioning (e.g. some diagnosed degenerative diseases) (2011, 1:14).
- A small number of people for whom individualised support would lead to large, identifiable benefits that would not otherwise be realised. This cohort was intended to capture anyone who might fall through the gaps of the first two definitions, but who nonetheless had significant disability-related support needs (2011, 1:15).
- A small number of carers under great strain, who needed support (2011, 1:15).

The amount of support provided to tier three individuals was expected to vary. Support needs would be assessed on a case-by-case basis, considering and complementing—rather than crowding out—informal support which was provided by families, carers and community members (Productivity Commission 2011, 1:83, 1:13). It would also exclude those whose support needs would be better met by other systems, including those who had recently acquired catastrophic injuries as the result of an accident (to be covered by the NIIS), those with certain health conditions for whom the public healthcare systems would be best suited (e.g. people with terminal cancer) and those who acquired their disability at or after the age pension age of 65 (Productivity Commission 2011, 1).[5]

[4] According to the Productivity Commission (2011, 2:14), 'permanent' refers to the irreversible nature of the disability even if it may be of chronic episodic nature.

[5] An exception to the aged care requirement was to be made for people reaching pension age while already in the NDIS. These people could elect to either stay with the NDIS or move to the aged care system. If moving to the aged care system, they would be governed by the support arrangements for that system, while staying with the NDIS would mean their previous care arrangements would continue. Either way, people at or over the pension age would be required to make a capped co-contribution to their care on the same basis as the general population with other costs to be met by the Commonwealth

'Reasonable and Necessary' Support

The NDIS, as originally envisioned by the Productivity Commission, was to provide the tier three cohort with access to specialised disability supports funded directly by the scheme. The level of paid support each individual would receive through the NDIS would be determined through an individualised planning process, involving a planner employed or contracted by the National Disability Insurance Agency (NDIA)—the organisation set up to oversee the NDIS—working with the person and their family to discuss what they wanted to achieve, assess the nature, frequency and intensity of their support needs, and combine these elements into a plan for the supports that they would receive. Individuals would then engage not-for-profit organisations, state and territory service providers and businesses to deliver the disability services outlined in their plans (Productivity Commission 2011, 1:30, 39–40).

An individual's paid NDIS supports would not simply be based on their wants. Support entitlements were to be assessed independently, using valid, reliable and rigorous needs assessment tools (Productivity Commission 2011, 1:315–318), and would consider what is 'reasonable and necessary' for the scheme to fund. The following criteria were offered by the Productivity Commission (2011, 1:258–260) for what 'reasonable and necessary' would mean for the NDIS in practice:

- The support should be likely to benefit the participant, being both consistent with their goals and supported by some evidence demonstrating its likely benefit;
- It should be appropriate, by being the best available and in keeping with clinical and evidence-based practice or relevant clinical guidelines;
- It should be delivered by an appropriate provider, considering factors such as the provider's experience and any potential conflicts of interest they might have;
- It should be cost effective, with benefits which are likely to outweigh the costs and without any other, more cost-effective ways to produce the same or better results; and

Government under the National Health and Hospital Network Agreement (Productivity Commission 2011, 1:16–17).

- It should be most appropriately provided through the NDIS, and not another service system or by the individual's informal support network such as their family and friends.

Reasonable and necessary supports would therefore include a broad range of things, such as aids and appliances, home and vehicle modifications, personal care (e.g. support showering or dressing), help to access the community and enjoy social independence, respite and specialist accommodation support, domestic and transport assistance, case management services, supported employment, specialist transition to work programs and a range of therapy services (Productivity Commission 2011, 1:23).

The Productivity Commission (2011, 1: 21, 1: 323–325) advised that reasonable and necessary support budgets for each NDIS participant be 'benchmarked' against the budgets of other participants with similar characteristics, as a mechanism to ensure consistency of care between individuals and the sustainability of the scheme. This would mean that each participant's package budget would be considered against the budgets provided to other participants in similar situations. Major funding outliers or inconsistencies would need to be reviewed, to ensure each individual budget was not too generous or overly stringent (Productivity Commission 2011, 1:20–21).

Empowerment, Choice and Control for People and Their Families

The NDIS was designed to offer people with disability, their families and carers greater choice and control over their lives, compared to the previous system. The highly individualised approach to funding for tier three individuals, described above, departed from the way funding had often historically been provided to people with disability. Prior to the NDIS, as covered in Chapter 2, funding was often allocated in annual lump sums paid to service providers (Productivity Commission 2011, 1:36; 50–52). Under these so-called block funding arrangements, individuals would often need to approach providers, who would determine whether they were eligible for support, if there were enough funds left in that year's budget to support them, and what kind and amount of support they would receive. These funding arrangements meant that people with disability were not guaranteed choice over the types of supports they would receive or who would provide them.

With the NDIS, these arrangements would be turned on their head. Similar to the individualised funding programs and pilots available in states and territories before the NDIS, funding would be notionally allocated to participants, not their providers. NDIS participants would then get to choose how and by whom their supports would be delivered by:

- Choosing and, if they wanted to, switching between support providers;
- Opting to have all their support needs met by a single provider, or choosing different providers for different needs;
- Choosing (subject to the conditions below) to 'cash out' their support package and manage details around allocating and trading off between their supports themselves, known as 'self-directed funding'. Self-directed funding would also allow individuals to employ anyone they wanted as support workers, including friends and neighbours, not just those who had registered to provide supports with the NDIS;
- Appointing a disability support organisation to assist with brokering their supports. Similar to a mortgage or stock broker, this person would provide personal planning services over and above what the person could get through the NDIS, help them get the best value from their self-directed funding and support them to develop skills and confidence to exercise informed choices in the future; and
- Opting to self-direct some parts of their plan (such as the employment of attendant carers to assist them with their daily activities), but elect to have other parts of their plan managed by a disability service organisation (Productivity Commission 2011, 1:31).

Self-directed plans would come with contingencies. The overall budget that a person could work with would be determined based on their needs, and some components of their plan could not be cashed out (e.g. funds earmarked for essential long-term assets such as wheelchairs) (Productivity Commission 2011, 1:32). Strong accountability measures would be introduced, such as not allowing 'high-risk' individuals to self-manage (e.g. those with a history of fraud) and some blanket restrictions would apply (e.g. gambling) (Productivity Commission 2011, 1:32).

A Nationally Consistent Approach Which Provides Certainty for People with Disability

Australia's disability system before the NDIS was described by the Productivity Commission (2011, 1:6) as a 'lottery' which allowed people with similar levels of functionality to get vastly different levels of support, depending on where they lived and the timing and origin of their disability. Before the NDIS, as discussed in Chapter 2, some jurisdictions were offering no-fault insurance to people who acquired disability as a result of a motor vehicle accident, while others still operated fault-based systems which meant people who had been catastrophically injured would have to sue the at-fault party in order to gain lifetime support.

The original design of the NDIS sought to address inequities by creating a system which was fairer, more consistent and provided greater certainty for people with disability. The whole scheme was to be overseen by one agency—the NDIA—which would apply nationally consistent eligibility criteria and benchmark people's support needs using consistent needs assessment tools (Productivity Commission 2011, 1:76, 1:315). Unlike the previous system, support entitlements were also guaranteed to follow a person around, meaning 'tier three' individuals would not need to worry about losing their supports if they moved suburbs or states (Productivity Commission 2011, 1:2).

To provide greater certainty to people with disability and their families, the Productivity Commission recommended that the NDIS be entirely funded by the Commonwealth Government. The Commission (2011, 1:85) recommended that the scheme be funded from national consolidated revenue, paid into a National Disability Insurance Premium Fund, using an agreed formula entrenched in legislation. If this funding approach were not adopted, it recommended two alternative, less desirable options: either that a levy on personal income (the National Disability Insurance Premium) be legislated to pay for the NDIS with no further special purpose payments to State and Territory Governments for disability supports provided; or, if the Commonwealth did not accept that it should be the sole funder of the NDIS, through intergovernmental agreement with State and Territory Governments that created a pooled funding arrangement, again using a formula entrenched in legislation to ensure the total pool size was sufficient to meet people's entitlements (Productivity Commission 2011, 1:86).

The Productivity Commission (2011, 1:88) also recommended that State and Territory Governments create insurance schemes to provide fully-funded care and support for all catastrophic injuries on a no-fault basis—known collectively as the NIIS. While nationally consistent but federated approach, the management, operation and financing of the NIIS would be undertaken by states and territories not the Commonwealth Government (Productivity Commission 2011, 1:88–89). State-based accident schemes were instructed to draw on the best arrangements already in place around Australia (such as the NSW Long Term Care and Support Scheme discussed in Chapter 2) and broaden their scope to cover all catastrophic injuries (Productivity Commission 2011, 1:854). Consistency would be ensured through the setting and monitoring of national minimum requirements for eligibility, the standard of care and benefits offered. The NIIS would cover all medical treatment, rehabilitation, home and vehicle modifications and care costs, and cover catastrophic injuries from motor vehicle, medical (excluding cases of cerebral palsy associated with pregnancy or birth, which would be covered by the NDIS), criminal and general accidents. Common law rights to sue for long-term care and support were to be removed, though access to damages for financial and economic loss, and general damages, would remain (Productivity Commission 2011, 2:913).

Efficient and Effective Corporate Governance

Unlike Australia's disability arrangements previously, the governance of the NDIS—the system of rules, practices and processes by which it would be directed—was designed to protect the financial sustainability of the scheme while also promoting good outcomes for people with disability and their families. The Productivity Commission (2011, 1:76–78) designed a corporate model of governance for the NDIS which would see the scheme administered by an independent statutory agency (i.e. an agency set up by law which is authorised to enact legislation), overseen by commercial board, advised by disability stakeholders and monitored continuously by Treasury. This proposed corporate governance model was considered a way of preventing the cost blowouts which had characterised Australia's previous disability support system, thus ensuring the NDIS's enduring sustainability (Productivity Commission 2011, 1:11).

Administration by an Independent Commonwealth Statutory Agency
The Productivity Commission (2011, 1:76) argued that the combination of high-quality care and cost containment would be best achieved if the NDIS were administered by a single, national agency: the NDIA. The NDIA would be responsible for day-to-day scheme management, including researching best practice interventions, assessing participant needs, managing claims, supporting people with disabilities, determining efficient prices for supports, authorising funding proposals and coordinating services. It would also play a role capacity building, workforce development and sharing best practice innovations with the not-for-profit sector and would employ Local Area Coordinators (LACs) to act as the primary point of contact for people with disability and their families engaging with the scheme (Productivity Commission 2011, 1:36, 39). The NDIA would also have an explicit mandate to protect the long-term sustainability of the scheme through the strict management of its future liabilities (its legal financial debts or obligations) and costs, and by collecting and analysing data about services uses, outcomes, efficacy of interventions and provider performance (Productivity Commission 2011, 1:39).

While ultimately accountable to government, the NDIA would be positioned at arm's length from it to mitigate political interference in daily NDIS operations (Productivity Commission 2011, 1:431). The NDIA would be set up as an independent Commonwealth statutory authority, whose key functions would be clearly defined in national legislation. Interactions between the NDIA and its relevant Commonwealth Minister would be strictly prescribed, as would mechanisms to ensure the NDIA retained operational independence from the government of the day (Productivity Commission 2011, 1:431). The Commonwealth Minister for the NDIS would be the Treasurer, reflecting the importance of controlling the long-term cost of the scheme (Productivity Commission 2011, 1:432).

The Commission believed the NDIA would need well-developed and rigorous processes for reviewing disputes and complaints. It recommended a layered approach to dispute resolution within the NDIA, beginning with informal, low-cost mechanisms, with unresolved and serious disputes escalated to an independent, statutory Inspector-General's office (within the NDIA, but appointed by the government). The Inspector-General's role and independence would be specified in legislation, including that it would act fairly and impartially, basing decisions on the available evidence, and could not be directed in its decision-making (Productivity Commission 2011, 1:454).

Oversight by a Commercial Board

According to the Productivity Commission (2011, 1:428), keeping the NDIS on track and within funding limits would require: "a single-minded commercial focus to avoid loss of strategic direction, indecision, and cost overruns... and to keep sight of the scheme's main objectives". The Commission (2011, 1:76) recommended that an independent commercial board—the NDIA Board—be responsible for overseeing the NDIA's performance. The NDIA Board would actively manage the balance of costs and benefits of the NDIS over time, providing strategic direction and oversight of the scheme's success and ensuring its financial sustainability. It would ensure that structures and procedures were in place to monitor and control the scheme liabilities (Productivity Commission 2011, 1:424). To this end, the NDIA Board was to be made up of people chosen for their commercial and strategic skills, and expertise in insurance, finance and management, and should include some people with these skills who also have experience and understanding of disability (Productivity Commission 2011, 1:76).

Advice from a Council of Stakeholders

The Productivity Commission agreed a need for mechanisms to give disability stakeholders the capacity to advise the NDIA Board. It recommended that an independent disability advisory council be set up to advise the NDIA Board on the scope and activities of the NDIS. This council would represent the perspectives of people with disability, carers, suppliers of equipment and services, and state and territory service providers, with representatives from each of these groups (Productivity Commission 2011, 1:76).

Funded Sustainably to Meet Current and Future Need

A central goal of the NDIS was to eliminate chronic underfunding and unmet need which were defining characteristics of Australia's disability system previously. The Productivity Commission (2011, 1:3) recognises that "[r]esourcing might be good one year, but insufficient the next, with many people missing out". Prior to the NDIS, funding flowing into the disability system each year was split across Commonwealth, State and Territory Governments, with the amount provided annually linked to what had historically been contributed. This funding approach, as highlighted by the Commission (2011, 1:11), meant that funding for disability services bore no consistent relationship with the actual level of need in any given year.

By comparison, the NDIS would be funded entirely by the Commonwealth Government based on actual levels of need in the community (Productivity Commission 2011, 1:33). It would not be means tested and would not require participants to make individual financial contributions towards their own supports (Productivity Commission 2011, 1:67). Introducing the NDIS and bridging the gap between supply and need was estimated to cost approximately $13.5 billion in the scheme's first full year of operation—nearly double what was being spent prior to this (Productivity Commission 2011, 2:747)—although the actual cost of the NDIS would depend on the number of people who chose to access the scheme and the level of support necessary to meet their needs.

The Productivity Commission (2011, 1:2) considered whether the NDIS should be 'fully funded' to ensure its longevity and sustainability. This would mean adopting a similar funding approach to the NSW Lifetime Care and Support scheme and the Victorian Transport Accident scheme, with each individual's estimated lifetime care costs paid into the scheme at their point of entry.[6] A fully-funded approach would help ensure the financial sustainably of the NDIS, as it would mean there would always be enough funding set aside to pay for the lifetime cost of care for all current participants.

The Commission (2011, 2:672) ultimately considered a fully-funded approach unrealistic and not essential to achieving the long-term sustainability of the NDIS. Instead, the scheme was to be set up as a 'pay as you go' arrangement where funding would be allocated each year, based on the estimated cost of running the scheme in that year. To ensure the NDIS's financial sustainability, the scheme was to be: "…managed and reported as if it were a 'fully-funded' scheme in which each year's funding is considered in the context of the scheme's expected future

[6] Unlike the NDIS, the NIIS was to be 'fully funded' with each jurisdiction responsible for underwriting its own scheme. This was considered more feasible for these state-funded schemes, which would be funded from various sources, and would allow the NIIS to use of price signals to encourage safe choices and reduce accidents (e.g. higher premiums on dangerous vehicles, such as motorbikes) (Productivity Commission 2011, 2:858–859).

liabilities" (Productivity Commission 2011, 2:690). It would be underpinned by actuarial analysis and monitoring—a way of assessing risk to determine whether future liabilities can be paid for—including requirements to report trends in scheme usage and costs. The NDIA would be subject to regular, independent professional actuarial assessment, which would monitor the organisation's capacity to meet future scheme liabilities, as well as key scheme cost drivers and emerging risks (Productivity Commission 2011, 1:78). A specialist unit within Treasury would also be established to provide additional external monitoring, and a reserve fund made available to smooth out annual cost fluctuations (Productivity Commission 2011, 1:78, 1:437, 2:669).

Intervening Early for Long-Term Benefit

The NDIS described by the Productivity Commission would take a lifetime view of disability funding and support provision. Unlike Australia's disability system previously, the NDIS would aim to minimise long-term costs and introduce strong incentives to undertake early intervention which would lead to greater benefits down the track (Productivity Commission 2011, 1:11). In other words, the scheme would spend money in the short term to save on more expensive crisis-driven care later on. It would aim to ensure people do not have to wait a long time for basic supports like wheelchairs and personal care (Productivity Commission 2011, 1:11).

As part of taking this long-term view, the NDIS would contribute to a growing evidence base about effective interventions. A research arm of the NDIA would "build an early intervention evidence base to guide the development of protocols governing the optimal intensity, timing and duration of interventions" (Productivity Commission 2011, 1:175). In many cases, this would involve other key stakeholders such as health departments and research institutions (Productivity Commission 2011, 1:175). The aim was to build a continually growing body of research to help the NDIA understand which interventions were effective, and where funding should be directed.

A Flexible Approach to Supporting Indigenous Communities

The Productivity Commission (2011, 1:82) recommended that overcoming barriers to service delivery for Indigenous Australians with a disability should be a key goal of the scheme. The Commission (2011, 2:531) found scope for the NDIA to attempt to address the high rate of disability among Indigenous Australians through prevention measures and early intervention. It also argued that the additional barriers to service delivery faced by Indigenous Australians meant that a purely market-based service delivery system may deliver inadequate care and support to Indigenous people with a disability, particularly in remote communities. While Indigenous Australians should have access to individual support packages on the same basis as non-Indigenous Australians, the Commission (2011, 1:82) recommended that block funding for some service providers be considered, to overcome barriers faced by Indigenous Australians. Flexibility, regionally based staff, locally determined strategies and ongoing and open program evaluation were also to play an important role in improving the disability supports in remote communities (Productivity Commission 2011, 2:531).

Why is the NDIS an 'Insurance' Scheme?

As its name suggests, the NDIS was intended to operate as an insurance scheme. The scheme, according to the Productivity Commission, would be based on insurance principles and would offer "...insurance where there was no insurance before" (Bonyhady 2015, 3). Its introduction was intended to entirely supersede Australia's so-called welfare approach to disability support provision, which had been characterised by block funding transactions between funders and service providers and significant unmet need.

While some have argued that the NDIS should not be called an insurance scheme, the scheme does closely resemble insurance in several important ways (Baker 2012, 7). The Productivity Commission (2011, 1:12) notes that use of the word 'insurance' in the context of the NDIS "...simply reflects the need to ensure the community pools resources to provide reasonable long-term supports for people acquiring a significant disability". Other key similarities, discussed further in Chapter Sixteen on the role of the actuary in the NDIS, are summarised below.

A Sophisticated, Lifetime Approach to Funding

The NDIS takes a lifetime approach to cost and risk. Australia's previous approach to funding disability supports was characterised by governments planning for expenditure "over a 12-month period to – at most – a five-year time frame" and, as a consequence, funds for disability varying "...depending on the economy, tax revenues and the requirements of other portfolios" (Bonyhady 2015, 3). The NDIS would instead consider the entire cost of the scheme, over its lifetime, from the outset. Scheme actuaries would be appointed to regularly estimate the expected future liability of the NDIS and track this against previous estimates to monitor cost, and target action to ensure sustainability. Sophisticated data collection and analysis techniques, and a national research capacity, would be drawn upon in support of this lifetime approach to scheme funding (Productivity Commission 2011, 1:36).

Carefully Monitored Incentives for Early Intervention

Similar to insurance schemes generally, the NDIS would create structural incentives for early intervention to improve outcomes and reduce the need for expensive interventions later (Productivity Commission 2011, 2:608–609). The scheme was designed to fund early intervention supports in order to minimise the impact of disability from its earliest appearance (Productivity Commission 2011, 2:610–611). Its tier one and tier two functions—including promoting opportunities for people with disability (tier one) and referring people with disability to relevant mainstream agencies for support (tier two)—were also intended to form part of the scheme's broader early intervention approach (Productivity Commission 2011, 2:608). Like all insurance schemes, actuarial analysis would also allow tracking and adjustment of early intervention investments to ensure they effectively enhanced outcomes and/or reduced costs over time.

Efficient Corporate Governance

Governance arrangements for the NDIS, as described by the Productivity Commission, likewise drew influence from government insurance schemes predating its introduction. Like the NSW Lifetime Care and Support scheme and the Victorian Transport Accident scheme before it, the Commission designed a corporate model of governance for the NDIS which included administration by an independent statutory agency and commercial board oversight (Productivity Commission 2011, 1:39). NDIA responsibilities would resemble those of insurers generally including assessing need, determining funding to be paid to participants, coordinating services, collecting and using data to manage efficiency and costs and making recommendations to government regarding the setting of future 'levies' for the scheme (Productivity Commission 2011, 1:410).

Peace of Mind for Current and Future Participants

A further benefit associated with public and private insurance schemes which would also be offered by the NDIS was peace of mind, for both those who 'claim' and those who don't. The Productivity Commission (2011, 2:573) recommended that the NDIS: "...lock in tax revenue to meet its annual liabilities, without a yearly battle through the budget process to secure sufficient funding in competition with other government spending initiatives ...". In effect, the NDIS will be funded by a mandatory annual insurance premium. The scheme was hence designed to ensure all Australians could take comfort in the fact that if they, their child or loved one is born with or acquires a permanent and significant disability, they can access as much support as they need. Support was to be viewed as an entitlement, with anyone meeting the scheme eligibility criteria guaranteed (at least in theory) access to reasonable and necessary which could last a lifetime.

From Theory to Practice: What Changed When the NDIS Was Introduced?

Following release of the Productivity Commission's final report in 2011, the then Prime Minister the Hon. Julia Gillard MP announced that the government would "start work immediately with states and territories on measures that will build the foundations for the National Disability Insurance Scheme" (Gillard 2011). Urged on by strong advocacy from the disability sector, the Commonwealth Government, and State and Territory Governments came together through COAG over several years to negotiate details of whether and how the scheme could be introduced.

On 21 March 2013, the *National Disability Insurance Scheme Act 2013* (the Act) was passed into legislation with bi-partisan support, enabling the NDIS to commence through a series of launch sites from 1 July 2013 (a year earlier than recommended). The Act outlined broad parameters for how the NDIS would work, including principles and objects for the scheme and high-level descriptions of eligibility, accessible supports, provider requirements and governance for the scheme. The original Act was silent on elements critical to delivery of the scheme including how it would be funded, detailed explanations of eligibility and what specific types of supports would be accessible through the scheme. Many of these characteristics were instead defined through a combination of multilateral and bilateral agreements negotiated for the launch (later changed to the 'trials' by the Abbott Government) and additional agreements for transition and full scheme. Further details still were defined via the introduction of rules (legislative instruments made under the NDIS Act), policies and operational guidelines. This progressive approach to introducing the NDIS through legislative, intergovernmental and policy instruments reflects that a scheme of this nature would be, as the Commission (2011, 2:929) noted, "…too large and complex to implement fully at a single start date".

The framework for the NDIS, introduced in 2013 through the initial Act and intergovernmental and bilateral agreements for the NDIS trials, in many ways, resembled the vision for the scheme put forward by the Productivity Commission. They also, however, contain several important differences between Commission's blueprint and the scheme that was introduced. Notable discrepancies relating to scheme financing, eligibility, governance and initial provisions (or lack thereof) for tier one and two cohorts and Indigenous people are discussed below. Further details on the intergovernmental and bilateral agreements underpinning the NDIS are outlined in Chapter Five on the NDIS trials and Chapter Six on the transition and full scheme.

Joint Funding Arrangements

Contrary to the recommendations of the Productivity Commission, the Act itself does not include a legislated formula prescribing funding contributions to be made towards the NDIS and is silent how and by whom the scheme will be funded. Details for scheme funding are instead outlined in intergovernmental agreements and various government budget papers, which establish the NDIS as a jointly funded initiative between the Commonwealth Government, and State and Territory Governments. Rather than positioning the Commonwealth as the single funder of the scheme, the NDIS would instead see the Commonwealth responsible for just over half of scheme costs for launch and full scheme (COAG 2012a, b, 2013a, b, c, d, e, f). Funding was to come from a mix of sources, including:

- Existing Commonwealth Government funding for disability care and support and new and existing state and territory funding for disability care and support. The exact details of these funding arrangements would be different between states, as outlined in their bilateral agreements with the Commonwealth.
- An increase to the Medicare levy from 1.5 to 2.0% for all eligible Australians. Revenue from this would be directed to a special fund: the DisabilityCare Australia Fund (DCAF), designed to reimburse governments for NDIS expenditure.
- Commonwealth revenue derived from the general budget or which is borrowed, to cover any costs not offset by the above sources.

The decision not to enshrine funding arrangements for the NDIS into legislation, and to adopt joint funding arrangements, departs from the Productivity Commission's vision for the scheme. Establishing the Commonwealth Government as sole funder—the Commission's preferred funding approach—was intended to put an end to cost shifting and debate about who should bear which costs. Introducing a legislative formula for determining funding to be paid into the scheme was likewise recommended to ensure funding for the scheme largely independent of annual budget pressures. Both measures were intended to provide confidence to people with disability, their families and carers about their future supports.

Attempts have been made since the NDIS was introduced to set aside enduring and dedicated funding sources to cover the full cost of the scheme. In March 2016, the then Minister for Social Services the Hon. Christian Porter MP introduced the Disability Insurance Scheme Savings Fund Special Account Bill 2016 into parliament. The Bill sought to establish a special account to ring-fence funds from consolidated revenue for the NDIS, but has since lapsed in the Senate (Parliament of Australia 2019). The Commonwealth also planned to increase the Medicare levy by a further 0.5 percentage point to be paid into the Fund (Productivity Commission 2017, 44). These plans were later scrapped, with the then Treasurer the Hon. Scott Morrison MP stating that "all planned expenditure on the NDIS will be able to be met in this year's budget and beyond without any longer having to increase the Medicare levy" (Greber 2018).

'In-Kind' Services

Another important compromise struck as the NDIS was introduced was permitting governments to make 'in-kind' contributions to help cover their financial commitments to the scheme (COAG 2012a, b, 2013a, b, c, d, e, f). In-kind services were to be existing disability services and supports delivered by, or contracted directly to, government departments, which would continue to be funded as they had been prior to the scheme (typically through block-funded arrangements). In-kind services could be accessed by scheme participants, would appear in participant plans, but would not be directly funded by the NDIA. Where comparable in-kind options were available, participants would need to 'use up' these services before other providers could be paid for similar services through their plans (Carey et al. 2017; Carey et al. 2019). 'In-kind' arrangements were intended to be temporary, allowing governments and providers more time to adjust to the new individualised funding arrangements under the NDIS (NDIA 2019).

The Productivity Commission has, since introduction of the NDIS, argued that continuation of in-kind services adversely affects the transition of existing providers, market entry, the quality of supports and overall scheme costs (Productivity Commission 2017, 281). The Commission (2017, 284) has emphasised that in-kind funding arrangements should only be continued where they ensure continuity of support for existing participants, and that a timetable for when in-kind supports will be 'cashed out' following transition to the NDIS should be included in future bilateral agreements. Although the Commonwealth has tried to wrap up in-kind contributions wherever possible, it is unclear whether or for how long they will continue (Carey et al. 2019).

Eligibility Criteria

The Act's eligibility criteria are broader than those were originally recommended by the Productivity Commission. Key differences are the inclusion of people who have substantially reduced functional capacity in learning or social interaction activities, adding to the Commission's eligibility recommendations for people with significant mobility, self-care, self-management and communication difficulties (Productivity Commission 2011, 1:198). Children with developmental delay were also made eligible for the scheme under its early intervention requirements (ss.21–25, *NDIS Act* 2013 (Cth); Productivity Commission 2017, 1:153–154).

This expansion of eligibility allows for more people to qualify for individualised supports under the NDIS than was assumed as part of the original scheme modelling. In its 2017 review of NDIS costs, the Productivity Commission noted that data was not yet available to assess the impact of these changes on the overall cost of the scheme (Productivity Commission 2017, 155–156). It argued that these costs should be continually monitored by the NDIA as the scheme continues to be rolled out (Productivity Commission 2017, 160).

Governance, Including Oversight and Complaints Processes

The joint approach to funding agreed for the NDIS meant changes to how the scheme would be governed. Although the NDIS would still be administered by an independent statutory agency and overseen by a commercial board, Ministerial oversight would be provided by a joint Ministerial Council, consisting of Ministers from the Commonwealth Government and all States and Territories. This council would be responsible for making recommendations about NDIS policy matters or issues that arose under the Act (s.12, *NDIS Act 2013* (Cwth), version: C2013C00240).

The Act's provisions in relation to NDIS complaints and appeals were also different to those proposed by the Commission. The original Act did not establish an independent statutory Office of the Inspector-General (OIG) to hear complaints, review and direct the NDIA in relation to contested decisions and oversee quality assurance of service providers. Instead, it specified that NDIS participants (or prospective participants) could request the CEO of the NDIA to review a decision (s.100) and, if still not satisfied with the outcome, could make an application to the Administrative Appeals Tribunal (AAT) (s.103, *NDIS Act 2013* (Cwth), version: C2013C00240). Amendments to the Act in 2017 established a new NDIS Quality and Safeguards Commission and office of the NDIS Quality and Safeguards Commissioner, to register and oversee the operation of NDIS providers and manage and resolve complaints about providers (Chapter 6A, *NDIS Act 2013* (Cwth), version: C2019C00332). The new Commission would not, however, handle grievances or review decisions of the NDIA itself. Complaints would instead be handled by the NDIA itself or, if required, by the Commonwealth Ombudsman, with the Administrative Appeals Tribunal responsible for reviewing NDIA decision-making issues unable to be resolved via internal review processes (NDIS Quality and Safeguards Commission 2020).

The OIG envisioned by the Productivity Commission was intended to play a dedicated and active role, with powers to follow up on complaints and undertake his or her own investigations in relation to both service providers and the NDIA itself (2011, 1:462). While the Quality and Safeguards Commission may play this proactive investigative role in relation to service providers, no such dedicated body exists to handle complaints regarding the planning process or the NDIA itself. The extent to which this will have implications in terms of the quality of participant planning, and interactions with the NDIA generally, remains to be seen.

Absent Cohorts: Indigenous Australians and Tier One and Two Cohorts

The Act and agreements for launch remain mostly silent on two cohorts highlighted in the Productivity Commission's report: Indigenous Australians and non-participants receiving support through the scheme (the tier one and tier two cohorts). The Act and intergovernmental agreements exclude reference to the NDIS as it will relate to Indigenous Australians. For tier one and two cohorts, the Act provides authority to the NDIA to fund supports to, or in relation to, people with disability who are not participants (sec. 13–15, 20–21) but does not further describe the role, scope, eligibility or mechanisms which will enable this. The agreements underpinning scheme refer at various points to 'tier two' referrals (e.g. COAG 2012b, 3), local area coordination and 'other' general supports (e.g. COAG 2012a, 3; 2013a, 4) but provide limited clarity on how these supports will work.

The initial lack of attention paid to how the NDIS would work for Indigenous Australians, tier one and tier two cohorts, could mean these considerations prove less fundamental to scheme implementation than originally envisioned. Although measures such as an Aboriginal and Torres Strait Island Engagement Strategy, and the activation of tier two supports through the Information Linkages and Capacity Building (ILC) program, have since refocused attention on these cohorts, the scheme's prioritising and quality of support provided to these important cohorts over the long term remains to be seen.

Conclusion

This chapter has outlined what the NDIS is by describing its original design and the underlying principles intended to drive its operation, as articulated by the Productivity Commission. It has further described how the NDIS can be interpreted as an 'insurance approach' by outlining several design features which resemble insurance schemes generally. Finally, it has commented on critical changes made to the design of the NDIS when it was first introduced in 2013, compared to the Productivity Commission's original design blueprint. This chapter has not attempted to offer a comprehensive analysis of how the NDIS has been operationalised or implemented since its launch in 2013. Commentary on these elements of the scheme delivery is covered throughout Part 2 of this book.

References

Baker, Andrew. 2012. The New Leviathan: A National Disability Insurance Scheme. *CIS Policy Monographs* 131: 1–34.

Bonyhady, Bruce. 2015. Reducing the Inequality of Luck, Australasian Society for Intellectual Disability Annual Conference, Melbourne. ParlInfo. https://parlinfo.aph.gov.au/parlInfo/download/media/pressrel/6624161/upload_binary/6624161.pdf;fileType=application%2Fpdf#search=%22media/pressrel/6624161%22. Buckmaster, Luke. 2013. 'DisabilityCare Australia' in Department of Parliamentary Services. Research Paper no. 3, Budget Review 2013. ParlInfo. https://parlinfo.aph.gov.au/parlInfo/download/library/prspub/2891592/upload_binary/2891592.pdf.

Carey, Gemma, Adrian Kay, and Ann Nevile. 2017. Institutional Legacies and "Sticky Layers": What Happens in Cases of Transformative Policy Change? *Administration & Society* 51: 491–509.

Carey, Gemma, Helen Dickinson, M. Fletcher, and Daniel Reeders. 2018. *Australia's National Disability Insurance Scheme: The Role of Actuaries*. Oxford Handbook of Public Administration. UK: Oxford University Press.

Carey, Gemma, Ann Nevile, Adrian Kay, and Eleanor Malbon. 2019. Managing staged policy implementation: Balancing short-term needs and long-term goals. *Social Policy & Administration* 54: 148–162.

COAG. 2012a. Intergovernmental Agreement for the National Disability Insurance Scheme Launch. NDIS. https://www.ndis.gov.au/about-us/governance/intergovernmental-agreements#western-australia.

COAG. 2012b. Heads of Agreement Between the Commonwealth and NSW Governments on the National Disability Insurance Scheme—Agreed 6

December 2012. NDIS. https://www.ndis.gov.au/about-us/governance/intergovernmental-agreements.

COAG. 2013a. Heads of Agreement Between the Commonwealth and Victorian Governments on the National Disability Insurance Scheme—Agreed 4 May 2013. NDIS. https://www.ndis.gov.au/about-us/governance/intergovernmental-agreements.

COAG. 2013b. Heads of Agreement Between the Commonwealth and Queensland Governments on the National Disability Insurance Scheme—Agreed 8 May 2013. NDIS. https://www.ndis.gov.au/about-us/governance/intergovernmental-agreements.

COAG. 2013c. Heads of Agreement Between the Commonwealth and South Australia Governments on the National Disability Insurance Scheme—Agreed 18 April 2013. NDIS. https://www.ndis.gov.au/about-us/governance/intergovernmental-agreements.

COAG. 2013d. Heads of Agreement Between the Commonwealth and Tasmanian Governments on the National Disability Insurance Scheme—Agreed 2 May 2013. NDIS. https://www.ndis.gov.au/about-us/governance/intergovernmental-agreements.

COAG. 2013e. Heads of Agreement Between the Commonwealth and Australian Capital Territory Governments on the National Disability Insurance Scheme—Agreed 19 April 2013. NDIS. https://www.ndis.gov.au/about-us/governance/intergovernmental-agreements.

COAG. 2013f. Heads of Agreement Between the Commonwealth and the Northern Territory Governments on the National Disability Insurance Scheme—Agreed 11 May 2013. NDIS. https://www.ndis.gov.au/about-us/governance/intergovernmental-agreements.

Commonwealth of Australia. 2011. 2010–2020 National Disability Strategy: An Initiative of Council of Australian Governments (COAG) Disability Reform Council. 2015. National Disability Insurance Scheme: A Framework for Information, Linkages and Capacity Building. NDIS. https://www.ndis.gov.au/community/information-linkages-and-capacity-building-ilc/ilc-policy-framework.

National Disability Insurance Scheme Act 2013 (Commonwealth). Version: C2013C00240. https://www.legislation.gov.au/Details/C2013C00240.

Gillard, J. 2011. *Productivity Commission's Final Report into Disability Care and Support*, Media Release, 10 August 2011, viewed 11 May 2012.

Greber, Jacob. 2018. Scott Morrison Scraps Medicare Levy Hike. *Financial Review.* April 25. https://www.afr.com/policy/economy/morrison-scraps-medicare-levy-hike-20180425-h0z86e.

NDIA. 2019. In-kind Supports—Participants: Fact Sheet. NDIA website. https://www.ndis.gov.au/participants/working-providers/kind-supports-participants.

NDIS Quality and Safeguards Commission. 2020. "Feedback About the NDIS". NDIS Quality and Safeguards Commission website. https://www.ndiscommission.gov.au/about/complaints-about-ndia

Parliament of Australia. 2019. National Disability Insurance Scheme Savings Fund Special Account Bill 2016. Australian Parliament website. https://www.aph.gov.au/Parliamentary_Business/Bills_LEGislation/Bills_Search_Results/Result?bId=r5682.

Productivity Commission. 2011. Disability Care and Support: Productivity Commission Inquiry Report. Commonwealth of Australia. https://www.pc.gov.au/inquiries/completed/disability-support/report.

Productivity Commission. 2017. National Disability Insurance Scheme (NDIS) Costs. https://www.pc.gov.au/inquiries/completed/ndis-costs/report/ndis-costs.pdf.

Thill, Cate. 2014. Listening for Policy Change: How the Voices of Disabled People Shaped Australia's National Disability Insurance Scheme. *Disability and Society*.

CHAPTER 5

The NDIS Trials

Mhairi Cowden, Claire McCullagh, and Jennifer Tran

Introduction

In April 2012, the then Prime Minister the Hon. Julia Gillard MP announced that the National Disability Insurance Scheme (NDIS) would be progressively rolled out across Australia, beginning with up to four sites across the country (Gillard and Macklin 2012). These sites were initially referred to as 'launch sites' and then later 'trial sites', and eventually there would be sites in every state and territory except for Queensland (which commenced full scheme without a trial). The first trial sites began operating from July 2013: a full year earlier than what the Productivity Commission had recommended in its Disability Care and Support report outlining the scheme (Productivity Commission 2011, 1:59).

This chapter provides an overview of this initial phase of the NDIS roll out—the trial phase.[1] It describes how governments cooperated through intergovernmental agreements for the trials, and summarises the approaches to trialling the NDIS taken in each state and territory. It then

M. Cowden (✉) · C. McCullagh (✉) · J. Tran
Nous Group, Perth, WA, Australia

[1] We recognise that some of the trial/launch documents refer to the NDIS 'launch'. For simplicity, we refer to the initial trial/launch period of the NDIS as the 'trial' phase, as this is now the more common understanding of the initial operation of the scheme.

M. Cowden and C. McCullagh (eds.), *The National Disability Insurance Scheme*, https://doi.org/10.1007/978-981-16-2244-1_5

describes some initial lessons learned through NDIS trial evaluations and reports, which characterise the NDIS trial period as a time of continual negotiations, fast roll out speeds and variable outcomes for participants.

Cooperation Through Intergovernmental Agreements

Intergovernmental cooperation through agreements is a critical part of policymaking in Australia. Our federated system including national, state and local governments, combined with constitutional limitations to the powers of each level of government, means that agreements become an important mechanism for intergovernmental initiatives. In addition, 'vertical fiscal imbalance'—where the Commonwealth Government holds the majority of the power to raise tax revenue, while State and Territory Governments hold most of the legislative powers to spend money in key areas (Burton et al. 2016)—means that the Commonwealth can use agreements as a way to ensure state and territory spending aligns with agreed aims.

As discussed in Chapter 4, the NDIS trial sites were to be jointly funded by the Commonwealth Government, and State and Territory Governments. This meant intergovernmental agreements would play a critical role in codifying joint funding arrangements for the scheme. While some obligations for the NDIS are legislated through the *National Disability Insurance Scheme (NDIS) Act 2013*, others are by agreement only, such as scheme finances and responsibility for risk. It is also worth noting that intergovernmental agreements of this nature are not legally binding: they are often described as 'political undertakings' and in most cases do not contain legally enforceable obligations (Chordia 2013). Although there is a strong convention of honouring intergovernmental agreements, they are open to being renegotiated or reinterpreted over time.

Intergovernmental Agreements for the NDIS Trials

On 7 December 2012, the Commonwealth Government, and State and Territory Governments, came together at the Council of Australian

Governments (COAG)—Australia's then peak forum for domestic intergovernmental cooperation—to sign an Intergovernmental Agreement for the NDIS trials (NDIS Intergovernmental Agreement). The NDIS Intergovernmental Agreement outlined the consistent principles, roles and responsibilities that would apply across jurisdictions for the trials. These included that governments would jointly fund the cost of the trial, participate in a Ministerial Council responsible for agreeing policy for the trial, share information and data, monitor progress and continue to support people with disability not eligible for NDIS support (COAG 2012a, 3–4).

The Commonwealth Government was to be solely responsible for introducing the National Disability Insurance Scheme Bill 2012 and for funding 100% of the risk of cost overrun due to increased client numbers or higher than expected support costs. The Commonwealth would also pay the cost of establishing and administering the agency set up to deliver the NDIS: the National Disability Launch Agency (known as the National Disability Insurance Agency or the NDIA) (COAG 2012a, 5–6). Beneath the NDIS Intergovernmental Agreement, COAG later agreed to a set of principles guiding the responsibilities of the NDIS and other service systems, such as the health, education and housing systems (COAG 2013).

Bilateral Agreements between the Commonwealth Government and individual State and Territory Governments were negotiated and attached as schedules to the NDIS Intergovernmental Agreement (Trial Bilateral Agreements). The Trial Bilateral Agreements outlined the specific arrangements which would apply for the NDIS in each trial site. Five Trial Bilateral Agreements were originally signed with New South Wales (NSW) (Schedule A), Victoria (Schedule B), South Australia (SA) (Schedule C), Tasmania (Schedule D) and the Australian Capital Territory (ACT) (Schedule E). Agreements were later signed with the Northern Territory (NT) (Schedule F) and Western Australia (WA) (Schedule G). As Queensland transitioned directly to a full NDIS without a trial, it did not sign a Trial Bilateral Agreement. Key arrangements agreed for the trial of the NDIS in each state and territory are outlined and discussed below.

NSW

Trial Bilateral Agreement for the NDIS in NSW was signed on 7 December 2012, in parallel with the overarching NDIS Intergovernmental Agreement. This followed an announcement on 1 August 2012 that the Commonwealth and NSW Governments had reached an agreement to establish a trial site in NSW's Hunter region from mid-2013 (Macklin and Constance 2012). The NSW NDIS trial would operate for three years from July 2013, in the three local government areas: Newcastle, Lake Macquarie and Maitland, for all eligible residents. It was expected that approximately 10,000 residents would become NDIS clients during the trial (COAG 2012b, 3).

The NSW Trial Bilateral Agreement outlined a shared funding approach that would apply for the trial. The Commonwealth Government agreed to:

- Fund NDIS supports for people with disability through both 'in-kind' (existing government-funded disability services) and cash contributions. The Commonwealth Government's total contribution towards NDIS-funded supports in NSW trial would add up to approximately $200 million—around 40% of the total cost of direct supports[2] (COAG 2012b, 8);
- Bear 100% of risks during the trial, including population, financial and transition risks (COAG 2012b, 3);
- Cover 100% of the risk during transition between the end of the trial and full scheme commencement, or until an alternative arrangement is made (COAG 2012b, 4);
- Fund all NDIA-related administrative and system support costs associated with the trial (COAG 2012b, 9);
- Meet all scheme costs associated with participants over 65 years (or 50 years for Indigenous participants) who choose to remain in the NDIS rather than transitioning to the aged care system (COAG 2012b, 3–4).

The NSW Government would contribute a fixed amount to the Hunter region trial, capped at a maximum of $550 million over three years. This would include $293 million for individual support packages and local support coordination roles: approximately 60% of total funded support

[2] Values calculated through summing annual values in Table 3—Commonwealth's funding for NDIS funded supports. Percentages calculated in combination with total values in Table 7—NSW funding for individual support packages and local support coordination.

costs for the trial.[3] Like the Commonwealth Government, the NSW Government's share of funding for the NDIS trials was to be provided in cash, and through direct provision of services (in-kind services) (COAG 2012b, 10).

The NSW Trial Bilateral Agreement included a commitment to uphold the rights of people with disability by guaranteeing the quality and safety of their NDIS services. The NSW Government's existing quality assurance framework would apply during the trial in the Hunter site, subject to the further development of, and transition to, a nationally consistent, risk-based quality assurance framework over the longer term. Participants would have access to a range of NSW complaints mechanisms: they could lodge complaints with the NDIA, Administrative Appeals Tribunal, Ombudsman, Health Care Complaints Commission or any other NSW or Commonwealth body or tribunal as appropriate (COAG 2012b, 5). Governments also committed to ensuring continuity of support arrangements for clients receiving support under existing contracts, who then entered the NDIS (COAG 2012b, 3).

Through the NSW Trial Bilateral Agreement, the Commonwealth Government and the NSW Government agreed that services to support individuals with decision-making (such as Local Area Coordination roles to support service planning and coordination) would be needed from the date of trial commencement. The NSW Government's in-kind funding contribution for the trial therefore included the provision of its Ability Links NSW and Aboriginal Ability Links programs, as well as diagnosis support workers and other coordination and decision-making services (COAG 2012b, 4). While the NSW trial was to be delivered by the NDIA, the NSW Government would continue to provide access points, through shopfronts and service outlets, for disability services in the trial site. Interfaces and protocols were established to provide cross-referral, transfer participant information and refer participants to local services, as required (COAG 2012b, 3).

By the end of the trial, there were 7,805 participants with approved support plans in the NDIS Hunter trial site (NDIA 2016a). Surveys of participants during and after the NSW NDIS trial indicated that most

[3] Total calculated through summing annual values in Table 7—NSW funding for individual support packages and local support coordination. Percentages calculated in combination with total values in Table 3—Commonwealth's funding for NDIS funded supports.

of their experiences with the NDIA were good or very good. In 2014, around 98% of participants in NSW rated their planning process experience as either good or very good (Commonwealth of Australia 2014a). Similarly, in 2016, 98% of participants and their carers and families rated their experience of the NDIA as good or very good (NDIA 2016b, 49).

Victoria

On 7 December 2012, a Trial Bilateral Agreement for commencement of an NDIS trial was signed by the Commonwealth Government and the Victorian Government. This Agreement followed a Commonwealth Government announcement on 12 August 2012 that it had reached agreement with Victoria to establish a trial site in the Barwon region from mid-2013 (Macklin et al. 2012). The Victorian trial was to commence from July 2013 and would take place over a three-year period. It would cover all eligible residents in the City of Greater Geelong, Colac-Otway Shire, Surf Coast Shire and the Borough of Queenscliffe areas. The trial was expected to benefit around 5,000 residents. Unlike the NSW Hunter Region trial, which rolled out geographically, the Victoria Barwon trial site was to be rolled out by program areas (COAG 2012c, 2).

The Commonwealth Government and the Victorian State Government agreed to similar roles and responsibilities for the Victorian trial as had been struck for the NSW trial. Funding terms were to be broadly similar to those outlined in the NSW agreement, with both parties agreeing to contribute a fixed amount, including both cash and in-kind components (COAG 2012c, 3). NDIS-funded supports would, as in NSW, be covered by both the Commonwealth Government (contributing approximately 40%)[4] and the Victorian Government (contributing approximately 60%)[5] for the duration of the trial, with the Commonwealth Government responsible for 100% of the support costs for participants who turn 65 (50 for Indigenous participants) and chose to stay in the scheme

[4] Values calculated by summing Table 3—Commonwealth's funding for NDIS funded supports. Percentage calculated by combining with the sum of values from Table 7—Victoria's funding for NDIS funded supports.

[5] Values calculated by summing Table 7—Victoria's funding for NDIS funded supports. Percentage calculated by combining with the sum of values from Table 3—Commonwealth's funding for NDIS funded supports.

(COAG 2012c, 9). Similar to the NSW Trial Bilateral Agreement, Victoria's existing quality and safeguarding arrangements would apply during the trial and continuity of support arrangements for trial participants would be assured (COAG 2012c, 3–4).

By the end of the trial period, there were 5,284 participants with approved support plans in the Barwon trial site (NDIA 2016a). Surveys of participants during and after the NDIS launch indicated that most of their experiences with the NDIA were good or very good. In 2014, around 97% of participants in Victoria rated their experience with the planning process today as good or very good (Commonwealth of Australia 2014b). In 2016, 97% of participants and their carers and families rated their experience with the NDIA as either good or very good (NDIA 2016b, 49).

SA

A Bilateral Agreement for the SA trial was signed on 7 December 2012. This followed announcement on 25 July 2012 that in-principle agreement had been reached for trial sites in SA, Tasmania and the ACT (COAG 2012d). Unlike the agreement with NSW, the trial in SA would cover the entire state but eligibility would be restricted to children with disability aged 0–14 and their families. The SA Trial Bilateral Agreement outlined that the NDIS trial would operate for up to three years from July 2013. NDIS services would be available to eligible children aged 0–5 years from July 2013, to eligible children aged up to 13 years from July 2014 and to eligible children aged up to 14 years from July 2015. It was initially expected that approximately 5,000 children with disability would benefit from the SA trial (COAG 2012e, 3).

The Commonwealth Government and the SA Government agreed to similar governance arrangements, roles and funding responsibilities as those agreed for the NSW and Victorian NDIS trials. A key difference in the SA Trial Bilateral Agreement is that it recognises uncertainty around the number of children with developmental delay who may be found eligible for the trial, and so commits governments to revisit trial population estimates in 12 months (COAG 2012e, 7). Higher than expected numbers of children with developmental delay, and Autism Spectrum Disorder, did indeed enter the SA NDIS during the trial period. This led to governments revising the estimated trial participant numbers for 2014–2015 from 5,000, up to 8,500 (COAG 2016a, Schedule A, 1).

By the end of June 2016, there were 7,117 participants with approved support plans in SA (NDIA 2016a, 33). Surveys of participants during and after the SA NDIS trial indicated that most of their experiences with the NDIA were good or very good. In 2014, around 88% of participants in SA rated their experience with the planning process today as good or very good, 10 percentage points lower than the satisfaction rate at the same time in NSW (Commonwealth of Australia 2014c). In 2016, 93% of participants and their carers and families rated their experience with the NDIA as good or very good, slightly lower than the same time in NSW (NDIA 2016b, 49).

Tasmania

A Bilateral Agreement for the Tasmanian NDIS trial was signed on 7 December 2012, following the July 2012 COAG announcement that in-principle agreement for a Tasmanian NDIS trial had been reached. Like SA, the trial in Tasmania was designed to cover the entire state and was limited to a specific age cohort—this time, to eligible individuals aged 15–24. Over the course of the trial—running for three years from July 2013—residents were permitted to enter the scheme as they turned 15 years old. In recognition of the need for continuity and ongoing support, once a resident entered the trial, participants were to remain in the scheme even once they turned 25 and beyond. Around 950 Tasmanian residents were expected to benefit from the NDIS trial (COAG 2012f, 3).

Governance and funding arrangements, roles and responsibilities for the Tasmanian trial were agreed on similar terms to the Trial Bilateral Agreements already discussed. A key difference was that Tasmania already had a well-established regional access point—the Gateway Service—which, prior to the NDIS, acted as an intake, referral, assessment and Local Area Coordination service for people with disability. Under the Tasmanian Trial Bilateral Agreement, community members would be able to access information about the NDIS from a range of service points in the community, with referrals to the scheme able to be made either directly to the NDIA or through the Gateway Service. The Gateway Services would provide background materials, diagnoses and previous assessments of people with disability to the NDIS where relevant, and with consent (COAG 2012f, 3–4).

By the end of the trial period, there were 1,162 young people with approved support plans participating in the Tasmanian NDIS trial (NDIA 2016a). Surveys of participants during and after the NDIS trial indicated that most of their experiences with the NDIA were good or very good. In 2014, 100% of participants in Tasmania rated their experience with the planning process today as good or very good (Commonwealth of Australia 2014d). In 2016, 97% of participants and their carers and families rated their experience with the NDIA as good or very good (NDIA 2016b, 49).

ACT

A Bilateral Agreement for the ACT trial was signed on 7 December 2012, following the July 2012 COAG announcement that in-principle agreement had been reached. The ACT's Trial Bilateral Agreement sets out that the trial would operate across the whole territory. Around 5,000 residents were expected to benefit, with roll out to occur from July 2014 across two financial years. NDIS intake would be in 'ages and stages', involving transitioning clients by specific age cohorts determined by date of birth or by academic year for children and young people of school age concurrently (COAG 2012g, Appendix C, 1).

As the ACT is located within the state of NSW, many people live in NSW but work or travel into the ACT for services. Considering this, the Commonwealth Government and the ACT Government agreed that people living outside the ACT trial area, but receiving their disability support services within the trial site, would not be affected by the trial (COAG 2012g, 3).

By the end of the trial period, there were 4,098 participants with approved support plans in the ACT (NDIA 2016a). Surveys of participants after the NDIS trial indicated that most of their experiences with the NDIA were good or very good. In 2016, 96% of ACT participants, their carers and families rated their experience with the NDIA as either good or very good (NDIA 2016b, 49).

NT

On 19 April 2013, the Commonwealth Government announced that an in-principle agreement had been reached with the NT Government to establish a trial site in Barkly—a remote region of the NT—from July

2014 (Gillard and Giles 2013). A Trial Bilateral Agreement signed on 2 May 2014, outlining that the NDIS trial would operate over a two-year period. It was expected that approximately 150 residents would benefit from the Barkley NDIS trial (COAG 2014a, 2–3).

Similar governance, roles and funding arrangements were agreed for the NT compared to other jurisdictions. However, the NT Trial Bilateral Agreement also included explicit aims concerning the delivery of the NDIS in rural and remote settings, including around:

- Exploring and evaluating service delivery models required for remote Indigenous people who might be eligible for the NDIS;
- Exploring rural and remote workforce attraction approaches;
- Examining how choice and control can work with limited provider options;
- Examining how the disability service marked can be stimulated in remote environments; and
- Exploring options for employment and training for people with disability in rural and remote environments (COAG 2014a, 2–3).

By the end of the trial period, there were 155 participants with approved plans in the Barkley trial site (NDIA 2016a). An evaluation of the NDIS looked specifically at the outcomes of the NDIS trial in the Barkly region. The evaluation highlighted that the prevalence of disability and associated health and social support needs in Barkley was likely to be higher than the number of NDIS participants (Mavromaras et al. 2018, xxiii). This indicates there is likely to be a significant number of people with disability in Barkley who, although eligible, did not access the NDIS trial in the NT.

The Barkly trial led to some participants receiving additional funding and supports than they had previously. However, participant outcomes and experiences of the scheme during this trial were variable. Participants with poor English literacy, without strong advocates or living in remote Indigenous communities had especially limited positive outcomes under the NDIS (Mavromaras et al. 2018, xxiii). In addition, choice and control in the region was 'an almost theoretical concept' due to the absence of a viable disability support market; therefore, levels of unmet demand—where participants had a plan, but no access to organisations able to provide them with services—were high among Barkly participants (Mavromaras et al. 2018, xxiii).

WA

Unlike other states and territories, negotiations between the Commonwealth and WA Governments did not initially result in an agreement on the model of the NDIS to be rolled out. The WA Government argued that the strong history of disability service reform within the state, the relationship between the WA Government and the disability service sector, and the geographic challenges associated with delivering services across a large state with a dispersed population meant that the NDIS would be better delivered by the WA Government rather than a newly established Commonwealth agency (the NDIA).

Consequently, on 5 August 2013, the Commonwealth Government announced that it had reached an agreement with the WA Government to establish two two-year trials from July 2014, one operating under the national NDIS model to be delivered by the NDIA and the other operating under the WA Government's My Way model to be delivered by the WA Disability Services Commission (Buckmaster and Clark 2018). Two subsequent agreements were signed in 2014, one to support each trial site:

- A Trial Bilateral Agreement was signed on 31 March 2014 to cover arrangements for the NDIA-operated NDIS trial sites from July 2014 in Perth Hills suburbs of Kalamunda and Mundaring, extending into Swan in 2015. Approximately 4,300 residents were expected to benefit (COAG 2014b, 2–3).
- A National Partnership Agreement on Trial of My Way sites, also signed on 31 March 2014 and supporting a WA Government-operated My Way trial. This trial was to commence from July 2014 in WA's Lower South West region and from July 2015 in the Cockburn-Kwinana region (COAG 2014c).

WA's approach was intended to allow for the assessment and comparison of the merits of the two different approaches to disability services (COAG 2014b, 2). Both governments agreed to co-fund an independent comparative evaluation of the services and outcomes in the

NDIA-operated trial site and the WA Government-operated My Way sites (COAG 2014b, 7–8).

Like trials in other states and territories, the Commonwealth Government would provide a financial contribution equivalent to approximately 40% of individual support package costs and the WA Government agreed to provide a financial contribution equivalent to 60% of package costs to support trial participants in both the NDIA and WA Government-operated trial sites. This funding was to be provided as both cash and in-kind contributions (COAG 2014b, c). Similar to other jurisdictions, where a person over 65 years (or 50 years for Indigenous participants) chose to remain in the NDIS rather than transitioning to the aged care system, the Commonwealth Government would be responsible for meeting these participant costs. The Commonwealth would also meet 100% of any costs associated with higher population numbers or higher per person NDIS-funded support costs in the NDIA-operated Perth Hills trial site, and 100% of the NDIA's cash flow risk during the trial (COAG 2014b, 7–8).

However, the WA Government agreed to meet 100% of any costs associated with higher population numbers or higher per person funded support costs in the My Way trial. It also agreed to cover 100% of the cash flow risk of the Disability Services Commission during the trial (COAG 2014c, 5–12). The WA Government was also required to nominate its own actuary for the My Way trials, to assess and prepare reports on its participants, expenditure, sustainability, risks and key trends (COAG 2014c, 8).

As part of the WA Trial Bilateral Agreement for the Perth Hills trial site, the WA Government agreed to make best endeavours to ensure appropriate staff were available to undertake Local Area Coordinator roles for both WA-based trials (COAG 2014b, 5). At this time, Local Area Coordinators were already an established part of WA's disability system, working to support people with disability to build their capacity to access other support systems, influence community attitudes about inclusion and address systemic barriers to participation for people with disability. The WA Government agreed that during both WA NDIS trials, existing Local Area Coordinators would assist people with disability in the community by:

- Providing general information about the scheme, the types of supports available through the NDIA and other supports available in the community at relevant community-based activities;
- Providing information to other stakeholders likely to play a key role in the lives of people with disability;
- Linking people with disability to providers of supports so that less complex needs are met efficiently;
- Helping to build the independence of people with disability through building their capacity and their informal networks of support;
- Identifying and working with community organisations to build their capacity to understand and respond to needs and to become more inclusive and meet the needs of people with disability;
- Providing information about how to make an access request, what information will be needed and what to expect in working with the NDIA;
- Assisting people to access the NDIA and making appointments with the NDIA on their behalf where requested; and
- Participating in planning discussions where they have an existing relationship with the participant (COAG 2014b, 4–5).

Two Local Advisory Groups were also established—one for each trial—to advise on how the trials were progressing. These Local Advisory Groups were not decision-making forums; they were a mechanism for the NDIA and the Disability Services Commission to discuss and seek resolution to issues at a local level, within existing policy frameworks (COAG 2014b, 19–20; Disability Services Commission, n.d.). A Joint Steering Committee was also established to oversee progress and the evaluation of the NDIS trials in WA (COAG 2014c, A-1–2).

Portability arrangements for the NDIS and My Way trials allowed participants to move into different disability service systems (this included moving within different parts of WA, or to another state outside WA) and be ensured continuing support and funding for up to 12 months. This was intended to allow an individual time to secure services, support and funding when they moved to a new place of residence. Trial participants in both the NDIS and My Way trials were also assured that they would receive ongoing support until transition to a full scheme commenced or an agreement is made covering ongoing support to trial participants (Disability Services Commission 2017).

Negotiations between the Commonwealth and WA Government continued during the two-year trial period, but no agreement on how the scheme would be rolled out in WA was reached. As a result, on 27 April 2016, the Commonwealth Government and the WA Government signed additional agreements to extend the period of operation of the both trials for 12 months until 30 June 2017, and to expand both trials into new geographic areas. From 1 January 2017, the NDIA-operated trial was to expand into Bayswater, Bassendean, Chittering, Toodyay, York and Northam, covering an additional 1,223 participants by the end of the trial (COAG 2016b, 1). The My Way trial would expand to include Armadale, Murray and Serpentine-Jarrahdale from 1 October 2016 to 30 June 2017, to support an estimated additional 1,479 participants (COAG 2016c, 2 and 13).

Queensland

There was no NDIS trial in Queensland. Rather, there was an early transition to full scheme agreed in three sites: Townsville, Charters Towers and Palm Island. This transition is discussed in Chapter 6. By 2016, when most trials in other states and territories ended, 361 people in Queensland were NDIS participants (NDIA 2016a).

Lessons from the NDIS Trial Phase

There have been many reviews and reports commissioned into the early operations of the NDIS. Lessons from the trial phase are outlined in three main reports—the 'Review of the Capabilities of the National Disability Insurance Agency', the 'Final Report of the Evaluation of the NDIS' and the 'WA NDIS Trials Evaluation Final Report'. Key insights from each of these reports are outlined and discussed below.

A Review of the Capabilities of the NDIA

The Review of the Capabilities of the NDIA (Capability Review) was an independent review that used the Australian Public Service Commission's own methodology to identify the strengths and weaknesses of the leadership, strategy and delivery capabilities of the NDIA as an organisation (Whalan et al. 2014, 3). The Review found the NDIA opening its doors in Barwon, Hunter, Tasmania and SA in July 2013 to be a remarkable achievement, but that there were key lessons to be learned from the trials.

The Capability Review found that bringing the commencement date for the trial phase of the NDIS forward by one year from what was originally recommended came at a cost. There were notable implementation and organisational challenges, which included operating with an Information and Communications Technology (ICT) system that was not fit for purpose, poor recruitment and retention of staff, poor data on eligible participants and a lack of clear guidance for staff on the way the scheme was intended to operate, including on key definitions such as eligibility and reasonable and necessary support (Whalan et al. 2014, 5–6). Delivering the trials ahead of the initial date also meant insufficient effort devoted to preparing for the next phase of roll out of the scheme after the trial period had ended (Whalan et al. 2014, 6). This raised concerns for the next phase of the NDIS—transition to full scheme—and whether the NDIA had the capacity to scale up to achieve this.

The Capability Review was prophetic, highlighting that the ambition of the NDIS and the proposed timetable for its roll out may not be achievable (Whalan et al. 2014, 6). It famously described the NDIS as being like 'a plane that took off before it had been fully built and is being completed while it is in the air' (Whalan et al. 2014, 7). Not only was the reform and program of service delivery new, but it was being undertaken by an agency—the NDIA—that had itself just been set up and had less capability to take on a new project than an established organisation may have had. These are challenges that the NDIS continues to face today.

Another key observation from the Capability Review was a potential conflict in the role of NDIA planners—core delivery staff who were expected to be both 'stewards of sustainability', who contained scheme costs, and advocates and enablers for people with disability (Whalan et al. 2014, 11). This tension has continued to play out as the scheme has rolled out.

NDIS Evaluation Final Report

Throughout the trials of the NDIS, the Commonwealth Government commissioned and ran an ongoing evaluation of the trial operations and outcomes for participants. The Final Report of the NDIS Evaluation (NDIS Evaluation) was released in 2018. The NDIS Evaluation assessed the many impacts of the trials that took place in SA, Tasmania, NSW,

Victoria, the ACT and the NT; it did not cover Queensland or WA, given their different arrangements.

The Evaluation found that the types and number of supports received by many NDIS participants increased due to their participation in the scheme. In general, the NDIS trials were found to have led to increased levels and quality of services and support.

However, not all people with disability were found to experience improved outcomes under the NDIS. In particular, people with disability who did not have the capacity to advocate for themselves, or navigate the complex NDIS processes, were at risk of, and in some cases were shown to be, receiving lower levels of services than they had previously (Mavromaras et al. 2018, xv). In addition, most NDIS participants wanted to have more choice and control over the supports they received, with one-fifth of NDIS participants reporting that they had little choice and control over their supports (Mavromaras et al. 2018, xv). Participants also reported experiencing a lack of service providers, long waiting lists, limited information regarding options and inflexibility of service provision. Only a minority of participants chose to self-manage their NDIS funding, and this uptake did not increase over time (Mavromaras et al. 2018, xvii).

While most participants reported a high level of satisfaction and that their NDIS supports were 'reasonable and necessary', results varied according to the characteristics of the participants. People with developmental or congenital disability were mostly satisfied, while those with intellectual or psychosocial disability were the least satisfied with the support received through the NDIS (Mavromaras et al. 2018, xvii). Dissatisfaction was commonly because of the variability of, and gaps within, individualised plans, and due to perceived inequality between the plans of participants with similar disabilities. There NDIS Evaluation also found a perceived inconsistency in decision-making, a lack of transparency, and variable levels of skills and experience held by NDIA planners to be additional issues (Mavromaras et al. 2018, xvii).

The NDIS Evaluation provided a range of specific findings particular to the trial in the NT, ruling its 'approach and implementation' to be 'ineffective' (Mavromaras et al. 2018, xxiii). It recommended the adoption of a model that was 'more culturally sensitive and appropriate to remote needs and service delivery' (Mavromaras et al. 2018, xxiii).

Overall, the results of the NDIS Evaluation demonstrated that the trial left a large minority (about a third) as well off as they were before, and a small minority (between 10 and 20%) feeling worse off. This finding pointed towards the need for closer monitoring and more targeted and person-centred policy responses (Mavromaras et al. 2018, xxiii). Echoing the early warning signs of the Capability Review, the NDIS Evaluation concluded that the speed of roll out was too fast and more thought would be needed regarding the practical aspects of roll out in future.

WA Independent Evaluation

As outlined previously, the Commonwealth and WA Governments co-funded and commissioned an independent comparative evaluation of the services and outcomes in the NDIA-operated trial site and the WA Government-operated My Way sites (WA Evaluation). The WA Evaluation found that there were many similarities between the two models being trialled in WA: both operated within the nationally consistent parameters of the NDIS legislation and rules, adopted common eligibility requirements and the same definition of 'reasonable and necessary support' (Stantons International 2016, 2–3).

Despite these similarities, the WA Evaluation found that the two models were derived from different starting points. The WA My Way model was based on 20 years of reform and practice within WA whereas the NDIA model was found to be 'newly developed to meet the specific needs of the NDIA at a national level' (Stantons International 2016, 3). The WA Evaluation found that after assessing the process, capabilities and systems of the two trials, the WA Government-operated model was the closest fit to the key features of an effective model for WA; however, it needed to continue to change and evolve (Stantons International 2016, 6).

Conclusion

The first phase of the NDIS roll out occurred through the launching of trial sites in locations across Australia. These trials were conducted in different ways—through providing services to all eligible participants in a geographic location, limiting services to participants of certain age cohorts, rolling out geographically, rolling out by program area and trialling two different operating models.

The speed by which the trials were launched was likely driven by a political imperative to see the NDIS launched and underway prior to the

2013 federal election. Launching the NDIS may have helped ensure that it was a policy reform unable to be reversed as future governments came to power, but this appears to have come at a price in that it put quantity (the number of people entering into the scheme) over service quality and outcomes for participants during these early years.

Evaluations show us that the NDIS trials seemed to function well in areas with an established disability services market, and participants have the capacity to navigate systems. In areas with thin or non-existent markets, and for participants with complex needs, the NDIS trials did not appear to function according to its original intent. Addressing these problems and finding a way that the NDIS could work for everyone was one of the key challenges faced by the scheme as it entered the next phase—transition to full scheme operations.

References

Buckmaster, Luke, and Shannon Clark. 2018. The National Disability Insurance Scheme: A Chronology. Parliament of Australia. https://www.aph.gov.au/About_Parliament/Parliamentary_Departments/Parliamentary_Library/pubs/rp/rp1819/Chronologies/NDIS.

Burton, Therese, Brian Dollery, and Joseph Wallis. 2016. A Century of Vertical Fiscal Imbalance in Australian Federalism. *History of Economics Review* 36: 26–43.

Chordia, Shipra. 2013. Legally Binding or Not: Why Breaking the Gonski Funding Deals Matters. The Conversation.

COAG. 2012a. Intergovernmental Agreement for the National Insurance Scheme (NDIS) Launch. https://www.coag.gov.au/about-coag/agreements/intergovernmental-agreement-national-disability-insurance-scheme-launch#:~:text=Intergovernmental%20Agreement%20on%20the%20National%20Disability%20Insurance%20Scheme%20Launch,-On%2029%20May&text=On%207%20December%202012%2C%20COAG,Agreement%20for%20the%20NDIS%20Launch.

COAG. 2012b. Bilateral Agreement for NDIS Launch Between the Commonwealth and New South Wales. Intergovernmental Agreement for the National Insurance Scheme (NDIS) Launch. https://www.coag.gov.au/about-coag/agreements/intergovernmental-agreement-national-disability-insurance-scheme-launch#:~:text=Intergovernmental%20Agreement%20on%20the%20National%20Disability%20Insurance%20Scheme%20Launch,-On%2029%20May&text=On%207%20December%202012%2C%20COAG,Agreement%20for%20the%20NDIS%20Launch.

COAG. 2012c. Bilateral Agreement for NDIS Launch Between the Commonwealth and Victoria. Intergovernmental Agreement for the National Insurance Scheme (NDIS) Launch. https://www.coag.gov.au/about-coag/agreements/intergovernmental-agreement-national-disability-insurance-scheme-launch#:~:text=Intergovernmental%20Agreement%20on%20the%20National%20Disability%20Insurance%20Scheme%20Launch,-On%2029%20May&text=On%207%20December%202012%2C%20COAG,Agreement%20for%20the%20NDIS%20Launch.

COAG. 2012d. Meeting Communique, 25 July 2012. https://www.coag.gov.au/meeting-outcomes/coag-meeting-communique-25-july-2012.

COAG. 2012e. Bilateral Agreement for NDIS Launch Between the Commonwealth and South Australia. Intergovernmental Agreement for the National Insurance Scheme. https://www.coag.gov.au/about-coag/agreements/intergovernmental-agreement-national-disability-insurance-scheme-launch#:~:text=Intergovernmental%20Agreement%20on%20the%20National%20Disability%20Insurance%20Scheme%20Launch,-On%2029%20May&text=On%207%20December%202012%2C%20COAG,Agreement%20for%20the%20NDIS%20Launch.

COAG. 2012f. Bilateral Agreement for NDIS Launch Between the Commonwealth and Tasmania. Intergovernmental Agreement for the National Insurance Scheme (NDIS) Launch. https://www.coag.gov.au/about-coag/agreements/intergovernmental-agreement-national-disability-insurance-scheme-launch#:~:text=Intergovernmental%20Agreement%20on%20the%20National%20Disability%20Insurance%20Scheme%20Launch,-On%2029%20May&text=On%207%20December%202012%2C%20COAG,Agreement%20for%20the%20NDIS%20Launch.

COAG. 2012g. Bilateral Agreement for NDIS Launch Between the Commonwealth and Australian Capital Territory. Intergovernmental Agreement for the National Insurance Scheme (NDIS) Launch. https://www.coag.gov.au/about-coag/agreements/intergovernmental-agreement-national-disability-insurance-scheme-launch#:~:text=Intergovernmental%20Agreement%20on%20the%20National%20Disability%20Insurance%20Scheme%20Launch,-On%2029%20May&text=On%207%20December%202012%2C%20COAG,Agreement%20for%20the%20NDIS%20Launch.

COAG. 2013. Principles to Determine the Responsibilities of the NDIS and Other Services. https://www.coag.gov.au/sites/default/files/communique/NDIS-Principles-to-Determine-Responsibilities-NDIS-and-Other-Service.pdf.

COAG. 2014a. Bilateral Agreement for NDIS Launch Between the Commonwealth and Northern Territory. Intergovernmental Agreement for the National Insurance Scheme (NDIS) Launch. https://www.coag.gov.au/about-coag/agreements/intergovernmental-agreement-national-disability-insurance-scheme-launch#:~:text=Intergovernmental%20Agreement%

20on%20the%20National%20Disability%20Insurance%20Scheme%20Launch,-On%2029%20MaCOAy&text=On%207%20December%202012%2C%20C OAG,Agreement%20for%20the%20NDIS%20Launch.

COAG. 2014b. Bilateral Agreement for NDIS Launch Between the Commonwealth and Western Australia. Intergovernmental Agreement for the National Insurance Scheme (NDIS) Launch. https://www.coag.gov.au/about-coag/agreements/intergovernmental-agreement-national-disability-insurance-scheme-launch#:~:text=Intergovernmental%20Agreement%20on%20the%20National%20Disability%20Insurance%20Scheme%20Launch,-On%2029%20May&text=On%207%20December%202012%2C%20COAG,Agreement%20for%20the%20NDIS%20Launch.

COAG. 2014c. National Partnership Agreement on Trial of My Way Sites: An Agreement Between the Commonwealth of Australia and Western Australia. COAG. http://www.disability.wa.gov.au/Global/Publications/WA-NDIS-My-Way/National-Partnership-Agreement-on-trial-of-My-Way-sites-March-2014.pdf.

COAG. 2016a. Bilateral Agreement Between the Commonwealth and South Australia: Transition to a National Disability Insurance Scheme. https://www.coag.gov.au/sites/default/files/communique/NDIS_SA.PDF.

COAG. 2016b. Schedule H: Bilateral Agreement for the Extension and Expansion of the National Disability Insurance Scheme National Disability Insurance Agency Trial Between the Commonwealth and Western Australia. https://www.coag.gov.au/sites/default/files/agreements/sched-h-wa-bilateral-agreement-signed.pdf.

COAG. 2016c. National Partnership on the Extension and Expansion of the Trial of WA NDIS Sites. http://www.federalfinancialrelations.gov.au/content/npa/community_services/national-partnership/past/Extension-Expansion-Trial-WA-NDIS-Sites-NP.pdf.

Commonwealth of Australia. 2014a. 'Chapter 4—The Hunter Trial Site': First Progress Report on the Implementation and Administration of the National Disability Insurance Scheme. Parliament of Australia. https://www.aph.gov.au/Parliamentary_Business/Committees/Joint/National_Disability_Insurance_Scheme/JNDIS-44th/First_progress_report/c04.

Commonwealth of Australia. 2014b. 'Chapter 2—The Barwon Trial Site': First Progress Report on the Implementation and Administration of the National Disability Insurance Scheme. Parliament of Australia. https://www.aph.gov.au/Parliamentary_Business/Committees/Joint/National_Disability_Insurance_Scheme/JNDIS-44th/First_progress_report/c02.

Commonwealth of Australia. 2014c. 'Chapter 5—The South Australian Trial Site': First Progress Report on the Implementation and Administration of the National Disability Insurance Scheme. Parliament of Australia. https://

www.aph.gov.au/Parliamentary_Business/Committees/Joint/National_Disability_Insurance_Scheme/JNDIS-44th/First_progress_report/c05.
Commonwealth of Australia. 2014d. 'Chapter 3—The Tasmanian Trial Site': First Progress Report on the Implementation and Administration of the National Disability Insurance Scheme. Parliament of Australia. https://www.aph.gov.au/Parliamentary_Business/Committees/Joint/National_Disability_Insurance_Scheme/JNDIS-44th/First_progress_report/c03.
Disability Services Commission. 2017. WA NDIS Operational Policy: Portability. Government of Western Australia. http://www.disability.wa.gov.au/Documents/WANDIS_OpPol_Portability%20(Internet%20only).pdf.
Disability Services Commission. n.d. WA NDIS Reference Group—Terms of Reference. http://www.disability.wa.gov.au/Global/Publications/WA%20NDIS/Minutes/Terms-of-Reference.pdf.
Gillard, Julia, and Adam Giles. 2013. Launch of Disability Care Australia in Barkley region of the Northern Territory. Joint Media Release—19 April 2013.
Gillard, Julia, and Jenny Macklin. 2012. Budget 2012: Funding the First Stage of the National Disability Insurance Scheme. Parliament of Australia. https://parlinfo.aph.gov.au/parlInfo/download/media/pressrel/1601478/upload_binary/1601478.pdf;fileType=application%2Fpdf#search=%22media/pressrel/1601478%22.
Macklin, Jenny, and Andrew Constance. 2012. Launching a NDIS in the Hunter. Press Release. https://parlinfo.aph.gov.au/parlInfo/search/display/display.w3p;query=Id:%22media/pressrel/1822395%22.
Macklin, Jenny, Ted Bailieu, and Mary Woodridge. 2012. Transcript of Joint Press Conferences: 12 August 2012: National Disability Insurance Scheme Launch in the Barwon Region. Press Release. https://parlinfo.aph.gov.au/parlInfo/search/display/display.w3p;query=Id:%22media/pressrel/2183315%22.
Mavromaras, Kostas, Megan Moskos, Stéphane Mahuteau, and Linda Isherwood. 2018. Evaluation of the NDIS: Final Report, National Institute of Labour Studies. National Institute of Labour Studies Flinders University. https://www.dss.gov.au/sites/default/files/documents/04_2018/ndis_evaluation_consolidated_report_april_2018.pdf.
NDIA. 2016a. Infographic of Quarter 4: 2015–16 Report. NDIS https://www.ndis.gov.au/about-us/publications/quarterly-reports/archived-quarterly-reports-2015-16.
NDIA. 2016b. Quarterly Report to COAG Disability Reform Council (Quarter 4 of Year 3). NDIS. https://www.ndis.gov.au/about-us/publications/quarterly-reports/archived-quarterly-reports-2015-16.

Productivity Commission. 2011. Disability Care and Support. Commonwealth of Australia. https://www.pc.gov.au/inquiries/completed/disability-support/report.

Stantons International. 2016. WA NDIS Trials Evaluation: Final Report. http://www.disability.wa.gov.au/Global/Publications/WA%20NDIS/Reports/Western%20Australian%20NDIS%20Trials%20Evaluation%20Report%20-%20Attachments.pdf.

Whalan, Jeff, Peter Acton, and Jeff Harmer. 2014. A Review of the Capabilities of the National Disability Insurance Agency. https://parlinfo.aph.gov.au/parlInfo/download/media/pressrel/3062257/upload_binary/3062257.pdf;fileType=application%2Fpdf#search=%22media/pressrel/3062257.

CHAPTER 6

Transition to Full Scheme

Mhairi Cowden, Claire McCullagh, and Jennifer Tran

Introduction

The trials of the National Disability Insurance Scheme (NDIS) were time-limited and covered only some of those who would eventually become eligible for the scheme. Next came the transition period: where Commonwealth, State and Territory Governments negotiated agreements that allowed full roll out and operation of the scheme nationally. During this period, states and territories progressively moved to make the NDIS available to people with disability in all age cohorts and geographic locations across Australia.

This chapter outlines the various agreements reached between Australian governments, first for transition to the NDIS and then for the full scheme (scheduled to be fully operational in most states and territories by 2020). It also discusses some of the early issues experienced during this transition period, including the impacts of fast roll out speeds, shared governance and funding arrangements and market and workforce challenges. Part II of this book, which examines how the NDIS has interacted

---

M. Cowden (✉) · C. McCullagh · J. Tran
Nous Group, Perth, WA, Australia

M. Cowden and C. McCullagh (eds.), *The National Disability Insurance Scheme*, https://doi.org/10.1007/978-981-16-2244-1_6

with specific cohorts and sectors, provides further analysis on these implementation issues, as well as a range of other challenges faced during the early days of the scheme.

NDIS Transition and Full Scheme Agreements

Transition to a full NDIS began in all states and territories except Western Australia (WA) from 1 July 2016. Funding and operational arrangements for transition to the NDIS, and for full scheme, were negotiated between the Commonwealth Government and individual State and Territory Governments through a series of two-party (bilateral) agreements. As discussed in previous chapters, these agreements were underpinned by legislation—the *National Disability Insurance Scheme Act 2013* (NDIS Act)—which established the scheme principles, eligibility and planning and governance arrangements, and created the National Disability Insurance Scheme Launch Transition Agency (known as the National Disability Insurance Agency or the NDIA).

Key agreements sitting alongside the NDIS Act, and which governed how the NDIS would work during transition and at full scheme, are described below.

Heads of Agreement

Heads of Agreement documents, signed by the Commonwealth Government with each individual State and Territory Government, set out a high-level commitment and broad parameters for a full NDIS, including transition timelines, full scheme funding arrangements and provisions for a separate National Injury Insurance Scheme to support people who had been catastrophically injured in an accident. Heads of Agreement were signed bilaterally throughout 2012 and 2013 between the Commonwealth Government and each State and Territory Government except WA, where a Heads of Agreement was not signed until 2017. (Council of Australian Governments (COAG) 2012, 2013a, b, c, d, e, f, 2017a).

Bilateral Agreements for NDIS Transition

Following on from the Bilateral Agreements that had been negotiated for the NDIS trials (Trial Bilateral Agreements), new Bilateral Agreements covering the transition to the full scheme were signed (Transition Bilateral Agreements). These Transition Bilateral Agreements set out the roles, responsibilities and arrangements for NDIS transition up until the point of full NDIS coverage in each state and territory. They included details on participant transition arrangements, financial contributions, continuity of support arrangements, sector and workforce readiness, quality and safeguarding arrangements, and how the NDIS would interface with other services such as health, education and housing.[1]

Transitional Bilateral Agreements were signed by the Commonwealth Government with each individual State and Territory Government. Agreements were struck with New South Wales (NSW) and Victoria in September 2015 (COAG 2015a, b), South Australian (SA) and Tasmania in December 2015 (COAG 2015c, d), Queensland in March 2016 (COAG 2016a) and the Northern Territory (NT) in May 2016 (COAG 2016b). As the Australian Capital Territory (ACT) had reached full scheme at the end of its trial, a Transitional Bilateral Agreement was not required.

In January 2017, a Bilateral Agreement was agreed by the Commonwealth and WA Governments which resolved that a nationally consistent but state-run NDIS would be implemented in WA with transition beginning from July 2017 (Porter and Barnett 2017). However, in December 2017, this agreement was replaced by a joint Heads of Agreement and Bilateral Agreement document which outlined that WA would transition to the NDIS administered by the NDIA, consistent with other states and territories (COAG 2017a). As discussed in Chapter 5, WA was unique in that it conducted two two-year trials of the NDIS before agreeing to transition to the scheme: one trial operated under the national NDIS model and the other under the WA Government's My Way model to be delivered by the WA Disability Services Commission (Buckmaster and Clark 2018). WA's unique transition arrangements are discussed later in this chapter.

Bilateral Agreements for Full Scheme

A final set of bilateral agreements were negotiated between the Commonwealth Government, and each State and Territory Government, for the

[1] Operational Plans also set out detailed implementation arrangements for the transition period.

full scheme (Full Scheme Bilateral Agreements). These agreements superseded both Heads of Agreement documents and Transition Bilateral Agreements, outlining arrangements for the NDIS operations after both trial and transition periods had come to an end.

NSW became the first state to officially sign up to the full NDIS. It signed a Full Scheme Bilateral Agreement in May 2018 to commence operations from 1 July 2018 (COAG 2018a). This was followed by SA (signed in June 2018, commencing 1 July 2018) (COAG 2018b), Tasmania (signed in December 2018, commencing 1 July 2019) (COAG 2018c); ACT (signed March 2019, for 1 July 2019) (COAG 2019a); the NT (signed March 2019, for 1 July 2019) (COAG 2019b); Victoria (signed June 2019, to commence on 1 July 2019) (COAG 2019c) and Queensland (signed July 2019, for 1 July 2020) (COAG 2019d). At the time of writing this book, no Full Scheme Bilateral had been negotiated for WA, although WA's Transition Bilateral Agreement does not expire until 2023 (COAG 2017a, 4).

As envisioned by the Productivity Commission in its 2011 Report first describing the NDIS, the Heads of Agreement and Bilateral Agreements for each individual state and territory shared many consistent provisions, to ensure that the NDIS would operate in a nationally consistent way. These agreements outlined common scheme governance, funding and risk arrangements, and a range of other features that would shape the way that the NDIS-operated during transition and at full scheme. Key operational elements of the NDIS described in these agreements are outlined and discussed below.

Scheme Governance

The NDIS Act requires that the scheme be administered by an independent, statutory body (the NDIA), overseen by a Board and advised by an Independent Advisory Council representing the voices of scheme participants (NDIS Act 2013, Chapter 6, version: C2014C00386). Heads of Agreement for each state and territory outline more details of the NDIA's responsibilities during both transition and full scheme. The NDIA's role would, according to these Heads of Agreement, include managing scheme funds, administering access to the scheme, approving the payment of individualised support packages, managing the financial sustainability of the scheme, developing the disability sector, building community awareness about disability and undertaking data collection and research responsibilities (COAG 2012, 2013a, b, c, d, e, f, 2017a).

Under the Act, a Ministerial Council was also established to advise on all NDIS policy issues and to make recommendations to COAG about such matters. The Council (known as the Disability Reform Council) was to consist of Ministers from the Commonwealth and all states and territories, with the Commonwealth Minister acting as chair and able to give directions by legislative instrument to the NDIA and provide strategic guidance to the NDIA Board (NDIS Act 2013, s.121, version: C2014C00386). Under Commonwealth, State and Territory Heads of Agreement, it was further described that this Ministerial Council would include Ministers with responsibility for both Disability and Treasury portfolios.

The diffuse governance arrangements for the NDIS, which split decision-making responsibilities across multiple entities and levels of government, have been identified as a challenge for policymakers and practitioners (Carey et al. 2017; Malbon et al. 2017). During transition to the NDIS, more streamlined governance arrangements were introduced through the National Disability Insurance Scheme Amendment (Streamlined Governance) Bill 2019 (the Bill). The Bill amended the NDIS Act to include new requirements for the appointment of the Board and the Independent Advisory Council, and establish a 28-day requirement for consultations with host jurisdictions for various matters under the Act (with the ability for host jurisdictions to seek an extension for up to 90 days if needed). Amendments also re-categorised several of the NDIS Rules made under the Act, so that some rules previously requiring unanimous or majority agreement of the Commonwealth Government, and States and Territory Governments, could instead be made simply after consultation (National Disability Insurance Scheme (Streamlined Governance) Bill 2019).

The Roll Out Schedule

Transition to the NDIS began earlier than anticipated in some jurisdictions. In NSW, transition commenced in the Nepean-Blue Mountains Region for children aged 0–17 years on 1 July 2015—a year ahead what had been agreed in the NSW Heads of Agreement. Other clients rolled in, by region, between July 2016 and June 2018 (COAG 2015a, Schedule A). Queensland also commenced early transition in three sites: Townsville and Charters Towers for children and young people aged 0–17 years, and Palm Island. Transition for the rest of the state occurred by region between July 2016 and July 2019 (COAG 2016a, Schedule A).

Other states and territories began transitioning to a full NDIS throughout 2016 and 2017, with transition complete by 2020 in all states and territories (except WA where the transition period extends to 2023). SA's transition took place over around two and a half years, starting in February 2016. It focused, in its first year, on bringing any remaining eligible children aged 0–14 into the scheme, after focusing on this age group during the trial. Young people aged 15–17 then transitioned from January 2017, with all remaining cohorts moving into the scheme, region by region (COAG 2015c, Schedule A). Both Victoria and the NT transitioned over three years from July 2016, by region (COAG 2015b, Schedule A; 2016b, Schedule A) while Tasmania transitioned over three years from 2016 prioritising eligible participants accessing complex level supported accommodation services, then by age group (COAG 2015d, Schedule A). In the ACT, as previously discussed, all eligible individuals had already been rolled into the scheme through the trials. In WA, transition occurred later than most, on a staged geographic basis commencing 2017 with the transition period complete by 2023 (COAG 2017a).

Each Transitional Bilateral Agreement included an initial estimate of the number of people who would benefit from the NDIS at the end of the transition period. These initial estimates are summarised in Table 6.1.

Table 6.1 Estimated participant numbers at the end of the NDIS transition period, by state and territory[2]

	NSW	*VIC*	*QLD*	*WA*	*SA*	*TAS*	*NT*	*ACT*
Estimated participant No.	140,000	105,000	91,217	47,941	32,284	10,587	6,500	5,075

[2] Tables have been drawn from the Transitional Bilateral Agreements (Schedule A) for each State and Territory. As there is no Transitional Bilateral Agreement for the ACT, this table has been drawn from the final year (2015–2016) of the Trial Bilateral Agreement (Appendix A, Table 1, 2016–2017).

Concerns about the speed of NDIS roll out were raised before the first Transition Bilateral Agreement was signed. The 2014 Review of the Capabilities of the NDIA, discussed in Chapter 5, raised concerns regarding the pace of the roll out during the NDIS trials (Whalan et al. 2014). The National Commission of Audit (NCOA) echoed similar sentiments in a 2014 Report, recommending that the NDIS be implemented more slowly than planned (2014, 94). In response, the Commonwealth Government commissioned work on the optimal transition and roll out arrangements for the scheme, which was undertaken by KPMG and released in July 2014.

Despite these early recommendations, governments persisted with a roll out schedule described by the Productivity Commission as "highly ambitious" (2017, 10). Most state and territories did not meet the participant targets set out in their Transition Bilateral Agreements, resulting in some people with disability experiencing delays in accessing NDIS services. By September 2017, there were over 34,500 people across Australia who should have already been NDIS participants, but who had not yet accessed the scheme (Parliament of Australia 2018, ix). Long waiting times were also reported for participants between being found eligible for the scheme and receiving a support plan which would allow them to access NDIS-funded services (Parliament of Australia 2018, 6).

The pace of the NDIS roll out has also been associated with challenges with individualised planning. The NDIS envisioned by the Productivity Commission was intended to provide people with disability with access to an individualised planning process, involving a planner working with the person and their family to discuss what they wanted to achieve, assess the nature, frequency and intensity of their support needs, and combine these elements into a tailored plan for the supports that they would receive (2011, 1:30, 39–40). During the early days of transition, however, participants reported poor and inconsistent planning experiences, including plans being made over the phone, concerns about planners' skills and competencies and inadequate levels of support resulting in potentially avoidable requests for plan reviews (Parliament of Australia 2018, 39).

In response to feedback from various stakeholders, the NDIA reviewed the journey of participants through the NDIS and announced a 'new participant pathway' in 2017. This new pathway was intended to improve participant and organisational experiences with the NDIS (NDIA 2017a). In December 2018, a pilot of the new pathway began in two NDIS regions in Victoria (NDIA 2017b), and in October 2019, it was announced that the NDIA would progressively roll out changes to improve plans across the country. Changes to be implemented included: clearer links between the NDIS and community, mainstream, informal and employment supports, and the use of face-to-face planning support for participants during critical pre-planning and implementation stages (NDIA 2019).

Funding and Risk

Similar to the trials, shared funding arrangements for the NDIS were agreed between Commonwealth Government and State and Territory Governments, for transition and full scheme. During transition, State and Territory Governments (except WA) committed to fund approximately 60% of package costs for an agreed number of participants aged 0–64 (0–50 for Indigenous Australian participants) who entered the NDIS, with the Commonwealth Government contributing the remaining 40%[3] (COAG 2012, 2013a, b, c, d, e, f). In all states and territories, the Commonwealth agreed to fund 100% of the costs associated with non-Indigenous participants 65 years and over (50 or over for Indigenous people) choosing to stay in the scheme, and the NDIA operational and administration costs (COAG 2012, 2013a, b, c, d, e, f, 2017a).

Through the initial Heads of Agreement documents, the Commonwealth Government also committed to fund 100% of the risk associated with higher NDIS participant numbers and/or higher average per person care and support costs, during transition and at full scheme (COAG 2012, 2013a, b, c, d, e, f, 2017a). Transition Bilateral Agreements for Victoria, SA and Tasmania walk back this commitment, inserting an additional clause which states that Commonwealth and State Governments will share the risks of higher than expected clients under 65 transitioning from State specialist disability services (COAG 2015b, c, d). These risk-sharing arrangements were activated on several occasions during transition, including the Commonwealth and SA sharing the cost from higher than anticipated numbers of children aged 0–14. Here, the Commonwealth Government did not fully fund the cost overruns because

[3] These percentage contributions are explicitly stated in the Victorian, Queensland, SA, Tasmanian, NT and ACT Heads of Agreement. The NSW Heads of Agreement instead outline a fixed, annual contributions during the transition period which equates to a similar proportionate funding split.

it did not consider the original trial participant estimates to be reasonable (Department of Social Services 2017, 11).

For full scheme, all State and Territory Governments committed to contribute a fixed, upfront funding amount for the cost of the scheme. This agreed amount would be escalated annually to account for factors such as inflation, at a fixed, agreed rate, until these arrangements were reviewed. State and Territory Government fixed, upfront contributions would partially cover participant support costs, including individualised support packages and general supports described by the NDIS Act. The Commonwealth Government would pay the remaining balance of scheme costs (COAG 2017a, 2018a, b, c, 2019a, b, c, d).

Funding for both transition and the full NDIS was to include a mix of cash and 'in-kind' contributions. In-kind services were existing disability services delivered by, or contracted directly to, government departments. They were originally included in Trial Bilateral Agreements to ensure continuity of support in the short term and to give disability support providers time to adapt to new, individualised funding models. In-kind services have also been observed to carry a number of disadvantages, including that they adversely affect the transition of existing providers, as well as market entry, the quality of supports and the overall cost of the scheme (Productivity Commission 2017, 281). As part of their Full Scheme Bilateral Agreements (and in WA's case, its Transition Bilateral Agreement), the Commonwealth Government and State and Territory Governments have agreed to phase out in-kind funding contributions as soon as possible, except in exceptional circumstances (COAG 2017a, 2018a, b, c, 2019a, b, c, d).

Continuity and Portability of Supports

Agreements for both NDIS transition and full scheme outline continuity of support arrangements for people accessing specialised disability services prior to the NDIS. Through their Transition and Full Scheme Bilateral Agreements, the Commonwealth Government and State and Territory Governments confirmed that continuity of support arrangements would be made available for any existing clients of specialist disability services who were not eligible for individualised support through the NDIS. Recognising that roll out of the NDIS should be managed so that nobody was disadvantaged, all governments committed to ensuring similar outcomes for anyone in this cohort compared to what they had experienced prior to the NDIS (COAG 2015a, b, c, d, 2016a, b, 2017a, 2018a, b, c, 2019a, b, c, d).

Governments also agreed that, once the NDIS was fully implemented, the supports participants received would be fully portable across Australia (2017a, 2018a, b, c, 2019a, b, c, d). This meant participants could move around, and change their residential address, without losing their NDIS supports or needing to re-establish eligibility for the scheme. During transition, the Commonwealth Government, State and Territory Governments, agreed that portability arrangements would only apply for sites transitioning to the NDIS, meaning participants could move between NDIS transition sites and still be guaranteed support (COAG 2015a, b, c, d, 2016a, b, 2017a).

Market Readiness

Transition and Full Scheme Bilateral Agreements for the NDIS all reference the critical importance of supporting the disability services market and workforce. In their Transition Bilateral Agreements, the Commonwealth Government, and State and Territory Governments recognise that disability service providers must be prepared for the NDIS at the point of scheme transition: understanding the cost of their business and how to operate in a contestable funding environment. In support of this aim, governments agreed to leverage existing investment in sector development to support NDIS readiness, and to work with the NDIA to determine how existing tools, resources and systems could best be adopted or funded to support the NDIS. Governments also agreed to do everything practicable to attract and employ suitably skilled staff to roles within the NDIA, including State and Territory Government for staff working on programs that would transition into the NDIS, and to monitor market, sector, participant, workforce and system readiness through various measures (COAG 2015a, b, c, d, 2016a, b, 2017a).

Establishing a consistently strong disability services market proved challenging during transition. The 2018 Joint Standing Committee Inquiry into the NDIS Transition found that thin markets—that is, market where there are low numbers of service providers and in some cases market failure—were being experienced by participants living in rural and remote areas, people with complex needs, those involved in the criminal justice system, people from Culturally and Linguistically Diverse (CALD) backgrounds and Indigenous people (Parliament of Australia

2018, 65). The NDIS transition to a market-based system was also found to result in gaps in the areas of advocacy, assertive outreach and support coordination (Parliament of Australia 2018, 71–75). The Productivity Commission has described the negative consequences of thin markets as including higher prices, less variety, lower quality services and unmet demand. In the disability support sector, the Commission describes thin markets as potentially resulting in poor participant outcomes, increased demand for services outside of the NDIS and pressure on informal carers (2017, 268).

Recognising the comparatively high costs of establishing and delivering services in small communities and a lack of economies, the Transition Bilateral Agreement for the NT includes a specific schedule describing 'provider of last resort' arrangements in the Territory (COAG 2016b, Schedule K). Through this agreement, the Commonwealth and NT Governments agreed that an effective, timely mechanism would be needed during transition to ensure access to the reasonable and necessary supports in regional and remote communities or where there have been consistently thin or non-existent markets. Both Commonwealth and NT Governments agreed that the NDIA would be the entity responsible for ensuring services were in place for all NDIS participants in the NT during transition, including where no other services were available (COAG 2016b, Schedule K, 1).

Workforce Readiness

As part of their Full Scheme Bilateral Agreements, the Commonwealth Government, and State and Territory Governments committed to the development of a healthy workforce and market of disability service providers. Commonwealth Government responsibilities were to include engaging in good faith to develop, consider and implement market policies, implementing market regulation and monitoring the impact of pricing policies on the sector. State and Territory Government responsibilities would include activities such as working with the Commonwealth Government on market policies and facilitating the sharing of relevant market intelligence from state-based agencies to inform effective market oversight (COAG 2017a, 2018a, b, c, 2019a, b, c, d).

Disability workforce shortages have been identified as a significant barrier to the delivery of NDIS services during transition and at full scheme. In its 2017 Review of NDIS Costs, the Productivity Commission found that the disability care workforce was not growing fast enough to meet demand and would likely not be sufficient to deliver the supports expected to be allocated by the NDIA by 2020 (2017, 36). The Commission argued that the disability sector workforce would need to be double, and in some regions more than triple, to meet new demand, and that greater attention should be paid to the long-term development of the disability workforce (2017, 36–37).

Quality and Safeguarding

The Heads of Agreement, Transition and Full Scheme Agreements for the NDIS include a range of commitments and measures to ensure NDIS participants are kept safe and able to consistently access high-quality supports. As part of the Transitional Bilateral Agreements, the Commonwealth Government agreed to work with respective State and Territory Governments, and the NDIA, to design of a nationally consistent quality and safeguard system to be agreed in early 2016. Until this time, it was agreed that existing quality assurance arrangements for specialist disability services—which were different in each state and territory—would apply for NDIS participants (COAG 2015a, b, c, d, 2016a, b, 2017a).

From 1 July 2018, the NDIS Quality and Safeguards Commission (NDIS Commission) was established and began operating in NSW and SA. The NDIS Commission subsequently began in Queensland, Tasmania and Victoria from 1 July 2019, and in WA from 1 December 2020 (Quality and Safeguards Commission 2020). Once operational, the Commission became responsible for regulating NDIS providers, providing national consistency, resolving problems and identifying areas for scheme improvement. It is also to be responsible for improving the quality and safety of services in the NDIS, so that participants can access services and supports that promote choice, control and dignity (Department of Social Services 2019).

Interfaces with 'Mainstream' Service Systems

The NDIS was never designed to function as 'the whole system' for people with disability. Transitional and Full Scheme Bilateral Agreements recognise that participants in the scheme will continue to access a range of other 'mainstream' services such as health, housing and education services, and that interfaces between these systems and the NDIS would need to be carefully managed to ensure good outcomes.

Transitional Bilateral Agreements include guidelines and arrangements for the interface between the NDIS and mainstream services during transition. Attached to each agreement is a schedule entitled: Principles to Determine the Responsibilities of the NDIS and Other Service Systems. This principles document was originally agreed to by COAG in April 2013 and then updated in November 2015. It commits jurisdictions to an agreed set of principles which delineate between NDIS supports and those that will remain the responsibility of other service systems. Generally, the principles define 'reasonable and necessary' personalised supports that are related to a participant's disability needs to fall within the NDIS's responsibility. Where supports form part of another service system's universal obligation, or can be covered by reasonable adjustments, they remain the responsibility of other so-called mainstream services (COAG 2015a, b, c, d, 2016a, b Schedule I, 2017a Schedule H).

The interface between the NDIS and other service systems proved difficult to navigate during transition. The 2018 Joint Standing Committee Inquiry into the NDIS Transition received evidence that the principles to determine the NDIS responsibilities were open to interpretation and lacked clarity (Parliament of Australia 2018, 11–12). The Inquiry found boundary issues and funding disputes to be leading to reduced (and in some cases no) access to services for both NDIS participants and other people with disability. In addition, the transition of government programs into the NDIS was found to be contributing to emerging service gaps and a lack of clear funding responsibilities between the NDIS and other services. Significant evidence of these boundary issues was found between the NDIS and health, aged care, education, transport, housing and justice services (Parliament of Australia 2018, 11–35).

Tier Two Supports (Information, Linkages and Capacity Building)

The NDIS was originally designed to support a broader group of people with disability than just those eligible for individualised packages of support. In its 2011 report, the Productivity Commission recommended the NDIS provide bridging and capacity building support ('Tier 2' services) to enable anyone affected by disability to connect with relevant disability, community and mainstream services (2011, 1:163–165, 198).

Some examples of these Tier 2 supports include Local Area Coordinators (LAC) to help link people with disabilities to local community groups, and web services to provide information and educate people about specific disabilities and where to get help (2011, 13, 163–164).

The Heads of Agreement, Transition and Full Scheme Bilateral Agreements provide limited information about how Tier 2 supports would operate. Instead, the COAG Disability Reform Council endorsed a separate Policy Framework for Information, Linkages and Capacity Building (ILC) (effectively Tier 2 supports) in August 2015—a month before the first Transition Bilateral Agreements were signed. This ILC Policy Framework described ILC services as inclusive of five streams:

1. Information, Linkages and Referrals. Connecting people with disability, their families and carers with appropriate disability, community and mainstream supports;
2. Capacity building for mainstream services. Ensuring people with disability connect with and access mainstream supports;
3. Community awareness and capacity building. Supporting organisations (such as not-for-profit organisations, local councils and businesses) and people within communities to be inclusive of people with disability and understand the needs of families and carers;
4. Individual capacity building. Fostering the principle of choice and control, improving outcomes for people with disability, their families and carers
5. Local Area Coordination (LAC) (which will also deliver the other streams). Developing relationships between the NDIS, people with disability, their families and carers, and the local community (NDIA 2015, 9–13).

It was initially determined that the NDIA would be responsible for administering the ILC program, although responsibility has since transitioned to the Department of Social Services (DSS) (Department of Social Services 2019). ILC roll out began in July 2017 and was initially focused on a series of state-based and national grant opportunities, which were designed to support a staged move towards a more national approach (NDIA 2018, 4).

Many submissions to the 2018 Joint Standing Committee Inquiry outlined concerns that insufficient funding was allocated to the ILC

Program during NDIS transition (Parliament of Australia 2018, 58–59). The Victorian Government's submission also noted concern that LACs were not performing their core function during transition, focusing disproportionately on participant planning at the expense of their critical role in building community infrastructure and mainstream capacity (Victorian Government 2017, 15).

In 2018, the NDIA developed a "more strategic approach to ILC" through a new ILC strategy (Strengthening Information, Linkages and Capacity Building (ILC): a national strategy towards 2022) (NDIA 2018, 5). This new strategy included explicit investment principles and objectives for ILC and specified that the NDIA would fund and deliver four ILC programs: Individual Capacity Building, National Information, Economic and Community Participation and Mainstream Capacity Building (NDIA 2018, 4–7).

WA's Transition Bilateral Agreement

In January 2017, the Commonwealth and WA Governments resolved that WA would commence transition to a nationally consistent, but WA Government-run NDIS from July 2017 (Porter and Barnett 2017). An original bilateral agreement was signed, outlining that the NDIS would in WA be delivered by a newly established WA Government agency, instead of by the NDIA. Under this original agreement, the cost of individual support packages would be shared between the Commonwealth and WA Governments, but the WA Government would be responsible for funding the NDIS administrative costs. The Commonwealth Government would also fund just 25% of the risk of any increase in costs associated with higher than expected participant numbers of higher package costs under the scheme, unlike other states and territories where it would fund 100% of these costs (COAG 2017b).

The WA Government claimed that the delivery of the scheme through the WA Government agency reflected a commitment to local decision-making and would allow Western Australians "the benefits of the national scheme with the added benefit of support informed by local knowledge and connections" (WA Government 2017, 1). The core principles of the national NDIS legislation would still be reflected in WA legislation, including identical definitions of key concepts such as eligibility, reasonable and necessary supports, and choice and control. The WA run scheme would also be portable across the national scheme operating in other jurisdictions (COAG 2017b).

The WA Government argued that a locally delivered NDIS would mean people with disability would have access to a properly person-centred service compared with the national scheme that used "1800 number Centrelink-style contact or over-the-phone planning" (WA NDIS 2017). At the time the agreement was reached, the WA Government-operated NDIS trial sites had the highest rate of plans that were self-managed plans—where participants, and not the NDIA or another service provider, managed the spending of their NDIS funding themselves—across all Australian jurisdictions. The WA Government argued that this demonstrated that the state-operated model delivered a higher level of choice and control.

Responses to this announcement were mixed. Many WA-based service providers and people with disability who had positive experiences under the WA Government's My Way NDIS trial welcomed the decision. However, some disability advocates criticised it. The inaugural chair of the NDIA Board, Bruce Bonyhady (2017), publicly criticised the move, stating that it would create a separate bureaucracy in WA and disadvantage Western Australians with a disability as they would not have access to the same national scheme as the rest of country.

Less than two months after this agreement was signed, the incumbent WA Government, led by Liberal Premier the Hon. Colin Barnett MLA, lost the State Government election in March 2017. The new government reopened negotiations between the WA and Commonwealth Governments on the roll out of the NDIS. On 12 December 2017, a new bilateral agreement was announced which saw WA agree to join the nationally delivered NDIS. From 1 July 2018, the NDIA assumed responsibility for the delivery of the NDIS in WA, which would continue to be implemented on a geographic basis and fully transitioned by 2023 (COAG 2017a).

The new agreement struck between the WA and Commonwealth Governments mirrored similar agreements made between the Commonwealth Government and other State and Territory Governments. In handing over responsibility to deliver the NDIS to the Commonwealth Government, the WA Government would not need to pay the administration costs of delivering the scheme locally, or cover potential cost overruns. The parties also agreed that, for the period 2017–2018 to 2019–2020, the State Government would fund approximately 60% of agreed package costs, and the Commonwealth Government would be responsible for the remaining 40%. Unlike other Transition Bilateral Agreements, the Commonwealth would assume responsibility for 50% of agreed package costs for those under 65 for the 2020–2021 to 2022–2023 period—an arrangement more favourable to the State Government than provisions outlined in other Transition Bilateral Agreements (COAG 2017a, Schedule B).

The new WA Premier, the Hon. Mark McGowan MLA, stated that the new Transition Bilateral Agreement gave: "people confidence that over their lifetimes they will have good support, not subject to the whims of state budgets but subject to a national agreement and the underpinning of the Medicare Levy arrangement that supports the [NDIS]" (Ceranic 2017). The WA Government has maintained that the decision to move into an NDIA-administered NDIS was driven by the needs of people with disability, although it is also reported that WA Government could save $1.3 billion over a decade by transitioning to an NDIA-operated scheme (Ceranic 2017).

Conclusion

This chapter has sought to provide an overview of the NDIS transition and full scheme arrangements negotiated between the Commonwealth Government and all State and Territory Governments, as reflected in intergovernmental agreements. While the agreements and approaches negotiated during the trial period varied somewhat across jurisdictions, the agreements for transition and full scheme operation appear to have brought the operations and funding under more nationally consistent arrangements. This chapter has not sought to analyse the success of the transition to full scheme operation period, although it has highlighted some of the early issues experienced during the scheme. Transition and full scheme implementation challenges are discussed at length in Part II of this book.

References

Bonyhady, Bruce. 2017. The Difference Between the WA NDIS and the Real NDIS. https://probonoaustralia.com.au/news/2017/03/difference-wa-ndis-real-ndis/.

Buckmaster, Luke, and Shannon Clark. 2018. The NDIS: A Chronology. Parliament of Australia. https://www.aph.gov.au/About_Parliament/Parliamentary_Departments/Parliamentary_Library/pubs/rp/rp1819/Chronologies/NDIS.

Carey, G., A. Kay, and A. Nevile. 2017. Institutional Legacies and 'Sticky Layers': What Happens in Cases of Transformative Policy Change? *Administration and Society* 51: 491–509. https://doi.org/10.1177/0095399717704682.

Ceranic, Irena. 2017. WA Has Signed on to the Federal NDIS—What Does This Mean for West Australians? ABC News, December 12.

COAG. 2012. Heads of Agreement Between the Commonwealth and New South Wales Governments on the National Disability Insurance Scheme. https://www.ndis.gov.au/about-us/governance/intergovernmental-agreements#new-south-wales.

COAG. 2013a. Heads of Agreement Between the Commonwealth and South Australia Governments on the National Disability Insurance Scheme. https://www.ndis.gov.au/about-us/governance/intergovernmental-agreements#south-australia.

COAG. 2013b. Heads of Agreement Between the Commonwealth and the Australian Capital Territory Governments on the National Disability Insurance Scheme. https://www.ndis.gov.au/about-us/governance/intergovernmental-agreements#australian-capital-territory.

COAG. 2013c. Heads of Agreement Between the Commonwealth and Tasmanian Governments on the National Disability Insurance Scheme. https://www.ndis.gov.au/about-us/governance/intergovernmental-agreements#tasmania.

COAG. 2013d. Heads of Agreement Between the Commonwealth and Victorian Governments on the National Disability Insurance Scheme. https://www.ndis.gov.au/about-us/governance/intergovernmental-agreements#victoria.

COAG. 2013e. Heads of Agreement Between the Commonwealth and Queensland Governments on the National Disability Insurance Scheme. https://www.ndis.gov.au/about-us/governance/intergovernmental-agreements#queensland.

COAG. 2013f. Heads of Agreement Between the Commonwealth and Northern Territory. https://www.ndis.gov.au/about-us/governance/intergovernmental-agreements#northern-territory.

COAG. 2015a. Bilateral Agreement Between the Commonwealth and New South Wales: Transition to a National Disability Insurance Scheme.

https://webarchive.nla.gov.au/awa/20151020011806/, http://www.coag.gov.au/node/525.
COAG. 2015b. Bilateral Agreement Between the Commonwealth and Victoria: Transition to a National Disability Insurance Scheme. https://webarchive.nla.gov.au/awa/20151020003310/, https://www.coag.gov.au/node/526.
COAG. 2015c. Bilateral Agreement Between the Commonwealth and South Australia: Transition to a National Disability Insurance Scheme. https://www.ndis.gov.au/about-us/governance/intergovernmental-agreements#south-australia.
COAG. 2015d. Bilateral Agreement Between the Commonwealth and Tasmania: Transition to a National Disability Insurance Scheme. https://www.ndis.gov.au/about-us/governance/intergovernmental-agreements#tasmania.
COAG. 2016a. Bilateral Agreement Between the Commonwealth and Queensland: Transition to a National Disability Insurance Scheme. https://www.ndis.gov.au/about-us/governance/intergovernmental-agreements#queensland.
COAG. 2016b. Bilateral Agreement Between the Commonwealth and Northern Territory: Transition to a National Disability Insurance Scheme. https://webarchive.nla.gov.au/awa/20161017023746/, http://www.coag.gov.au/node/539.
COAG. 2017a. Heads of Agreement Between the Commonwealth and Western Australian Governments on the National Disability Insurance Scheme; and Bilateral Agreement Between the Commonwealth and Western Australia: Transition to a National Disability Insurance Scheme. http://www.disability.wa.gov.au/Global/Publications/NDIS/NDIS-Landing-Page/Helpful%20documents%20Oct%202018/Heads-of-Agreement-and-Bilateral-Agreement-NDIS%20.pdf.
COAG. 2017b. Bilateral Agreement Between the Commonwealth and Western Australia: Transition to a National Disability Insurance Scheme in Western Australia (original Transition Bilateral Agreement signed January 2017). http://www.disability.wa.gov.au/Global/Publications/WA-NDIS-My-Way/NDIS%20in%20WA%20Bilateral%20Agreement%20and%20Schedules.pdf.
COAG. 2018a. Bilateral Agreement Between the Commonwealth of Australia and the State of New South Wales on the National Disability Insurance Scheme. https://www.coag.gov.au/about-coag/agreements/bilateral-agreement-between-commonwealth-australia-and-state-new-south-wales.
COAG. 2018b. Bilateral Agreement Between the Commonwealth of Australia and the State of South Australia on the National Disability Insurance Scheme. https://www.coag.gov.au/about-coag/agreements/bilateral-agreement-between-commonwealth-australia-and-state-south-australia.
COAG. 2018c. Bilateral Agreement Between the Commonwealth of Australia and the State of Tasmania on the National Disability Insurance

Scheme. https://www.coag.gov.au/about-coag/agreements/bilateral-agreement-between-commonwealth-australia-and-state-tasmania.

COAG. 2019a. Bilateral Agreement Between the Commonwealth of Australia and the Australian Capital Territory on the National Disability Insurance Scheme. https://www.coag.gov.au/about-coag/agreements/bilateral-agreement-between-commonwealth-australia-and-australian-capital.

COAG. 2019b. Bilateral Agreement Between the Commonwealth of Australia and the Northern Territory on the National Disability Insurance Scheme. https://www.coag.gov.au/about-coag/agreements/bilateral-agreement-between-commonwealth-australia-and-northern-territory.

COAG. 2019c. Bilateral Agreement Between the Commonwealth of Australia and the State of Victoria on the National Disability Insurance Scheme. https://www.coag.gov.au/about-coag/agreements/bilateral-agreement-between-commonwealth-and-victoria-national-disability.

COAG. 2019d. Bilateral Agreement Between the Commonwealth of Australia and the State of Queensland on the National Disability Insurance Scheme. https://www.coag.gov.au/about-coag/agreements/bilateral-agreement-between-commonwealth-australia-and-queensland-national.

Department of Social Services. 2017. Submission 29. Joint Standing Committee on the NDIS. https://www.aph.gov.au/Parliamentary_Business/Committees/Joint/National_Disability_Insurance_Scheme/Transition/Submissions.

Department of Social Services. 2019. NDIS Quality and Safeguards Commission. Accessed 1 December 2020. https://www.dss.gov.au/disability-and-carers-programs-services-for-people-with-disability/ndis-quality-and-safeguards-commission.

Malbon, Eleanor, Gemma Carey, and Helen Dickinson. 2017. Accountability in Public Service Quasi-Markets: The Case of the Australian National Disability Insurance Scheme. *Australian Journal of Public Administration* 77: 468–481. https://doi.org/10.1111/1467-8500.12246.

National Disability Insurance Scheme Act 2013 (Commonwealth). Version: C2014C00386. https://www.legislation.gov.au/Details/C2014C00386.

National Disability Insurance Scheme Amendment (Streamlined Governance) Bill. 2019. https://parlinfo.aph.gov.au/parlInfo/search/display/display.w3p;query=Id%3A%22legislation%2Fems%2Fs1218_ems_a0cbc30c-db42-4e94-9e06-fb7f245afaf5%22.

NCOA. 2014. Towards Responsible Government: Report of the NCOA Phase One, recommendation 16. Parliament of Australia. https://parlinfo.aph.gov.au/parlInfo/search/display/display.w3p;query=Id:%22library/lcatalog/00818002%22.

NDIA. 2015. A Framework for Information, Linkages and Capacity Building, Geelong. https://www.dss.gov.au/disability-and-carers-programs-services-

for-people-with-disability-information-linkages-and-capacity-building-ilc/ilc-building-policy-framework.
NDIA. 2017a. New NDIS Pathway Released to Improve Participant and Provider Experience. Media Release, 17 October 2017. https://www.ndis.gov.au/news/426-new-ndis-pathway-released-improve-participant-and-provider-experience.
NDIA. 2017b. NDIS Pathway Pilot Released. Media Release, 16 November 2017. https://www.ndis.gov.au/news/420-ndis-pathway-pilot-released.
NDIA. 2018. Strengthening Information, Linkages and Capacity Building (ILC): A National Strategy Towards 2022. https://www.ndis.gov.au/community/information-linkages-and-capacity-building-ilc/ilc-investment-strategy.
NDIA. 2019. NDIS Pathway Reform. Media Release, 16 January 2019. https://www.ndis.gov.au/news/1215-ndis-pathway-reform#:~:text=The%20NDIA%20initiated%20a%20'Pathway,consistent%20and%20positive%20NDIS%20experience.
NDIS Quality and Safeguards Commission. 2020. Website accessed 14 November 2020. https://www.ndiscommission.gov.au/.
Parliament of Australia. 2018. Joint Standing Committee Inquiry into the NDIS Transition. https://www.aph.gov.au/Parliamentary_Business/Committees/Joint/National_Disability_Insurance_Scheme/Transition/Report.
Porter, Christian, and Colin Barnett. 2017. Governments Sign Bilateral Agreement on Local Delivery of NDIS in WA: Media Release. Parliament of Australia and Government of WA. https://parlinfo.aph.gov.au/parlInfo/download/media/pressrel/5073513/upload_binary/5073513.pdf;fileType=application%2Fpdf#search=%22media/pressrel/5073513%22.
Porter, Christian, Colin Barnett, and Donna Faragher. 2017. Governments Sign Bilateral Agreement on Local Delivery of NDIS in WA. Media Release, 1 February 2017. https://parlinfo.aph.gov.au/parlInfo/search/display/display.w3p;query=Id:%22media/pressrel/5073513%22.
Productivity Commission. 2011. Disability Care and Support: Productivity Commission Inquiry Report. Commonwealth of Australia. https://www.pc.gov.au/inquiries/completed/disability-support/report.
Productivity Commission. 2017. National Disability Insurance Scheme Costs. https://www.pc.gov.au/inquiries/completed/ndis-costs/report.
Victorian Government. 2017. Submission to the Joint Standing Committee on the NDIS. https://www.aph.gov.au/Parliamentary_Business/Committees/Joint/National_Disability_Insurance_Scheme/Transition/Submissions.
WA Government. 2017. WA NDIS: The National Disability Insurance Scheme Delivered Locally. http://www.disability.wa.gov.au.
WA NDIS. 2017. WA NDIS: The National Disability Insurance Scheme Delivered Locally. Fact Sheet. http://www.disability.wa.gov.au/Global/Publicati

ons/WA-NDIS-My-Way/Fact%20Sheet%20-%20Agreement%20on%20the%20NDIS%20in%20WA.pdf.

Whalan, Jeff, Peter Acton, and Jeff Harmer. 2014. A Review of the Capabilities of the National Disability Insurance Agency. https://www.ndis.gov.au/about-us/publications/review-capabilities-ndia-2014.

CHAPTER 7

The Philosophy of the NDIS

Mhairi Cowden and Claire McCullagh

Introduction

The rights of people with disability are central to current political and legal discussions about a just society. However, philosophers have historically had surprisingly little say on the subject. People with significant disability often feature as an afterthought to mainstream moral theories. Perhaps because of this, the extension of equal moral consideration to those with disability (particularly people with intellectual disability) poses a problem for many traditional ethical theories, which have tended to exclude or marginalise them.

This chapter explores the philosophical principles relating to theories of rights that guide the design and implementation of the National Disability Insurance Scheme (NDIS). It looks at the concept of rights as it has been applied to people with disability by the scheme and considers why traditional philosophical explanations of rights and moral consideration frequently, and troublingly, overlook or exclude those with intellectual disability. It also considers how alternative theories about the justification of rights can begin to make sense of disability rights, in a more inclusive way, as they have been conceived of by the NDIS.

M. Cowden (✉) · C. McCullagh
Nous Group, Perth, WA, Australia

M. Cowden and C. McCullagh (eds.), *The National Disability Insurance Scheme*, https://doi.org/10.1007/978-981-16-2244-1_7

Rights for People with Disability

Rights are at the centre of current political discourse about what is, and is not, permissible treatment of people with disability. The United Nations Convention on the Rights of Persons with Disabilities, ratified by Australia in July 2008, requires that people with disability participate in society on the same basis as all people. It highlights the importance of those with disability having the opportunity to participate in economic and social life, and recognises their right to make choices about their own lives (United Nations 2006, art. 19).

In Australia, disability legislation makes explicit reference to the fact that people with disability have the same rights as other community members, regardless of the degree and nature of their disability. The Disability Discrimination Act 1992 protects individuals across Australia from unfair treatment. The Act makes disability discrimination unlawful and promotes equal rights, opportunities and access for people with disability. Similarly, the first object of the *National Disability Insurance Scheme Act 2013* (NDIS Act), even before it provides for the creation of the NDIS, is to "in conjunction with other laws, give effect to Australia's obligations under the Convention on the Rights of Persons with Disabilities done at New York on 13 December 2006" (part 2, object 1a).

People with disability have historically been treated paternalistically, with decisions about their lives being made by others acting in their "own good" (noting that what is considered in someone's "own good" can vary considerably). As highlighted in Chapter 2, this historical approach saw many people with disability confined to institutions under a "banner of benevolence", living lives predominantly governed by the choices of others (Friedman 1995, 1285).

The disability rights movement represents a departure from the paternalistic view. It recognises not only the right of people with disability to life, participation and humane treatment, but also their right to have their own decisions and choices dictate the direction of their lives. This may seem like a simple and obvious move to many people—however, it represents a significant shift for traditional liberal philosophy because of two key arguments. First, liberal philosophy has a long history of not affording people with disability the same moral status as the rest of humanity, and second (and sometimes related), liberal philosophy has often argued that some people with disability cannot hold rights.

What Are Rights?

While rights discussions have preoccupied philosophers for centuries, the rights of people with disability have only recently entered discussions. Rights are entitlements or protections that ensure the possessor the free performance of certain actions, choices, or the guaranteed provision of certain benefits. Most agree that rights are grounded in certain features or capacities, which grant special worth to the right-holder, rendering them protected from, or entitled to, some condition.

Philosophers offer different explanations of the content, function and justification of rights. These different theories have implications for how people with disability (particularly those with intellectual disability) are accounted for. Three major debates about the content and function of rights, and how these relate to the NDIS's characterisation of disability rights, are outlined below. As will be seen, many rights descriptions discriminate against those who lack the ability to conceptualise their idea of the good life and act consistently according to reasons, which in many cases means those with intellectual disability (Stark 2009).

Claim and Liberty Rights

The American legal theorist Wesley Hohfeld, in seeking to best describe the structure of rights, has argued that when we talk about rights we are often talking about multiple different concepts and this creates confusion (1913, 16). Hohfeld identified four different 'pairings' that he deemed to be different types of rights. The most common pairings are: Claim and Duty, and Liberty and No Claim. A claim (also referred to as a 'claim right') is held by an individual and always produces a corresponding duty in others to either act or refrain from acting. The most famous claim is the right to life, which produces a corresponding duty to not kill. This claim right demonstrates how an individual can simultaneously hold claims and be bound by duties. For example, I hold a claim right to life, which produces duties in all other people not to take my life. At the same time, I am bound by duties to not take the lives of other people. These duties arise directly from their own corresponding claims to life.

A liberty right, however, is defined by the lack of duty. I have a liberty right to walk down the street, to cook myself dinner and to write this book because I am free from any duties that would stop me from doing so. Most of the time, when we speak of rights that we think should be protected in some way, we are speaking of claim rights and their corresponding duties. However, it is also the case that some of our most famous rights are liberty rights. For example, many hard-won civil rights, such as the right of women to work in any profession of their choosing, or the right of Indigenous Australians to attend the same schools and restaurants as non-Indigenous Australians, are liberty rights. These rights are defined by an absence of duty to do or not do an action.

Although liberty rights are important, it is claim rights that attract the primary attention when we speak of the NDIS. As we will argue later in this chapter, the NDIS Act codifies a number of claim rights for people with disability that produce corresponding duties in others. Given this, we will focus the rest of this chapter's discussion on claim rights.

Legal and Moral Rights

Not all claim rights are treated the same. One debate within philosophy is whether rights must be enshrined within a legal system to be considered rights, or whether they can exist outside of the law. Some philosophers believe that only legal rights are "true rights". Jeremy Bentham (1970) argued that the concept of moral rights external to the law is "conceptual nonsense". Rights which are not based on commands issued by the state can only tell us, in a vague sense, what we should do; they cannot serve as practical restriction which creates duties or obligations upon others (Bowring 2019). Hence, "moral rights", which are not codified by laws, are not really rights, as they do not enforce obligations as rights should do.

Other philosophers argue that rights can exist as moral imperatives outside of the law (Wellman 1985; Raz 1984, 165). The idea is that moral rights tend to be grounded in moral reasons, and rights of this nature exist independently of legal systems. For example, Joseph Raz argues that someone may have rights if an aspect of their wellbeing is sufficiently pressing to place a duty upon others. These rights are hence argued to exist, whether they are legally recognised or not.

The NDIS is established and described in the NDIS Act 2013, which is seen to 'give effect to Australia's obligations under the Convention on the Rights of Persons with Disabilities' (part 2, object 1a). It is unclear whether the architects of the scheme viewed the rights of people with disability as pre-dating the existence of the Act, pre-dating the Convention on the Rights of Persons with Disabilities or that such rights only truly existed once the NDIS Act came into operation. Disability advocates, however, have argued that the rights that are enshrined within the NDIS Act have always existed and it is in recognising the moral status of people with disability that we have been able to make the case for legal change. Due to the existence of the NDIS Act, the rights of people with disability now exist in law as legal rights. Disability rights as moral rights are discussed later in this chapter.

Positive and Negative Rights

In addition to moral vs legal rights, philosophers commonly distinguish between negative rights and positive rights. If we return to the concept of a claim right, the distinction between positive and negative relates to what type of duty the right produces. Negative claim rights produce duties of non-interference with an individual choice or interest. They secure 'a whole field of action unhampered by legal precepts...[and] a general condition of free exercise of natural [human] faculties' (Pound 1942, 78–79). Examples of negative rights drawn from the Universal Declaration of Human Rights (UDHR) include freedom from slavery (article 4) and from torture or cruel, inhuman or degrading treatment or punishment (article 5). In this sense, negative claim rights produce a duty to refrain from a particular action.

By contrast, positive conceptions of claim rights produce duties that include the active intervention of another to bring about some benefit or service to the right-holder. Positive rights directly obligate a third party, usually the government, to act (Jackman 2010). Examples of positive rights, also from the UDHR, include the right to work (article 23), to health (article 25) and to free education (article 26) all of which explicitly impose a duty upon governments to bring about a state of affairs.

Carrying out the duties required by positive rights often involves infringing upon negative rights. For example, if I have a right to health care, the provision of this service by the government using public money could be argued to infringe upon the negative property rights of other individuals by subsidising my service through their taxation. For this reason, political philosophers continue to argue about whether positive or negative rights apply and, if both, how they should be weighed against each other.

It is sometimes said that negative rights are easier to protect than positive rights, requiring only that people refrain from interfering with each other. However, when it comes to the enforcement of rights, this difference collapses, as implementing negative rights often requires a protection role performed by a third party. For example, funding a justice system that enforces negative property rights could be even more resource-intensive than funding a social service system that provides healthcare assistance.

We will argue below that the NDIS outlines claim rights that produce duties both to act and to refrain from acting, and that these duties interrelate in important ways.

The Justification of Rights

The discussion so far has addressed the structure of rights including the relationship between claim and duty, whether a right is enshrined in law or not and what kind of duty the right produces—to act or refrain from acting. This section discusses why people hold rights: that is, the purpose or justification for rights.

There are two distinct philosophies that explain the purpose of rights: will theory and interest theory. Philosophers who adhere to the will theory, such as H L A Hart and Hillel Steiner, argue that the core function of a right is to protect or enable an individual's will or choices (Hart 1982, 183; Steiner 1998). The idea of rights, according to will theory, is to protect a certain sphere of an individual's choices from interference by others. Having a right to something thus means that you have control over others' free will regarding it. Someone violates your right by acting against your will in relation to the object of your right. According to the will theory, an individual has the power to enforce or waive their right, and so the duties rights place on others can shift in line with the right-holder's decisions.

In order to hold a claim right under will theory, the right-holder must have the 'factual competence' to make a rational choice regarding the enforcement of waiver of their right. For example, I may have a property right over my computer that produces a duty in others to not take or use my computer. However, if my friend asks to borrow my computer for the afternoon, I can temporarily waive that claim right, but if my friend takes my computer without asking I can enforce my right by demanding it back, or even go to the police if she doesn't comply. Enforcement or waiver of the duties that correspond to a claim right involves my choice. According to will theory, people or animals who do not have the competence to make these rational choices cannot hold claim rights. Will theory therefore has a confining effect on rights. They can only be held by rational adults. Children, animals and some people with intellectual disability cannot be seen as right-holders under this definition.

Interest theory, put forward by philosophers including Joseph Raz, Neil MacCormick and Matthew Kramer, asserts that the function of a right is to protect a certain pressing interest (Raz 1986; MacCormick 1977; Kramer 2001, 28–95). Hence, individuals have rights, not because they have choices, but because having that right makes them presumptively better off. Someone violates my right by not doing her duty to provide me with something important that is in my interest.

According to the interest theory, not all interests are grounds for rights claims. For example, I may have an interest in my employer giving me a pay rise, so I can fund my various hobbies. However, this does not mean that I necessarily have a right to a promotion. Only certain, urgent interests are proper grounds for a right. According to Raz, for example, an interest must be of sufficient importance to justify requiring some corresponding duty from another person or entity (Raz 1986).

Importantly for our purposes, there is nothing within the interest theory of rights that would restrict rights to only those that have the capacity for rational choice. Indeed, interest theory argues that people who may lack the power to obtain goods or services for themselves, who lack capacities or are powerless and vulnerable to oppression, are often those that need the protective force of rights the most.

The NDIS as a Rights Scheme

Taking into account the discussion above, and the discussion of the scheme design provided in Chapter 4, we argue that the NDIS acknowledges two key claim rights held by people with disability:

1. The right to 'reasonable and necessary' supports and
2. The right to 'choice and control' over the design and delivery of these supports.

We will discuss each of these claim rights in turn, unpacking the different duties they produce. In doing so, we identify how the claim rights outlined by the NDIS may not, according to traditional rights theories, apply equally or in the same way to all people with disability.

The Right to Reasonable and Necessary Supports

The first right is central to the NDIS that eligible people are entitled, or have a claim to, 'reasonable and necessary' supports to help them to achieve their vision of a good life. These supports are defined as those which, among other things, help a participant to reach their goals, objectives and aspirations in a range of areas. This may include education or employment goals, social participation, independent living arrangements and health and wellbeing.

By recognising the right of NDIS-eligible individuals to 'reasonable and necessary supports', the scheme appears to endorse a positive conception of rights; that is, scheme administrators play an interventionist role to bring about certain positive wellbeing conditions for people with disability. In order to fully realise this claim right, we can articulate three distinct duties that fall to those responsible for operating the scheme:

1. A duty to fund supports to the individual: this duty is fulfilled by the National Disability Insurance Agency (NDIA) providing funding packages to individuals based on their personalised plan. Using these funding packages, individuals can purchase supports.
2. A duty to ensure that supports are available to be purchased by the individual: this duty recognises that it is not sufficient to simply provide funding packages to individuals if supports are not available to be purchased. Governments can therefore be seen to also have a duty to ensure that there are disability service organisations that provide the required supports operating in Australia. This could include regulating the market through quality registration, pricing structures and oversight and providing market stewardship to assist organisations to enter the market and develop areas where the market is thin.
3. A duty to be a provider of last resort: for some types of support services, there may be no providers available to operate and provide individuals with the services they need. This may be the case, for example, in rural and regional areas. In these cases, the government (State or Commonwealth) will hold a duty to be the provider of last resort to ensure that an individual's claim right under the legislation can be fulfilled.

The Commonwealth Government playing an interventionist role to bring about wellbeing conditions is an important claim right. The previous approach to disability service provision in Australia allowed differential treatment between those who acquired a disability through a workplace or motor vehicle accident and those who acquired a permanent disability in another way, or were born with a permanent disability. Place of residence also influenced eligibility for funding and support, creating a system described famously as a 'postcode lottery'. The NDIS, by contrast, has nationally consistent eligibility criteria. This ensures that all those with a permanent, significant disability, no matter where they live or how their disability is acquired, can access an individualised plan and associated supports.

However, the duties imposed on the Commonwealth Government to fulfil an individual's claim to supports have limits. An individual is entitled to supports only when they meet six criteria for 'reasonable and necessary', outlined in section 34 of the NDIS Act. These criteria outline the types of considerations that must be taken into account when determining what supports an individual is entitled to. These criteria include consideration of the likely benefit of the support to the participant, whether it is evidence based and cost effective, and whether it is appropriately delivered by the NDIS and/or another service system. This reflects the philosophical principle argued by Raz that duties have limits and should not impose an unreasonable burden onto other people's liberties, or that the duty imposed should be proportionate to the importance of the interest that is being protected.

The Right to Choice and Control

The second claim right recognised by the NDIS is the claim of participants to 'choice and control' over the design and delivery of their supports. Here, the NDIS goes beyond the assumption that people with disability have the right to have their welfare needs met: the scheme emphasises the centrality of participants' rights to directing and making decisions about what is important to them in leading a good life, and the types of services they need to make this happen.

The idea behind individualised funding—a central pillar of the NDIS—is that, instead of expecting people with disability to fit into existing programs and services, services respond to the choices and goals of people with disability. Disability advocate Belinda Epstein-Frisch offers a useful distinction between three different domains of choice, which are useful when considering the different ways in which the NDIS can uphold individual choices:

1. Pervasive choices affect significant milestones in a person's life and their aspirations. These choices are the most significant for an individual and include decisions about school education, employment, housing, social relationships and community participation.
2. Lifestyle choices are connected to a person's identity. Lifestyle choices can be choices about how a person dresses, how they spend their time, what sports they play and the equipment they purchase.
3. Everyday choices that are made throughout each day; these include decisions about what to eat, what movies to watch and the type of care that an individual may want (Epstein-Frisch 2013).

Individualised planning and funding is a way to promote choice across all three domains but is particularly relevant to the most significant domain: pervasive choices.

The design of the NDIS allows individuals with disability to make choices and have control over their support plan and funding. In this way, the scheme also appears to support rights in a negative sense—that is, the freedom of individuals in the scheme to make choices about their lives, with reasonable and necessary supports acting as a mechanism to assist with the implementation of these rights.

At first glance, the right to choice and control may be seen to produce duties of simple non-interference. This is true in the basic sense, but when we look at what is needed to fully realise the benefit of this claim right, there may be additional positive duties imposed on governments, carers, family and friends of people with disability. The claim right of choice and control can be understood as producing three distinct duties:

1. A duty not to choose for the individual and to refrain from paternalistic decision-making: this is a duty that falls on the NDIA to allow individuals with disability the freedom to choose their own goals and aspirations, but also where appropriate to manage their funded packages themselves. This duty may also fall on the carers, family and friends of people with disability to refrain from speaking or choosing for them or acting inappropriately as their proxy.

2. A duty to support informed and structured decision-making: in many cases, it may not be enough to simply refrain from choosing for people with disability. The claim to choice and control also produces a duty for this choice to be supported. For the NDIA, this may include a duty to provide clear information and guidance for individuals so that they are able to make choices and navigate the system. For carers, family and friends, this may include supporting an individual to make decisions and facilitating structured decision-making. This becomes particularly important for those with limited decision-making capacity.
3. A duty to ensure a range of choices are available: a claim to choice and control cannot be fully realised if there is no choice to be made. The Commonwealth Government, through the administration of the NDIS, will hold a duty to ensure choice is available through the healthy development of a disability service market but also direct operation of the scheme to ensure individuals have the opportunity to make choices during the planning process.

The claim right to choice and control is central to the NDIS functioning as it was originally intended. As we have discussed above, respecting this right may not be as simple as fulfilling a duty of non-interference but includes duties to provide active assistance to promote and support choice.

People with Intellectual Disability

An underlying principle of the NDIS is that all people with disability who meet the eligibility requirement have a right to reasonable and necessary supports, and to have choice and control over the supports and services, they need to achieve this. These two claim rights have been clearly set out in the section above.

However, holding that all people with disability uniformly have both of these claim rights does not fit neatly with either the will or the interest theory of rights. The will theory stipulates that those who are not rational decision-makers cannot have rights, as they do not have the capability to determine whether to enforce or waive their rights. Those with intellectual disability who cannot exercise rational choice to claim or waive rights therefore cannot possess them, according to the will theory. For our purposes then, will theory would not support the argument that people with intellectual disability hold either claim right one—the right to 'reasonable and necessary' supports—or claim right two—the right to choice and control over these supports.

Interest theory conversely argues that rights need only be plausibly beneficial to the claim-holder to qualify as a right. The claim-holder hence does not need to be capable of understanding, asserting or withdrawing rights claims. This means that, according to interest theory, it is possible for those with significant intellectual disability to possess rights. However, if a prospective right-holder does not have the capability to realise any benefits from having a right, then that interest may not qualify as important enough to ground a rights claim. For example, a baby with no grasp of language cannot be argued to have a present right to attend university (although she may have this right in future), as she lacks the present capacity to act on, or benefit from, this right. Under this conception of rights, people with intellectual disability would clearly hold claim right one—the right to 'reasonable and necessary' supports—as these supports are clearly of benefit to the right-holder. However, it is not so clear that people with intellectual disability will always hold claim right two—the right to choice and control over their support services—according to the interest theory of rights.

While those with a profound intellectual disability have clear interests in being treated well, a right to self-determination (choice and control) without the capacity to conceive of the good, or act rationally and independently towards it, is less clear grounds to an interest-based claim. Immediate preference satisfaction can work against overall interests for those with intellectual disability quite dramatically, making this tenuous ground for interest-based choice rights. Clegg et al. (2017) identify several real-world examples of the consequences of paying attention only to the immediate choices. For example, support staff working with Robert (a young man with significant intellectual disability) comply with Robert's refusal to eat or drink for nearly a week. While the support staff are concerned with Robert's choices, his mother considers this failure to intervene pure negligence (Clegg et al. 2017, 359–372).

It should be noted at this point that not all people with intellectual disability lack the capacity to make rational choices. Intellectual disabilities encompass a wide range of disabilities with differing cognitive function. However, it is sufficient for the purposes of this discussion to accept that some people with intellectual disability, particularly if the cognitive impacts are significant, lack the capacity for rational decision-making as it is traditionally defined within liberal rights theory.

On this argument, both traditional will-based and interest-based rights theories appear to lead to a troubling conclusion—that we have different duties to those whose intellectual disability inhibit their ability to act as "rational agents". Both theories seem to lead us to conclude that (contrary to the central principles of the NDIS) some people with intellectual disability cannot have a right to freedom of choice, as they lack an ability to conceive of their own idea of the good life and make rational choices in pursuit of it. This is one of the reasons why those with intellectual disability have rarely been seen by traditional liberal philosophers as people with an equal entitlement to fulfilment (Carlson and Kittay 2003, 257).

The majority of this chapter has concerned itself with liberal theories of rights that are still centrally concerned with the concept of choice and rationality. A critique of this approach may be that it places too much importance on the concept of rationality or capacity.

The final part of this chapter outlines some alternative philosophical theories or considerations that do not provide rationality such a central position. Rejecting traditional liberal assumptions about the central importance of rationality, these accounts attempt to explain why people of varying capabilities are owed equal consideration, including rights to self-determination and to make choices about their lives. These philosophies demonstrate how equal rights can extend to all NDIS participants, by considering those with intellectual disability from the very start.

Dignity of Risk

A central rallying cry of disability advocates in the lead up to the introduction to the NDIS was the 'dignity of risk'. This phrase originally comes from a 1972 article by Robert Perske. In the article, Perske (1972) argues that the traditional paternalistic approach to people with intellectual disability, such as the need to 'protect', can endanger the '...person's human dignity and tends to keep him from experiencing the normal taking of risk in life which is necessary for normal human growth and development'. In the modern literature, dignity of risk is 'the principle of allowing an individual the dignity afforded by risk-taking, with subsequent enhancement of personal growth and quality of life' (McDougall 2005; Robertson 2011).

The concept of dignity of risk recognises that there is risk in allowing people with intellectual disability to have choice and control over their lives but argues that enabling this choice provides human dignity and improved wellbeing that justifies taking it on. The dignity of risk also relates to the concept of the 'right to fail' (Soyer 1963). The concept of the right to fail argues that having a right to make a choice does not necessarily mean that we only have a right to make *correct* choices. People without intellectual disability who are seen as holding rational decision-making capacity routinely make bad choices or choices that are seen as irrational. The right to make these choices is regarded as an important part of recognising and protecting one's self-determination.

The dignity of risk and right to fail view this as equally important for people with reduced cognitive capacities. Within a reasonable realm that does not put people in significant risk of harm, people with intellectual disability should be afforded choice and control over their lives even if this means that at times, they do not make rational choices. There is debate within the healthcare literature on how to balance the dignity of risk with care-giver's duty of care, with some believing that a balance cannot be properly struck. However, this is a problem of implementation, not of conceptual clarity (Ibrahim and Davis 2013).

The focus on human dignity shifts the emphasis from rationality and asks us to begin our thinking from an enabling place. The concept of dignity of risk allows us to think of people with intellectual disability as equally holding rights to choice and control over their lives and disability support services. The concept of dignity, and some objections, is discussed further when we address the capabilities approach below.

The Potentiality View

Some philosophers have argued for equal consideration of those with intellectual disability based on their potential for rational thought. Sophia Wong (2009) argues that, as it is impossible to predict which individuals will develop capacity for rational decision-making,[1] we owe all those with intellectual disability (as well as those without) access to the "enabling conditions" necessary for them to develop as fully rational agents. These "enabling conditions" require that we continue to treat and support all those with intellectual disabilities (and those without) as though they will become capable of conceptualising their own good, and communicating it with us, as this might one day become a reality (Wong 2009, 389). The antithesis of this—assuming people with intellectual disability will never conceptualise their own good, and providing them with little choice and control over their lives—is considered morally impermissible.

Using developmental potential as the basis for equal moral consideration in this way is more inclusive than many traditional liberal philosophies. However, it only provides the basis for equal treatment for those with significant intellectual disability where their future developmental potential remains unknown, and the possibility of future rationality persists. While it may not currently be possible to predict which individuals could grow to be fully capable of rational decision-making, medical advancements may mean this is far easier to predict this sort of thing in future. Invariably, Wong's potentiality approach will exclude some individuals where they can be accurately predicted to never develop the rational capabilities, and hence will leave some individuals behind (Berube 2009). While this conclusion may be acceptable to some, the NDIS stipulates a need to respect the choice-rights of all those with disability, regardless of their future developmental trajectory. Wong's view thus seems to stand in opposition to this fundamental principle of the scheme.

The Capabilities View

The capabilities view argues that there are a set of central capabilities which are objectively valuable, and that society should be organised to foster these capabilities equally among its members (Nussbaum 2006, 74–76). Originally put forward by Amartya Sen and advanced by Martha Nussbaum, this view considers rights as meaningful only where they provide people with opportunities to flourish. For example, the right to free association simply implies freedom from coercion that would prevent

[1] Indeed, medical professionals have tended to be inaccurate with these predictions, with many historically thought to be incapable of thought or speech learning to do both with the right support.

a person from meeting with others, while having this capability means actually being able to freely meet with others of one's choice. The latter could require providing access to transportation, physical and economic support to ensure this capability is actually able to be realised (Khader 2008).

The capabilities approach is argued to offer a single standard that justifies the social entitlements of those with intellectual disability by the same logic as all other people (Khader 2008, 8). For example, Nussbaum (2006) argues that human dignity can serve as the justification for personhood, an entitlement to moral consideration and, hence, development of important central capabilities. Human dignity, she argues, is often characterised by a kind of rationality, but also includes other qualities typical of our "animality" such as our sociability and bodily needs (e.g. the need for care). To 'count', in a moral sense, one simply needs to possess just some of the many aspects that make up our human dignity (Nussbaum 2006, 160). Those whose disability in some way impedes them from arriving at and articulating complex accounts of their own good can still possess human dignity by this account. Hence, according to Nussbaum, even those with profound intellectual disability are entitled to develop the central capabilities entitled to all those possessing of human dignity. These capabilities include the ability to form a conception of the good and to engage in critical reflection about the planning of their life—both central principles underpinning the design of the NDIS (Nussbaum 2006, 77).

Collaborating on Notions of the Good Life

Silvers and Francis argue that liberal theories, while committed to protecting many different ideas about the good life, tend to be prescriptive on how conceptions of the good life must be formed and sustained. They argue that, while some people don't possess the cognitive capabilities to arrive at a conception of their own good independently, ideas of the good can be articulated, validated, and maintained in a collaborative fashion. They argue that in many cases, normally autonomous individuals do not arrive at, nor do they express, notions of their own good in isolation from, or independent of, their interactions with other people. In this sense, conceptions of the good are "socially scripted and interactively developed" for both those with intellectual disability and those without. Hence, a more collaborative conception of choices is appropriate to everyone, but especially useful for those with intellectual disability (Silvers and Francis 2009, 485).

Silvers and Francis (2009, 486) argue that, as a prosthetic arm or leg executes some of the functions otherwise undertaken by their biological counterparts, an appointed trustee can use their reasoning and communicating to execute part or all of someone else's own thinking processes, without substituting the trustee's own idea as if it were the subject's own. Hence, while conceptualising goals is considered important, Silvers and Francis's view allows for this process to be undertaken collectively, with others assisting in their formation. This theory hence has implications for the legitimate role of trustees or proxies (such as family members or support workers) in planning with those with intellectual disability.

Conclusion

The NDIS Act clearly articulates that those with disability, including those with intellectual disability, have the same rights and entitlements as all other citizens. These include liberty rights, including choice and control over the supports they receive. Yet rights philosophies have struggled to reconcile the notion of equal treatment with those who don't possess certain capacities for rational thought and action. For this reason, contrary to the principles underpinning the NDIS, liberal philosophers have tended to exclude or treat as special cases, those whose intellectual disability mean they cannot arrive at their own idea of the good life, or make rational decisions that lead them towards it.

This chapter has presented some alternative philosophical theories that attempt to be more inclusive of the idea that those with intellectual disability also have choice rights, consistent with the principles of the NDIS. Without landing on any particular theory, this chapter attempts to demonstrate some of the philosophical complexities of any liberal philosophy that wishes to include all people on equal footing, including those with disability.

References

Bentham, Jeremy in John Bowring. 2019. *The Works of Jeremy Bentham*, vol. 2 (Judicial Procedure, Anarchical Fallacies, works on Taxation) [1843], ed. John Bowring. Online Library of Liberty.

Bentham, Jeremy. 1970. *Of Laws in General*, ed. H.L.A. Hart. London: Athlone Press.

Berube, M. 2009. Equality, Freedom and/or Justice for All: A Response to Martha Nussbaum. *Metaphilosophy* 40: 353–365.

Carlson, Licia, and Eva Feder Kittay. 2003. Introduction: Rethinking Philosophical Presumptions in Light of Cognitive Disability. *Metaphilosophy* 40: 307–330.

Clegg, Jennifer, Elizabeth Murphy, and Katherine Almack. 2017. Liberal Individualism and Deleuzean Relationality in Intellectual Disability. *Philosophy, Psychiatry and Psychology* 24: 359–372.

Disability Discrimination Act 1992 (Commonwealth). Commonwealth Consolidated Acts. http://www5.austlii.edu.au/au/legis/cth/consol_act/dda1992264/.

Epstein-Frisch, B. 2013. Advocate, Family Advocacy NSW, member of the National People with Disability and Carers Council 15 August 2013.

Friedman, Lawrence. 1995. Review of James Trent, Inventing the Feeble Mind: A History of Mental Retardation in the United States. *American Historical Review* 100: 1284–1286.

Hart, H.L.A. 1982. *Essays on Bentham: Studies in Jurisprudence and Political Theory*. Oxford: Clarendon Press.

Hohfeld, Wesley. 1913. Some Fundamental Legal Conceptions as Applied in Judicial Reasoning. *Yale Law Journal* 23: 16–59.

Ibrahim, Joseph, and Marie-Claire. Davis. 2013. Impediments to Applying the 'Dignity of Risk' Principle in Residential Aged Care Services. *Australian Journal of Aging* 32: 1–6.

Jackman, Martha. 2010. Charter Remedies for Socio-Economic Rights Violations: Sleeping Under a Box? In *Taking Remedies Seriously*, ed. Robert J. Sharpe and Kent Roach. Montreal: Canadian Institute for Administrative Justice.

Khader, Serene. 2008. Cognitive Disability, Capabilities and Justice. *Essays in Philosophy* 9 (1): 11.

Kramer, Matthew. 2001. Getting Rights Right. In *Rights, Wrongs, and Responsibilities*, ed. Matthew Kramer. London: Macmillan.

MacCormick, N. 1977. Rights in Legislation. In *Law, Morality and Society. Essays in Honour of H.L.A Hart*, ed. P. Hacker and Joseph Raz. Oxford: Oxford University Press.

McDougall, Tim. 2005. The Dignity of Risk. United Kingdom: National Children's Bureau, Council for Disabled Children & Shared Care.

National Disability Insurance Scheme Act 2013 (Commonwealth). http://www8.austlii.edu.au/cgi-bin/viewdb/au/legis/cth/num_act/ndisa2013341/.

Nussbaum, Martha. 2006. *Frontiers of Justice: Disability, Nationality and Species Membership* (The Tanner Lectures on Human Values). Harvard: Harvard University Press.

Perske, Robert. 1972. The Dignity of Risk and the Mentally Retarded. *Mental Retardation* 10: 24–27.

Pound, Roscoe. 1942. *Social Control Through Law*. New Haven: Yale University Press.

Productivity Commission. 2011. Disability Care and Support, Productivity Commission Inquiry Report no 54 (July). Commonwealth of Australia. https://www.pc.gov.au/inquiries/completed/disability-support/report.

Raz, Joseph. 1984. The Nature of Rights. *Mind* 93: 194–214.

Raz, Joseph. 1986. *The Morality of Freedom*. Oxford: Oxford University Press.

Robertson, John. 2011. Positive Risk Taking: Whose Risk Is It? An Exploration in Community Outreach Teams in Adult Mental Health and Learning Disability Services. *Health, Risk & Society* 13: 147–164.

Silvers, Anita, and Leslie Pickering Francis. 2009. Thinking About the Good: Reconfiguring Liberal Metaphysics (or Not) for People with Cognitive Disabilities. *Metaphilosophy* 40: 475–498.

Soyer, Davis MS.. 1963. The Right to Fail. *Social Work* 8: 62–78.

Stark, Cynthia A. 2009. Respecting Human Dignity: Contract Versus Capabilities. *Metaphilosophy* 40: 366–381.

Steiner, Hillel. 1998. *Working Rights in a Debate Over Rights: Philosophical Enquiries* eds. Matthew Kramer, N.E. Simmonds, and Hillel Steiner. Oxford: Oxford University Press.

United Nations. 1948. The Universal Declaration of Human Rights. https://www.un.org/en/universal-declaration-human-rights/.

United Nations. 2006. Convention on the Rights of Persons with Disabilities (CRPD). https://www.un.org/development/desa/disabilities/convention-on-the-rights-of-persons-with-disabilities.html.

Wellman, Carl. 1985. *A Theory of Rights*. Totowa, NJ: Rowman & Allanheld.

Wong, Sophia. 2009. Duties of Justice to Citizens with Cognitive Disabilities. *Metaphilosophy* 40: 382–401.

Part II

CHAPTER 8

Implementation Challenges in the NDIS

Gemma Carey and Eleanor Malbon

Introduction

As one of the most complex and challenging reforms in recent times, the National Disability Insurance Scheme (NDIS) has experienced a range of implementation challenges. We think of implementation as everything that happened after the NDIS was passed in Parliament in March 2013—from the creation of governance structures to organisational arrangements and changes to scheme design in areas such as planning and Local Area Coordination. Establishing the NDIS has involved unprecedented changes in both the structure and culture of government and the disability sector. To date, implementing the NDIS has involved the creation of a new agency co-owned by the Federal, State and Territory Governments, a new regulatory body, the creation of complex disability markets and over 13,000 new public sector positions from the local to national level. It has required policymakers to utilise new policy instruments and shift the rules and norms of institutions and the goals of government and providers. These changes, coupled with the diversity of support needs met by the NDIS, distinguish it from many other public service reforms which have

G. Carey (✉) · E. Malbon
UNSW, Kensington, NSW, Australia

M. Cowden and C. McCullagh (eds.), *The National Disability Insurance Scheme*, https://doi.org/10.1007/978-981-16-2244-1_8

come before—giving policymakers little in the way of a 'blue print' to follow.

This chapter draws on longitudinal research into the implementation of the NDIS to discuss key challenges that have emerged in implementation to date. Specifically, the chapter examines the interplay of politics and implementation, along with 'path dependency', whereby new policies fall into old traps and legacies of former initiatives. Dismantling old systems has been a major barrier to the implementation of the scheme—with many elements of the previous system being brought into the NDIS as a result. An interrelated challenge for the implementation of the NDIS has been balancing short-term, often politically driven, goals and the longer-term vision of the scheme. Meeting participant targets and roll out deadlines has compromised the core values of choice and control, which sit at the heart of the reform. This chapter explores how these tensions have played out during the implementation of the NDIS and their implications for the future of the scheme.

Bringing the 'Old' into the 'New'

There is a branch of policy theory known as historical institutionalism that is concerned with how institutions—such as governments, administrative systems and so forth—change or fail to change over time. One of the central arguments to this work is that change is often very difficult to achieve because we are, so to speak, stuck in the same grooves of working. This is referred to as 'path dependency'—whereby the legacies of former ways of working drive future ways of working. Interconnected with this idea is that of 'policy layering', whereby new policies get layered onto old ones—rather than replacing them (Mahoney and Thelan 2010; Powell and DiMaggio 1991; Streeck and Thelen 2005). As a result, we see forms of 'policy drift' (where policies drift back to previous models), or 'conversion' where parts of the system are converted to meet alternate goals (Mahoney and Thelan 2010; Streeck and Thelen 2005). In short, policy change never starts with a clean slate—which is central to why policy implementation is messy and often fraught. In practice, what citizens end up with can be very different from policy 'as designed'.

The NDIS is envisaged as a transformative policy change—it entails the dismantling of an entire system, which is then being rebuilt from a different value set. As outlined in previous chapters, these values are about empowerment, agency and rights of people with disability to exercise decisions about their lives. Despite this, the NDIS did not start with a 'clean slate'. For example, the process of moving from a largely state-funded disability service market to a federally funded service market created a number of complexities around NDIS funding, including how 'in-kind' funding from the states should be used. We detail this and other complexities that have arisen through the implementation of the NDIS that may change the trajectory of the scheme. Policy layering, drift, conversion and path dependency have played out in the implementation of the scheme in unexpected, and often unhelpful, ways. We explore a number of elements of the scheme where these processes have come into play, taking the NDIS away from the original blueprint set out by the Productivity Commission (2011), to a scheme that is perhaps more accurately described as a hybrid between the old and new disability systems (at least at the time this chapter was written). Specifically, we will examine the four core areas where various forms of layering and path dependency have taken the scheme away from its original goals: funding, planning, market management and administration.

Funding

In transitioning from a state-funded to a federally funded approach to funding disability services, those responsible for policy design and implementation have faced serious complexity in how to convert old block and grant funding into the new 'individualised' scheme. This has necessitated, or at least resulted in, a range of interim measures which mix old and new approaches to disability funding. For example, existing services offered either by State and Territory Governments directly, or through contracts between State and Territory Governments and third-party providers, could not be immediately dismantled. That is, programs that had already been funded for a set period of years (some of which stretched right through to full implementation of the scheme). To account for these issues, an agreement was negotiated between the Commonwealth Government and the various State and Territory Governments which required participants to use state- and territory-funded services (referred to as 'in-kind' services) before 'cash' services (i.e. those contained in plans) where individuals are given money to purchase alternatives from the market (Carey et al. 2017, 2019). This is a form of policy layering where new policy goals are layered onto an old arrangement, thereby compromising the goals of the reform.

The requirement for individuals to continue to use existing government services limits both choice and control for participants and, over time, hinders the growth of the disability services market. By using in-kind, you're also restricting choice and control of the participations, because you're saying, 'well we've still got this service that we're going to have for the next three years, as a contract'. So, although we're telling you, 'you can go and get whatever provider you want', you actually have to use this [provider] first because otherwise we'll run out of money (senior public servant, quoted in Carey et al. 2019).

There has been a growing recognition that this policy layering is creating a legacy of distortions that could be difficult, or at least take considerable time, to 'wash out' (Carey et al. 2019). The Commonwealth Government has tried to wrap up the in-kind contributions by making it non-negotiable that in-kind comes to an end, but some say it will continue into 2023 (10 years into scheme) (Carey et al. 2019). The hang-over effects in terms of market development and the ability of individuals to exercise choice and control will have gone well past early implementation, placing limits on market development and also the development of capabilities of individuals to exercise choice and control (rather than continuing to receive standard government services). Hence, while the in-kind arrangement met the immediate priority of managing the financial transition from State and Territory Governments to the Commonwealth Government, it also has the potential to entrench expectations, practices and cultures that are inconsistent with the ultimate goals of the NDIS.

Participant Planning

One of the major innovations of the NDIS is the creation of 'Local Area Coordinators' (LACs). In the original blueprint for the scheme, the role of LACs was to provide local level support by linking people with disability to local community groups, providing small grants to assist individuals access community activities, identifying voluntary resources that people with disability could access, as well as case management and brokerage functions (Productivity Commission 2011). However, the shape of this important 'street level' role has undergone significant change as the scheme has moved through its various implementation phases.

The 'transition phase' of the NDIS saw an increase of enrolments in the scheme from 20,000 to 460,000. Not surprisingly, implementation priorities centred on getting participants enrolled and drawing up personalised budget plans as quickly as possible, with less consideration given to the quality of the plans (Knaus 2017). The focus on increasing enrolments as quickly as possible was driven by political imperatives and targets—no government wants to be responsible for the NDIS 'falling behind'. However, the main implementation agency—the National Disability Insurance Agency (NDIA)—has experienced significant resource constraints compared to the original NDIS blueprint, due to a cap on public servant staffing. For example, the NDIA was originally intended to employ around 10,000 individuals to support the planning and administrative aspects of the scheme, but the Commonwealth Government initially restricted the number of staff who could be employed directly to 2,500 (Productivity Commission 2011; Nevile et al. 2019).

To reach the targets, LACs were redirected away from their original role of providing local level support and required to focus their attention on enrolling participants and placing them on plans (Carey et al. 2019). Early on in implementation, the Abbott Government outsourced LACs to non-government organisations (again, as part of a broader small government agenda) (Carey et al. 2019). This outsourcing—to a diversity of NDIS partner organisations across the country—created ambiguity and diversity around the LAC functions. Arguably, the LAC position was exploited to cover the shortfall of planners within the NDIS. This is reflected in LAC contracts, which now stipulate key performance indicators around planning activities, with less emphasis on the diversity of their original planned activities which were intended to help participants build capacity by accessing local services (NDIA 2016). The change in LAC roles was noted in early research evaluating aspects of the scheme.

> LACs are… not doing what they were employed to do. Many felt the specific skills and connections to the community that they brought to the position were not being utilised. All of the LACs who were interviewed described being required to spend the largest portion of their time supporting the planning process and plan implementation. (Mavromaras et al. 2018, 107)

While the intention is that in time LACs will return to their original roles, there are many indications from broader public administration literature suggesting that the process of returning LACs to original LAC duties may not be as easy as has been hoped. Pressures on street level bureaucrats to meet performance targets have been shown to increase standardisation of service in other quasi-markets in Australia such as the jobs market (Considine et al. 2011; Marston and McDonald 2008). As argued in Malbon et al. (2019), cultural norms established early on in the LAC position could become intractable. Theories of institutional change show that institutional norms, informal rules and cultural practices can become difficult to change or return (Mahoney and Thelan 2010). The longer that LACs play the role of planning rather than the broader role of the 'glue' that holds the NDIS together at a local level, the harder it will be to return them to their role as originally envisaged.

The planning process within the NDIS remains fraught. There have been significant financial cuts to the amount of money available to participants and major inconsistencies in care plans on both a case-by-case and year-by-year basis (Commonwealth Ombudsman 2018; Joint Standing Committee on the NDIS 2018). The Commonwealth Ombudsman found that the NDIS had around 8,100 requests for revisions or alterations to NDIS care plans in February 2018, with around 600 new requests occurring per week at that time (Commonwealth Ombudsman 2018). There was significant attention on the NDIS's plan revision process at this time, with media highlighting the backlog and the Ombudsman's report recording 400 complaints relating to the plan revision process (Commonwealth Ombudsman 2018). This has the potential to erode community trust in the planning process and lessen the ability of the LACs, who have become the face of the planning process in many locations, to fulfil the original vision of their role.

Disability Markets

The success of the NDIS hinges on the development of robust disability markets across the country. Robust NDIS markets are crucial, as without multiple care options for participants to choose from, participants cannot exercise choice and control over their care services. The establishment and maintenance of markets for disability support services rely on participants having funds to purchase services, thereby creating demand and driving provider growth in the markets (Productivity Commission 2011).

During transition, the scheme has been characterised by higher numbers of participants and larger funding packages than anticipated in early modelling (Productivity Commission 2017). While the scheme remains within its budget envelope, this is because participants have not utilised the full funding within their plans, highlighting a major budgetary problem within the NDIS (Productivity Commission 2017). Lack of spending on care plan budgets is no doubt driven by a range of factors; however, a lack of markets from which to purchase services has been identified as major cause of participants not spending their allocated budgets (Productivity Commission 2017).

In response to pressures to keep the NDIS within the current funding allotment, underspent money in plans has been withdrawn from participants' budgets.

Similarly, while there is no systematic evidence, there are reports in the media that participants' plans are being reduced over time, particularly if people are perceived to be doing well (Morton 2017).

Pulling unspent money back into the scheme, and reducing participant's packages over time, meets the immediate demands on the NDIS to rapidly reduce costs and prevent a budget blowout. However, it places longer-term goals in jeopardy—without money in the hands of participants there is no means by which to stimulate market growth. This is a form of policy drift, with high stakes. If the service markets do not develop as a result of a lack of funds to stimulate growth, the NDIS will fail to deliver on choice and control (Productivity Commission 2017).

This policy drift, as well as other logistical challenges of establishing new NDIS markets, has led to low market capacity issues. Low market capacity, also referred to as thin markets, has been a major implementation challenge in the NDIS. NDIS market readiness was the subject of a senate inquiry in 2018 (Hansard 2018). Many major providers around Australia were tasked with transitioning from a block-funded model to a business model that has a weekly or daily cash flow. While support was offered by the NDIA for transitioning providers, many challenges remain and some service providers have been withdrawing from the NDIS or certain NDIS participants, unable to find appropriate business models for the new NDIS system.

The slow development of NDIS markets comes with a set of implementation issues, including the need to define responsibility for market function in the NDIS. Responsibility ultimately rests with the NDIA, but also intersects with the Department of Social Services and the Quality and Safeguards Commission (Malbon et al. 2016, 2018).

Administrative Burden

The NDIA was originally designed with the staffing resources to better orientate and support users to the new scheme. With the cap on public servant staff numbers, however, the burden of helping NDIS participants navigate the new NDIS system has been pushed out of government and onto providers and individuals. At present, providers report they are picking up unpaid and un-costed work created by the scheme—which may be exploited by government for the purposes of cost containment.

At the time of writing, providers in the NDIS have reported higher than sustainable levels of administrative burden (Carey et al. 2019). There are multiple sources of this burden—some of which were anticipated and associated with the new NDIS individualised funding system, while others have been 'brought over' from old ways of working or unanticipated needs.

In terms of genuinely new and important administrative burdens, the NDIS has created a range of new responsibilities for providers. Administrative processes for quality and safety assurance are essential for the NDIS, ensuring that government and providers are ensuring safe service practice. This has been necessarily compounded as the new NDIS regulatory body—the Quality and Safeguards Commission—rolls out.

The Quality and Safeguards Commission is bringing with it further important administrative processes regarding compliance, oversight and financial reporting (Commonwealth Department of Social Services 2015, 2017).

However, providers have reported doing large amount of unfunded work during implementation. There have been significant time investments by providers in helping participants navigate the new NDIS system. Many service providers have been supporting their clients since before the NDIS and are a known 'face' to them (Carey et al. 2019). Consequently, many service providers feel motivated to assist clients in navigating the NDIS systems, despite there being specific NDIS-funded people in place to do this (such as LACs and planners). A high proportion of those providers that are mission-driven may find their goodwill towards clients means they pick up additional work that others are not undertaking.

While the scheme may be intended to reduce pressure on carers, rather than ameliorating pressure for carers, these burdens have in part been shifted onto service providers. Many providers report that given their link with users and their families, they inevitably undertake an amount of bridging activities in terms of skilling up individuals and their families (Carey et al. 2019). This is particularly important when something goes wrong with the planning process or payment systems—increasing the administrative burden on providers. Simultaneously, administrative burden for carers remains high as they navigate the new NDIS bureaucratic complexities (Mavromaras et al. 2018).

One particular point that seems to have created significant stress for providers and users alike is transitioning between plans (Carey et al. 2019). As the NDIS has been in a roll out phase and therefore charged with getting significant volumes of individuals on to plans, there have been delays in reviewing plans in some areas. In many cases, this has been compounded by workforce difficulties. If a plan ends before a new one can be created, this poses somewhat of a gap for individuals and providers. Providers can continue to deliver services, under the promise that they will be paid once a new plan is delivered, but it means going without payment for a period of time. Even where plans do exist, they may not be high quality for a number of reasons and may therefore need to be re-done or need significant work to make these relevant and useful for consumers.

This latter set of administrative burdens relates to transitioning between systems. However, with cuts to resources around staffing and the NDIA, much of this work appears to be falling onto providers during implementation. The unexpected and unfunded administrative burdens falling on the disability sector are likely to prove problematic for the NDIS. Either organisation will be forced to withdraw from the scheme due to financial pressures, or abandon the additional, unfunded work that may place more burden on remaining providers, or on families who are left with nowhere to turn if this administrative burden is not picked up by government or advocacy organisations. It is worth noting that growth in administrative burdens has been a feature of personalisation schemes internationally (Fleming et al. 2019). Generally, these have been attributed to the design of overly complex systems that have emerged naturally out of poor design and could therefore be corrected through re-design (Fleming et al. 2019).

Discussion

It is not surprising that the implementation of the NDIS has been and will continue to be challenging. As Whelan et al. (2014) memorably pointed out, implementing the NDIS is like 'building the plane while flying it'. As we have identified in this chapter, the implementation of the NDIS exhibits many challenges common to other large-scale reforms and government programs. Alongside the successes of the scheme, instances of policy layering, policy drift and intractable cultural norms define the implementation process. There are a number of core drivers for these diverse areas of the NDIS that are experiencing implementation challenges. One of these is a genuine struggle for policymakers in balancing short-term and long-term goals of the scheme. Within the areas discussed, the need to meet short-term priorities, which were often political in nature, set in motion the creation of structures and cultures that are likely to become entrenched. Indeed, our longitudinal research has enabled us to show that some changes are indeed becoming intractable. Three years ago, policymakers raised concerns about LACs becoming 'locked' into planning roles, and in 2018, we find that planning now takes up 80% of LACs' time and has been written into contracts. In response to short-term needs, processes of policy drift, layering and conversion have occurred. In Table 8.1, we outline these, their consequences and the long-term adjustment that is needed.

Overall, this raises questions about what the NDIS has actually become during implementation, and what the future holds. When we look back at the original blueprint for the NDIS put forth by the Productivity Commission, one might reasonably argue we have arrived at a different scheme through implementation. One which is a hybrid of ideas put forth in the Productivity Commission report, hangovers from the previous system and elements drawn from broader and long-running trends in policy and administration. In the remainder of this chapter, we attempt to outline the NDIS 'as exists', in contrast to the 'NDIS as designed'.

A crucial slippage that has occurred within the NDIS is a shifting from personalisation to individual budgets. Leadbeater (2004) argues that personalisation exists on a continuum—with personalisation at one end (whereby participants can create truly personalised solutions to their service needs) and individual budgets at the other (merely giving individuals control of funding, but services are not tailored or bespoke). During

Table 8.1 Implementation changes and their consequences

Aspect	*Short-term needs*	*Unintended consequences*	*Long-term needs*
Funding	Make use of in-kind supports	Stagnated market growth	Secure adequate funding
Participant Planning	A high demand for planning activities in the early stages of the scheme	Loss of LAC function	Ensuring that the planning process remains directed by people with disability, equitable and in keeping with the ideal of the scheme
NDIS markets	Reduce costs and prevent budget blowout	Loosing means to stimulate market growth as participants spend less funds	Offer a basis for choice and control
Administrative burden	Capping NDIA staff to reduce costs	Lack of implementation capacity within NDIA, transfer of administrative burden	Better bureaucratic processes that reduce burden/burden placed back onto government

the implementation of the NDIS, the scheme has shifted towards the individual budgets end of the spectrum. Limitations in planning, shifting role of LACs and lack of robust markets have meant that for many participants, they may hold the budgets but have limited say in how it is spent and whether tailored services can be accessed.

Another driver of the 'individual budget' slide has been an overemphasis on free-market solutions. While the Productivity Commission report outlines markets as the mechanism by which choice and control would be operationalised, these markets were to be supplemented by other efforts such as commissioning and micro-commissioning (whereby the NDIA or other parties contract out for specific services that are missing from the market). During implementation, free-market ideals took hold among scheme implementers, with a reluctance to mix markets and other forms of public service provision in order to ensure personalisation (Carey et al. 2017).

This same market emphasis can be seen in how advocacy has been treated within the scheme. There has been a distinct step away from government funding of advocacy organisations, particularly by State Governments, on the notion that within a market environment, individuals are responsible for their own advocacy (Carey et al. 2017). This is despite research demonstrating that engaging advocates can significantly boost the size of packages received (Malbon et al. 2019). The original Productivity Commission report noted that:

> Advocacy plays an important role in the disability system. Systemic advocacy pushes for broad policy and social change, while individual advocacy promotes the interests of particular individuals by acting on their behalf to resolve specific issues. These functions should lie outside the NDIS... Current funding arrangements through [Commonwealth Government] and various State and Territory governments should continue. (2011, 26)

The LAC position has also changed significantly through implementation and is now focused on very procedural and efficiency-based aspects of the scheme such as getting an increasing number of participants onto plans. LACs were envisaged as providing oversight for service delivery, participant interactions with NDIA and links to the community, as well as independently assessing the quality of service providers (Productivity Commission 2011, 411). However, due to pressures to increase the number of participants with NDIS plans, LACs' work was refocused. Interviews with LACs show that they have key performance indicators around the number of plans they institute a week, leaving less time for the softer parts of the LAC role that can help support people with disability to find and keep good services (Malbon and Carey 2021).

At present, the NDIS constitutes a hybrid scheme—influenced by its original design, elements of the previous system and changes that have occurred during implementation (e.g. a greater emphasis on market mechanisms). Changes which occur through policy drift and layering often become intractable and difficult to rectify (Mahoney and Thelan). This means that the NDIS may now be set on a course from which it is unlikely to be able to return to the original design. This does not, however, mean that the scheme has 'failed' as is often reported in the media, or that there is nothing that can be done to overcome the challenges that have occurred during implementation. We want to emphasise that changes and shifts in the implementation of large-scale reforms are commonplace, and that a focus on the core goals of the scheme can help to reorient implementation efforts towards scheme betterment.

One of the drivers behind the continuing challenges is a separation between authority and knowledge within the scheme. Predominately, authority continues to sit at the 'top' of the scheme in the hands of actuaries, the NDIA board and to a lesser extent Commonwealth Government. Knowledge of how the scheme is working (or not) exists at the local level, held by people with disability, service providers, advocates, LACs and more. This indicates that we need to shift towards a more devolved model of decision-making, which will encourage local responsiveness in the NDIS. At the time of writing, there are several actions that could be taken which, while not shifting the NDIS back to its original design, will relieve pressures and improve the experiences of scheme participations. These include reorienting the role of Local Area Coordinators within the scheme, lifting staffing and resource caps on the NDIA, and finding ways to develop local level markets by empowering participants to drive change (e.g. through advocacy).

Conclusion

The NDIS is one of the most complex reforms to be implemented in Australia in a generation. Not surprisingly, there have been challenges during its implementation. While throughout 2018 and 2019 media reports have increasingly suggested that the NDIS has 'failed', the challenges that have emerged are in fact common to the implementation of many reforms. Rather than 'failure', we propose that the NDIS has emerged as a hybrid scheme, encompassing some of the original design and ideals, alongside elements of the previous system and new features which have emerged during implementation. The goal is to work with this hybridity to secure choice and control for people with a disability.

References

Australian Productivity Commission. 2011. *Disability Care and Support: Productivity Commission Inquiry Report*. Melbourne, VIC: Productivity Commission.

Carey, G., and E. Malbon. 2018. Strange Magic: What Can the Emergence of 'Magic Concepts' Tell Us About Policy Implementation? *Policy Design Practice* 1 (3): 169–182. https://doi.org/10.1080/25741292.2018.1499414.

Carey, G., A. Kay, and A. Nevile. 2017. Institutional Legacies and "Sticky Layers": What Happens in Cases of Transformative Policy Change? *Administration & Society*. https://doi.org/10.1177/0095399717704682.

Carey, G., H. Dickinson, E. Malbon, et al. 2017. The Vexed Question of Market Stewardship in the Public Sector: Examining Equity and the Social Contract through the Australian National Disability Insurance Scheme. *Social Policy & Administration Online First*. https://doi.org/10.1111/spol.12321.

Carey, G., A. Nevile, A. Kay, et al. 2019. Managing Staged Policy Implementation: Balancing Short-term Needs and Long-term Goals. *Social Policy & Administration*: spol.12530. https://doi.org/10.1111/spol.12530.

Carey, G., M. Weier, E. Malbon, et al. 2019. How Is the Disability Sector Faring? Report from the National Disability Services Annual Market Survey. Sydney, NSW: Centre for Social Impact, UNSW Sydney.

Commonwealth Department of Social Services. 2015. Proposal for a National Disability Insurance Scheme Quality and Safeguarding Framework: Consultation Paper. Canberra: Commonwealth Government of Australia.

Commonwealth Department of Social Services. 2017. NDIS Quality and Safeguards Commission. Available at: https://www.dss.gov.au/disability-and-carers/programs-services/for-people-with-disability/ndis-quality-and-safeguards-commission.

Commonwealth Ombudsman. 2018. Administration of Reviews Under the National Disability Insurance Scheme. Commonwealth Government of Australia.

Considine, M., J.M. Lewis, and S. O'Sullivan. 2011. Quasi-Markets and Service Delivery Flexibility Following a Decade of Employment Assistance Reform in Australia. *Journal of Social Policy* 40 (04): 811–833. https://doi.org/10.1017/S0047279411000213.

Fleming, P., et al. 2019. Individualised Funding Interventions to Improve Health and Social Care Outcomes for People with a Disability: A Mixed-Methods Systematic Review. *The Campbell Collaboration*. https://doi.org/10.4073/csr.2019.3.

Green, C., E. Malbon, G. Carey, et al. 2018. Competition and Collaboration Between Service Providers in the NDIS. Centre for Social Impact.

Hansard, Commonwealth Government of Australia. 2018. Joint Standing Committee on the National Disability Insurance Scheme: Market Readiness for Provision of Services Under the National Disability Insurance Scheme. Hansard, Commonwealth Government of Australia.

Joint Standing Committee on the NDIS. 2018. Joint Standing Committee on the National Disability Insurance Scheme Public Inquiry. Hansard Report. Hansard, Commonwealth Government of Australia.

Knaus, C. 2017. NDIS Rollout Targets in Doubt Because of Lack of Resourcing. *The Guardian*, 20 September.

Leadbeater, C. 2004. *Personalisation through Participation: A New Script for Public Services*. London: Demos.

Mahoney, J., and K. Thelan. 2010. *Explaining Institutional Change: Ambiguity, Agency and Power*. Cambridge: Cambridge University Press.

Malbon, E. & Carey, G. (2021). Stewardship of Quasi-Markets by Street Level Bureaucrats. *Social Policy & Administration* 55 (1): 18–33.

Malbon, E., G. Carey, and H. Dickinson. 2016. Accountability in Public Service Quasi-Markets: The Case of the Australian National Disability Insurance Scheme. *Australian Journal of Public Administration.*

Malbon, E., G. Carey, and D. Reeders. 2018. Mixed Accountability Within New Public Governance: The Case of a Personalized Welfare Scheme in Early Implementation. *Social Policy & Administration.*

Malbon, E., G. Carey, and A. Meltzer. 2019. Personalisation Schemes in Social Care: Are They Growing Social and Health Inequalities? *BMC Public Health* 19 (1): 805. https://doi.org/10.1186/s12889-019-7168-4.

Marston, G., and C. McDonald. 2008. Feeling Motivated Yet? Long-Term Unemployed People's Perspectives on the Implementation of Workfare in Australia. *Australian Journal of Social Issues* (Australian Council of Social Service) 43 (2). Available at: http://search.ebscohost.com/login.aspx?direct=true&profile=ehost&scope=site&authtype=crawler&jrnl=01576321&AN=33410967&h=tdtHfLMrJs16aDMI9uMqQRjyxMH0%2BobOGqeqAzmCqEhQzu0s3t4zQ%2Bm%2Bgtj05iUn4RCvU%2BxfPtJPH93gHpTeBg%3D%3D&crl=c. Accessed 16 May 2014.

Mavromaras, K., M. Moskos, S. Mahuteau, et al. 2018. Evaluation of the NDIS: Final Report. National Institute of Labour Studies, Flinders University.

Morton, R. 2017. Families' NDIS Support Slashed in Crackdown. *The Australian.*

NDIA. 2016. Draft Grant Agreement Terms and Conditions NDIS Partners in the Community Program. Commonwealth Government of Australia.

Nevile, A., E. Malbon, A. Kay, et al. 2019. The Implementation of Complex Social Policy: Institutional Layering and Unintended Consequences in the National Disability Insurance Scheme. *Australian Journal of Public Administration Early View.*

Powell, W., and P. DiMaggio. 1991. *The New Institutionalism in Organisational Analysis*. Chicago: University of Chicago Press.

Productivity Commission. 2011. *Disability Care and Support: Productivity Commission Inquiry Report*. Canberra: Commonwealth Government of Australia.

Productivity Commission. 2017. National Disability Insurance Scheme (NDIS) Costs: Issues Paper. Canberra: Commonwealth Government of Australia.

Streeck, W., and K. Thelen. 2005. *Beyond Continuity: Institutional Change in Advanced Political Economies*. Oxford: Oxford University Press.

Whelan, J., P. Acton, and J. Harmer. 2014. A Review of the Capabilities of the National Disability Insurance Agency. National Disability Insurance Agency.

CHAPTER 9

Mental Health and the NDIS: Making It Work for People with Psychosocial Disability

Theresa Williams and Geoffrey Smith

Mental health came late to the National Disability Insurance Scheme (NDIS; 'the scheme') and this has shaped much of what has followed. In August 2012 Professor Alan Fels, as Chair of the National Mental Health Commission, addressed the National Press Club and spoke in favour of the decision to include psychiatric disability in the NDIS observing that:

> The National Disability Insurance Scheme is very welcome...it is critical that it not only applies to persons with physical disability but also to persons with significant and enduring psychiatric disability. After some debate the Productivity Commission recommended this and I believe the government broadly supports this. It is a key need for the mental illness agenda. We are conscious there will be pressure to reduce costs by restricting the scope of the program. The National Mental Health Commission will closely watch to ensure that current policy is maintained. (Fels 2012)

T. Williams (✉) · G. Smith
University of Western Australia, Perth, WA, Australia

M. Cowden and C. McCullagh (eds.), *The National Disability Insurance Scheme*, https://doi.org/10.1007/978-981-16-2244-1_9

While the mental health sector broadly supported being included, the NDIS was largely designed to meet the needs of people with physical, sensory or intellectual disability with limited reference to the needs of people with psychosocial disability (MHCA 2013; CMHA 2017). Many issues relating to the design of the scheme and the way it has been implemented have been attributed to this late inclusion (CMHA 2017; MHA 2018a). Two issues have been of particular concern to the mental health sector, namely that:

1. The eligibility requirement that an impairment is or is likely to be permanent has been considered incompatible with the recovery philosophy which underpins mental health care (Williams and Smith 2014). And
2. the implementation approach has not adequately recognised that '...psychosocial disability differs from physical and sensory disabilities in important ways and presents the Scheme with significant challenges' (JSC 2017, ix).

These issues underpin much of the ongoing debate over (i) whether key aspects of the NDIS design should be changed, particularly the eligibility requirement for permanent impairment, (ii) what adaptations are required to the way the scheme is implemented to address the specific needs of people with psychosocial disability and (iii) whether adaptations made within the existing framework will be sufficient to overcome the difficulties or whether more substantial reform to the legislation and rules will be required.

So while there is widespread recognition by the mental health sector that the NDIS has the potential to offer significant tangible benefit to people with psychosocial disability, there remains concern about how well the scheme is working in practice to deliver these benefits (MHA 2017, 2018a, 2019a; Productivity Commission 2017).

When Two Worlds Collide

The NDIS suddenly brought the mental health and disability sectors together. This has highlighted underlying differences between the sectors, including deep-seated issues of identity, described as follows by Professor Peter Beresford, a UK academic and mental health service user:

> Many psychiatric system survivors are unwilling to see themselves as disabled...Similarly, some disabled people do not feel that psychiatric survivors are disabled, because they do not have a physical impairment or their situation is not permanent. There are also fears and anxieties on both sides of being linked with the negatives that are often associated with the other. (Beresford 2000, 169)

Both in Australia and internationally, the mental health and disability sectors have emerged from their own social movements; each with a distinct identity, history, culture, ideas, agenda and way of doing things (Beresford 2000; NDA 2010). Within Australia, these differences have been magnified in the period since the inception of the NDIS with the debates being characterised by a leading mental health advocate as 'the great narrative wars' (CMHA 2017, 4). These different worldviews, largely rooted in the separate development of the two sectors, provide the lens through which many of the discussions about the design of the scheme and the implementation challenges can be viewed.

A brief recap of the key disability and mental health legislative and policy milestones in Australia over the past four decades highlights a history of separate development and provides an important context for understanding the NDIS in relation to people with psychosocial disability.

The Handicapped Persons Assistance Act 1974 was the first attempt to address services for people with disability at a national level and was followed by the Disability Service Act 1986 enshrining the principles of citizenship, equal opportunity and community inclusion. From 1991 the National Disability Agreements between the Commonwealth, States and Territory Governments provided the framework which shaped the delivery, funding and development of disability care and support services across Australia (Soldatic and Pini 2012). Although both Acts specifically included psychiatric disability within their remit, importantly the funding and provision of treatment and support services for people with mental health issues developed separately from those for people with sensory, physical or intellectual disability; the former remaining primarily the responsibility of health and the latter of the disability sector.

At the same time as disability services were being shaped through the National Disability Agreements, mental health was undergoing its own transformation leading to the National Mental Health Strategy in 1992 and the development of a series of rolling National Mental Health Plans (COAG Health Council 2017). Over the past quarter of a century, these nationally agreed 5-year plans have set the strategic direction for the development of mental health services across the country.

The NDIS arose, in large part, from the sustained efforts of disability advocates representing people with physical, sensory or intellectual disability, reflecting their voice and world view (Soldatic and Pini 2012; Thill 2015; Buckmaster and Clark 2018a). As a consequence, the scheme espouses the core values and language which underpins the disability sector, namely that of person-centred, self-directed and individualised services that promote independence, community inclusion and participation underpinned by the UN Convention on the Rights of Persons with Disabilities (United Nations 2006; Productivity Commission 2011; NDIS Act 2013).

The dominant philosophy underlying contemporary mental health services has been the concept of recovery, described by Anthony (1993, 14) as 'a deeply personal, unique process … a way of living a satisfying, hopeful and contributing life, even with the limitations caused by illness'. It is not the same as clinical recovery but instead the focus is on living a meaningful life with or without symptoms (RMI 2016). Core principles which underpin the recovery paradigm are hope, self-determination, self-management and empowerment together with the right to full inclusion to be able to live a meaningful life free of stigma and discrimination. Recovery permeates the language of mental health and is embedded in policies, plans and service delivery across all jurisdictions (NMHC 2014; WAMHC 2015; COAG Health Council 2017).

There are substantial similarities between the philosophies which underpin the disability and mental health sectors and people with different types of disability have much in common (Pilgrim and Tomasini 2012). Despite these commonalities, the importance of each sector retaining their independent and distinct identities, philosophy and language has been argued by many (Beresford 2000; Beresford et al. 2002).

Reconciling the disability and mental health perspectives is achievable; however, it will require substantial change to the NDIS to reflect the lens through which people with psychosocial disability see the world so that the scheme can realise its potential.

'Psychiatric Disability' or 'Psychosocial Disability': What's in a Name?

There has been widespread concern within the mental health sector that the NDIS places a heavy reliance on the formal diagnosis of a mental illness, rather than functional impairment, to determine eligibility (RANZCP 2017; JSC 2017). This has been partly attributed to the difficulty of assessing and predicting functional impairment and also to the eligibility requirement outlined in Section 24(1)(a) of the NDIS Act 2013 for an impairment 'attributable to a psychiatric condition' (NDIS Act 2013, 28). The genesis of this language can be seen in the early stages of the formation of the NDIS when the Productivity Commission referred to 'people with significant and enduring psychiatric disabilities' (Productivity Commission 2011, 14).

At the same time as the Productivity Commission was undertaking its inquiry, the national body for mental health consumers and carers published a position paper entitled Unravelling Psychosocial Disability (NMHCCF 2011). It unequivocally endorsed the use of the term psychosocial disability as the one favoured by mental health consumers and carers, primarily because it emphasises the social consequences of a disability, as opposed to the term psychiatric disability with its emphasis on a medically defined illness or impairment. It drew heavily on the seminal work of the World Network of Users and Survivors of Psychiatry who, from 2002 to 2006, participated in the negotiations at the United Nations to develop the Convention on the Rights of Persons with Disabilities. In that process they developed new terminology to actively shift away from the language of persons with psychiatric disability and its associated medical model of individual pathology (WNUSP 2008).

> We described ourselves as persons with psychosocial disabilities. The word psychosocial refers to the interaction between psychological and social/cultural components of our disability. The psychological component refers to ways of thinking and processing our experiences and our perception of the world around us. The social/cultural component refers to societal and cultural limits for behaviour that interact with those psychological differences/madness as well as the stigma that the society attaches to labelling us as disabled. (WNUSP 2008, 9)

The term 'psychosocial disability' has been adopted by the NDIA and the mental health sector. The NDIA has publishing a detailed definition of

Table 9.1 NDIS definition of psychosocial disability

Psychosocial disability—the term used to describe a disability arising from a mental health condition or conditions. Not everyone who has a mental health condition will have a disability, but for those who do it can be severe and longstanding and it can have a significant impact on someone's life and potential recovery. Psychosocial disability is the term preferred by people living with mental health issues, families, and carers
'Psychosocial disability' is an internationally recognised term under the United Nations Convention on the Rights of Persons with Disability and is used to describe what is often the outcome for a person with mental health condition attempting to interact with a social environment that presents barriers to their equality with others
Psychosocial disability may also describe the experience of people with impairments and participation restrictions related to mental health issues such as the loss of or reduced abilities to function, think clearly, experience full physical health and manage the social and emotional aspects of their lives (NDIS 2018, 3)

psychosocial disability (outlined in Table 9.1) which largely reflects the position of the National Mental Health Consumers and Carers Forum and the World Network of Users and Survivors of Psychiatry by:

- recognising consumer, carer and family preference for the term psychosocial disability;
- outlining the psychological and social aspects of the impairment;
- recognising the interaction between the person with impairments and the environmental barriers that hinder societal participation; and
- including the concept of recovery (NDIS 2018).

Design Challenges: Is the Legislative Framework Fit for Purpose?

Difficulties with the design of the NDIS for people with psychosocial disability have been recognised since its inception (CMHA 2017). The peak national body that represents and promotes the interests of the mental health sector observed:

> Some of the core design problems relating to eligibility, funding and scope were raised with the government prior to the scheme's commencement, and even prior to the passing of the National Disability Insurance Scheme Act (2013). The failure to address these issues, after such a long period of consideration and after such clear articulation over time, suggest the

current governance arrangements for the NDIS, and for the systems that interact with it are not fit for purpose. (MHA 2017, 3)

The most contentious aspect of the NDIS design relates to the eligibility requirement in Section 24(1)(b) of the NDIS Act 2013 which specifies that 'the impairment or impairments are, or are likely to be, permanent' (NDIS Act 2013, 28). Central to the argument from the mental health sector has been the contention that the language of disability, impairment and illness contained within the NDIS Act is at odds with the concepts of hope, empowerment and recovery which underpin contemporary mental health care.

The issue of permanent impairment has been considered in three key inquiries into the NDIS with varying conclusions being reached (Ernst and Young 2015; JSC 2017; Productivity Commission 2017). Within their broader deliberations, each inquiry considered the appropriateness of the current legislative framework for people with psychosocial disability and the key issues and conclusions are outlined below.

Independent Review of the NDIS Act (Ernst and Young 2015*):* This independent review of the NDIS Act was commissioned by the Commonwealth Government, in consultation with State and Territory Governments, to assess the operation of the NDIS and to consider whether any amendments should be made to the legislative framework.

Concerns were raised by a number of stakeholders during the Review about the appropriateness of the concept of permanency in the context of mental illness. Three key arguments were mounted. Firstly, that the episodic nature of some mental illness, such as bi-polar disorder, may result in fluctuating or episodic impairment rather than permanent impairment, and that people can and do recover. Secondly, that permanency is at odds with the recovery principle which underpins the delivery of mental health services. Finally, that the requirement for permanency will limit the effectiveness of the Scheme by (i) reducing participation and (ii) providing supports which assume permanent impairment rather than recovery resulting in people receiving support for longer than needed.

The Review recommended no change to the legislation in relation to the eligibility criteria of permanence, mainly on the grounds that it is a core feature of the NDIS and could expand the scope and cost of the scheme. They were of the view that there was sufficient flexibility within the current framework to accommodate concerns and that the NDIA should be given the opportunity to continue their efforts to make the scheme more responsive to people with psychosocial disability. They gave four reasons for reaching their decision not to recommend legislative changes to the permanency provision:

- The concept of permanency is central to the design of the NDIS and the risk in making an amendment is that it could broaden the scope and cost of the scheme.
- The legislative framework already accommodates some of the stakeholder concerns by allowing fluctuations in impairment (Rule 5.5).
- Current evidence does not suggest a dampening of participation.
- The NDIA have invested considerable effort in attempting to 'enhance the responsiveness of the NDIS to people with mental illness' and these efforts should 'be exhausted before determining whether amendments to the permanency provisions are required' (Ernst and Young 2015, 38).

In concluding, the Review acknowledged the level of stakeholder interest in the issue and left the door open to future change noting that there would be value in re-visiting the appropriateness and effectiveness of the permanency provisions when the NDIS Act was next reviewed.

Joint Standing Committee on the NDIS: Psychosocial Disability (JSC 2017): The Joint Standing Committee on the NDIS (the Committee) reports annually to the parliament and has a broad remit, including inquiring into the implementation, performance, governance, administration and expenditure of the NDIS. In November 2016 the Committee decided to undertake an inquiry into the provision of services by the NDIS to people with psychosocial disability.

The Committee heard from several stakeholders that the eligibility requirement for permanent impairment in Section 24(1)(b) is viewed as being incompatible with the principle of hope which is central to the recovery journey (NDIS Act 2013; MHA 2017). It was argued that the language of disability, impairment and illness used in the legislation represents a backward step from the more empowering recovery-based discourse which underpins contemporary mental health care (RANZCP 2017). There is emerging evidence that some people are declining to engage with the NDIS because they do not consider that they have a psychosocial disability which is permanent.

As discussed in the previous section, it was also argued that the eligibility requirement for an impairment 'attributable to a psychiatric condition' in Section 24(1)(a) (NDIS Act 2013, 28) has led to a heavy reliance on diagnosis rather than functioning and may exclude people with psychosocial disability despite their ongoing need for support (JSC 2017).

There were proposals to amend Rule 5.4 of the NDIS (Becoming a Participant) which states that an impairment is or is likely to be considered permanent '...only if there are no known, available and appropriate evidence-based clinical, medical or other treatment that would be likely to remedy the impairment' (NDIS Rules 2018, 9). Many people with psychosocial disability continue to receive mental health clinical, medical and other psychosocial services and this is not reflected in Rule 5.4.

The Committee agreed that the language of disability does not readily translate into a mental health context and that using concepts of permanence may, on the surface, be seen to conflict with recovery principles. They recommended a review of the permanency requirement in Section 24(1)(b) and also to reference to a psychiatric condition in Section 24(1)(a). In relation to the Rules they recommended a change to Rule 5.4 to clarify that it should not apply to people with psychosocial disability to reflect the appropriateness of individuals continuing to receive ongoing treatment and care to support their recovery.

The Productivity Commission Report on NDIS Costs: As part of the Heads of Agreement signed by Commonwealth, State and Territory Governments in 2012 and 2013, it was agreed that the Productivity Commission would review NDIS costs in 2017 to inform the final design of the full scheme (Productivity Commission 2017). As part of the terms of reference the Productivity Commission was to consider whether there were any issues with the design of the NDIS.

The Productivity Commission report devotes a section to psychosocial disability—the only specific disability where this is the case. This reflects the complexity of the issues and recognition of the unique challenge of providing services for people with psychosocial disability. As in previous inquiries, concerns were raised by stakeholders about the incompatibility of the legislative requirement for permanence with a recovery approach. However, the Commission concluded that the 'investment approach of the NDIS and the recovery model of mental health are both about building capacity, and appear to be well aligned' and that the 'NDIS Rules and operational guidelines accept that a permanent condition may be episodic requiring different levels of support at different times' (Productivity Commission 2017, 23). It cautioned against changing the permanence requirement on the grounds that it may impact on the financial sustainability of the scheme.

However, given the particular challenges for people with psychosocial disability and having identified this group as being at higher risk of having poorer outcomes, the Productivity Commission accepted that 'some aspects of psychosocial disability do not sit that well in the NDIS given the design of the scheme and how it operates' (Productivity Commission 2017, 176). As a consequence, they recommended establishing a specialised entry gateway for people with a psychosocial disability.

Where to Next with the Legislation and Rules?

Overall, despite repeated attempts by the mental health sector to persuade the various inquiries and reviews of the need to change the legislative framework, the results have been mixed, with two of the three key investigations not supporting amendments to the Act and the Rules. The Commonwealth Government, in responding to the recommendations from the Joint Standing Committee, did not support the recommendation regarding permanency and reference to a psychiatric condition within the Act. Nor did it support the recommendation to assess an amendment to the Rules to include the principle of recovery-oriented practice or to clarify that people with mental conditions will receive ongoing treatment to aid recovery (Australian Government 2018).

Overall, there appears little appetite from the majority of the inquiries or from government, at this point in time, to amend the legislative framework. This position appears to be primarily driven by a concern about potential cost increases which could result from any change to the boundaries of the scheme with 'permanency' being seen as a key design tenet. Despite this reluctance to amend the legislation or the Rules, each of the inquiries has recognised that there are significant challenges in improving the NDIS for people with psychosocial disability. The preferred approach, at this point in time, is for the NDIA to work within the existing legislative framework to address any identified shortcomings by modifying the way they administer and implement the scheme (Productivity Commission 2017, 176; MHA 2018b). However, there now appears to be more readiness to develop specific strategies which are tailor-made for people with psychosocial disability rather than relying on improving the 'general pathways' (Productivity Commission 2017). The development of a psychosocial pathway exemplifies this change of approach (Fletcher and Henderson 2018).

Implementation: Learning from the Initial Trials

Given the scale and complexity of the NDIS is it unsurprising that a number of significant difficulties have arisen. Many of these, such as the need to provide flexible support in response to episodic illness, were foreseen early in the development of the scheme (Williams and Smith 2014). As the implementation has progressed operational issues, such as the way in which assessment and planning is undertaken and the pricing of psychosocial support services, have also emerged (Productivity Commission 2017; MHA 2019a). Much has been learned through the implementation process and the NDIA continues to work to improve the responsiveness of the scheme for people with psychosocial disability (NDIA 2019a, b) (Table 9.2).

Insights from the NDIS Trials

The progressive roll out of the NDIS through a series of launch sites provided a unique opportunity for a structured approach to identifying problems and trialling innovative solutions. A significant amount of

Table 9.2 NDIS challenges identified early for people with psychosocial disability (Williams and Smith 2014)

- The estimated 57,000 eligible people with psychosocial disability is a significant underestimate
- Whether the scheme has the flexibility to respond to the fluctuating disability support needs of people with a mental illness of an episodic nature
- The difficulty in the early prediction of 'permanent' impairment, which is one of the criteria for access to early intervention psychosocial support
- How the concept of recovery fits with a scheme that appears to be framed around lifelong support and maintenance
- The degree of readiness of the workforce and service providers for this fundamental change in the way that services are to be delivered
- How States and Territories will respond to the support needs of people who are not eligible for entry to the scheme
- The difficulty in defining the boundaries between support services that are the responsibility of the health system or the NDIS

learning in relation to psychosocial disability came from two of the initial sites launched in July 2013—the Hunter area of NSW and the Barwon region in Victoria (PDSV 2015; MHC NSW 2015; MHCC 2016a). This knowledge base expanded when the NDIS was launched in the ACT, the Perth Hills in Western Australia and the Barkly region in the Northern Territory in July 2014 (NDIA 2014; MHCC ACT 2018).

A number of themes emerged from the trial sites including:

- the lack of knowledge of the NDIS among potential participants and providers;
- a requirement for greater clarity regarding eligibility and improvements to the planning process which is currently complex and resource intensive;
- the need for optimal evidence-based packages of individual supports;
- the necessity for services to support families and carers and increased sensitivity to their role in supporting the participant; and
- the importance of advocates to provide support and assist participants navigate the system.

Indigenous people, migrant and refugee communities were identified as having specific needs (PDSV 2015). The importance of creating strong links between the NDIS and mental health services was emphasised because of their key role in advocating for and supporting participants to access the NDIS (MHCC 2016a).

The challenge for consumers who are ineligible for the NDIS was highlighted, particularly as funding from programs such as Partners in Recovery is transferred to the scheme, potentially leaving people who were previously eligible without support (MHCC ACT 2018). There is a lack of clarity about the role of the States and Territories in providing services to fill these gaps (PDSV 2015). From the perspective of service providers, it has been complex and challenging to transition from block funding to a new business model based in individually funded packages. This has been made more difficult in the context of a pricing framework which fails to recognise both the increased administrative impost and the higher costs of an expert workforce necessary to deliver specialist psychosocial disability supports (PDSV 2015; MHCC ACT 2018).

Some interesting innovations have emerged from the NDIS trials. They signal opportunities to build these approaches into the 'fabric' of the way that the NDIA operates so as to address some of the implementation challenges in relation to people with psychosocial disability. Selected examples are outlined below.

Bringing the NDIS to people living in psychiatric hostels: A key initiative during the Perth Hills trial in Western Australia was to actively reach out to people in five psychiatric hostels to support them to access and engage with the NDIS (Stopher and Hughes 2017). It recognised that people with severe and persistent mental health issues are often isolated from community, family and friends and as such, are likely to require tailored supports to effectively engage with the NDIS. The project ran from October 2015 to November 2016 and brought 110 people into the NDIS from an estimated 135 considered to be eligible. The evaluation of the project concluded that residents would not have effectively engaged with the NDIS without many, if not all, of the following strategies being implemented:

- Establishing a **stakeholder collaborative**, including Community Managed Organisations (CMOs), the Public Advocate, clinical mental health services, the WA Mental Health Commission and the consumer peak organisation, to oversee and shape the project.
- Employing a **project manager** for 18 months to coordinate the project.
- Developing close working arrangements with the **National Access Team** to clarify the evidence required to assess eligibility.
- Developing **information templates** to assist residents and providers with the application process.
- Assigning four **dedicated NDIA planners** to work with residents and at the same time increasing their specialist knowledge of psychosocial disability.
- **Support coordinators** from CMOs assisting residents to interview potential support workers to enable them to choose their community access worker.
- **Peer facilitators and peer workers with lived experience** supporting hostel residents through the process by designing and delivering support to assist them to explore their experiences as they engaged with each stage of the NDIS process (CoMHWA 2016). The peak mental health consumer organisation recruited and supervised the peer support facilitators.

Supporting consumers of clinical mental health services engage with the NDIS: The Hunter New England Mental Health Service appointed NDIS 'champions' in each mental health team to act as a local resource and facilitate a seamless transition for participants of the NDIS. In addition, a full-time project manager was appointed for 12 months to support consumers, carers, families and clinical staff through the transition phase. This proactive approach to capacity building also led to the clinical mental health services engaging with CMOs, including with some services which had not traditionally had a strong connection to or history of collaborating with health services. This extra capacity also enabled the clinical mental health services to engage with CMOs who had newly entered the mental health sector and to discuss ways they could assist them to enhance their capacity to support clients with complex mental health needs, such as through shared care arrangements (MHCC 2016a).

Local 'communities of practice' to build links and enhance learning: An NDIS and mental health community of practice was established in the Hunter trial as initial experience showed that learning was occurring in silos (MHCC 2016a). Rather than using existing networking structures, participating organisations decided to establish a specific NDIS community of practice to share information, learn from each other and solve problems facing the group. Meetings were held every 3 months and were open to anyone with an interest in the NDIS and mental health/psychosocial disability. Consumers and carers attended the forums as well as participants from a wide range of mental health/health, disability, drug and alcohol, homeless, housing, emergency services, education, university and advocacy services.

It resulted in closer working relationships between government agencies and CMOs, encouraged intersectoral innovation, learning, leadership and local level action. As a result of these positive outcomes, guidelines for establishing a local NDIS community of practice were published to assist other local communities to establish similar mechanisms (MHCC 2016b).

National Evaluation of the Trial Sites

An independent evaluation of the NDIS was undertaken to assess the impact of the five original trials, as well as the Barkly site in the Northern Territory, during the period 2013–2017. This comprehensive evaluation drew on qualitative data from in-depth interviews as well as quantitative data from a large-scale survey (Mavromaras et al. 2018). It found that people with psychosocial disability had poorer outcomes across a number of measures when compared with people with other types of disability, including:

- They were less satisfied with the **quality of their supports** under the NDIS compared to participants with other types of disability and reported worse outcomes in terms of the quality of their support than they would have had without the NDIS.
- In regard to **choice and control**, one of the key tenets of the NDIS, people with psychosocial disability reported having less say over what supports they received compared with NDIS participants with other disability types. Those who cared for a person with psychosocial disability also reported lower than average satisfaction with their choice and control.
- People with psychosocial disability, along with those with intellectual disability, were least satisfied that their **supports were reasonable and necessary**.
- People with psychosocial disability reported average lower levels of **wellbeing and social connections** than other types of disability. Furthermore, carers of NDIS participants with mental/psychosocial disability had lower levels of wellbeing than those caring for people with other types of disability.

In their concluding comments, the evaluation authors noted that:

> ...the NDIS is working well for the majority of the people that it touches, which is a major achievement. However, the NDIS also leaves a large minority (about a third) as well off as they were before, and it makes a small minority (between 10 and 20 per cent) feel worse off. These proportions come up time and again in many of the evaluation's findings. In most cases of a new policy, leaving a clear minority feeling worse off because of the policy would be a cause for concern. In the case of often highly vulnerable people with disability not clearly benefiting from the new system, such a finding points towards the need for closer monitoring and for more targeted and person-centred policy responses. (Mavromaras et al. 2018, xxiv–xxv)

Making Adaptations in an Evolving Scheme

From its inception, the NDIA has been aware of the need to refine and improve its responsiveness to meet the specific needs of people with psychosocial disability (IAC 2017). It has continued to increase specialist mental health expertise within the agency to better understand the issues and to adapt and refine existing processes including the appointment of a Mental Health Strategic Advisor (IAC 2017).

The NDIA have continued their efforts to improve the implementation of the scheme through a range of initiatives including refining the standardised assessment tool, clarifying eligibility criteria, developing psychosocial reference support packages, developing and implementing a range of improvement initiatives (fact sheets, practice guidance and training), supporting provider readiness, building the evidence base and strengthening the capacity of providers (Australian Government 2018). Most recently, the NDIA are working with the States and Territories to develop a Psychosocial Disability Capacity Framework with a strong focus on recovery and supporting episodic needs, which aims to ensure that NDIA staff and partners have the skills required to support people with mental health conditions (COAG DRC 2019; MHA 2019b).

The NDIA actively engages with the mental health sector including establishing a National Mental Health Sector Reference Group with broad sector representation and commissioning projects designed to build capacity and address implementation challenges (MHCC 2018; NDIA 2019a). There has been ongoing, significant collaboration between the NDIA and Mental Health Australia, the peak national body of the mental health sector, including funding projects designed to build the evidence base and inform future implementation strategies (MHA 2018a, b).

A Psychosocial Disability Stream

Despite the ongoing endeavours of the NDIA, the mental health sector has sustained its position that further significant accommodations are needed to enable the NDIS to meet the needs of people with psychosocial disability (JSC 2017; Productivity Commission 2017; Smith-Merry et al. 2018). In response to widespread advocacy from the mental health sector, the Productivity Commission (2017, 51) recommended the development of a 'psychosocial gateway' as the 'primary pathway' for people with a psychosocial disability to enter the NDIS. Key features were the use of specialised staff, operating on a face-to-face basis, outreaching to people who were unlikely to approach the scheme and linking to clinical and non-clinical services.

The NDIA subsequently engaged Mental Health Australia to consult with key stakeholders to give detail to the proposed psychosocial gateway concept (MHA 2018a). The result was a report which made 29 recommendations underpinned by these key messages which arose from their consultations:

- **Psychosocial disability differs** from most others forms of disability.
- The psychosocial disability **journey starts well before Phase 1** of the current NDIA pathway and requires assertive outreach and personalised engagement support.
- The skills, knowledge and experience of **front-line staff** are crucial.
- **Access, planning and review processes** need to be consistent, fair and transparent and key to this is to develop a validated, psychosocial disability-specific access assessment tool, to provide opportunities to check and confirm decisions and the evidence on which they're based, and to recognise the critical role of family and carers.
- The NDIA has a **responsibility towards people experiencing psychosocial disability who do not access the NDIS** including those who are 'hard to reach', those who are reluctant to test their eligibility and those found to be ineligible.
- Certain **support types** should be discussed in every planning conversation with the NDIS participants including support coordination, capacity building, carer support and respite and provision for urgent and unplanned need due to episodes of illness and disability.
- **Implementation** of reforms to the psychosocial disability pathway should be collaborative and subject to transparent evaluation, i.e. major design elements are to be tested with participants through piloting; the NDIA is to ensure close engagement with the mental health sector including mainstream systems and regular targeted reporting on outcomes for people seeking access to the scheme and the content and effectiveness of psychosocial disability plans.

Importantly, the report noted that minor adjustments to current pathways would not be sufficient to achieve the change necessary for the NDIA to engage people with psychosocial disability. It concluded by recommending that the NDIA develop an overarching psychosocial disability strategy, beyond reforming pathways, which will be required to address many wider issues raised by stakeholders during the consultation process. These included improving the skills, knowledge and experience of NDIA staff, reforming typical support packages and developing a communications strategy.

In October 2018 the Commonwealth Government, informed by the recommendations in the Mental Health Australia report, announced that the NDIA would progressively implement a 'psychosocial disability stream' with specialised planners and Local Area Coordinators who understood psychosocial disability, better linkages between mental health services and the NDIA and a focus on recovery-based planning and episodic-needs (Fletcher and Henderson 2018, 1). The development of the Psychosocial Disability Service Stream represents a hard won, significant step forward that explicitly acknowledges the unique needs of people with psychosocial disability, recognises the episodic nature of the illness for some people and proactively supports a recovery approach (NDIA 2019b). Key operational features include more specific pre-planning, being supported by a trusted family members/advisor and working with a specialist planner. The NDIA established a working group with broad sector representation including consumers to inform the design of the stream, with a staged roll out commencing in every State and Territory by June 2020 (MHA 2019b).

The NDIA has also introduced a Complex Support Needs Pathway to provide specialised support for participants living with disability who have complex and often multiple needs (Henderson 2018). While the pathway is not exclusively for people with psychosocial disability, it is anticipated that approximately one-third of participants with primary psychosocial disability will receive support through this pathway. National roll out of the pathway is underway (NDIA 2019b). These two initiatives hold promise for improving both the responsiveness of the NDIS and outcomes for people with a psychosocial disability, representing what could arguably be the most significant attempt to date to address many of the concerns which have been consistently raised by the mental health sector.

What Can Australia Learn from International Experience?

Over the past two decades a number of countries, including the USA, the Netherlands and the UK, have implemented national disability support programs with individualised funding which share many similarities to the NDIS (Alakeson 2010; Da Roit and Le Bihan 2010). To date there has been little reflection in Australia on this international experience either in learning from the pitfalls or building on success. In particular, many of the challenges which have arisen in relation to implementing self-directed support in Scotland and personal budgets in England for people with mental health issues resonates with the Australian experience with the NDIS. The good news is that, as the NDIS continues to evolve, it is not too late to learn from the experience of other disability support schemes (Williams 2012).

Key Lessons from International Experience

Psychosocial disability is different and implementation needs to be adjusted: The difference between psychosocial disability and other types of disability was captured in a consultation with mental health consumers and providers in Scotland in relation to their Self-Directed Support scheme where:

> In every meeting, discussion highlighted differences between mental health and other forms of impairments, and made suggestions as to how system providers might adjust to facilitate implementation in mental health. This was the lens through which challenges and opportunities in process, choice and information were seen. (MHF 2013, 8)

Uptake is lower than expected: Low uptake for people with psychosocial disability, when compared with other disability groups, has been identified as a key challenge in Scotland and England. In England, only 9% of adults with mental health problems who were eligible for a Personal Budget received one compared with 41% of eligible adults with a learning disability (RCP 2013). An evaluation of three Self-Directed Support test sites in Scotland found that mental health accounted for only 3% of individual support budgets (Ridley et al. 2011). When a follow-up evaluation was undertaken, the absolute number of individual budgets for people with mental health issues had increased but the overall percentage remained low at 2% compared with 59% for people with learning disability and 19% for those with physical disability (Ridley et al. 2012).

Sector capacity building and innovation requires partnership, time and resources: The Scottish Government responded to the findings of low uptake by funding a number of capacity-building initiatives designed to address identified barriers and actively involve mental health consumers and carers as active co-design partners (Williams 2014). Examples include Pilotlight—a co-production project undertaken by teams of people who use and those who deliver services which specifically aims to improve access to self-directed support for people with mental health problems (SCN 2014).

Evidence from England and Scotland suggests that to effectively support sector capacity building and innovation it needs to (i) be based on local partnerships and shared learning between all key stakeholders including consumer and carer organisations, clinical mental health services and CMO's; (ii) foster an approach of 'learning by doing' with evaluation being built into the process; and (iii) be funded over an extended period to encourage sustained effort, recognising that complex system change takes time (Williams and Smith 2014).

Engaging with mental health professionals increases access: The separation of disability support and mental health services has been identified as a key access barrier in both Scotland and England. While most people's route to support is through clinical mental health services, many clinicians have little knowledge of the disability support systems (MHF 2013; NDTI 2013; RCP 2013). The active engagement of key mental health professional bodies has been recognised as key to supporting people with psychosocial disability to access disability support programs (Alakeson et al. 2016). A significant step forward was the publication of a position paper by the influential Royal College of Psychiatrists, jointly developed with the Association of Directors of Adult Social Services, which supported the use of personal budgets as a way of facilitating recovery and made a commitment to work to increase the low uptake of people with mental health problems (RCP 2013).

Early intervention is challenging: The challenges in providing disability support for young adults in the early stages of their illness were highlighted in demonstrator mental health personal budget site in England. The evaluation found that although overall uptake could be largely improved by tailoring the program and working closely with the mental health clinical team, it proved difficult to engage young people as they were '...often at a stage where they wanted to keep official interaction with mental health teams to a minimum, and still felt they had their health under control' (Eost-Telling 2010, 23).

Infrastructure is needed to support 'real' choice and control: To effectively exercise choice and control requires the development of support infrastructure to ensure people have real choice. This includes assistance to access information, advocacy, support to develop individual support plans, choice of provider and selecting/employing support workers.

User-led organisations such as Onafhankelijk Leven in Belgium and Per Saldo in The Netherlands are based on maximising choice and control. These organisations are long established and provide considerable support to individuals with physical, sensory or intellectual disability. There are fewer consumer-led disability support services for people with psychosocial disability, however, one innovative example was the commissioning of a mental health consumer-led social enterprise ('All Together Positive') to engage peer workers to support individuals navigate the complexity of the process, assist in developing their individual plans, provide advocacy and engage with policymakers and service providers (Williams 2012; Dean et al. 2014).

The Challenges Ahead

While the NDIA are continuing to implement a range of initiatives to better meet the needs of people with psychosocial disability, there remain significant challenges ahead. There are varying levels of optimism/pessimism with some seeing the NDIS as being '...on the cusp of exciting changes...' but others noting a lack of progress where '... the challenges associated with the transition to the NDIS for eligible participants and continuity of support for those outside the scheme remain significant' (MHA 2019a, 5; JSC 2019, 18).

Amending the NDIS Legislation and Rules

This issue has persisted since the start of the NDIS. The multiple attempts by the mental health sector to lobby government to amend the NDIS legislation and rules were outlined in Section 4 and continue unabated (MHA 2019a). Despite the lack of success to date, the mental health sector is likely to continue to give voice to what they perceive as a compelling case for change.

Improving the NDIS Participant Experience for People with Psychosocial Disability

There remain a number of challenges in the way in which the NDIS is being operationalised for people with psychosocial disability including inconsistency in eligibility and planning outcomes, the lack of an agreed, validated and transparent assessment tools and the adequacy of plans and concern about the skills and knowledge of NDIA staff (JSC 2019). These issues were identified in the trial sites and remain largely unresolved. While initiatives such as the psychosocial disability stream and the complex support needs pathway show promise, the mental health sector is emphasising the need to evaluate these programs as they are rolled out to ensure that they are having the intended impact (JSC 2019).

Active Outreach to Bring the NDIS to People with Psychosocial Disability

> We will not reach the 64,000 goal unless we reach out more to those who will be eligible but are unlikely to apply…What we're understanding is that, for many people with psychosocial disability, often relating to a large government bureaucracy is at times traumatising and threatening. So, one of the issues we need to look at more closely is how do we outreach much more. (Naughtin quoted in McInerney 2018)

This observation from Dr Gerry Naughtin, NDIA Strategic Advisor on Mental Health and Psychosocial Disability, highlights a significant shift from the early approach which he describes as 'we'll set up our system and you'll need to come to us' (McInerney 2018). Access remains a key issue. As at 30 June 2019 some 9% (25,192) of all participants who were accessing and receiving support through the NDIS were people with psychosocial disability, whereas it was expected that by full scheme it would be 14% (64,000) of all participants (NMHC 2019). This highlights the need for the NDIA to continue its efforts to work with key stakeholders to provide assertive outreach and personalised engagement support, particularly for those who are 'hard to reach' or who are reluctant to test their eligibility.

Engaging with Health Professions

International experience highlights the key role of health professionals in supporting people with mental health issues to access disability support (Williams and Smith 2014). Within Australia, an extensive consultation process has been conducted with health professional organisations (HPOs) who reported that while they recognise that clinical care can be complemented by NDIS supports, their members have limited knowledge of the scheme—both who it is for and what it offers (MHA 2019b). While the HPOs support their members having a role in facilitating access to the NDIS, they identified barriers such as (i) a lack of perceived understanding and respect by the NDIA for the role and clinical opinion of health professionals; (ii) a lack of clear expectations from the NDIA for the role of each health profession; and (iii) little clarity about eligibility criteria. Specific actions have been recommended to address these barriers.

Early Intervention for Young People

Despite the option for early intervention supports within Section 25(1)(a) of the NDIS Act, it has been argued that young people in the 12 to 25-year age group in particular may have difficulties accessing these supports because they are unlikely to receive a diagnosis of permanent impairment. Clinical experts advise that even when a young person is experiencing severe and functionally disabling mental ill-health, it is neither possible nor clinically advisable for it to be diagnosed as a permanent disability (Orygen 2017). Furthermore, young people in the early stage of their illness are often reluctant to engage with mental health services, to view their illness as permanent or to see themselves as disabled (Eost-Telling 2010; Orygen 2017). This makes it unlikely that they will try to access the NDIS. An opportunity to minimise impairment and optimise outcomes risks is being lost without providing assertive outreach and assistance in system navigation, particularly for those young people who are not in contact with services (Orygen 2017). It is important that the NDIA further understand the access barriers for this group, estimate the numbers who may be impacted and identify potential strategies to address this challenge.

People with Psychosocial Disability Who Are Ineligible for the NDIS

The majority of people with mental ill-health will not be eligible to access the NDIS. It has been estimated that about 300,000 people with a serious mental health condition will require support but only about 64,000 are expected to be eligible (JSC 2019).

There is concern about clients of existing Commonwealth community mental health programs transitioning to the NDIS with about 50% of participants of these programs having applied for the NDIS with half having being found eligible and about one quarter ineligible and the remaining quarter awaiting an outcome (CMHA 2019). There is a call for Commonwealth community mental health programs to be extended to ensure that all current clients can test their NDIS eligibility and maintain continuity of support. Importantly, it has been argued that longer-term arrangements for existing clients who are not eligible for the NDIS need to be put in place before these programs close (JSC 2019, NMHC 2019).

Once the process to transition current participants from Commonwealth programs to the NDIS has been completed, it remains unclear as to the level of funding which will be provided by all jurisdictions for those who are ineligible for the NDIS but who require psychosocial support (JSC 2019; NMHC 2019). The provision of support outside the NDIS will present a significant funding challenge.

Conclusion

The final word goes to former Prime Minister the Hon. Julia Gillard MP whose Government introduced the NDIS. Speaking at a NDIS and mental health conference in 2018, some six years after the scheme was introduced, she acknowledging the frustration felt by families and those with mental health issues but observed:

> Some say including psychosocial disability was a mistake. I don't believe it was. If it wasn't included, people would be advocating for it to be now...great reform does take time to grow deep roots. (Gillard quoted in McInerney 2018, 9)

References

Alakeson, Vidhya. 2010. Active Patient: The Case for Self-direction in Healthcare. The Centre for Welfare Reform. https://www.birmingham.ac.uk/Documents/college-social-sciences/social-policy/HSMC/publications/active-patient-paper.pdf.

Alakeson, Vidhya, Jed Boardman, Billy Boland, Helen Crimlisk, Charlotte Harrison, Steve Iliffe, Masood Khan, Rory O'Shea, and Janet Patterson. 2016. Debating Personal Health Budgets. *BJPsych Bulletin* 40: 34–37.

Anthony, William A. 1993. Recovery from Mental Illness: The Guiding Vision of the Mental Health Service System in the 1990's. *Psychosocial Rehabilitation Journal* 16: 11–23.

Australian Government. 2018. Australian Government Response to the Joint Standing Committee on the National Disability Insurance Scheme (NDIS) Report: Provision of Services Under the NDIS for People with Psychosocial Disability related to a Mental Health Condition. Australian Government. https://www.dss.gov.au/sites/default/files/documents/03_2018/australian_government_response_to_the_jsc_on_ndis_inquiry_into_the_provision_of_services_under_the_ndis_for_people_with_psychosocial_disabilities_related_to_a_mental_health_condition_2.pdf.

Beresford, Peter. 2000. What Have Madness and Psychiatric System Survivors Got to Do with Disability and Disability Studies? *Disability and Society* 15: 167–172.

Beresford, Peter, Chris Harrison, and Anne Wilson. 2002. Mental Health Service Users and Disability: Implications for Future Strategies. *Policy and Politics* 30: 387–396.

Buckmaster, Luke, and Shannon Clark. 2018a. The National Disability Insurance Scheme: A Chronology. Research Paper Series, 2018–19. Parliamentary Library. https://apo.org.au/sites/default/files/resource-files/2018/07/apo-nid182336-1130211.pdf.

Buckmaster, Luke, and Shannon Clark. 2018b. The National Disability Insurance Scheme: A Quick Guide. Research Paper Series, 2018–19. Parliamentary Library. https://parlinfo.aph.gov.au/parlInfo/download/library/prspub/6665574/upload_binary/6665574.pdf.

CMHA (Community Mental Health Australia). 2017. National Mental Health Conference Report. CMHA https://cmha.org.au/wp-content/uploads/2017/12/CMHA-National-NDIS-Mental-Health-Conference-Report.pdf.

CMHA (Community Mental Health Australia). 2019. Tracking Transitions of People from PIR, PHaMs and D2DL into the NDIS. CMHA. https://cmha.org.au/wp-content/uploads/2017/04/CMHA-and-University-of-Sydney-NDIS-Tracking-Transitions-Phase-2-Report-version-3.pdf.

COAG DRC (The Council of Australian Governments (COAG) Disability Reform Council). 2019. Meeting of the COAG Disability Reform Council

Sydney – 9 October 2019 communiqué.COAG DRC. https://www.dss.gov.au/sites/default/files/documents/10_2019/communique-drc-9-october_2019.pdf.

COAG Health Council. 2017. The Fifth National Mental Health and Suicide Prevention Plan. Commonwealth of Australia. https://www.coaghealthcouncil.gov.au/Portals/0/Fifth%20National%20Mental%20Health%20and%20Suicide%20Prevention%20Plan.pdf.

CoMHWA (Consumers of Mental Health Western Australia). 2016. Report on the NDIS Peer Support in Psychiatric Hostels Project. CoMHWA. https://waamh.org.au/assets/documents/sector-development/ndis-peer-support-in-psychiatric-hostels-report.pdf.

Da Roit, Barbara, and Blanche Le Bihan. 2010. Similar and Yet so Different: Cash-for-Care in Six European Countries' Long-Term Care Policies. *Milbank Quarterly* 48: 286–309.

Dean, Shirley, Doreen Roberts, Ian Roberts. 2014. Learning from Mental Health Personal Health Budgets in Stockport. All Together Positive. https://www.centreforwelfarereform.org/uploads/attachment/505/learning-from-mental-health-phbs.pdf.

Eost-Telling, C. 2010. Final Report of the Evaluation of the Self-Directed Support Pilot. University of Chester. https://centreforwelfarereform.org/uploads/attachment/255/assetsdocsattachment255pdf.pdf.

Ernst and Young. 2015. Independent Review of the NDIS Act. Department of Social Services. https://www.dss.gov.au/sites/default/files/documents/04_2016/independent_review_of_the_ndis_act.pdf.

Fels, Allan. 2012. National Press Club Address: Allan Fels on Mental Health and Suicide Prevention. *The Conversation*, August 1. https://theconversation.com/national-press-club-address-allan-fels-on-mental-health-and-suicide-prevention-8567.

Fletcher, Paul, and Sarah Henderson. 2018. Government Announces Improved NDIS Mental Health Support. Australian Government. https://www.ndis.gov.au/news/400-government-announces-improved-ndis-mental-health-support.

Henderson, Sarah. 2018. Improved NDIS Planning for People with Complex Support Needs. Australian Government. https://formerministers.dss.gov.au/18797/improved-ndis-planning-for-people-with-complex-support-needs/.

IAC (Independent Advisory Council to the National Disability Insurance Agency). 2017. Submission to the Joint Standing Committee Inquiry into the Provision of Services under the NDIS for People with Psychosocial Disabilities Related to a Mental Health Condition. IAC. file:///C:/Users/he06404/Downloads/Submission%20125%20(2).pdf.

JSC (Joint Standing Committee on the National Disability Insurance Scheme). 2017. Provision of Services Under the NDIS for People with Psychosocial Disabilities Related to a Mental Health Condition. Commonwealth of Australia. https://www.ntmhc.org.au/wp-content/uploads/2017/10/Joint-Standing-Committee-on-the-national-Disability-Insurance-Scheme.pdf.

JSC (Joint Stand Committee on the National Disability Insurance Scheme). 2019. *Joint Standing Committee on the National Disability Insurance Scheme Progress Report*. Commonwealth of Australia. file:///C:/Users/he06404/Downloads/Report%20(2).pdf.

Mavromaras, Kostas, Megan Moskos, Stephane Mahuteau, Linda Isherwood, Alison Goode, Helen Walton, Llainey Smith, Zhang Wei, and Joanne Flavel. 2018. Evaluation of the NDIS: Final Report. National Institute of Labour Studies, Flinders University. https://www.dss.gov.au/sites/default/files/documents/04_2018/ndis_evaluation_consolidated_report_april_2018.pdf.

McInerney, Marie. 2018. Outlining Plans to Improve the NDIS for People with Serious Mental Health Issues. https://croakey.org/outlining-plans-to-improve-the-ndis-for-people-with-serious-mental-health-issues/.

MHA (Mental Health Australia). 2017. *Submission to the Joint Standing Committee on the National Disability Insurance Scheme into the Provision of Services Under the NDIS for People with Psychosocial Disabilities Related to a Mental Health Condition*. MHA. https://mhaustralia.org/sites/default/files/docs/mental_health_australia_submission_on_the_ndis_and_psychosocial_services.pdf.

MHA (Mental Health Australia). 2018a. National Disability Insurance Scheme: Psychosocial Disability Pathway. MHA. https://mhaustralia.org/sites/default/files/images/ndis_psychosocial_pathway_consultation_project_-_final_report_-_may_2018.pdf.

MHA (Mental Health Australia). 2018b. Optimising Psychosocial Supports: Project Report. MHA. https://mhaustralia.org/sites/default/files/docs/optimising_psychosocial_supports_project_report_final_web_0.pdf.

MHA (Mental Health Australia). 2019a. Submission to the Review of the National Disability Insurance Scheme (NDIS) Act and the New NDIS Participant Service Guarantee. MHA. https://mhaustralia.org/sites/default/files/docs/mha_cmha_and_mifa_-_submission_to_the_ndis_legislation_review.pdf.

MHA (Mental Health Australia). 2019b. Health Professionals, Psychosocial Disability and NDIS Access. MHA. https://mhaustralia.org/sites/default/files/images/health_professionals_psychosocial_disability_and_ndis_access_w_attachments_0.pdf.

MHCA (Mental Health Council of Australia). 2013. Mental Health and the National Disability Insurance Scheme, Position Paper. Canberra. MHCA. http://mhca.org.au/publication/mhca-position-paper-mental-health-and-national-disability-insurance-scheme-2013.

MHCC (Mental Health Coordinating Council). 2016a. Disability Insurance Scheme (NDIS) and Mental Health in NSW—Navigating the NDIS: Lessons Learned Through the Hunter Trial. MHCC. https://www.mhcc.org.au/wp-content/uploads/2018/05/ndis_lessons_final_200117.pdf.
MHCC (Mental Health Coordinating Council). 2016b. The National Disability Insurance Scheme (NDIS) and Mental Health in NSW—Guidelines for Establishing a Local NDIS Community of Practice to Enhance Learning and Sector Reform. MHCC. https://www.mhcc.org.au/wp-content/uploads/2018/05/ndis_cop_guidelines_final_200117.pdf.
MHCC (Mental Health Coordinating Council). 2018. View from the peak. MHCC. https://www.mhcc.org.au/wp-content/uploads/2018/10/VFP-Web_October_2018_v1_20181010.pdf.
MHCC ACT (Mental Health Community Coalition ACT). 2018. When the NDIS Came to the ACT: A Story of Hope and Disruption in the Mental Health Sector. MHCC ACT. https://static.wixstatic.com/ugd/672a33_7ac3cd4b1e774808b30258e0fb94cfe6.pdf.
MHC NSW (Mental Health Commission of New South Wales). 2015. The NSW NDIS and Mental Health Analysis Partnership Project: Insights from the First Two Years of the NDIS Rollout in the Hunter Region. MHC. https://www.google.com/search?source=hp&ei=zWHCXfODGeTez7sPyoax-As&q=The+NSW+NDIS+and+Mental+Health+Analysis+Partnership+Project%3A+Insights+from+the+first+two+years+of+the+NDIS+rollout+in+the+Hunter+region&oq=The+NSW+NDIS+and+Mental+Health+Analysis+Partnership+Project%3A+Insights+from+the+first+two+years+of+the+NDIS+rollout+in+the+Hunter+region&gs_l=psy-ab.12...2272.2272..3643...0.0..0.0.0.......1....2j1..gws-wiz.&ved=0ahUKEwiznuLG9NTlAhVk73MBHUpDDL8Q4dUDCAw.
MHF (Mental Health Foundation). 2013. Self-Directed Support in Mental Health: Capacity Building for Third Sector Providers Summary Findings. MHF. https://www.mentalhealth.org.uk/sites/default/files/Self-directed-support.pdf.
NDA (National Disability Authority). 2010. Advice Paper to the Value for Money and Policy Review of Disability Services Programme. NDA. http://nda.ie/nda-files/Advice-paper-to-the-Value-for-Money-and-Policy-Review-of-Disability-Services-Programme1.pdf.
NDIA (National Disability Insurance Agency). 2014. NDIS Opens at First NT Trial Site. https://www.ndis.gov.au/news/428-ndis-opens-first-nt-trial-site.
NDIA (National Disability Insurance Agency). 2019a. Annual Report NDIS 2018–19. NDIA. file:///C:/Users/he06404/Downloads/PB%20Annual%20Report%202019%20PDF.pdf.
NDIA (National Disability Insurance Agency). 2019b. National Disability Insurance Agency Submission Joint Standing Committee on the NDIS

Inquiry into Planning. NDIA. file:///C:/Users/he06404/Downloads/sub_20PLAN.pdf.

NDIS Act. 2013. Commonwealth of Australia. file:///C:/Users/he06404/Downloads/C2013A00020.pdf.

NDIS Rules. 2018. National Disability Insurance Scheme (Becoming a Participant) Rules 2016 Made Under Sections 22, 23, 25, 27 and 209 of the National Disability Insurance Scheme Act 2013 Compilation No. 4 Compilation date: 27 February 2018. Australian Government. https://www.legislation.gov.au/Details/F2018C00165.

NDTI (National Development Team for Inclusion). 2013. Self-Directed Support and Mental Health—Data. NDTI. https://otbds.org/wp-content/uploads/2017/10/SDS-and-mental-health-Background-Paper-3.pdf.

NMHC (National Mental Health Commission). 2014. The National Review of Mental Health Programmes and Services. NMHC. https://www.mentalhealthcommission.gov.au/media/119896/Summary%20%20-%20Review%20of%20Mental%20Health%20Programmes%20and%20Services.PDF.

NMHC (National Mental Health Commission). 2019. Monitoring Mental Health and Suicide Prevention Reform: National Report 2019. NMHC. https://nacchocommunique.files.wordpress.com/2019/09/national_report_2019.pdf.

NMHCCF (National Mental Health Consumer and Carer Forum). 2011. Unravelling Psychosocial Disability: A Position Statement by the National Mental Health Consumer & Carer Forum on Psychosocial Disability Associated with Mental Health Conditions. NMHCCF. https://nmhccf.org.au/sites/default/files/docs/nmhccf_psychosocial_disability_booklet_web_version_27oct11.pdf.

Orygen. 2017. Submission Joint Standing Committee on the NDIS: Provision of Services Under the NDIS for People with Psychosocial Disabilities Related to a Mental Health Condition. Orygen. https://www.orygen.org.au/Policy-Advocacy/Policy-Areas/Government-policy-service-delivery-and-workforce/Government-policy/The-NDIS-for-people-with-psychosocial-disabilities/Orygen-Provision-of-services-NDIS-psychosocial-dis?ext.

PDSV (Psychiatric Disability Services of Victoria). 2015. Learn and Build in Barwon: The Impact of the National Disability Insurance Scheme on the Provision of Mental Health Services in the Barwon Launch Site. Key Issues for Consumers, Families and the Victorian Mental Health Service System. Vicserv. https://www.mhvic.org.au/images/PDF/VICSERV_publications/June_2015_Learn-and-Build-in-Barwon_Final.pdf.

Pilgrim, David, and Floris Tomasini. 2012. On Being Unreasonable in Modern Society: Are Mental Health Problems Special? *Disability & Society* 27: 631–646. http://dx.doi.org/10.1080/09687599.2012.669108.

Productivity Commission. 2011. Disability Care and Support, Report Number 54. Commonwealth of Australia. https://www.pc.gov.au/inquiries/completed/disability-support/report/disability-support-overview-booklet.pdf.

Productivity Commission. 2017. National Disability Insurance Scheme (NDIS) Costs, Study Report. Commonwealth of Australia. https://www.pc.gov.au/inquiries/completed/ndis-costs/report/ndis-costs.pdf.

RANZCP (Royal Australian and New Zealand College of Psychiatrists). 2017. The Provision of Services Under the National Disability Insurance Scheme for People with Psychosocial Disabilities Related to a Mental Health Condition. Submission to the Joint Standing Committee on the National Disability Insurance Scheme. RANZCP. https://www.ranzcp.org/files/resources/submissions/0622o-president-to-committee-secretary-re-ndis-sub.aspx.

RCP (Royal College of Psychiatrists). 2013. The Integration of Personal Budgets on Social Care and Personal Health Budgets in the NHS: Joint Position Statement of the Royal College of Psychiatrists and the Association of Directors of Adult Social Services: Position Statement PS01/2013. RCP. https://www.rcpsych.ac.uk/pdf/PS01_2013.pdf.

Ridley, Julie, Helen Spandler, Ann Rosengard, Simon Little, Michelle Cornes, Jill Manthorpe, Susan Hunter, Tony Kinder, and Bill Gray. 2011. Evaluation of Self-Directed Support Test Sites in Scotland. Scottish Government Social Research. http://clok.uclan.ac.uk/2888/4/0121078.pdf.

Ridley, Julie, Helen Spandler, Helen Rosengard, and Angela Menhennet. 2012. Follow-Up Evaluation of Self-Directed Support Test Sites in Scotland. Scottish Government Social Research. https://pdfs.semanticscholar.org/2d94/0d741b5e2b0dedd22edfeebac3fa78b8fab8.pdf.

RMI (Rethink Mental Illness). 2016. Recovery Fact Sheet. Rethink. file:///C:/Users/he06404/Downloads/recovery-factsheet.pdf.

SCN (Scottish Co-Production Network). 2014. Pilotlight Case Study: Co-designing a Pathway to Self-Directed Support for People who have Mental Health Problems. https://www.seemescotland.org/media/7292/pilotlight-case-study-april-2014.pdf.

Smith-Merry, Jennifer, Nicola Hancock, Amanda Bresnan, Ivy Yen, John Gilroy, and Gwynnyth Llewellyn. 2018. Mind the Gap: The National Disability Insurance Scheme and Psychosocial Disability. Final Report: Stakeholder Identified Gaps and Solutions. University of Sydney. http://sydney.edu.au/health-sciences/documents/mind-the-gap.pdf.

Soldatic, Karen, and Barbara Pini. 2012. Continuity or Change? Disability Policy and the Rudd Government. *Social Policy and Society* 11: 183–196. https://doi.org/10.1017/S1474746411000510.

Stopher, Kerry, and Denise Hughes. 2017. Building New lives: Bringing the NDIS to People Living in Psychiatric Hostels Perth Hills Trial Site WA:

Overview and Stakeholder Reflections. NDIA. https://valuedlives.org.au/wp-content/uploads/2017/09/Bringing-the-NDIS-to-people-living-in-psychiatric-hostels-Final-002.pdf.

Thill, Cate. 2015. Listening for Policy Change: How the Voices of Disabled People Shaped Australia's National Disability Insurance Scheme. *Disability and Society* 30: 15–28. https://doi.org/10.1080/09687599.2014.987220.

United Nations. 2006. Convention on the Rights of Persons with Disabilities and Optional Protocol. United Nations. https://www.un.org/disabilities/documents/convention/convoptprot-e.pdf.

WAMHC (Western Australian Mental Health Commission). 2015. Better Choices. Better Lives. Western Australian Mental Health Alcohol and Other Drug Services Plan 2015–2015. WAMHC. https://www.mhc.wa.gov.au/media/1301/the-plan_final.pdf.

Williams, Theresa, and Geoffrey Smith. 2014. Can the National Disability Scheme Work for Mental Health? *Australian and New Zealand Journal of Psychiatry* 48: 391–394. https://pdfs.semanticscholar.org/0740/7f87776167c3c9fd0cd23228c2e8e4e12b77.pdf.

Williams, Theresa. 2012. To Investigate the Policy and Practice of Self-Directed Support for People with a Mental Illness. Winston Churchill Memorial Trust of Australia. http://www.churchilltrust.com.au/media/fellows/2011_Williams_Theresa.pdf.

Williams, Theresa. 2014. The NDIS: What Can Australia Learn from Other Countries? *NewParadigm: The Australian Journal on Psychosocial Rehabilitation*. Summer Edition: 30–33. https://cmha.org.au/wp-content/uploads/2017/05/2014NewParadigmSummer.pdf.

WNUSP (World Network of Users and Survivors of Psychiatry). 2008. Implementation Manual for the United Nations Convention on the Rights of Persons with Disabilities. WNUSP. http://www.wnusp.net/documents/WNUSP_CRPD_Manual.pdf.

CHAPTER 10

The National Disability Insurance Scheme and Health Care

Ian Thompson

Introduction

People with disability generally have poorer health status and face more access barriers to health care than the general population. Many require continuing health care support, coordinated between health and disability service providers. Inadequate health service provision or inadequate coordination between the disability and the health services sectors can have very significant negative impacts on their health and quality of life, and often place additional burden on providers in the other sector to try to meet support needs. For these reasons, the interface between the disability and health sectors is crucial to the wellbeing of National Disability Insurance Scheme (NDIS) participants.

This chapter discusses the potential benefits and challenges associated with the NDIS and health, and the experience from the roll out of the NDIS to date. It will also discuss the long-standing difficulties between the health and disability sectors, and some of the implications these difficulties have had on the roll out of the NDIS. In addition to the sources

I. Thompson (✉)
Nous Group, Perth, Australia

M. Cowden and C. McCullagh (eds.), *The National Disability Insurance Scheme*, https://doi.org/10.1007/978-981-16-2244-1_10

referenced, this chapter draws on my experience of managing a tertiary hospital and associated community and mental health services through the roll out of the NDIS as well as consultancy work over the last three years with health and humans services providers working at the interface between the NDIS and health systems.

The NDIS and Participant Health and Wellbeing

Evidence shows that people with disability experience higher levels morbidity and mortality than the general population, and that support for access to health care is particularly important. For example, a retrospective population-based standardised mortality study of adults with intellectual disability compared with a comparison group in NSW found that adults with intellectual disability experience premature mortality and over-representation of potentially avoidable deaths (Trollor et al. 2016, 7). Similarly, the Australian Institute of Health and Welfare's (AIHW) 2019 People with Disability in Australia report found that:

- 24% of adults with disability experience very good or excellent health, compared with 65% of without disability.
- 32% of adults with disability experience high/very high psychological distress, compared with 8% without disability.
- 1 in 6 people with disability aged under 65 experienced discrimination by health staff (GP, nurse, hospital staff).
- 2 in 5 people with disability aged under 65 had difficulty accessing medical facilities (GP, dentist, hospital).
- 1 in 8 people with disability aged under 65 who needed help with health care had no source of assistance.
- 1 in 6 who saw three or more different health professionals for the same health condition reported there were issues caused by lack of communication among different health professionals (AIHW 2019).

The AIHW drew on the Australian Bureau of Statistics Survey of Disability, Ageing and Caring for this report and notes that the survey only collected information from people with disability and their carers. This means that comparative data for the overall population of people without disability for access to health services are not available. However, the report argues that "while not directly comparable, information from the ABS' Patient Experience Survey 2015–16, which looked at the use of health services by the general Australian population, suggests that people with disability are more likely to face barriers such as cost when accessing some types of health services" (AIHW 2017).

These results are comparable with the baseline indicators for participants in the NDIS, collected on entry to the scheme. As reported in the September 2019 quarterly report to the COAG Disability Reform Council, 68% of 15 to 24-year olds and 46% of 25-year olds reported their health as good, very good or excellent, with 69 and 65%, respectively, reporting that they did not have any difficulties accessing health services.

The health needs, access to care and need for coordination between health and disability services varies considerably between NDIS participants. For many people with disability, there is little or no reason for coordination between the health and disability services they receive, for example, general practice attendances for minor illness for people whose disability doesn't impact on their ability to engage with their GP or impact on the severity of the illness. However, many people with disability need continuing health care as part of their support and/or their disability affects their ability to access or receive health care. For people in this situation, coordination and interaction between health and disability services is essential.

The promise of the NDIS to provide improved levels of support has potential to allow people with disability to manage their health needs more effectively, and evidence suggests that this has been achieved to some degree. While the numbers vary between age groups and time of joining the NDIS, participant survey data indicate that generally between about 40 and 50% of participants believe that the NDIS has improved their health and wellbeing and that this rate is improving, slowly, over time with increases generally in the 4–7% range. Results for families of people with disability are less positive, with between 30 and 40% of families believing that the NDIS has improved their health and wellbeing, with little or no improvement over time (NDIA 2019, 86). The participation survey does not ask specifically about the effect of the NDIS on access to health services. While these figures show evidence of some improvement, at least half of participants, and more than half of families do not report improvements in their health and wellbeing as a result of participation in the NDIS, indicating that further attention on these issues is required.

Work is underway to try to improve the interface between the NDIS and mainstream health services. A focus of this work is the NDIS Information, Linkages and Capacity Building (ILC) framework, with the Mainstream Capacity Building Program being developed under the ILC Strategy, Towards 2022, having an initial focus on mainstream health services (NDIA 2019, 55). Additionally, at the June DRC meeting, Commonwealth and State and Territory Disability Ministers clarified the boundaries between the NDIS and health-related services. As a result, as reported by the NDIA, "from 1 October 2019, NDIS participants commenced receiving funding for the disability-related health supports they need as a direct result of their disability, and as part of their daily life, through their NDIS plans" (NDIA 2019, 57). This is potentially a significant step forward for the NDIS, but it is telling that it took more than three years from participants first entering the scheme for this decision to be made.

In addition to potentially improving health and wellbeing for participants, the NDIS is also planned to reduce the burden on the health system and need for health services to supplement or respond to gaps in disability service provision. In its submission to the Productivity Commission's Study of NDIS Costs, the NDIA's submission provided preliminary estimates suggesting that the NDIS will reduce "costs for the health system by between $140 and $300 million each year (by reducing hospitalisations for people with disability and limiting the need for people with disability to remain in hospital due to a lack of more appropriate arrangements)" (Productivity Commission 2017, 148). If realised, these benefits will take some time to be achieved, and currently, the evidence is not available to assess progress.

Implementation Challenges from a Healthcare Perspective

At the current stage of NDIS roll out, many in the health system argue that the NDIS is not achieving reductions in demand for health services and is in fact increasing the burden on the health system in a number of ways. From a health sector perspective, these opportunities are balanced with significant risks, five of which are outlined below.

Role Ambiguity

Principles and indicative role descriptions have been developed to assist in clarifying roles and responsibilities of health and disability services under the NDIS but translating these principles and role descriptions into a clear operational role delineation has been the source of significant contention. Role ambiguity has fuelled the perception among many health service providers that the NDIS planners have managed costs by defining out services that they feel can be shifted onto the health system. The ambiguity around responsibilities between the NDIS and mainstream services, including health services was highlighted in the Productivity Commission's costs study, which noted that the lack of clarity can impact on "the effectiveness and efficiency of service delivery in multiple ways, including: scope creep; cost shifting from mainstream services to the NDIS and vice versa; gaps in service provision; inconsistent support access decisions; and duplication of services" (Productivity Commission 2017, 247). From the work already done in relation to the interface between the health system and the NDIS, there is significant concern among elements of the health system that this is in fact occurring, and the lack of data to monitor the impact is reinforcing this concern.

Limited Flexibility in the NDIS Approach

The national consistency of the NDIS is in many ways a strength and is helping to overcome the highly variable service access and provision across different regions in Australia that previously characterised disability services. However, limitations of the NDIS approach for regional and remote areas, Indigenous people and people from culturally and linguistically diverse backgrounds, and for people with specialised, complex, fluctuating and deteriorating conditions are being observed.

There has been extensive discussion about the difficulties created for market-based service provision systems in areas where there is specialised, limited and/or dispersed demand, and limited service provision. These markets are described as thin markets. The problem of thin markets for the NDIS is well recognised and solutions are being pursued, including through provider of last resort arrangements, but the perception of many health service providers is that, pending the development of alternative solutions, they are filling the gap with limited support. Exacerbating this is the perception that the NDIS is inflexible, and that there is not the capacity for health services to work locally and flexibly with disability service providers to broker solutions that was available previously with State Government funded or provided services.

Health services can be, and many have, registered as NDIS providers to receive revenue for providing eligible services to NDIS participants. Where this has happened, it is usually seen as a partial solution at best due to the NDIS prices, slower than expected uptake of the NDIS, the content of plans and workforce supply. Health service providers, like many other providers, frequently argue that the NDIS prices are too low to support care provision of a reasonable quality. The rates of pay for staff in the health sector are often higher than in the disability sector, and health services are often constrained industrially from employing staff on different pay scales. The utilisation expectations of staff are also seen to be too high, and to preclude provision of the quality improvement and training activities required to maintain a high quality of care.

The Effectiveness and Efficiency of the NDIS Planning and Processes

The content of plans is critical to ensuring that people with disability receive the support they need. In addition to the personal cost for participants, any shortfalls or gaps in the plans can result in increased demand across many parts of the health system. Health services report that they are required to provide support when other services are unable to manage, and gaps or shortfalls in plans result in increased presentations at hospital emergency departments or hospital admissions, particularly for patients with more complex or higher-level support needs.

These challenges are heightened for people whose care needs are not stable over time. The impact on people with psychosocial disability has received particular attention, and the situation can be similar for people whose care needs increase over time due to degenerative conditions, who have long-term rehabilitation goals due to, for example, acquired brain injury or spinal cord injury or involve early childhood intervention services to reduce their long-term disability. The core model of the NDIS is aligned best to people who have stable, long-term disability. Providing varying intensity of support to respond to changing needs and more frequent review of support levels is not aligned with this core model.

The expertise of NDIS planners is raised as a particular concern in this respect. Health professionals report that they do not feel that their expertise is being drawn on adequately in the planning process to ensure the plans provide the range and level of support needed by clients. Some successful approaches have been developed at local levels to improve coordination and draw on the expertise of health professions. However, in line with the feedback provided to the 2018 final report of the Evaluation of the NDIS, this is not done consistently, and a lack of coordination across the health and disability sectors predominates (National Institute of Labour Studies, 207–208).

Slower than expected uptake of the NDIS, and the content of plans, are also of concern for health services in the context of 'cashing out' of services. This is where funding previously provided to services directly is instead re-allocated to the NDIS, to be spent as part of participant plans. Where people who are potentially eligible for the NDIS are not participating in the scheme, or when participants choose not to include services provided by a health service provider in their plans, services can effectively end up still providing and paying again for the service that had been cashed out. Particularly in areas where there are limited or no alternative service providers this leaves the health services with the choice of either providing the service at additional cost, or participants being left with inadequate or no support. Access to funding through the NDIS also does not address workforce shortages experienced by health services, particularly for allied health professionals. Shortages of allied health professionals are experienced across many health services, particularly in regional and more remote areas, and this constrains the capacity to take on services for NDIS.

A final concern that will be discussed here is one that has been raised consistently and highlights the long-standing differences between the health and disability sectors discussed further below. This concern relates to the timeframes associated with the NDIS processes. This again has been the subject of considerable focus since the commencement of the NDIS, but the way the health system operates, and public acute hospitals specifically, amplifies these concerns.

Efficient performance of public acute hospitals is contingent on maintaining patient flow. This involves patients move through the different parts of the hospital, and out of the hospital, in a timely manner so that new patients can be admitted through the emergency department or through planned admission processes like elective surgery. Timeliness indicators for patient flow are often expressed in terms of minutes, hours and at times days. In contrast, NDIS timeframes comprise weeks and months. Consequently, if discharge of a patient is contingent on applying for, planning and receiving NDIS supports the timeframes will be much greater than the expected hospital timeframes. This can reinforce the sense of mistrust or lack of confidence between health professionals and the NDIS, and the perception that the NDIS is not responsive to the needs of patients or the health system.

Extended length of stay in hospital can have significant negative effects for patients. Acute hospitals are not designed for extended stays, and lack facilities to support physical and intellectual activity, social connection and entertainment. Clinically, long stays have been associated with loss of muscle strength, sleep deprivation, increased risk of falls and fracture, and increased risk of healthcare-associated infections (NHS Improvement 2018, 2). Patients also risk social isolation and difficulty maintaining employment and housing. Reducing the timeframes to access NDIS supports for patients in hospitals would have a significant positive benefit for patients affected as well as on the operation of hospitals.

In summarising concerns about the interface between mainstream services and the NDIS, the 2018 NDIS Evaluation referred to "boundary issues and conflict between the NDIA and mainstream organisations around their responsibilities, poor communication between the NDIA and mainstream organisations, and also delays in referrals and the ability of NDIS participants to be able to access services as a result of NDIA processes" (National Institute of Labour Studies 2018, 212). As described above, these concerns continue to be expressed by health services and can have a significant impact on NDIS participants given their poorer health status, difficulties in access and discrimination within the health system, and the detrimental effects of delayed access to care. These concerns however did not originate with the NDIS.

In its 2011 inquiry report into Disability Care and Support, the Productivity Commission found that in 2009–2010 almost 85,000 bed days in hospital were occupied by long stay patients under the age of 65. The report concluded that "the numbers of long stay patient separations and bed days appear to vary from year to year, showing no long-term downward trend. Hence, the issue of bed blocking in hospitals is likely to continue unless further action is taken" (Productivity Commission 2011, 128). Similarly, the National Disability Services 2014 Background Paper on People with Disability and Hospitalisation: Challenges and Opportunities in NSW, argued that "At present, NSW Health is spending more than it should on the health and hospitalisation of people with disability due to longer hospital stays, poorer outcomes, and repeated, unnecessary admissions. In addition, disability service providers are often footing the bill for the hospital support NSW Health has been unable to provide – despite not being funded to do so" (National Disability Services 2014, 3). Evidence like this, and the Australian and international evidence of poorer health outcomes, access barriers to health services and discrimination towards people within the health system, demonstrates the potential improvements the NDIS could deliver. However, importantly, it also demonstrates the significant and long-standing operational and cultural challenges that need to be overcome to deliver those benefits.

It is not reasonable to expect the NDIS to overcome these long-standing issues overnight, but the absence of attention to the existing interface challenges and how to overcome them was arguably one of the most significant flaws in the NDIS roll out. As the terminology implies, mainstream interfaces have typically been seen to be at the edges of the roll out of the core scheme, and the timeframes and the resourcing of the roll out did not allow for adequate attention to be paid to the interfaces. The ILC Mainstream Capacity Building Program was established, in part to address the interfaces, but one thing that was not adequately recognised was the extent to which mainstream interfaces directly affect the core objectives of the NDIS, including what "reasonable and necessary" means in term of NDIS supports and the core concept of choice and control.

Coordination and Interface Challenges Between the Health System and the NDIS

As has been described earlier in this book, the NDIS commits to provide reasonable and necessary supports for participants. Determining what is reasonable and necessary "should take into account support given to you by other government services, your family, carers, networks and the community" (NDIA website 2020). Consequently, the access to, and the interface with mainstream services, including health services, is an integral part of determining what are reasonable and necessary supports. Concerns about the delineation between health and disability services and what was in scope for the NDIS were apparent, and expressed very early on in roll out at trial sites, but as noted above, the boundaries between the NDIS and health-related services were still being considered by DRC in June 2019. There was evidence from the trials that clarifying the boundaries was crucial to ensure many participants received reasonable and necessary supports, and the time taken to achieve clarification has fed a perception that the haste of the roll out, and Commonwealth/State funding responsibilities have taken a higher priority than participant support and outcomes.

The situation is similar for participants seeking to exercise choice and control. In market-based systems, exercising choice and control to achieve the best outcomes for clients is contingent, among other things, on having access to a choice of services, and sufficient information to understand which services are needed and will deliver the best outcomes. The gaps in integration and coordination of health and NDIS services compromise both factors for clients.

Joint action to address thin markets has been recommended, including by the Productivity Commission who recommended that "the Australian, State and Territory Governments should [...] coordinate their market stewardship actions across all sectors, particularly with other care sectors and mainstream services" (Productivity Commission 2017, 396). This remains a priority, but of equal priority should be action to ensure that health professionals and NDIS planners work in a coordinated way to ensure that the expertise needed to enable participants to get comprehensive information about their support needs is made available. This is particularly important for people with complex, fluctuating and changing needs. Further work to directly address mistrust, a lack of confidence and competing priorities and timeframes between the health and disability sector is needed to achieve this.

Monitoring of the Impacts of the NDIS

Significant gaps remain in the data available to monitor the impact of the NDIS, and notable gaps related to health include evidence to support the expectations about the extent to which the NDIS is improving health service access for participants, the NDIS' impact on avoidable use of health services and the health and financial benefits that would accrue, and improvements in the experience of using health services (including reduced experience of discrimination). In the absence of data, anecdote predominates, and it is easy in the current situation for the perceived failings of the NDIS to be focused on. This represents another lost opportunity arising from the implementation of the NDIS. Given the history of problems at the interface of health and disability services, it is possible that improvements being generated by the NDIS are not being recognised and built on due to the lack of data to identify them.

Conclusion

The NDIS is still in its early stages. Against the historical difficulties associated with health and disability, and despite the problems associated with roll out of the NDIS, much of the criticism levelled at the scheme is arguably a consequence of problems that arose well before the development of the NDIS. Improving the interface between health and the NDIS remains a high priority and is, as we've outlined in this chapter, a focus of attention. However, learning the lessons arising from the implementation to date of the scheme and providing the time, process and effort to put in place the changes is necessary to ensure that the NDIS achieves its promise.

References

Australian Institute of Health and Welfare. 2017. Access to Health Services by Australians with Disability. https://www.aihw.gov.au/reports/disability/access-health-services-disability.

Australian Institute of Health and Welfare. 2019. People with Disability in Australia. https://www.aihw.gov.au/reports/disability/people-with-disability-in-australia.

National Disability Services, NSW. 2014. People with Disability and Hospitalisation: Challenges and Opportunities in NSW.

National Institute of Labour Studies. 2018. Evaluation of the NDIS Final Report. Department of Social Services. https://www.dss.gov.au/sites/default/files/documents/04_2018/ndis_evaluation_consolidated_report_april_2018.pdf.

NDIA. 2020. Reasonable and Necessary Support. https://www.ndis.gov.au/understanding/supports-funded-ndis/reasonable-and-necessary-supports.

NDIA. 2019. COAG Disability Reform Council Report. NDIS. file:///Users/kittymuirhead/Downloads/QR%20Q2%20201920%20Part%20A%20PDF_0%20(2).pdf.

NHS Improvement. 2018. Guide to Reducing Long Hospital Stays. https://improvement.nhs.uk/resources/guide-reducing-long-hospital-stays/.

Productivity Commission. 2011. Disability Care and Support, Volume 1, Report no. 54, Canberra. https://www.pc.gov.au/inquiries/completed/disability-support/report/disability-support-volume1.pdf.

Productivity Commission. 2017. National Disability Insurance Scheme (NDIS) Costs, Study Report, Canberra. https://www.pc.gov.au/inquiries/completed/ndis-costs/report/ndis-costs.pdf.

CHAPTER 11

Housing and the National Disability Insurance Scheme

Ilan Wiesel

This chapter discusses the housing needs of the National Disability Insurance Scheme (NDIS) participants and considers the adequacy of provisions both within the scheme and beyond it in meeting these needs. The NDIS was designed such that it operates in accordance with a set of 'General Principles' defined by the National Disability Insurance Scheme Act 2013 (Sect. 4). Among these principles are recognition that people with disability have the same rights as other Australians to realise their potential, including the right to live independently and to be included in the community as fully participating citizens, free from abuse, neglect and exploitation, the right to exercise choice and control, and the right to have their privacy and dignity respected.

In this chapter, I argue that the success of the NDIS in fulfilling these principles depends on the adequacy of participants' housing. Yet, housing options for people with disability in both the private market and the social housing system are extremely constrained, and the NDIS itself was not designed to address the housing needs of most of its participants. To date,

I. Wiesel (✉)
University of Melbourne, Melbourne, Australia

M. Cowden and C. McCullagh (eds.), *The National Disability Insurance Scheme*, https://doi.org/10.1007/978-981-16-2244-1_11

no policy commitments have been made to address an estimated unmet need in affordable housing for over 100,000 NDIS participants.

The first part of the chapter discusses the housing rights and needs of people with disability. The second part considers the factors limiting housing options for people with disability, addressing barriers associated with both the disability services system and the housing system in Australia. The third part of the chapter estimates the impact the NDIS is likely to have on demand for affordable housing, and the capacity to meet such demand through provision of Specialist Disability Accommodation (SDA), as well as access to mainstream housing, including both the social and private housing sectors. In the chapter's conclusion, I argue that it is time to review and expand the housing responsibilities of the NDIS beyond the funding of SDA, such that the scheme plays a more proactive and meaningful role in addressing the unmet need in housing for such a large number of its participants.

The Right to Housing

People of all abilities need a home to provide them with shelter from the elements, a personal space for sleep, self-care and leisure, a secure place in which to engage in both intimate and other social relations with others, and an anchor in space from which to access material and non-material resources located elsewhere, such as jobs, services and social networks. For many, home is the place where they feel most in control of their lives (Easthope 2004). A secure home is a fundamental condition for health and wellbeing, including a sense of ontological security. For many young adults, moving out of the parental home to make a home of their own is an important life transition, associated with independence. Recognising these multiple and fundamental roles of home in people's lives, the right to housing is more than simply a right to any form of shelter. Beyond the right not to be homeless, the right to housing is a right to housing of a certain standard that is adequate for meeting diverse human needs (Wells 2019).

The right to adequate housing has been recognised in recent years as a fundamental right for people with disability. The United Nations (2006) Convention on the Rights of Persons with Disabilities (CRPD)—of which Australia is a signatory—states that people with disability have the right to an adequate standard of living with adequate food, clothing and housing and to the continuous improvement of living conditions (Article 28).

The CRPD specified that people with disability should have the opportunity to choose their place of residence; where and with whom they live on an equal basis with others (Article 19); and have access to public housing programs (Article 28). In the CRPD, the right to housing is interconnected with the right to independent living and full inclusion and participation in the community (Article 19). In Australia, the Council of Australian Governments (COAG) initiated the 2011 National Disability Strategy, which, in accordance with the CRPD, states that people with disability should have access to affordable and secure housing across all tenures, as a key element of their right to participate as equal citizens in Australian society.

Some of the key aspects to consider in assessing the adequacy of housing for people with disability include affordability, scale and community integration, choice and control, secure occupancy, location and design.

Affordability: Low-income households paying more than 30% of their income on housing are considered to be in affordability stress (Disney 2004). The consequences of housing affordability stress are multifaceted, from extreme financial hardship through to negative health impacts and risk of homelessness. Housing affordability stress is prevalent among people with disability because of relatively low rates of participation in paid employment and low incomes. In Australia, only around 25% of people with profound or severe disability aged between 15 and 64 years old—used here as a proxy for the population of NDIS participants—are in the labour force compared with 83% of the population without disability (ABS 2018, Table 8.3).

Scale and community integration: The research evidence suggests that smaller-scale, non-congregated housing in the community is a critical condition for social inclusion, self-determination and wellbeing of people with intellectual disability (Walsh et al. 2010; Kozma et al. 2009).

Choice and control: Ability to choose where and with whom one lives is a key aspect of adequate housing. As argued by Wells (2019), people of all abilities have a right to freedom of association: the freedom to enter into relations with others, to refuse to enter into them and to leave them once they have begun. Such freedoms are not adequately protected when people are forced to share with others, and more so when they have no control over whom they share with.

Secure occupancy: Security of occupancy relates to the stability of existing housing arrangements and is associated with many aspects of human wellbeing, such as family functioning, economic and social participation, and physical and mental health. Having secure housing is an important condition for people's sense of ontological security, a deep psychological need for a sense of security and constancy (Hulse and Milligan 2014). For people with psychosocial and intellectual disability, security of occupancy is particularly vital, given the high underlying risk of homelessness (Beer et al. 2019a). Furthermore, the limited social networks for many people with intellectual disability further highlights the importance of stable housing that would enable them to develop and sustain long-term relationships with others in their community (Bigby 2008; Forrester-Jones et al. 2006).

Location: Geographic location with good access to material and non-material resources is necessary to ensure adequate access to jobs and services. For many people with disability, well-located housing is particularly important because of low rates of car ownership and barriers to driving. Therefore, people with disability require housing in locations with good access to services, including both mainstream services and specialist formal support services, as well as to their own families and informal support networks (Productivity Commission 2011; Wiesel et al. 2015).

Design: Adequate housing standard as applies to people of all abilities, in terms of housing size and quality. In addition to these universal standards, additional design considerations apply for people with disability. For people with physical or sensory disabilities, the design of housing must meet basic accessibility standards to ensure ability to move into, within and out of homes and be able to perform everyday living tasks with maximum autonomy (Franz et al. 2014). Likewise, research on housing design for people with autism highlights the importance of providing spaces for developing interests and skills; coherent design that minimises triggers of agitation and anxiety; design that is tolerant of unintended uses; and design that enables staff to provide person-centred support (Brand et al. 2010).

A study by Wiesel et al. (2015) examined the outcomes experienced by people with disability who moved into supported independent living in adequate housing. Many reported a growing sense of independence, and a strong sense of home, including a sense of ownership and control (regardless of whether they were renters or owner-occupiers in their new homes); they reported an improved sense of control over social interactions with others, including opportunities for both privacy and socialising with others; and improved physical and mental health, including reduced depression and anxiety, improved physical activity and improved sleep. In contrast, a study by the Disability Housing Futures Working Group highlighted the negative health and wellbeing implications for people with disability living in inadequate housing (DHF 2016a).

Barriers to Adequate Housing

Prior to the NDIS, the range of housing options available to people with disability had been very limited because of two primary factors: the cost and availability of support to live independently, and the availability of affordable and secure housing (Beer and Faulkner 2008). These two factors are elaborated below.

Disability Support System Barriers

Prior to the NDIS, limited access to and lack of choice about disability support services had limited housing options for many people with disability who require support in everyday activities at home. Since the bulk of support funding was tied to supported accommodation, those who did not wish or were unable to enter supported accommodation had very limited access to paid support. In the absence of paid support, many adults with disability lived with their parents as primary carers. Using Survey of Disability Ageing and Carers (SDAC) 2012 data, Qu et al. (2012) identified that more than 93,000 people with disability over 25 years of age were living with their parents (predominantly ageing parents).

People with disability who were successful in securing paid support services have also been extremely limited in their housing choices. Until the 1980s, institutional care was the major form of supported accommodation for people with intellectual or psychosocial disability. Since then, such institutions have been progressively closed or redeveloped and their residents rehoused. The implementation of deinstitutionalisation across Australia has been slow, haphazard and, as yet, incomplete (Wiesel and Bigby 2015). The closure of most large institutions led to the establishment of alternative models of housing and support, most notably the group home (shared supported accommodation), typically housing between four and six people with extensive paid staff support. According to AIHW (2014, 51), in 2012–2013, 16,433 people with disability (most with intellectual disability) lived in over 4,000 government-funded group homes across Australia. Outcomes for group home residents in terms of engagement, choice and participation have been highly variable due to variation in the implementation of the model, as well as a substantial shortage in group home placements and extensive waiting lists (Mansell et al. 2013). As discussed in the following section, the NDIS is expected to address some of the disability support system constraints described above, while also creating new challenges.

Housing System Barriers

People with disability seeking 'mainstream' housing—provided separately to the disability services system—face many barriers including affordability constraints, discrimination and inadequate housing in the private sector, and a major shortfall in supply of social housing. These barriers are underpinned by the absence of strategies and policies on housing for people with disability (Gilchrist and Charlton 2014, 30).

Housing affordability has become a key factor. A recent survey of 69 485 rental properties advertised across Australia found that less than 1% are affordable and suitable for a person living on a Disability Support Pension (DSP) (Anglicare 2019). According to SDAC (2012), of 94,272 (20%) people with severe or profound core activity limitation live in private rental, the majority (71%) have personal incomes below $580 per week. It can be estimated that close to a third of those experience affordability stress, with AIHW (2018, Table Financial.5), found that three in 10 persons receiving the DSP were spending more than 30% of gross household income on rent after Commonwealth Rent Assistance (CRA).

Where a rare affordable private rental property is to be found, people with disability often face disadvantage in the competition with other rental applicants due to lack of rental history, or stigma and discrimination associated with disability (Wiesel et al. 2015). Furthermore, in the absence of regulatory access requirements, housing in the private rental sector is largely inaccessible for people with mobility restrictions such as wheelchair users, and significant barriers prevent modification of existing stock to improve accessibility. As noted by Franz et al. (2014, 18) under the Disability Discrimination Act 1992 tenants have the right to modify a rental property within reason but are obliged to remove the modifications at the end of their tenancy. Many tenants are unwilling to make this financial commitment without security of tenure and landlords are often reluctant to allow modifications even when they are not obliged to pay for them.

Homeownership rates among people with disability, particularly those with profound or severe disability, are significantly lower than the general population. Of people 25–64 years old with severe or profound disability, the proportion of those living in owner-occupied housing (46%) is well below the general population (70%). Affordability is the primary barrier preventing people with disability on low incomes from entering home-ownership. People with intellectual disability face additional barriers, such as difficulty securing finance for home purchase due to perceived lack of legal capacity to enter the necessary contractual agreements (Wiesel et al. 2015).

Declining affordability in the private housing sector has increased demand for social housing. Social housing includes housing owned and managed by state governments, or increasingly by not-for-profit community housing providers. Rents are typically set up to a maximum of 25% of tenants' income to ensure affordability, and tenancy agreements provide an improved security of tenure relative to private rental. However, the supply of social housing has failed to keep pace with levels of demand. The proportion of Australian households who live in social housing fell from a high point of over 7% of all households in 1991 to the low point of 4.2% in 2016 (AHURI 2017). The shortfall in supply is evident in the waiting lists for social housing: across Australia 189,000 households were on a social housing waitlist in June 2017 (AIHW 2018).

People with disability are over-represented in housing assistance programs, at the same time as the system fails to meet their housing needs. In 2018, over 151,000 households living in social households had a member with a disability, representing approximately 42% of all households in social housing (AIHW 2019, Table S3). Approximately 258,000 people receiving a Disability Support Pension also received CRA, representing approximately 19% of all CRA recipients (AIHW 2018, table Financial.2). According to Wiesel et al. (2015), of people 25–64 years old with a severe or profound disability, a majority (79%) were on low or very-low income, yet only 13.5% were public renters. Thus, although significantly over-represented in this housing tenure (compared to 2.5% of people with no severe or profound disability), only a small minority of people with severe or profound disability benefit from the relative affordability and security of tenure in social housing. Indeed, while eligible for social housing, many people with disability are deprioritised in the allocation of social housing vacancies, since they are not deemed to be in immediate risk of homelessness, for example if they are living with their parents.

People with disability experience a greater exposure to risk of homelessness than the general population, and yet homelessness services are often irresponsive or poorly equipped to support them. Beer et al. (2019a) found that homelessness agencies fail to respond to requests for help by homeless people with physical or intellectual disability, and often refer them to other agencies. Similarly, such agencies fail to identify disabilities that are less visibly obvious and thus are unable to provide adequate support.

Housing Transitions Under the NDIS

While the NDIS was designed to fund primarily disability support services, it is likely to impact on participants' housing trajectories in two ways. Firstly, a small proportion of participants will be eligible for Specialist Disability Accommodation (SDA) funding as part of their NDIS support plans. Secondly, many NDIS participants will receive, for the first time, individualised funding for disability support services they can use wherever they live. This could potentially impact on demand for housing by participants who seek to move from their parents' homes, from group homes, or from institutional or congregate accommodation to more independent living in the community. Although it is hoped that the NDIS will support many people with disability to enter paid employment, it is expected that the majority of NDIS participants will have low incomes and will require affordable housing.

Analysis undertaken by the Disability Housing Futures Working Group (DHF, 2016b) estimated that, of 460,000 NDIS participants nationally, approximately 110,000 could potentially seek to move from their current housing or step out of housing affordability stress over the first 10 years of the NDIS. This includes adults with disability currently living with parents (50,000), in congregate accommodation (20,000), and those experiencing affordability stress in private rental (35,000), or homelessness (5,000). This estimation is consistent with the NDIA estimation of unmet need in affordable housing of 83,000–122,000 NDIS participants at full scheme (Bonyhady 2014). New SDA and existing social and affordable housing stock provide a very partial response to this unmet need.

Specialist Disability Accommodation (SDA)

Specialist Disability Accommodation (SDA) is a funding package offered by the NDIS not for support services, but for the dwellings managed by registered providers and occupied by eligible participants. SDA funding is narrowly targeted at NDIS participants who require an 'integrated housing and support model and the cost of the accommodation component exceeds a reasonable contribution from individuals' (Australian Government 2016). Funding is only provided to a small proportion (approximately 6%) of NDIS participants with who have an extreme functional impairment or very high need for personal supports (Australian Government 2016).

Existing stock of Shared Supported Accommodation (group homes)—previously owned and funded by state governments—will be fully funded under SDA. In addition, the NDIS seeks to use the funding to stimulate investment in the development of new SDA stock. Approximately $700 million annually has been allocated to the SDA program, costed for an estimated 28,000 NDIS participants, including 16,000 already living in existing purpose-built disability accommodation (primarily group homes) and an additional 12,000 who will be eligible for SDA and currently living with parents or in institutional settings (PWC and Summer Foundation 2017; Beer et al. 2019b).

The SDA was set up as a market-oriented program whereby funding is allocated on the basis of a pricing structure sensitive to the costs of building, maintaining and managing housing of different types in different locations, and designed to leverage substantial private investment—estimated at $5 billion—in SDA development (PwC and Summer Foundation 2017). Residents in SDA will contribute to the costs of housing through rent, limited to 25% of their disability support pension, plus CRA where applicable (PWC and Summer Foundation 2017). Each dwelling will be funded for a 20-year period, after which the dwelling is sold in the market (PwC and Summer Foundation 2017; Beer et al. 2019b).

Research by Beer et al. (2019b) found that the investment and affordable housing sectors are responding positively to the SDA program. Initial concerns about the affordable housing industry's ability to operate within a model driven by client choice, and without a safety net for investors, have given way to a consensus that the model can be made workable with adequate return on investment relative to the risk profile. At the same time, there is no return until the property is sold at the end of 20 years of SDA funding, a significant delay which deters investors, in addition to the reputational risk associated with selling an SDA property. Additional challenges and risks that need to be addressed to increase industry take-up of SDA include the need more and better information on the nature and location of demand for SDA; inconsistencies and uncertainties in the process of defining SDA eligibility; risk of continued regulatory and policy change, inconsistency and uncertainty; and, the risk of cost blowouts in building homes for specific needs.

From a consumer perspective, the SDA program has the potential to enhance choice and control through increase and diversification of supported accommodation options. Whereas existing shared supported accommodation has been criticised as a 'one size fits all' model lacking in diversity, new SDA stock will involve a greater variety of design categories (on a spectrum from 'Basic' design without specialist features to 'High physical support' design with high level of physical access provisions), and dwelling types (apartments; duplexes, villas and townhouses; houses; group homes of up to five residents; and larger dwellings with more than five residents). NDIS participants who are approved for SDA are allowed to register as their own housing provider, or to live in SDA with a partner or children who are not eligible for SDA payments. This creates opportunities for new types of housing tenure and arrangements funded under SDA, including shared equity and homeownership (Wiesel et al. 2017). Furthermore, in contrast to traditional group homes where residents have had little or no say in choosing their co-residents, in the case of SDA homes with more than one resident, providers must now 'consider the views of all participants (if any) already residing in an SDA dwelling before housing another participant in that dwelling'.

However, Beer et al. (2019b) argue that to date NDIS participants' choice and control have been 'critically compromised' within the SDA program. Whereas the NDIS individualised funding model has been touted as the primary mechanism to increase choice and control for participants, SDA was designed as a payment that is made to housing providers rather than individual participants, even if the funding is notionally allocated to individuals in their plans. Furthermore, while the delivery of housing and support by separate providers is often considered essential to increase the choice and control of people with disability, SDA rules impose no restriction on registration of disability support services as SDA providers.

SDA rules include 'density restrictions' that specify an upper limit on the number of SDA-recipients who can live on the same site: no more than ten people living on the same site if they are housed in groups of three or more, and no more than 15 people if they are housed individually or in pairs. However, the absolute number of people living on the same site while receiving SDA funding can exceed these limits if they only constitute up to 10 or 15% (for smaller homes) of the total number of people living on the site. This could include, for example, a high-rise building with a total of 107 residents, of which 16 are SDA-recipients living in eight two-bedroom units. These density restrictions do not apply to existing congregate accommodation ('legacy stock').

The proportion of people living on a site and receiving SDA funding can increase to 25% of the total number of residents if the development is an 'intentional community', defined in the SDA rules as a residential community where members have chosen to live together based on common social values and a commitment to mutual support. This could include ecovillages, income-sharing communes, student co-ops and spiritual communities. An intentional community, according to the rules, is not solely designed to provide supported accommodation services and is controlled by the members or residents and is not governed by a single entity such as a support provider.

These 'density restrictions' represent a minimum standard, however, the NDIS will also be able to influence the market to shift away from congregate settings (even within these limits) by changing its pricing formula for congregate housing. It is expected, for example, that SDA payments for 'legacy stock' with more than six participants on a single parcel of land will discontinue over time.

Despite these levers, the restrictions on congregate housing appear weak. Until recently, clusters of units with 10 or 15 people with high levels of disability were typically developed as part of institution closures, often in response to concerns by family members of institution residents. The new rules normalise such congregate developments even for people who have never lived in institutions before. Thus, although the National Disability Insurance Agency, and those who conceived it, envisaged a more radical shift away from congregate housing, as well as the separation of 'bricks and mortars' from support provision, the

SDA funding rules and its weak 'density restrictions' do not deliver on these promises. Indeed, leaving much to the discrepancy of the market—financiers, housing developers and disability support providers—there is a genuine risk of moving backwards towards higher levels of congregate housing.

NDIS Support in Mainstream Housing

From its very conception, the NDIS was envisaged as a scheme with limited responsibility for housing assistance beyond SDA. When outlining its recommendations for the design of the NDIS, the Productivity Commission (2011) argued that NDIS funding for housing would weaken the incentives for state governments to properly fund social and affordable housing and may result in the segregation of people with disability in specialist accommodation. Consequently, the vast majority (94%) of NDIS participants will not be eligible for SDA and will require mainstream housing solutions, including both social housing and housing in the private market. For these participants, the NDIS will not directly fund the costs of housing, and the housing-related support it will provide would be limited to supports for independent living as well as funding for home modifications for physical accessibility. Many of those who will miss out on SDA have significant disability support needs. The Productivity Commission (2011, 758–760) projected that approximately 25,000 NDIS participants will require intensive levels of support, yet just below the benchmark for SDA eligibility.

As discussed above, social housing is already playing an important role in providing housing for people with disability, and this role is likely to increase with the NDIS. Many NDIS participants are likely to be eligible to social housing because of their low income and in some cases will also qualify for high priority in the waiting list due to circumstances such as homelessness, leaving institutions or housing crisis following the illness or death of a carer. However, as discussed above, a severe shortage in social housing stock across Australia and lengthy waiting lists, means social housing has limited capacity to address unmet housing need for NDIS participants. With no government commitment to build new social housing supply at scale, NDIS participants' access to social housing will depend on turnover in existing stock. Nationally, since 2011–2012 approximately 21,000 households enter social housing each year, primarily filling vacancies arising from exits of previous tenants

(AIHW 2018). About half of new allocations are made to households that include a person with disability, but the proportion of NDIS participants will be smaller. If 20% of all new social housing allocations will be made to NDIS participants, over a decade this would enable over 40,000 more NDIS participants to enter social housing. However, this is likely to be constrained by incompatibilities between participants' need and the location and design of social housing stock, competition over vacancies with other high-priority applicants on the waiting lists, as well as concerns about the over-concentration of people with significant disability in social housing.

Considering the extreme affordability constraints in the private housing market discussed above (Anglicare 2019), in the absence of any government assistance beyond CRA, the majority of NDIS participants with low incomes will not be able to secure affordable private rental or home purchase. Nevertheless, a small group of NDIS participants might be able to overcome these barriers thanks to financial assistance from family or home sharing arrangements.

Many people with disability have no family members who are able or willing to provide financial assistance to support their housing costs, in part due to the lower incomes and assets generally owned by carers of people with disability, and in part due to the social isolation experienced by many people with disability. Nevertheless, previous research has indicated some people with disability are financially supported by parents, including retirees who withdrew funds from their superannuation savings, or equity from their own homes to assist their son or daughter enter and sustain private rental or homeownership. 'Unlocking' such financial support from families who are able and willing to contribute will require innovations in finance, social security, taxation and housing provision (Wiesel et al. 2015).

Housing models such as shared equity or mixed equity have been identified as mechanism to leverage finance from families which can afford to make only a small capital contribution to home purchase. In shared and mixed equity schemes, the ownership of a dwelling is divided between the person who lives in the house and a 'non-person' equity partner, such as a community housing provider. Such models enable people with disability to access homeownership, with enhanced choice of housing, long-term security and affordability and opportunities for accumulation of capital. At the same time, some models of shared equity can expose people with disability to the risks of debt in a volatile housing market. In any case, such schemes are yet to be scaled-up significantly (Wiesel et al. 2015).

Financial instruments such as Special Disability Trusts (SDTs) can be used to encourage and facilitate transfer of assets from families to people with disability. An SDT is established with the primary purpose of paying for the reasonable care, accommodation and other needs of a person with disability during their lifetime. SDTs are distinguished from a traditional family fixed or discretionary trust because of the significant tax and social security concessions made available for both the contributor and the beneficiary of the SDT. While acknowledging the potential of SDTs and similar to incentivise transfer of families' private assets to support housing for NDIS participants, existing research has also found SDTs to be highly restrictive and difficult to establish and maintain over time. Consequently, uptake among Australian families has been very limited to date (Davy et al. 2018).

Home sharing (co-residency) arrangements involving two or three NDIS participants, or pairs involving a person with disability and one without, could potentially reduce the affordability barrier in accessing private rental, and in some cases also home purchase. Beyond the sharing of housing costs, home sharing has the potential to offer additional advantages such as pooling together of individual support packages as well as informal supports, and opportunities for increased social connections. Setting up and sustaining sharing arrangements can be challenging, however, often requiring years of planning. The termination of a sharing arrangement when one co-resident chooses to move on can create difficulty for other co-residents to sustain their tenancy, highlighting the precarity associated with this living arrangement (Wiesel et al. 2015).

Conclusion

The NDIS will trigger significant demand for affordable housing, especially by adults with disability who for the first time will access the support funding necessary to move out of their parents' home or of institutional or congregate accommodation. However, the NDIS was not designed to meet the housing needs of its participants. While the SDA program offers a revitalised approach and much needed funding for provision of a more diversified range of specialist accommodation, the NDIS will not provide satisfactory housing solutions for most of its participants. Affordability constraints in the private housing market—less than 1 per cent of rental vacancies affordable for a person living on the DSP (Anglicare 2019)—and a massive shortfall in supply of social housing (AIHW 2018) will leave many thousands of NDIS participants stranded without adequate housing options.

Addressing the unmet need in affordable housing for NDIS participants at the scale described in this chapter, requires wide structural transformations in the Australian housing system, well beyond the remit of the NDIS itself. Not least, this must include a substantial increase in social housing supply. In addition, market-oriented strategies such as inclusionary zoning (requirement for affordable housing developer contributions as a condition for planning approvals for private housing developments) are also necessary to increase supply of affordable housing for all low-income Australians, including but not restricted to NDIS participants.

Notwithstanding, the NDIS too has a critical role to play in addressing the unmet housing need experienced by so many of its participants. The axiom that the NDIS's responsibility in relation to housing is primarily limited to the funding of SDA for only 6% of its participants is inconsistent with the scheme's General Principles, which uphold participants' right to live independently and to be included in the community as fully participating citizens, free from neglect (such as homelessness or inadequate housing) and exploitation (such as poor housing conditions in private rentals). Likewise, the rights to exercise choice and control and to have one's privacy and dignity respected cannot be fulfilled for those who are forced to share with others. In other words, the right to housing is at the heart of what the NDIS is all about.

The argument that housing assistance provided by the NDIS beyond SDA would somehow discourage state governments from properly funding social and affordable housing (Productivity Commission 2011) is hard to defend. For instance, the NDIS funds taxis and specialist transport for participants, which can be argued to weaken the pressure on state governments to deliver universally accessible public transport services as they are legally required to do. On the same token, the NDIS should also fund housing for participants who are excluded from mainstream housing systems.

There is therefore an urgent need to review and expand the role of the NDIS in relation to participants' housing. Specifically, these responsibilities should include, firstly, a more proactive role for the NDIS in promoting injection of new affordable housing supply by Commonwealth, state and local governments as well as the market, for instance by making public its data on participants' unmet housing need; secondly, ensuring both existing and new affordable housing supply is designed, managed and allocated in ways that are responsive to the needs of people with disability; thirdly, direct assistance for participants to move out of inadequate housing; and, finally, ongoing reworking of the SDA rules and its pricing framework in ways that will minimise new forms of congregated housing, and enhance deinstitutionalisation.

References

ABS (Australian Bureau of Statistics). 2018. Disability, Ageing and Carers, Australia: Summary of Findings. https://www.abs.gov.au/AUSSTATS/abs@.nsf/DetailsPage/4430.02018?OpenDocument. Accessed 14 November 2019.

AHURI. 2017. Census Data Shows Falling Proportion of Households in Social Housing. https://www.ahuri.edu.au/policy/ahuri-briefs/census-shows-falling-proportion-of-households-in-social-housing. Accessed 14 November 2019.

AIHW. 2014. Disability Support Services: Appendix 2012–2013. Australian Institute of Health & Welfare.https://www.aihw.gov.au/getmedia/14efafa1-871b-413f-ae7d-56c150eb1f76/17553-appendix.pdf.aspx.

AIHW. 2018. Housing Assistance in Australia 2018. Australian Institute of Health & Welfare. https://www.aihw.gov.au/reports/housing-assistance/housing-assistance-in-australia-2018/contents/housing-in-australia.

AIHW. 2019. People with Disability in Australia, 2019. https://www.aihw.gov.au/reports-data/health-conditions-disability-deaths/disability/data. Accessed 14 November 2019.

Anglicare. 2019. Rental Affordability Snapshot. https://www.anglicare.asn.au/docs/default-source/default-document-library/final---rental-affordability-snapshota302da309d6962baacc1ff0000899bca.pdf?sfvrsn=4. Accessed 14 November 2019.

Australian Government. 2016. National Disability Insurance Scheme (Specialist Disability Accommodation) Rules 2016 https://www.legislation.gov.au/Details/F2017L00209. Accessed 14 November 2019.

Beer, Andrew, and Deborah Faulkner. 2008. The Housing Careers of People with a Disability and Carers of People with a Disability: AHURI. https://www.ahuri.edu.au/research/nrv-research-papers/nrv2.

Beer, Andrew, Emma Baker, Laurence Lester, and Lyrian Daniel. 2019. The Relative Risk of Homelessness among Persons with a Disability: New Methods and Policy Insights. *International Journal of Environmental Research and Public Health* 16: 1–12.

Beer, Andrew, Kathleen Flanagan, Julia Verdouw, Braam Lowies, Elizabeth Hemphill, and Gina Zappia. 2019. Understanding Specialist Disability Accommodation funding. Australian Housing and Urban Research Institute Limited. https://papers.ssrn.com/sol3/papers.cfm?abstract_id=3357193.

Bigby, Christine. 2008. Known Well by No-One: Trends in the Informal Social Networks of Middle-Aged and Older People with Intellectual Disability Five Years After Moving to the Community. *Journal of Intellectual and Developmental Disability* 33: 148–157.

Bonyhady, Bruce. 2014. The National Disability Insurance Scheme: A Catalyst for Large Scale, Affordable and Accessible Housing for People with Disability. Housing, Disability and the NDIS Forum.

Brand, Andrew, and Rama Gheerawo. 2010. *Living in the Community: Housing Design for Adults with Autism*. London: Helen Hamlyn Centre.

Davy, Laura, Julian Laurens, Rosemary Kayess, Shona Bates. 2018. Special Disability Trusts. Social Policy Research Centre. https://parlinfo.aph.gov.au/parlInfo/search/display/display.w3p;query=Id:%22library/summary/summary.w3p;query=Author%3A%22Kayess,%20Rosemary.%22.

DHF. 2016a. People with Disability Living in Inadequate Housing: Prevalence, Trends, and Health and Workforce Participation Outcomes. https://www.nahc.org.au/pages/research/disability-housing-futures-working-group.

DHF. 2016b. Disability Housing Futures Working Group Final Report. National Affordable Housing Consortium. https://www.nahc.org.au/pages/research/disability-housing-futures-working-group.

Disney, Julian. 2004. Affordable Housing in Australia: Some Key Problems and Priorities for Action. National Forum on Affordable Housing. https://www.ahuri.edu.au/__data/assets/pdf_file/0018/2178/AHURI_Final_Report_No105_Housing_affordability_a_21st_century_problem.pdf.

Easthope, Hazel. 2004. A Place Called Home. *Housing, Theory and Society* 21: 128–138.

Forrester-Jones, Rachel, John Carpenter, Pauline Coolen-Schrijner, Paul Cambridge, Alison Tate, Jennifer Beecham, Angela Hallam, Martin Knapp, and David Wooff. 2006. The Social Networks of People with Intellectual Disability Living in the Community 12 Years After Resettlement from Long-Stay Hospitals. *Journal of Applied Research in Intellectual Disabilities* 19: 285–295.

Franz, Jill, Barbara Adkins, Andrea M. Petriwskyj, Grace Bitner, Margaret Ward, and Annie Rolfe. 2014. Person-Centred Approaches to Private Housing for People with Disability: Impediments, Difficulties and Opportunities. University of Queensland. https://core.ac.uk/download/pdf/33495746.pdf.

Gilchrist, David, and Alan Charlton.2014. Home Ownership and Affordability for People Living with Disability in Western Australia. University of Western Australia. https://research-repository.uwa.edu.au/en/publications/home-ownership-and-affordability-for-people-living-with-disabilit.

Hulse, Kath, and Vivienne Milligan. 2014. Secure Occupancy: A New Framework for Analysing Security in Rental Housing. *Housing Studies* 29: 638–656.

Kozma, Agnes, Jim Mansell, and Julie Beadle-Brown. 2009. Outcomes in Different Residential Settings for People with Intellectual Disability: A Systematic Review. *American Journal on Intellectual and Developmental Disabilities* 114: 193–222.

Mansell, Jim, Julie Beadle-Brown, and Christine Bigby. 2013. Implementation of Active Support in Victoria, Australia: An Exploratory Study. *Journal of Intellectual and Developmental Disability* 38: 48–58.

Productivity Commission. 2011. Disability Care and Support-Productivity Commission Inquiry Report. Australian Government Productivity Commission. https://www.pc.gov.au/inquiries/completed/disability-support/report.

PwC and Summer Foundation. 2017. NDIS Specialist Disability Accommodation: Pathway to a Mature Market. https://www.summerfoundation.org.au/wp-content/uploads/2017/08/pwc-summer-foundation-sda-market.pdf. Accessed 14 November, 2019.

Qu, Lixia, Ben Edwards and Matthew Gray. 2012. Ageing Parents of People with a Disability. Australian Institute of Family Studies. https://aifs.gov.au/publications/ageing-parent-carers-people-disability.

Walsh, Patricia Noonan, Eric Emerson, Carolyne Lobb, Chris Hatton, Valerie Bradley, Robert Schalock, and Charles Moseley. 2010. Supported Accommodation for People with Intellectual Disabilities and Quality of Life: An Overview. *Journal of Policy and Practice in Intellectual Disabilities* 7: 137–142.

Wells, Katy. 2019. The Right to Housing. *Political Studies* 67: 406–421.

Wiesel, Ilan, and Christine Bigby. 2015. Movement on Shifting Sands: Deinstitutionalisation and People with Intellectual Disability in Australia, 1974–2014. *Urban Policy and Research* 33: 178–194.

Wiesel, Ilan, Jane Bullen, Karen R. Fisher, Di Winkler, and Astrid Reynolds. 2017. Shared Home Ownership by People with Disability. Australian Housing and Urban Research Institute Limited. https://papers.ssrn.com/sol3/papers.cfm?abstract_id=2985296.

Wiesel, Ilan, Carmel Laragy, Sandra Gendera, Karen R. Fisher, Samantha Jenkinson, Trish Hill, Kate Finch, Wendy Shaw, and Catherine Bridge. 2015. Moving to My Home: Housing Aspirations, Transitions and Outcomes of People with Disability. Australian Housing and Urban Research Institute Limited. https://www.ahuri.edu.au/research/final-reports/246.

CHAPTER 12

Children and the National Disability Insurance Scheme

Mhairi Cowden

The National Disability Insurance Scheme (NDIS) is not only a major change to the disability service system, it represents a shift in assumptions about the capacities of people with disability, their decision-making rights, and the balance between self-determination and paternalism. These shifts have potential to radically change the way in which children with disability are treated, engage and flourish in society.

Furthermore, the NDIS is in many ways a large-scale experiment in the early intervention principles that complements the social insurance approach of the scheme. Children are the archetypal early intervention cohort. We are often told by policy professionals that if appropriate services are provided early in life then not only will we see better outcomes for individuals, but lower costs for our tertiary service systems. Children with disability should therefore be in a prime position to benefit in the short, and long term, from what the NDIS has to offer.

In this chapter, I examine the place for children with disability within the NDIS. To begin, I provide a brief overview of what we mean when

M. Cowden (✉)
Nous Group, Perth, WA, Australia

M. Cowden and C. McCullagh (eds.), *The National Disability Insurance Scheme*, https://doi.org/10.1007/978-981-16-2244-1_12

we talk about children with disability and the movement over the last 10–20 year to recognise that children, including children with disability, have certain rights over their lives. Importantly these rights include the right to be involved in decision-making regarding their own lives. I then outline the potential shift that the NDIS presents in thinking about choice and control.

I will provide an overview of how the NDIS views children as articulated in the original 2011 Productivity Commission report, the relevant NDIS legislation and briefly how this is being translated into policy particularly through the Early Childhood Early Intervention program. I will primarily talk about the NDIS as how it should work in theory but will also touch on some of the implementation challenges and varied outcomes for children with disability.

Finally, I consider some of the challenges and contradictions. Although the NDIS presents much promise for children with disability, it fails to fully embrace its potential. This is for two reasons: (1) a continued reliance on an assumption of incompetence for children with disability where this assumption does not exist for adults with disability; and (2) the absence of structured, sustained and well-resourced support to enable decision-making and choice from children themselves and/or their representatives.

Children with Disability

Children are young human beings. However, not all children are the same. The nature of childhood is that it is changing rapidly. The differences between a six-month-old and a 12-year-old child in terms of size, physical abilities, mental abilities and emotional development are enormous. Children with disability are no different. The type of disability or functional impairment that a child experiences may change and evolve as the child grows. The different types of disability children experience are also wide and varied. Furthermore, for some disability types and some cohorts of children, disabilities are not immediately apparent from birth. For example, in Australia the average age of diagnosis of children with autism is just over 4 years old (Bent et al. 2015, 317). In some parts of Australia, diagnosis or identification of disability can occur much later in childhood. Lack of access to services, culturally appropriate screening tools and different conceptualisations of disability can mean that Aboriginal and Torres Strait Islander children are often not identified as having a disability until later in life (DiGiacomo et al. 2013).

Children are usually defined by age. According to the United Nations Convention on the Rights of the Child (CROC), children are defined as 'every human being below the age of eighteen unless under the law applicable to the child, majority is attained earlier' (UN, article 1). Children are also defined by their level of competence. Children are often prohibited from doing many things that adults are allowed to do in society. This includes driving, voting, working and making direct decisions regarding their health or welfare. As Schapiro (1999, 717) points out, this indicates the existence of a deeper meaning attached to children—one of moral status. Much of this is based on a sensible approach to denying children, particularly very young children, the ability to do things that are going to bring about risk or harm. For example, it would be potentially harmful to allow a 4-year old to drive a car, not only to the child but also to other people on the road.

However, not all of the things we deny children are appropriately based on an accurate assessment of capacity, risk or harm. Throughout the 1980s many scholars grew increasingly dissatisfied with the superficial way in which many social science disciplines understood childhood (Prout 2005). Sociocultural theorists now argue that there is no one route to development dependent on innate biological stages but instead child development is based on cultural goals. The way we understand children as incompetent and developing in a linear way is not solely grounded in biological facts but rather socially constructed (Smith 2002). This interaction between the nature of childhood and our own cultural assumptions about children can often result in children being treated inconsistently or ascribed a lower moral status within society.

As earlier chapters of this book have discussed, throughout history people with disability have similarly been subject to blanket assumptions of incapacity, incompetence and a lower moral status. The way we understand disability is also informed by societal norms and is not solely rooted in biology. Therefore, children with disability can be seen as potentially battling two reinforcing norms of assumed incompetence and lower moral status. The existence of these norms, coupled with the still very real need to ensure children with disability are safe from risk and harm, presents a challenging conceptual landscape for any policymaker to navigate.

The United Nations Convention on the Rights of Persons with Disabilities recognises that children with disability have rights equal to all other children. Article 7 of the Convention outlines that:

- State Parties shall take all necessary measures to ensure the full enjoyment by children with disability of all human rights and fundamental freedoms on an equal basis with other children.
- In all actions concerning children with disability, the best interests of the child shall be a primary consideration.
- States Parties shall ensure that children with disability have the right to express their views freely on all matters affecting them, their views being given due weight in accordance with their age and maturity, on an equal basis with other children, and to be provided with disability and age-appropriate assistance to realise that right (United Nations 2006, 7–8).

The first part of Article 7 establishes that children with disability are on an equal footing to all children. The second part of Article 7 introduces the principle of the 'the best interests of the child'. The best interests principle is designed to ensure that decision-making for children is not captured by the interests of others (such as the parents and the State) but undertaken from a child-centred point of view (Cowden 2016, 111). The UN Committee on the Rights of the Child provides further insight to the best interests principle explaining it as:

1. A substantive right to have his or her best interests assessed and taken as a primary consideration when different interests are being considered;
2. A fundamental, interpretive legal principle to guide legal matters that are open to more than one interpretation; and
3. A rule of procedure whereby the decision-making process must include an evaluation of the possible impact (positive or negative) of the decision on the child or children concerned (UN Committee on the Rights of the Child 2013).

It is the third part of Article 7 that begins to challenge traditional assumption of children with disability. This part of the Article not only outlines that children with disability have the right to have their views taken into account regarding matters about their lives, it also enshrines that children with disability should be given the age appropriate and disability appropriate support to realise this right. This means that we cannot simply assume that children with disability, either because they have a disability, or because they are children, do not have the capacity to be involved in decision-making. It means that we must provide them with the right support to help them do so. The challenge then is to balance the risk or harm-based considerations inherent within the best interests principle, with the obligation to enable the self-determination of children with disability.

The Promise of the NDIS

As has been outlined in the first part of this book, the NDIS is a national reform to the way disability services are both funded and delivered. The NDIS seeks to place the individual at the centre of decision-making. The NDIS seeks to achieve this in two main ways: first by moving the disability service system from a rationed system to an entitlement system. Under this move, it is not only those that are the most in need who receive services, but in theory all of those that are entitled to receive services should be able to under the scheme. Second, it enshrines the concept of 'choice and control' of all people with disability over the services they receive. Choice and control challenge the previous paternalistic assumptions that have traditionally dominated the disability services space. Choice and control say that no matter your capacities or disability, you have a right to either directly determine, or be involved in the determination of, the types of services you receive. Within the disability advocacy world, this is often captured through the phrase, '*There is dignity in risk*' (Perske 1972).

On the face of it, this would seem to be a promising move for children with disability as the NDIS starts from a place of assuming that all people with disability have the capacity and the right to be involved in decision-making about their lives. In this sense, the NDIS seems to take seriously the third part of Article 7 of the UN Convention on the Rights of Persons with a Disability—that children with disability have the right to express their views freely on all matters affecting them, and their views being given due weight in accordance with their age and maturity.

The NDIS and Children

The 2011 Productivity Commission 'Disability Care and Support' report provided the blueprint for the NDIS. The report itself does not spend significant time discussing children with disability. However, the report addresses children in three main ways—individualised packages of support, early intervention and interaction with the education system. These have remained the three main ways in which children with disability interact with the NDIS.

Individualised Packages

Children with disabilities are eligible for tier three supports through individualised packages and plans. When referring to eligibility, the Productivity Commission spoke to 'persons with disability' with no reference to a lower age limit. The Commission report is silent on how the planning process or self-directed funding process will work for children with disability. In one sense this is consistent as the Commission recommended an 'individual choice' model of choice and control. Under this model, people with disability (or their guardians) can choose how much control they want to exercise. Therefore, the extent of choice and control should be determined on a case-by-case basis by the individual with a disability (Productivity Commission 2011, 30). This would seem to open the door to allowing children with disability, particularly older children, the option of being directly in control of the way they receive services. The way in which this has been translated into legislation and policy is not so straightforward. I will discuss this in detail later in this chapter.

Early Intervention

The Commonwealth Government, through their terms of reference, requested that the Productivity Commission look at the incentives to focus investment on early intervention (Productivity Commission 2011, iv). The Commission found that early intervention was consistent with the 'wellness approach' that focuses on 'optimising an individual's functional and psychosocial independence with a view to achieving positive and long reaching benefits' (Productivity Commission 2011, 169). Adopting a 'wellness approach' would mean that the scheme should not focus investment and services only on those that have catastrophic, severe or profound disability as this would not allow the scheme to delay the deterioration of conditions or reduce the need for downstream supports (Productivity Commission 2011, 169). The Commission stated that,

> the overarching objective of early intervention is to incur expenditure on a particular intervention today that, not only improves individual outcomes beyond that which would occur in the absence of the intervention, but lowers the costs and impacts associated with the disability for individuals and the wider community over the longer-term. (2011, 608)

This combined goal of early intervention, better outcomes and lower costs, is the holy grail of public policymaking. If early intervention works as it should do, it is clearly an attractive option for children with disability, their families and carers. For example, early intervention for children with a hearing impairment can ensure that language development occurs within the appropriate developmental period. This can assist with reading and writing and lead to better educational and economic outcomes later in life (Cowan et al. 2018). Children with developmental delay or disability can benefit from early intervention services to promote physical, mental and emotional wellbeing and prevent secondary health problems such as obesity (Royal Australian College of Physicians 2013). The review of the Footprints Program by Autism Behavioural Intervention NSW showed that early intervention services through the delivery of training and support for families of children with Autism helped address challenging behaviour, social skills and communication. These services led to better outcomes such as being able to enrol children in mainstream school (ABI 2010).

The Productivity Commission (2011, 14) recommended that in order to be eligible for tier three supports (individualised packages) all people needed to demonstrate permanent (or likely to be permanent) disability referring to the irreversible nature of the disability, even though it may be of a chronic episodic nature. Following this, the Commission recommended two pathways into the NDIS, either by demonstrating that the person with disability experienced significantly reduced functioning as a result of the disability, or to be in an early intervention group (Productivity Commission 2011, 14).

However, the Productivity Commission report identified that early intervention is not just bound by age. Early interventions can occur within the first few years of life, when a disability first arises or 'around specific transition points, such as leaving school or home, or entering the workforce' (Productivity Commission 2011, 170). Therefore, the Commission proposed that the early intervention group should encompass people 'for whom there is good evidence that the intervention would be safe, significantly improve outcomes and be cost-effective' (Productivity Commission 2011, 171). Many of these life transition points, such as leaving school, are relevant for people with disabilities under the age of 18.

The early intervention approach articulated by the Commission was translated into the NDIS legislation by outlining that a person meets the early intervention requirements if they have a permanent impairment or are a child who has developmental delay (Sect. 25 NDIS Act). In addition, the early intervention proposed must have evidence that it will reduce the need for future disability supports, mitigate or alleviate the impact of the disability, prevent deteriorations, improve functional capacity or strengthen the sustainability of informal supports (Sect. 25 of the NDIS Act).

In practice, this means that all children from 0 to 6 years with developmental delay or disability are eligible for the NDIS Early Childhood Early Intervention Approach. Early intervention for older children and adults is also available but delivered directly through the National Disability Insurance Agency (NDIA) or other nominated partner agencies as part of the traditional individualised package pathway. The Early Childhood Early Intervention approach is currently contracted out through Early Childhood Partners. Early Childhood Partners are community-based disability service organisations that are contracted to the NDIA to work with families, connect them to existing services and enable access specific funding for early interventions if appropriate. Early intervention services are delivered within a best practice framework developed by Early Childhood Intervention Australia (Gavidia-Payne 2020).

Education

The other way that the NDIS is relevant to children is through its interaction with the education system. The Productivity Commission noted that there has been significant change in the approach taken within Australia and internationally to educating children with disability. The move has been away from segregated settings and supporting the 'rights of students with a disability to be educated on the same footing within regular or 'mainstream' classrooms' (Productivity Commission 2011, 244). This is because children with disability need opportunities to learn and socialise with a broad range of other students if they are to maximise opportunities to participate in the workforce and community life (Productivity Commission 2011, 245). In addition, it is believed that educating children with disability within mainstream schools 'can reinforce positive attitudes to diversity, leading to social inclusion in the community…there is potential for long-term acceptance and mutual support' (Productivity Commission, 2011, 245). However, it should be noted that evidence also shows this is not something that happens automatically, and that educational staff, students and their peers need to work collaboratively to create inclusive environments (Morrison and Burgman 2009).

The Productivity Commission recommended that the NDIS should play a role in meeting some of the needs of some students with disability. The Commission noted that it would be perverse to insist that since the children were in a different setting that the costs regarding services should solely be met by the educational system. However, the Commission recommended that the types of support provided to students with disability should typically be the types of services that the child would need regardless of whether they were attending school or not. This would include goods and services such as personal attendant care, or a hearing aid or a wheelchair (Productivity Commission 2011, 248). The NDIS currently does this in two ways: first by providing support for children with disability within their NDIS-funded packages. NDIS funds can be used for services such as self-care at school related to the child's disability, or specialised training for teacher and staff at the school regarding the specific personal support needed for a student with disability. Second, the NDIS provides support directly to schools through the Education Systems Fund. The Fund covers things such as adjustment to buildings, ramps or hearing loops, aids and equipment to make curriculum materials accessible and support and training for teachers and other staff.

Children and Choice

The approach to choice and control underpinning the NDIS in theory sounds promising and is a really progressive approach to decision-making. It respects the individual, acknowledges that people with reduced decision-making capacities can be involved in decisions about their lives and takes seriously the concept of building the capacity of individuals to choose for themselves. This should be a great approach to children with disability. However, when we get to the detail of children with disability as set out in the NDIS legislation and policy, it is not so simple.

The starting point for adults with a disability (those over the age of 18) is a general assumption of capacity. The NDIS assumes that people with disability, even those with severe or profound intellectual disability, have the right to be in control over how services are delivered. From here it needs to be demonstrated if other arrangements are needed—i.e. a guardianship order, special assistance or even decision-making by the CEO of the National Disability Insurance Agency. When it comes to children, the starting point is an assumption of incapacity. The rules underpinning the NDIS Act recognise the provision within the Convention on the Rights of the Child where a child's ability to undertake acts and make decision on their own behalf increases as they develop (National Disability Insurance Scheme (Children) Rules 2013, 1.2). However, children with disability under the age of 18 are automatically appointed a representative that makes decisions on their behalf. In this sense, the capacity assumption is reversed and all individuals with disability under the age of 18, irrespective of their individual decision-making capacities. The child representative makes all decisions relevant to the NDIS for the child. In most cases, the child's representative will be their parent.

There are, however, some conditions around the role and duties of the child's representative. The NDIS Rules state that where things are done on behalf of the child the best interests of the child are paramount and full consideration should be given to protect them from harm, promote their development and strengthen/promote positive relationships between the child and their family (National Disability Insurance Scheme (Children) Rules 2013, 1.4, a–c). The Rules also outline that where acts or things are done on behalf of a person with disability:

- they should be involved in decision-making that affects them, including making decisions for themselves, to the extent possible; and
- they should be encouraged to engage in the life of the community; and
- the judgements and decisions they would have made for themselves should be taken into account; and
- their cultural and linguistic circumstances, and gender, should be taken into account; and

- their supportive relationships, friendships and connections with others should be recognised (National Disability Insurance Scheme (Children) Rules 2013, 1.4, d).

The explicit duties of a child's representative are to ascertain the wishes of the child and act in a manner that promotes the best interests of that child (National Disability Insurance Scheme (Children) Rules 2013, 6.2). However, this duty is not breached, so long as:

- the child's representative reasonably believes that they have ascertained the wishes of the child in relation to the thing; and
- the child's representative reasonably believes that doing the thing, or refraining from doing the thing, promotes the best interests of the child (National Disability Insurance Scheme (Children) Rules 2013, 6.3).

The CEO of the NDIA can make a determination that a child does not need a representative and can do things for him or herself. In order to make such a determination, the CEO must: be satisfied that the child is capable of making their own decisions; and be satisfied that it is appropriate in the circumstances for certain provisions of the Act not to apply to the child (National Disability Insurance Scheme (Children) Rules 2013, 5.1). Essentially, the CEO must be satisfied that it is appropriate for the child to do things for himself or herself. In making these types of the determination, the CEO of the NDIA must consult with the child and the child's representative; and have regard to the following:

- whether the child: is able to understand the kind of information relevant to decisions that need to be made under the NDIS; and
- is able to use information of that kind when making decisions; and
- is able to understand the consequences of decisions that need to be made under the NDIS; and
- is able to communicate decisions in some way;
- whether there are people in the child's life who can support them to make their own decisions (National Disability Insurance Scheme (Children) Rules 2013, 5.3).

The Productivity Commission stated that the NDIS focuses on one aspect of power—'the capacity of people to have decision-making power as consumers, and in the case of self-directed funding, control of their budgets' (2019, vol. 1, 345). By applying a blanket approach to children with disability under the age of 18, the NDIS is saying that children with disability should not have this power unless they can prove they should. Is this justified? One argument may be that a blanket approach must be taken as very young children such as newborns cannot articulate their preferences or life choices. Therefore, we should start from an assumption of incapacity, with a provision that a child can make their own decisions at the appropriate time. However, this logic does not hold within the broader logic of the NDIS. For if we were to take this approach seriously, then it is also clear that some adults with severe cognitive disability cannot articulate their preferences or life choices. Why should we not start from a point of assuming incapacity for these people too?

Another argument may be that the risk for children is lower. For example, in a situation where a 16-year-old child with physical disability is denied the right to make decisions about their care and support, we know that in two years' time this will change, and once they turn 18, they will have full decision-making powers. Therefore, the risk, or harm arising from an incorrect assessment of an individual's decision-making capacities, is fairly low. If an assumption of incapacity is made for adults with disability, there is no automatic age-related release mechanism to overturn it. Therefore, the burden of proof may be higher to prove incapacity, in order to guard against the higher life-time risk of denying someone their decision-making rights.

These arguments may have some elements that are compelling. Despite this, I argue here that they are unnecessary. A convincing case to start from a place of assuming incompetence and automatically appointing a child representative does not need to be mounted for one key reason. That is—the more nuanced approach of working with the individual's needs and capacities already exists and is set out in detail by the Productivity Commission. There is no reason why this approach could not be adopted for children with disability as well as adults. An adult with severe intellectual disability may not be able to make clear decisions as a consumer whereas a 14-year-old with a physical disability may have rational and relevant views regarding how services should be delivered to them. For the same reason that there is value in allowing an adult with disability to make decisions, there is value in stepping beyond just taking an individual's views into account and allowing them to make the decision themselves. This does not mean that all children must or should make decisions directly. The Productivity Commission (2011, 384–385) set out a range of different levels of choice and control an individual could have. The key thing here is that people should have 'choice about choice'. Currently children with disability do not have choice about choice.

The Commission's report recognised that there are different levels of risk and effort involved in the different types of choice and control mechanisms. For example, there is a high level of risk and effort associated with self-directed funding compared to provider choice. Provider choice can be compared to choosing off a menu where the options are all safe and pre-approved. Self-directed funding is more similar to shopping for ingredients and cooking at home. There could be a variety of outcomes and things could go wrong but there is more scope for control (Productivity Commission 2011, 348). The same approach could be taken for children. For example, it may be more appropriate for children, with the right support, to have the power to approve their own plans or choose the provider they want rather than to directly manage their own budgets.

In addition, the Productivity Commission report set out a number of considerations that would need to be taken into account when people are choosing for themselves:

- Some vulnerable people have preferences that can lead them to harm to themselves or others (Productivity Commission 2011, 356). These types of preferences, such as a 4-year-old driving a car, should not be supported.
- Some choices people make are based on false or misleading information (Productivity Commission 2011, 356). Therefore, consumer support and service screening may be needed to prevent advertising of services that do not work or individuals being vulnerable to making poor decisions. Noting that this is also true for people without disability.
- The NDIS in its early years and time will be needed to build people's confidence in making choices (Productivity Commission 2011, 356). This acknowledges that for people who have been denied choice and control for a long time, it is not always easy to begin exercising this right. Support to build decision-making capacity may be needed. This is true for children and the development of decision-making capacity too.

Some people with disability may not be able to make all their own decisions, such as people with profound intellectual disability. In these cases, the Productivity Commission (2011, 356) recommended that decisions be made jointly with or by their primary carers. These seem to be good principles that could equally apply to people with disability under the age of 18. Adopting a consistent individualised approach irrespective of age would allow the rights of children with disability to be respected. To be clear I am not advocating that six-month-old babies should be in charge of exercising consumer choice regarding services. In most cases, it will be simple and straightforward to determine that a very young child cannot make decisions for themselves and that a child representative will be needed. This may seem like a pedantic point but getting this right matters. Currently children with disability, as in those under the age of 18, comprise just over half of the NDIS's current participants (NDIA 2020, 87). In addition to children comprising the majority of participants in the NDIS, this chapter has also highlighted the importance of early intervention. Early intervention is also important to introduce and build decision-making capacity and independence.

Supported Decision-Making

The original Productivity Commission frequently conflated the decision-making or choice of the person with disability and the decision-making or choice of the parent or carer of that person with disability. The NDIS legislation introduced some clarity and the duties surrounding the role of the child's representative in many ways represent a big step forward in articulating the types of considerations that we should have when making decisions for others, particularly for children. However, the child's representative in most cases is their parent. There are limited ways to ensure that principles of decision-making such as these are being practised within the complexities of a family setting.

It is worth noting here that I am not saying that it is inappropriate for parents or carers to be making decisions or choices on behalf of children with disability. I am saying that it is helpful, conceptually and also for public policy design purposes, to be clear that there is an important distinction. As a mother of two young children, I recognise that it would be impractical and resource intensive for someone other than myself or my partner to make the million of different choices that are involved every day in the lives of small children. However, it is also my experience as a parent that tells me that the decisions I make are not always guided by rationality or considered in a structured framework. It is often easier to make decisions that suit my family's lifestyle, than to spend time seeking the input from my toddler. It is quicker for me to choose her clothes and dress her in the mornings than to allow her to do it herself. But it is in allowing her to do so that she develops independence and her own capacities. This may be in her best interests. My point here is that choosing for others, respecting independence and adopting strategies to develop independent decision-making, is complex. Parents and other carers need support to do this well.

Supported decision-making is recognised upfront by the Productivity Commission in the original NDIS design. The Commission outlined that,

> The proposed NDIS offers the opportunity to implement a better resourced and better focused version of case management. Currently, case managers often dedicate significant amounts of time and energy to determining the eligibility of their clients to different programs and securing funding. As this would be completed in the assessment phase of the proposed NDIS, their role would be appropriately be redirected to: providing their clients with the information needed to make informed decisions; assist in planning; see those decisions eventuate in the delivery of a disability goods and services; muster any community supports; and monitor their effect on the client over time. In that sense, the model of a 'local area coordinator', as used in Western Australia, may be the best form of case management. (Productivity Commission 2011, 484–485)

This is the vision for the role of Local Area Coordinators. They are to be a resource to participants, including children with disability and their families, to ensure that they have everything they need to make good and informed choices. The formal recommendation from the Productivity Commission was that,

> The NDIA should support consumer decision-making by providing...well resourced and effective provision of advice and information to clients, as well as monitoring of their wellbeing, through Local Area Coordinators. These services should be graduated in terms of the needs of the client and concentrated at key points, such as when entering the disability system or important transition periods. (Productivity Commission 2011, 486–487)

This seems to be particularly important for children with disability. Their needs and capacities are often evolving and there is a concentration of important transition periods in the first part of a person's life. Yet it is telling that it is this aspect of the scheme that is failing at the moment. The evaluation of the NDIS shows that overall LACs are spending most of their time on eligibility and access requests and putting together plans. Many people employed as LACs felt their skill set was being under-utilised and they were not being used for what they were employed to do (Mavromaras et al. 2018, 83). There has been much discussion of the NDIS's capacity to deliver on its promise to promote and bring about real choice and control, including in this book. Without this sort of well-resourced support, it would seem that the NDIS is setting up children with disability, and their families, to fail.

Outcomes for Children Under the NDIS

What does all of this mean for the kinds of outcomes that children with disability are experiencing under the NDIS? The NDIS is still in its early days of roll out and roll out schedules have differed between states and territories, and not all children with disability have had a similar path into or within the scheme. In addition, the types of long-term outcomes that were discussed in the early intervention section of this chapter can only be observed over the course of a longitudinal study. In other words, it is too early to say if the investment in early intervention will pay off through lower costs and better outcomes across a person's lifetime.

What we do know are the outcomes reported in the 2018 NDIS Evaluation that tracked the outcomes of participants in various NDIS trial sites. The evaluation found overall that the NDIS has led to modest improvements in the wellbeing of people with disability; this is further improving with time they spent in the NDIS (Mavromaras 2018, xviii). Although there was an improvement, the wellbeing of people with disability remains at a level well below that of all Australians (Mavromaras 2018, xviii). Wellbeing outcomes were found to be varied depending on the age of the participant. For adult participants, wellbeing increased with age and was highest for people in their mid to late 40s. However, the NDIS was not found to have an impact on the wellbeing of child participants (Mavromaras 2018, xviii). A negative impact of the NDIS on wellbeing was reported by those caring for children with disability. The evaluation noted, 'in particular those who cared for a child with a disability…reported lower than average satisfaction with their choice and control' (Mavromaras 2018, xvii). The evaluation found that,

> Many carers of NDIS participants (particularly of young children) reported that their own needs and those of the family more broadly were not addressed in the planning process. Respondents requested greater attention be paid to the family context, in particular the potential for parents/carers to require support and respite. (Mavromaras 2018, 32)

The evaluation also found that there were still unresolved issues regarding the NDIS's interface with mainstream sectors including the education system and the types of supports within the school environment for children with disability (Mavromaras 2018, xx). Children ages seven—15 years were about eight per cent more likely to experience unmet demand than their adult counterparts (Mavromaras 2018, 56).[1]

There are few other studies available that demonstrate the outcomes for children with disability, their families and carers under the NDIS. Howard et al. (2015) identified challenges faced by families in a regional NDIS trial site in NSW. The challenges experiences revolved around accessing, communicating and navigating the scheme. Gavidia-Payne's (2020) recent study demonstrated that families of children with disability experienced difficulties accessing the scheme, in developing plans or receiving services, that they had limited choice and control over services and that there was an overemphasis on the individual needs to the detriment of supports for the family or supports delivered in the family or community setting. More research is needed to know how the NDIS is performing for children with disability.

Conclusion

Children with disability have the right to treatment and life satisfaction equal to all other children. Children and people with disability have traditionally been treated as having a lower moral status and denied the right

[1] The evaluation did include people with disability of all ages but that children below the age of eight were not asked to provide any direct information and their surveys and instead the surveys were typically completed by their parents. No child participants were asked for choice and control information as part of the evaluation methodology. This information was only elicited from adult people with disability (Mavromaras 2018, 11).

to be involved in and make decisions regarding their own lives. The NDIS is underpinned by the principle of choice and control and seeks to provide people with the power to choose the services they receive and who they receive it from by being involved in planning, approving plans and even managing their own funds.

The NDIS provides supports for children in three ways: first by providing supports in traditional individualised plans, second by providing early intervention support to all children with developmental delay or disability under the age of seven and finally by providing support to children in the education system.

This chapter has argued that if the NDIS is to realise its potential in terms of a scheme that fully embraces the principle of choice and control, then consideration should be given to providing a consistent individualised approach to decision-making capacity for children with disability. In addition, appropriately resourced supported decision-making for children and their representatives, families and carers needs to be implemented.

References

Autism Behavioural Intervention NSW. 2010. Submission to the Productivity Commission on Disability Care and Support: submitted 16 August 2010. https://www.pc.gov.au/inquiries/completed/disability-support/submissions/sub0331.pdf.

Bent, Catherine, Cheryl Dissanayake, and Josephine Barbaro. 2015. Mapping the Diagnosis of Autism Spectrum Disorders in Children Aged under 7 Years in Australia, 2010–2012. *The Medical Journal of Australia* 202: 317–320.

Cowden, Mhairi. 2016. *Children's Rights: From Philosophy to Public Policy*. U.S.: Palgrave Macmillan.

Cowan, Robert, Brent Edwards, and Teresa Ching. 2018. Longitudinal Outcomes of Children with Hearing Impairment (LOCHI): 5 Year Data. *International Journal of Audiology* 27: S1–S2.

DiGiacomo, Michelle, Patricia Davidson, Penelope Abbott, Joanne Delaney, Tessa Dharmendra. 2013. Childhood Disability in Aboriginal and Torres Strait Islander Peoples: A Literature Review. *International Journal for Equity in Health* 12: 1–18. https://doi.org/10.1186/1475-9276-12-7 and https://equityhealthj.biomedcentral.com/articles.

Howard, Amanda, Tamara Blakemore, Lou Johnston, Darleen Taylor, and Rani Dibley. 2015. 'I'm Not Really Sure but I Hope It's Better': Early Thoughts of Parents and Carers in a Regional Trial Site for the Australian National Disability Insurance Scheme. *Disability and Society* 30: 1365–1381.

Mavromaras, K., M. Moskos, S. Mahuteau, et al. 2018. Evaluation of the NDIS: Final Report, National Institute of Labour Studies. National Institute of Labour Studies Flinders University. https://www.dss.gov.au/sites/default/files/documents/04_2018/ndis_evaluation_consolidated_report_april_2018.pdf.

Morrison, Rachel and Imelda Burgman. 2009. Friendship Experiences among Children with Disabilities Who Attend Mainstream Australian Schools. *Canadian Journal of Occupational Therapy* 76: 145–152. htps://journals.sagepub.com/doi/abs and https://doi.org/10.1177/000841740907600303.

National Disability Insurance Scheme (Children). 2013. COAG Disability Reform Council Quarterly Report: 31 March 2020. Rules 2013 National Disability Insurance Agency. https://www.ndis.gov.au/about-us/publications/quarterly-reports.

NDIS. 2019. Education. https://www.ndis.gov.au/understanding/ndis-and-other-government-services/education.

Payne, Gavinda. 2020. Implementation of Australia's National Disability Insurance Scheme: Experiences of Families of Young Children with Disabilities. *Infants and Young Children* 33: 184–194.

Perske, Robert. 1972. The Dignity of Risk and the Mentally Retarded. *Mental Retardation* 10: 24–27.

Productivity Commission. 2011. Disability Care and Support: Productivity Commission Inquiry Report. Commonwealth of Australia. https://www.pc.gov.au/inquiries/completed/disability-support/report.

Prout, Alan. 2005. *The Future of Childhood: Towards the Interdisciplinary Study of Children*. London: Routledge Palmer.

Schapiro, Tamar. 1999. What is a Child. *Ethics* 109: 717.

Smith, Anne. 2002. Interpreting and Supporting Participation Rights: Contributions from Sociocultural Theory. *The International Journal of Children's Rights* 10: 73–88.

The Australasian College of Physicians, Paediatric and Child Health Division. 2013. Position Statement: Early Intervention for Children with Developmental Disabilities. https://www.racp.edu.au/docs/default-source/advocacy-library/early-intervention-for-children-with-developmental-disabilities.pdf.

UN Committee on the Rights of the Child. 2013. General comment No. 14 (2013) On the Right of the Child to Have His or Her Best Interest taken as a Primary Consideration (art. 3, para 1), adopted 62nd session, January 14–February 1, 2013.

United Nations. 2006. Convention on the Rights of Persons with Disabilities. https://www.un.org/disabilities/documents/convention/convoptprot-e.pdf.

CHAPTER 13

Indigenous Ways of Knowing, Being and Doing, and Responding to NDIS Thin Markets

Jody Barney

Indigenous ways of knowledge transfer include the relationships that are built respectfully between the "teacher and listener" (Participant and NDIS Service Provider). The sharing of this knowledge is often determined by the experience, listening, space, sharing and telling of stories, as well as addressing and supporting those conversations to occur safely. Many Indigenous people with disabilities, and those who care for them, are often using profoundly different ways of engaging with the thin markets of the NDIS and its many issues compared to mainstream clients and services. These differences in perspective and service needs often relate to the natural world and the ways in which Indigenous people hold their governance. Importantly, the recognition and sharing of that vital Indigenous knowledge is often missing in the discussions with services. The growth and development of First Nations people with disabilities

J. Barney (✉)
Deaf Indigenous Community Consultancy, Melbourne, VIC, Australia

M. Cowden and C. McCullagh (eds.), *The National Disability Insurance Scheme*, https://doi.org/10.1007/978-981-16-2244-1_13

is to ensure that the learning, traditions and ownership of knowledge is culturally centred and holds true to their culturally lived experience.

This chapter takes you on a journey of those lived experiences and how they overcome and relate to the ongoing issues of thin markets of the NDIS. For this, I have utilised a narrative style that honours my lived experience as a Deaf Aboriginal and South Sea Islander woman and reflects how I interact and support other mob with disabilities.

The importance of NDIS thin markets is evident nationwide and particularly for those who need support systems within their communities. Herein, I define 'thin markets of the NDIS' as barriers to overcome whether relate to location (for regional, rural or remote settings) or for those with complex needs, including cultural needs. For those who are subjected to the 'thin markets', systems that perpetuate the inequities of the NDIS service scheme are often seen to be broken beyond repair. I argue that there is a misconception that the thin markets can be reversed with a move to a 'correct' method of engagement: one that is focused on, and provides support, with positivity and accessibility. Rather I challenge that there are structural deficiencies within the broader NDIS system and its underlying framework that cannot be easily remedied. One of the most urgent challenges faced by the communities in the thin markets is the requirement of services to be delivered by professionals that are qualified or subjected to non-cultural scrutiny, perpetuating interactions that are culturally unsafe, therapeutically inadequate and considered rigorous only from a mainstream, Western lens. How this preoccupation of ideals of mainstream service impacts the Indigenous ways of knowing, being and doing in service delivery continues to be *the* disconnect between effective and unsafe practice for people with disabilities.

Indigenous People are the FIRST Storytellers of This Continent

Imagine this, you are walking up to the gate of a home where you see that the path is broken up in spots, you see the family on the front steps having a yarn. You approach, you gesture hello, they gesture back. You see that they are wary, cautious, but they see that you have no papers, no books, no folders, and no police.... You sit with them on the step, you start sharing who you are, who your mob is, where you are from and thank them for their time to meet with you. You say that you are there to understand their needs, to listen to them unpacking their story from start to now, as it is not yet finished.... You hear the stories of constant barriers... sharing of emotional responses to not knowing what to do. So, you listen, these are their stories, their lived experience and their optimism and hope for greater social change with the NDIS....

Dave and His Story

Dave lost his leg to diabetes when he was 34 years old, but he's now in his 50s and struggles to get around his home. Dave also has family popping in and out who often take him to see other family on Country. However, Dave is also a proud man who now has been diagnosed with early onset dementia. Dave's daughter shares her experience of living with her dad: "He is always careful, wanting us to be mindful like, taking his time to get around the house real slow, it's frustrating when ya busy with the little one". Dave's daughter cares for him during the week. She lives there with Dave at the house with her two small children and makes sure Dave takes his medication on time.

Importantly, Dave has a different story, and he says "My daughter here all the time, it's not her place to care for me; like I need a man to help in the shower and that"... on asking Dave about the NDIS, he calls it "them mob" and that he has had too many yarns with them and gets more confused each time. Dave states: "they think I am leavin' my home, put me in a house in town with other mob like me? What they mean "other mob like me"? I ain't leaving my home to live where I don't know anyone cos, they won't give me help out here". Because if Dave did go live in a residential house with others, he would be leaving his community and home and the familiar places that he feels where he can be himself.

What Dave's Story Tells Us About the NDIS: Inadequate Support and Cultural Protocols not Adhered to

Dave is not alone; feelings of abandonment and leaving home and Country are a common concern for many people with disabilities living with limited services and supports. The thin markets of the NDIS, as it currently stands, have increased the impact of social isolation, cultural deprivation and removal of knowledge from the community. The view of many is that this removal and rehousing occurs only for the purpose of agencies and services to control the market and bring mob off country to town in ways that fulfil their revenue stream, but not the needs of their Indigenous clients. These are issues that tend to cause people like Dave to withdraw from the NDIS and put a much heavier burden and reliance on family and kin. The lack of prioritising support provided to Dave in his own home, where he is most comfortable and feels safe, also has an impact on his NDIS package: he is frightened that they will take his funding from him all together.

There are ongoing systemic abuses of power that undermine Dave's rights to remain in his own home, on his own country. Amidst a nation-wide burden of poor housing and the maintenance of his home, it is often difficult for services to be provided, due to the deterioration of his home and subsequent occupational health and safety issues for support workers to be onsite. However, this has not been discussed with Dave. Dave has expressed his views to family, however, the protocols for others to speak for him is problematic within the thin market sector of the NDIS. That there are "others" advocating without an authority to do so from a legal perspective—such as an enduring power of attorney, or being appointed by tribunals to be a guardian—takes away those cultural obligations and causes disharmony and shame for Dave and his family. The thin markets that impact on his life is not only the burden of disease but also the loss of connection and responsibility to care for him on country in the way Indigenous families have been doing for thousands of generations.

Cultural Incompetency: An(Other) NDIS Story

The lack of a cultural space for First Nations people with disability is not isolated to any jurisdiction—these issues are seen and heard on a national level. The inability of the NDIS to adequately respond to cultural ways to inform and support people in the thin market sector is apparent in the overall NDIS framework and its service translation and design. Many organisations that provide work in the thin market space are also ill-equipped to provide support when they have limited access to the required cultural voices and staff to do the work in a culturally safe way.

While we can all agree that there are various levels of thin markets, the impact of First Nations people is the stories of those experiences. I wish to share some of those with you to highlight the importance of culturally informed practice and the urgency to remove systemic racism and oppression so apparent in such a thin market area.

Naomi's Story

Naomi is a 48-year-old Aboriginal woman living with disabilities in a rural community. She has endured a lack of communication from NDIS on what is provided or accessible to her in her rural community and correspondence that is consistently lost in jargon, overuse of paperwork and the lack of face-to-face interactions. Naomi's mental health, post-traumatic stress disorder and sensory disorders are often overshadowed by behaviours of concern, however, what isn't addressed are the removal of services within the community: individual racism and dismissal of unmet needs always eclipse the lack of adequate service provision. By not having adequate access to the NDIS and the thin market of supports in her community, Naomi disengaged from services on a regular basis. Naomi shares her experience:

"I can tell ya, them mob with the fancy cars, fancy shirts and shoes, come up on me like I am no good, talk to me like I am crazy and slow in the head" Naomi's experience of interactions with service providers has been negative and inappropriate. Naomi continues "I know I am not right, that I play up sometimes, but I am trying to do good and have help, but they talk to me wrong way" when asking Naomi why she feels this is wrong way, she shares "They think all us mob with disabilities are dumb, that we don't know our way, it's not our way we don't know it's their way we can't do". Naomi experience of services being unconcerned; trivialising her experiences; and not meeting the cultural needs of participants is unfortunately experiences that are echoed across the country.

What Naomi's Story Tells Us About the NDIS: A Minimal and Menial Approach When Holistic Care is Needed

Thin markets are a struggle for all, the NDIS assumes that living on country and having plenty of people around will provide a lot of informal supports, while limiting and lessening the burden on the NDIS system. However, this assumption is (at best) simplistic in how supports should be delivered for very vulnerable community members. Another prominent feature is how the NDIS system interferes with or minimises the importance of relationships and cultural awareness; these factors should be considered a central prerequisite for good care for Indigenous clients.

Naomi's NDIS is rarely used in her local community, and her support needs are often at the mercy of agencies that want her to be supported while she is in their building, programs, cars and activities. However, the daily support needs in her home, on her country and her ability to respond to cultural events under cultural obligation is non-existent. Naomi has not had an Aboriginal support worker, and this lack of cultural knowledge among staff is a recognised gap nationally. There is an urgent need to strengthen capacity and upskill Aboriginal and Torres Strait Islander people to be support workers, to engage in the fundamental, culturally appropriate service delivery that is often overlooked or underrated by the NDIS.

Good Workers Doing Good Work: The Importance of Training and Cultural Supervision

Naomi tells her story in a way that makes sense to her, her ability to yarn with mob who are not familiar to her is daunting and strange: "them fellas keep telling me to go here, go there, how? I ain't gotta car". Her inability to have self-awareness of her behaviours towards others also limits her access to good workers. Naomi fears workers who do not understand her cultural responsibilities. This includes her giving away a lot of what she may have, in reciprocal and collectivist cultural practice, regardless of the consequences of agencies who do not reimburse her. Naomi has expressed how workers leave her for a long time then they return after time away, but they forget how to work with her, and therefore make her feel shame that they don't reconnect in an appropriate way.

The sharing of knowledge and the expectations of workers being replaced or shared among other organisations is evident in thin markets. The need for better training and supervision continues to have a national focus and is championed by lead advocacy and service agencies. What is essential for Naomi in the thin market space, but also has implications elsewhere, is to use what is locally available and upskill local community to assist not only Naomi but others in the community who require NDIS services.

Thin Markets Are Spread Thin Across the Continent

Thin market issues for Indigenous people are not only isolated to rural and remote communities, however, they remain the focus of much research and expenditure, especially in terms of inconsistent, fly-in-fly-out consultation. Sally, who lives in a remote community, shares her story...

Sally's Story

Sally is a young carer with a disability. She looks after her folks who both are unable to look after themselves. Sally is 25 years old and her parents are in their late 50s. Sally has the NDIS however her parents have had ongoing issues with government departments and don't want to be involved with the scheme. Sally explains how trying to get her folks connected will help them all, but this has proven to be exceedingly difficult as the opportunities she has had were irreparably damaged by the inappropriate behaviour of those from NDIS who came and spoke to her folks. Sally also was bound by her cultural obligation to care for her folks, which tends to fall outside her ability to get them to understand her current needs as a woman with a disability, and not just their daughter.

Arriving to speak to Sally, she introduces her folks: her father Bill and her mother Kath. Bill is a short fella with woolly grey hair and eyes that have seen a lot. Kath is much shorter and tends to dance about and make a fuss over Bill and Sally. When Kath shoos me inside, out of the weather, they give me the lay of the land straight up... Kath tell me "now listen here, I want you to know whatever you reckon, we ain't getting up with that "purple people eaters" [NDIS workers wear purple shirts] We been around a long time, and you look like you know a thing or two but what ya doing, but out here we go by the way of the land and if we need help we know how to be neighbourly, our Sally, she does a good job and we not complainin' about that- are we Bill?" Bill nods and agrees with Kath, but it's clear Bill didn't hear her at all, but the many years together has clued him in to face-watching (a process deaf people use to react to facial cues from others) that helps him understand his wife.

What Sally's Story Tells Us About the NDIS: Unequal Measures and Unequal Shares

It is often a huge concern for Indigenous people with disabilities when services are provided for just one person in the house, and that the NDIS system does not take into consideration some of the stresses that maybe caused by strangers having access to the home.

Sally has a community access worker that takes her to do the fortnightly shopping. The community access worker picks her up early in the morning to do the one-hour drive into town. Sally states that the community access worker provides a "buffer" for her when her folks are not with her and she's not humbugged by others in the community when she's conscious that her folks are at home alone. Being so far out of town Sally worries because of Bill's hearing loss and his dementia and her mother's needs around her post-traumatic stress disorder. The help she needs cannot be given from her NDIS plan as there she doesn't have enough hours of support, and she knows that both her folks needs a plan for themselves, before they turn 65. This will help them get the supports they need as they age. Both do not get ages care as they are on the disability support pension.

Bill, using cultural sign language systems and broken English, stated "all this mucking around, it's gammon, they say they give us a better life with all this help, but out here, in the bush, they tend to think we don't know our own culture and what it means to look after each other. I'm too old to listen to the same tripe I been getting since I was born". There is systemic racism inherent in the response that the only way to support rural Aboriginal people with needs like ours is to move them off country and put them into care. Bill explains "I'm stolen mob, you know, I been taken away from this country". By acknowledging the impact of these thin markets and the ongoing trauma of Stolen Generation members with disabilities only increases the barriers to good care.

Bill walks me on his country, sitting under the shady tree, he talks of the times that there were plenty of tucker before he was taken away, that he could go safely to the waterhole and swim. That he had the ability to know that when he was younger, he was strong and fit. He indicated via his gestures that he does not understand this world now, only the trees, the way to the waterhole and the times he has with others to talk of the business on country. He wishes to stay on country and live his days in peace, but that this is not possible as they do not have the supports to help them participate and live their best life, which only serves to further increase the stress and trauma they experience.

Kath calls out to Bill, but Bill cannot hear her, and she comes out and sits under the tree with us. She crosses her legs and yarns about the time they met. She also gestures to the far north and tells me that is her country up there. That there is no one there now, that they all moved to the big community. She met Bill at the local rodeo and how they knew they were meant to be...Bill looks on and pats her leg... she grins and tells how after four kids, and their life is now being difficult because they getting old. Kath asks “So what’s the deal with this purple people eater mob” ...

Kath later explains that when the NDIS came out, they had interpreters, but that they were confused about what this ‘purple people eater’ mob were on about, and how Aboriginal spoken language interpreters were unable to find the appropriate interpretation of concepts that are different to their traditional cultural life. Explaining to Bill and Kath that they can get help, but they can say what help they like. Bill could do things with the fellas and Kath could go do things with her friends meant that it would help Sally get things done she needs to do. That way they all could come home to yarn about their day and enjoy their family life without stress.

What Kath and Bill’s Story Tells Us of the NDIS: Boundaries and Respect

Kath explained that sometimes they had people come out and that they were into everything: “they were in my private places, they looked at my bed and that’s not proper why they do that”. I was then explaining the role of an Occupational Therapist, to ensure that while that should have been explained proper way the visit wasn’t for Kath, it was for Sally to get the help around doing the chores in the house- to see what Sally needed to care for them both. Kath said “Well they should’ve asked” ... there is a clear miscommunication of what therapists do and how the NDIS obtain and procure assessments. This has been the number one reason both Bill and Kath do not want the NDIS: they weren’t asked what they wanted, they were only told someone is coming to look at their house, and this caused Kath’s post-traumatic stress disorder to go into overdrive as she was worried they were welfare mob here to take away Bill and Sally from her.

The thin market NDIS assessment and service process often ignores the lived experience of trauma among people with disabilities, a scenario that is further amplified for Indigenous people with disabilities. This causes people like Sally, Bill and Kath to get stuck in a void owing to processes that are not culturally sound, safe and informed. Sally, Bill and Kath’s right to self-determination is forgotten during a process that disengages them, disempowers them and causes unnecessary angst that could've been avoided if it was communicated well and appropriately.

Building a Better System, Service and Workforce for Indigenous People with Disability: Making the Thin Markets Strong

What these case studies have provided are narrative pieces that speak to existing inequities in the NDIS for Indigenous people with disabilities. Some of these underlying assumptions that underpin the current framework of the NDIS and NDIA continue to perpetuate trauma, stress and harms that have long mired Indigenous experience with a mainstream, Western system of 'care'.

So what are some ways forward? How can we best bridge intent of the NDIS—to be respectful of individual choice within a social model of disability—and actual practice of care for Indigenous peoples with disability?

Some of these suggestions include building the client's capacity for self-determination and self-efficacy; improving the ways of working; and, most importantly, building respect and safety. For example, there is an important need to recognise that different ways of working are apparent in how the language and discourse of the NDIS concentrates on a deficit-based, clinical risk level: literal, diagnosis-focused and bureaucracy-speak. These all operate within narrow therapeutic windows, as compared to cultural ways of care that speak to carefully-bound commitments, expectations and protocols that have been practised on this continent for millennia. Indigenous social and cultural worlds that are responsive and are shaped and held within strengths-based models of kinship, responsibility and reciprocity. With these existing foundations, it is, therefore, unsurprising that the NDIS 'one-size-fits-all' model does not work!

If changes are not made, we run the risk of further disconnection between agencies and service users, and reinforcing existing vulnerabilities among mob. Transactional care will only continue to exacerbate prevailing inequities and perpetuate Australia's history of punitive and assimilationist government policies that have resulted in widespread disconnection, pain, grief and loss. The thin market space is notorious for failing clients, and rather than passing-the-buck or (even worse) blaming and silencing clients and communities, NDIS systems, agencies and the workforce need to put in the effort—in committing to critical self-reflection and undertaking cultural competency and capacity building among staff- in order to do better. There is no longer any excuse that any agency that works for and with Indigenous people with disabilities are not aware of existing community strengths and advocacy, nor can agencies rely on regurgitating generic, mainstream service models for Indigenous clients.

There are opportunities to improve the disability care sector for Indigenous clients. Cultural-informed practice, utilising appropriate and engaged supports tailored for the client, should be utilised to address needs, as well as provide opportunities to engage in cultural, community and kinship connection. Communication and use of language that is respectful, appropriate and clear. Prioritising cultural approaches to enrich physical and emotional safety, especially in complex settings. Working holistically and relationally, including connecting with informal supports and building trust within families and communities. There is also an area of the NDIS market that remains broadly unaddressed and underutilised but should be recognised within a unique range of service supports for Indigenous peoples: culturally enriched practices, including spiritual healing.

These improvements to practice and service delivery will not negate the continuing structural- and systems-level deficiencies within NDIS thin markets; but at least we have the prospect of promoting *Indigenous* ways of being, knowing and doing for *Indigenous* people with disabilities, and together, build a better path forward.

CHAPTER 14

"The Scheme Was Designed with a Very Different Idea in Mind of Who a Disabled Person Is": The National Disability Insurance Scheme and People with Intellectual Disability

Christine Bigby

The early optimism about the National Disability Insurance Scheme (NDIS) 'being on time and on budget' has been overtaken by harsh criticism of almost every aspect of the scheme. Implementation of the NDIS has faced extraordinary public scrutiny from the press, parliamentary enquiries, advocacy groups and public bodies. Media accounts of delays that have had devasting individual consequences, of market failure and inept decision-making illustrate more systemic problems. For example, reports have concluded that:

> ...some disability supports are not being provided because of unclear boundaries about the responsibilities of the different levels of government.

C. Bigby (✉)
Living With Disability Research Centre, La Trobe University, Melbourne, Australia

M. Cowden and C. McCullagh (eds.), *The National Disability Insurance Scheme*, https://doi.org/10.1007/978-981-16-2244-1_14

> [and there is] dissatisfaction with plans being developed over the phone; the skills and competence of planners; inconsistency of planning decisions; delays to plans and plan reviews (Productivity Commission 2017, 86).
>
> The NDIA is "unapproachable" and "lack fairness and transparency (Commonwealth Ombudsman 2018, 3).
>
> ...participants and families are overwhelmed, confused and anxious about the market and how to engage with the NDIS, let alone navigating to a new service provider (Joint Parliamentary Standing Committee 2018, 25).
>
> The NDIA is "creating imperatives for low quality provision [because] pricing is predicated on under-classification of workers and insufficient time for workers and supervisors to do their jobs well (Cortis et al. 2017).

The scheme's policies, procedures and external relationships have undergone significant change to manage increasing numbers of participants, respond to political demands and address public critique. Change continues as the NDIS nears full roll out in 2020; a legislative review is underway and the Minister announced a new NDIS Plan with six strands in November 2019 (Roberts 2019). The scale of change during its implementation phase has been necessitated, in part, by a hurried implementation that was thwarted by staffing restrictions, as well as the size and complexity of the scheme (Carey 2019). However, it is also indicative of some fundamental design tensions. These need to be explored if the NDIS is to deliver on its promises to all people with disability.

One tension is the scheme's dedifferentiated approach—that is, regarding participants as members of one group, people with disability (Sandvin and Soder 1996). Dedifferentiation emphasises individualism, functional capacity and choice of people with disability taking little account, either in policy or practice, of the specific impairment group to which they also belong.

There is growing evidence however of inequities between different NDIS participant groups with different types of impairment or different access to social capital; some impairment groups are experiencing better outcomes than others and the scheme is working much better for participants and families who are able to strongly advocate for themselves (Mavromaras et al. 2018). People with intellectual disability are one impairment group identified as having poorer outcomes who are also at risk of being without strong self or family advocacy.

The aim of this chapter is to use a lens of dedifferentiation to review how adults with intellectual disability have fared in the NDIS, explore the reasons for their poorer outcomes compared to other groups and consider what types of differentiated responses might redress this. I draw on analysis of multiple sources; the grey and academic literature about the NDIS from 2014 to 2019, a review of the mainstream media for the 12 months from July 2018, and semi structured interviews with 11 key informants, including senior public servants, academics and staff of disability support organisations.

Indications of Relatively Poorer Outcomes for People with Intellectual Disability

The first issue is how people with intellectual disability have fared in the NDIS. The dedifferentiated and anecdotal nature of much data about the NDIS and the significant changes to the scheme make robust conclusions about outcomes difficult. Nevertheless, a consistent trend in the small body of more systematic evidence suggests the scheme is failing to deliver benefits to people with intellectual disability similar to those experienced by other groups nor leading to their greater social inclusion, choice and control.

The rigorous mixed method evaluation of the pilot sites is the largest study of the scheme to date (Mavromaras et al. 2018). It found people with intellectual disability were at risk of receiving inadequate levels of support through the NDIS and relatively poor outcomes. Compared to other groups they: had higher levels of unmet demand, exercised less choice and control over supports, gained less clear benefits around social participation, had poorer average levels of wellbeing, were least satisfied with NDIS processes and were more likely to be unable to navigate the NDIA website and obtain information about services. While other groups, such as people with psychosocial disability or rural dwellers, were also relatively disadvantaged in the scheme, data available showed that people with intellectual disability generally fared the worse.

Notably, this study did not include people living in supported accommodation services many of whom have severe and profound intellectual disability. There is no reason however to think that their experiences are any more positive than their private dwelling counterparts. Indeed, for many of this group planning process were minimal as existing supports were simply rolled over into the NDIS as a result of bilateral agreements about 'in kind' contributions from states (Carey et al. 2019).

Three small-scale qualitative studies of the planning experiences of people with intellectual disability (Collings et al. 2019; Lloyd et al. 2019; Perry et al. 2019) illustrate these trends of relative disadvantage and some of the reasons behind them. The majority of the 38 adults with intellectual disability across the three studies had been excluded from meaningful engagement in planning and were heavily reliant on their parents to lead these processes. Lloyd et al. (2019, 8) concluded that it was clear these adults with intellectual disability were "not a contributing member of the planning team for most of the plans developed". Some adults had not been present at meetings and many who were, reported feeling confused and unsure what to expect. Parents expressed the view that planners had neither the skills nor were prepared to work with the adult with intellectual disability.

The two studies that interviewed adults with intellectual disability directly about their experiences suggested they felt planning processes had not captured their longer-term aspirations or real needs. This was particularly the case for aspirations about greater independence and intimate relationships. Participants talked about such issues either being ignored in plans when they had brought them up in meetings or a reluctance to raise such sensitive topics with their parent present.

Other reasons for the relatively low impact of the NDIS on wellbeing of adults with intellectual disability were evident from the problems with the translation of plans into action. Many of these adults were concerned about the lack of follow through or progress on plan goals, particularly those around social inclusion or friendships. For example, participants said,

> My sister took me to archery … but that's a one on one thing and the rest of I went umm into the mini golf … but I didn't know anyone there, so I went alone you know so … I think I'd prefer meeting people". Jacinta would also like to make more friends stating, 'It's just been a bit hard … I wouldn't even know where to get started' (Perry et al. 2019, 7).

Similar issues were raised in the study of parents, who felt that although the NDIS had provided more opportunities for activities, these were more likely to be solo or in segregated rather than inclusive groups (Lloyd et al. 2019).

Notably absent from these studies were the experiences of adults with severe or profound intellectual disability. Their lack of symbolic communication makes these participants totally dependent on others to engage with the NDIS on their behalf, meaning the representation of their aspirations is particularly challenging. The comment from a researcher who is also a parent of a young women with profound intellectual disability, that she is often asked to 'just put her [daughter] on the phone' is indicative of a fundamental lack of understanding of this group within the NDIS (King 2019).

There is also a dearth of academic research about the experiences of people with intellectual disability and complex support needs with the NDIS. There are, however, numerous case studies in the media and reports documenting their poor experiences (Office of the Public Advocate 2018). Early commentary from advocacy groups flagged their high risk of not gaining adequate support from the NDIS. They were seen as ill-equipped for the consumer demand approach of the NDIS; reluctant to make claims or identify as having intellectual disability, inexperienced in articulating their own support needs or exercising choice and control over support services (Clift 2014; O'Connor 2014). Predicted difficulties were evident in an account by Churchill, Sotiri and Rowe (2017) about the experience of a community justice centre in supporting two young men with intellectual disability and complex needs. These men maintained they wanted nothing to do with the NDIS, which meant they would loose much of the intensive assistance for community living and probation and parole obligations when the NDIS took over responsibility for its funding. Another example of a client whose NDIS funding was halved illustrated the disadvantages stemming from requiring people to nominate their own needs without access to skilled facilitation for the planning process.

The next sections explore why people with intellectual disability have fared so poorly in the NDIS.

Did the Design of the NDIS Take Account of People with Intellectual Disability?

As the quote at the beginning of this chapter suggests, the scheme was not designed with the needs of people with intellectual disability in mind. They were neither well represented 'at the table' nor was the knowledge about their experiences in other individualised funding schemes heeded.

People with disability were prominent in the early consultations and planning for the NDIS, but as a senior federal bureaucrat pointed out, people with intellectual disability and those representing their perspectives or needs were largely absent;

> ...probably over-represented and disproportionately represented were people in wheelchairs with physical disabilities who were resourceful, well resourced, articulate, brought to the table a whole set of life experiences, the capabilities and capacities that in fact people with intellectual disability don't bring.... [people with intellectual disability] weren't represented in proportionate numbers ...things that were part of original scheme design and quality and practice definitely didn't resonate and weren't sufficiently nuanced...the original membership of the Independent Advisory Council ... There was one woman, a fantastic woman...she was a mother, a carer, a provider and her son had a significant intellectual disability. But that was a sole voice.

Individualised funding schemes and market models of service delivery rely on people with disability being good consumers who can exercise choice and control. They privilege self-defined needs, and assume participants have capabilities to lodge claims, articulate needs, make decisions, identify and exercise control over service delivery and access social capital. Reflecting such assumptions, the NDIS legislation has clear expectations that participants will direct the preparation of plans and management of funding (NDIS 2013, s.31) and have capacity to determine their own best interests and make decisions that affect their lives (NDIS 2013, s.17A(1)). As the evidence reviewed earlier shows, these embedded assumptions about self-direction of plans and decision-making do not reflect the experience of people with intellectual disability with the NDIS. Nor do they not sit well with the difficulties in these spheres associated with intellectual disability unless people have "access to very considerable support and skills training" to make choice and control real (NSW Council for Intellectual Disability (CID) 2015, 12).

Significantly, the literature identifies mechanisms to support choice and control, such as, independent advocacy or systems of brokerage, as prerequisite design features of individualised funding models (Lord and Hutchinson 2003; Needham 2013; Williams and Dickinson 2016). Such mechanisms clearly benefit many groups but particularly people with intellectual disability who have been less likely than other groups to take up or benefit optimally from individualised funding:

> Evidence from the UK has shown that individuals with physical disabilities are able to take better advantage of these opportunities than those with intellectual impairments. In the latter, good outcomes appear to depend upon strong advocacy or brokerage support (Carey et al. 2018, 26).

The design of the NDIS acknowledged the imperatives for support mechanisms, to some extent, by asserting the principle that participants would be supported in their dealings with the NDIA. The qualifying statements that, self-direction of plans would be 'so far as reasonably practicable' and participants had capacity to make their own decisions 'so far as reasonable' could also be interpreted as recognition of the substantial support some participants would require to engage with the scheme. Yet the types of mechanisms suggested in the literature as necessary to support choice and control by people with intellectual disability were not well embedded in the implementation of the scheme. There were no provisions for brokerage or independent advocacy, no mandates for person-centred planning or supported decision-making and, at least in the early stages, no recognition of the necessity for long term or intensive support to implement plans. These omissions together with other features were inherently disadvantageous for people with intellectual disability.

Problematic Features of the NDIS for People with Intellectual Disability

NDIS planning processes do not take account of the communication and decision-making difficulties of adults with intellectual disability. They have been heavily criticised by many groups as not putting the person at the centre or delivering on "promises of individualized resource packages tailored to the needs of each participant" (Carney et al. 2019, 1). One of the reasons for this is the underpinning logic of planning, an ethic of justice—'treating like cases alike', leading to standardisation and undue weight to equity and efficiency goals (Carney et al. 2019). This type of approach facilitates data-driven planning necessary for the actuarial foundation of the NDIS, through the construction of typical participant profiles and reference packages to determine funding allocation.

A standardised approach is the very anathema of the type of person-centred planning found in the literature (Lyle O'Brien and O'Brien 2002) that was designed to accommodate the needs of people with intellectual disability. Carney et al. (2019, 783) capture the contrast between the two types of planning as:

> a tension between two types of ethics: an ethics of justice that seeks impartial planning, based on abstract principles applied consistently to all participants; and an ethics of care, that views each participant as unique and seeks a more relational approach to planning, that places at its centre the dialogue between the caseworker (or planner) formal and informal supporters rather than abstract standardized principles.

As this analysis implies, and, in line with a market model, NDIS planning, also prioritises self-expressed needs over facilitation of input from multiple sources by planners. The planning process has two core components. First a statement prepared by the participant about their goals and prescribed types of information about personal circumstances. This component relies on the self-articulation of needs by participants and a carefully prepared claim for support sought from the NDIS. Second is a statement of supports that specifies the amount funding from the scheme and how it is to be managed. This component is determined jointly by the participant and the NDIA, although there is no statutory requirement for this to occur through a prolonged or negotiated process or a face to face meeting.

In the absence of advocacy or formal requirements for supported decision-making participants have to rely on their own network of family or service providers for planning assistance. Figures suggest that over 90 per cent of participants received support for planning predominantly family (73%) or friends (3%) (Mavromaras et al. 2018). Qualitative studies reflect this trend for adults with intellectual disability (Collings et al. 2019; Lloyd et al. 2019). 27 of the 28 people with intellectual disability in these two studies were supported by a family member, leading to conclusion by Lloyd et al. (2019, 2) that "families play a central role in NDIS planning and plan implementation for many adults with intellectual disability". This role is onerous for many families, and one parent likened the work involved in negotiating contracts and searching for providers to having a new job.

The heavy reliance on parents also has significant costs for adults with intellectual disability in curtailment of their choices and control of planning. In these studies, parental power rather than the adults with intellectual disability largely determined what was included in plans, and at times this overrode, failed to listen to or silenced the adult participant's own perspective (Collings et al. 2019; Perry et al. 2019). The experiences recounted by this research might have been predicted from the wider literature about decision-making support for adults with intellectual disability. It points to their limited participation in decisions about their own lives, the often paternalistic or risk adverse stance of decision supporters, and the negative consequences of unregulated informal support (Antaki et al. 2009; Bigby et al. 2019; Dunn, et al. 2010; Pilnick et al. 2010). These issues were discussed in the NDIS context by Carney et al. (2019, 809):

> ... reliance on informal support may be problematic, not least because there is little evidence that NDIA planners scrutinise the approach taken by supporters, much less that they have some principles to guide a judgement about whether the way they are enacting the support is in tune with the intention of rights and principles in the legislation. Informal supports, while in theory closest to the person and thus most capable of knowing or 'reading' the will and preferences of the person being supported, may be unduly protective and risk-averse, and accountability can be difficult to ensure.

NDIS nominee provisions do enable the exercise of proxy decision-making powers but have been little used and heavily criticised as a form of 'guardianship light' without the due process or protections afforded by guardianship (McCarthy 2014). In practice this has left guardianship as the only formal alternative for those without informal support or for whom it is found wanting. The cost for adults with intellectual disability has been reversal of the long-term decline of guardianship orders made for adults with intellectual disability (Fougere 2014; OPA 2019). Victorian legislation requires guardians to make decisions based on the will, preference and rights of people with disability rather than best interests but this is not the case in all states. Regardless, whatever the regime, imposition guardianship means the removal of decision-making rights, that could be avoided through a supported decision-making scheme.

There is minimal research about the particular impact on people with intellectual disability of aspects of the scheme other than planning and decision-making. Early findings from several studies in progress do suggest, however, that there is little recognition within the NDIS of the skilled support necessary to enable this group to meaningfully participate in the social and economic life of communities. The strong individualism underpinning the scheme appears to have led to a default understanding that support needs of people with disability revolve around one-to-one direct contact with a support worker, either in the form of attendant care—doing things for people or as a paid companion—taking people to community places. Glimpses of reliance on this type of one-to-one companionship were evident from issues about plan implementation in the studies already discussed. There are also indications that bringing a support worker is becoming a prerequisite for people with disability to being included in mainstream activities.

Directly supporting a person with intellectual disability to be socially included is more complex than the type of attendant care or personal assistance suited to people without cognitive disability who are able to define tasks and direct workers. It will likely include facilitating engagement, social interaction or development of relationships, providing practical help and skill development, supporting choice or decision-making and giving advice and guidance (Askheim 2003; Bigby, Bould and Beadle-Brown 2017; Mansell and Beadle-Brown 2012). Research has begun to define the skills and judgements direct support workers require to assist people with intellectual disability with these things. For example, the nuanced 'behind the scenes' negotiations with an organisation or support to other group members necessary to enable inclusion of an individual with intellectual disability in a community group (Bigby & Anderson, 2021; Craig and Bigby 2015; Stancliffe et al. 2015); in the moment judgement that creates opportunities for convivial encounters (Bigby and Wiesel 2015) and; the use of graded assistance to enable engagement in a domestic task (Mansell and Beadle-Brown 2012).

Person Centred Active Support is at the core of the necessary skill set for staff supporting people with intellectual disability. There is robust evidence about the type of training and front-line Practice Leadership that support workers require to develop and sustain this practice (Bigby et al. 2019). Despite this, there are no mandatory requirements for staff working with people with intellectual disability to be trained in Active Support. Indeed, studies suggest that NDIS prices are insufficient for organisations to afford this type of staff training and supervision (Cortis et al. 2017). This does not bode well for the quality of support delivered by the burgeoning direct support workforce given that new recruits are less skilled, trained and experienced than existing support workers (Baines et al. 2019). Notably, after five years there remain no statement of the capabilities required for direct support work with people with intellectual disability, and the competences developed in the sphere of behaviour support give only a passing nod to Active Support, largely ignoring its foundational role in positive behaviour support (Ockendon, Ashman and Beadle-Brown 2014; NDIS Safeguard and Quality Commission 2019).

Differentiation in the NDIS and Adults with Intellectual Disability

Undoubtedly, adults with intellectual disability will benefit from many of the evolutionary changes made to address issues that have negatively affected a broad cross section of NDIS participants. For example, the abandonment of planning by phone, commitment to better trained planners and a more transparent and more consultative process before plans are finalised (Joint Standing Committee on the National Disability Insurance Scheme 2019). Interestingly, in responding to the many implementation problems, the early hard-line dedifferentiation of the NDIS has softened. Some changes are taking a more differentiated approach by tailoring operations more carefully to specific groups of people with disability, albeit in a fairly ad hoc manner. For example, by creating separate access pathways, recognising the need for specialist knowledge about impairment types, establishing impairment specific advisory or reference groups, appointment of very senior strategic advisers for autism and psychosocial disability, and, through the Information, Linkages and Capacity Building (ILC) program, funding for impairment specific information projects and self-advocacy groups (Joint Parliamentary Standing Committee 2018).

In parallel, advocacy and the constituency of people with disability and their families have also become more differentiated, splintering from the united voice presented in the dedifferentiated *Every Australian Counts* campaign, (or reverting) into impairment and issue specific groups, lobbying for their own needs. For example, campaigning by the Summer Foundation has contributed to the priority now accorded in the NDIS to young people with acquired disability and complex needs in nursing homes; $4.7 m allocated to a Joint Agency Task Force action plan, and a specialist team within the NDIS to prevent younger people with disability entering aged care (Probono 2019). Similarly, very strong advocacy has drawn attention to the needs of people with autism, helping to attract $9 m for grants towards independent evidence-based information, advice and assistance to people with autism, their families, professionals and the NDIA (ILC grant outcomes 2019).

The inherent risks of a shift towards differentiated initiatives generated by groups able to marshal strong advocacy are the exacerbation of emerging inequities between groups, leaving behind still further people with intellectual disability who as a group have little social or political capital.

Some sub-groups of adults with intellectual disability will benefit from inclusion in initiatives that cross disability types. For example, the specific pathways utilising more specialist knowledge for people with complex support needs, a decision support pilot targeting adults without family or informal support and potentially some of the autism specific initiatives given the high cooccurrence rates of autism and intellectual disability (at least 20 per cent of people with autism have intellectual disability and 10 per cent of people with intellectual disability have autism (Rydzewska et al. 2019).

Nevertheless, despite being the single largest group of participants, adults with intellectual disability are seldom distinguished in the NDIS as an impairment group facing distinctive issues. One of the few acknowledgements of this group was the establishment of an Intellectual Disability Reference Group to the Independent Advisory Council of the NDIS in 2014. Though symbolically important, in the absence of strong parallel advocacy about the issues raised, such as supported decision-making, this has led to few discernible changes. As one senior NSW state bureaucrat suggested in 2018;

> The NDIS at this point in its development does not really understand the unique issues associated with people who have an intellectual disability. And I think if there is not a voice to assist those people or their families to articulate what it is that they want and need to be supported appropriately, then that group is going to become a sub-group that is ignored in the new NDIS environment (senior NSW bureaucrat 2018).

One reason for the lack of understanding and limited advocacy is the absence of a national organisation sufficiently well-resourced to represent issues interest specific to people with intellectual disability. The small state bodies that make up *Inclusion Australia* the 'national voice for Australians with intellectual disability' are poorly funded, often on a project-by-project basis. Neither is there is a dominant profession or discipline that leads practice or research about adults with intellectual disability. Indicative of this is the low media profile of people with intellectual disability. For example, only 6 per cent of the 394 items about the NDIS in the major suburban press during the 12 months from June 2018 to 2019 mentioned intellectual disability. The emphasis on hearing directly from people with disability may exacerbate the low profile. It's difficult, for example, to gain media coverage unless one has a person with intellectual disability ready to front the story, which is rarely feasible for large-scale research that has used observations methods to tap into experiences of people with severe or profound intellectual disability.

Another reason for their low profile is the very characteristics that differentiate people with intellectual disability from other impairment groups; difficulties with self-advocacy and heavy reliance on skilled support to identify or articulate issues of concern. These issues were highlighted by an interviewee and a parent of an adult with intellectual disability in his letter to the Age;

> ...some of those physical disability groups, they can ramp up hundreds and hundreds of members who are all quite capable of ringing their local MP and writing a letter, and that's not the group of people with an intellectual disability. And often their families are fatigued, they're fatigued through a life of caring, and you know, they're just not going to be able to do that lobbying in the same way (senior bureaucrat).
>
> Thank you for the heartwarming story about a young woman whose life has been enhanced by the National Disability Insurance Scheme. It is well known that the NDIS works best for people who can self-advocate or have family or friends to advocate for them. You will not hear such glowing stories about the thousands of people with a disability who are living in disability accommodation, who are unable to self-advocate and do not have family support (The Age 2018).

The NDIS is a complex scheme and this chapter has analysed only a few of its facets, primarily those related to planning and decision-making. While the evidence is relatively limited about experiences and outcomes for people with intellectual disability, there are strong indications of the failure to deliver to them equal benefit or the promise of more choice and control and social inclusion. It has been argued, that as a group people with intellectual disability are particularly disadvantaged by some features of the NDIS. Somewhat paradoxically both by its predominant dedifferentiated approach and newer differentiated initiatives. The final section considers responses that might redress this.

Differentiation to Address the Needs of People with Intellectual Disability in the NDIS

Planning and decision-making attuned to adults with intellectual disability

An approach to NDIS planning more attuned to people with intellectual disability must reach a "balance between past excesses of professional planning of needs and promotion of UNCRPD-compliant, person-centred planning" (Carney et al. 2019, 787). Person-centred planning was developed specifically for people with intellectual disability in the 1980s. It starts from the aspirations and capacities of the person—visions of their future rather than immediate problems with the guiding question "what particular assistance do you need because of your specific limitations in order to pursue the life that has been envisaged together" (Lyle O'Brien and O'Brien 2002). The focus is on listening in all its guises, to build a shared picture of who the person is, their talents and gifts, their visions for their life, what matters most, what support they need to move towards that future, who will help them.

However, 'person centred planning' has become a catch all phrase, fraught with different interpretations and misapplication of its core principles (Bigby et al. 2007). It has lost many of its original features, as a process undertaken with the person by members of an informal circles of support, and outside the formal service system (Medora and Ledger 2005).

The principles and practice of person-centred planning in context of the NDIS will need careful definition if this concept is to guide NDIS planning processes. Care must also be taken to avoid implicit but erroneous assumptions of person-centred planning that people with intellectual disability always have others that know them well (Bigby 2008).

The logic and practice of planning must reflect an ethic of care, designed to elicit the best possible information about needs and aspirations of a person with intellectual disability. Knowledge from research and practice wisdom suggest planning for this group, regardless of the severity of impairment, should be relational, unhurried, based on trust and informed by multiple sources, including those with expert knowledge and who know the person well (Bigby and Frawley 2010; Lyle O'Brien and O'Brien 2002).

Studies with people with intellectual disability, able to express their views about planning in the NDIS, have found they are concerned that their perspectives are not heard and assumptions exist that carers or advocates know best. They want to be better prepared and more involved in planning processes; to be listened to, have their opinions respected and a relationship with planners (Collings 2019; Lloyd 2019). Advocates echo these views, suggesting that more time should be taken with planning, the voice of the person should be distinguished from their family, and planners better trained (NSW CID 2016).

Ascertaining the needs and preferences of people with intellectual disability takes time, skill and trusted relationships. As one experienced practitioner explained:

> goals and plans for our client group are usually developed via a long process. This involves staff developing a close working relationship with the client. By spending time together...workers are able to identify certain things over time that clients might bring up in a conversation. We can then reflect that back to them in terms of a goal or strategy. It's a process that takes time but is often very effective. But if we were to sit with them and ask, 'what are your goals?' we would inevitably draw a blank (Churchill et al. 2017, 15).

For people with severe and profound intellectual disability, unable to have conversations, planning requires spending time with them, and dialogue with others who know them well from different perspectives. Supporters also need to be committed to separating their own preferences and guiding the person's own self-determination (Crisp 2018; Douglas and Bigby 2018).

Planning processes must go at a pace that reflects each individual and the NDIS must have mechanisms to provide whatever type and intensity of support is needed to ensure their participation and preferences are not only elicited but prioritised in plan goals. The most effective path for this may be through specialist planning teams for adults with intellectual disabilities as proposed by NSW CID (2016). Such specialisation may need to incorporate sub-specialist teams with even more expert knowledge around for example, life course stages or severity of impairment. The alternative to avoid potential risks of labelling or devaluing, which may also benefit other groups, would be a redesign of the entire planning process, so it is more clearly relational, unhurried and draws on input from multiple sources facilitated by skilled planners.

A robust mechanism to support the decision-making of people with intellectual disability must be an integral part of the scheme; engaging, planning and plan implementation all require decisions to be made. Supported decision-making is promoted as a rights-based alternative to the binary options of unregulated informal support or guardianship. It is based on the concept of relational autonomy, and principles that people with disability should have access to the support necessary to make, communicate and participate in decisions that affect their lives and, the will, preferences and rights of people who require decision-making support must direct decisions that affect their lives (Bach 2017; ALRC 2014).

The legal and practice frameworks of supported decision-making schemes guide both supporters' actions and provide criteria by which to judge the quality of decision support. They may include mechanisms for building supporter's capacity through mentoring or training. In an NDIS context, a supported decision-making scheme could be an important safeguarding mechanism, equipping staff to be alert to coercion or undue influence by supporters (Bigby and Douglas 2020). Design of supported decision-making schemes may also incorporate strategies particularly important to people with intellectual disability to match paid or volunteer supporters to those without informal support or for whom it is working (Bigby et al. 2017).

A supported decision-making scheme will not replace some participants' needs for independent advocacy. Advocacy and supported decision-making are not the same although the practice of both draw on some of the same principles and skills. Advocacy generally starts from the point of failure of an already made choice or decision to be implemented, and is often short-term, meaning that advocates have little opportunity for getting to know a person well, one of the central components of decision support (Leadership + 2019).

There is a growing evidence about effective practice which can inform the design of a supported decision-making scheme for NDIS participants (Douglas and Bigby 2018). Such a scheme would help to ensure rights-based decision support for people with intellectual disability, and oversight of its quality of support. It would be far preferable to the current situation of little or no scrutiny of who provides informal support or its quality and stem the growth of guardianship orders for people with intellectual disability evident in recent years (OPA 2019).

Representation of people with intellectual disability and their issues

The NDIS has championed the inclusion of people with disability as staff, their representation in governance and consultative mechanisms, co-production teams and prioritised the lived experiences of disability over other sources of knowledge. Yet the underrepresentation of people with intellectual disability suggests engagement strategies are insufficiently adjusted to hear their collective and individual voices. More skilled and creative accommodations are needed to enable people with intellectual disability to be included as co-creators rather than simply consumers of the NDIS. In this respect, there is much the NDIS could learn from the best practice modelled by NSW CID, who as one interviewee said, "don't just pop people in there and just tick the box". Inclusion in any type of forum or activity cannot be left to chance, whatever their role or experience, people with intellectual disability need individual support to be suited to their needs, from working out the views they want to express and how to do so, to the practicalities of getting places. In parallel, inclusion depends on a supportive and welcoming milieu, which means attitudes and actions of others and ways of doing business also have to change (Frawley and Bigby 2011).

ILC initiatives are helping to strengthen the small state bodies, such as NSW CID that make up the national body that represents people with intellectual disability, *Inclusion Australia*. However, if people with intellectual disability are to gain prominence in proportion to their size as group of NDIS participants, affirmative action will be needed to maintain a strong independent representation outside of the NDIS apparatus. One strategy would be funding a network of organisations led by people with intellectual disability similar to NSW CID, as vehicles for people with intellectual disability to have their own voice in public debate and civil society (Bigby and Henderson 2018). Such organisations would require core funding at levels sufficient to employ skilled professional advocates and well educated and experienced supporters which are features of NSW CID. With a wider brief than traditional self-advocacy, systemic advocacy generated by organisations such as this would be grounded in experiences of self-advocates but planned and executed through an alliance of leaders with intellectual disabilities, family members and professionals working together. Their practice would involve supporters and people with intellectual disability working together "collecting, comparing and picking the pith out of individuals' stories and acting on the wider policy implications these throw up" (Bigby and Henderson 2018, 8).

A quick win too would be an internal strategy to carve out jobs for people with intellectual disability within the NDIS. Very few people have friendships or regular contact with a person with intellectual disability, so more contact between NDIS staff and this group would help to embed a deeper understanding of their lived experiences in the organisation.

Funding through ILC programs is strengthening self-advocacy groups and the expectations of the NDIS Quality and Safeguard Commission, raising the profile of self-advocates in governance roles on boards and advisory bodies. Such measures tend to heighten the collective voices of people with less severe intellectual impairments, as people with more severe and profound intellectual disabilities are seldom involved in self-advocacy groups and self-advocates struggle to act as proxies for them. There is a need for much more creativity and lateral thinking to find alternatives to direct representation for this group. One strategy may be testing the methods developed by the Openstorytellers organisation that use co-construction of personal narratives to enable people without language to engage an audience with stories about their lived experiences (Grove 2015). There is no one way to represent the perspectives of people with intellectual disability. The NDIS might need to be more open to the inherent challenges therein by adopting a more multifaceted approach that values, their direct voices, but also those of families and others who know them well, and knowledge from research that uses alternative methods such as observation to capture experiences of people with more severe and profound intellectual disability.

Regulation and funding to shape delivery of quality support practices to people with intellectual disability

Although, the NDIS does not directly deliver services, the provisions of the Act expect the scheme to proactively address service quality by promoting, "innovation, quality, continuous improvement, contemporary best practice and effectiveness of supports" (NDIS 2013, s.4 15). It does this through the funding and regulatory regime for disability supports. Policies about price and type of supports funded, and the requirements set by the NDIS Quality and Safeguard Commission heavily influence the nature and quality of support services.

There is considerable potential for both the NDIA and the Commission to use a differentiated approach to drive service quality for people with intellectual disability, by developing standards and requirements for staff skills that reflect of evidence about best practice. For example, in a similar way that evidence of qualifications is required to attract a higher level of funding for allied health staff—there could be provisions, that in order to receive funding for support of people with intellectual disability, organisations would have to demonstrate that their staff are trained in Active Support and that there is an appropriate ratio of trained front-line Practice Leaders. It may also be feasible to require services to provide more direct tangible evidence of service quality in order to receive funding, showing for example, delivery of Active Support at a level above the benchmark for good practice (Bigby et al. 2019).

As already discussed, there is potential for evidence-based competencies for staff working with people with intellectual disability to be set by the Commission. Importantly too, compliance and quality assurance mechanisms, such as audits and inspections must take into account evidence about the fallibility of paperwork as an indicator of service quality and the difficulties of relying on self-report by people with intellectual disability either to make complaints or provide feedback about quality. Observation of staff practice and levels of engagement of people with intellectual disability should be central rather than peripheral to judgements about compliance with quality standards. Research provides evidence-based indicators of what must be in place, at service and organisational levels, to deliver good quality active support which can be tailored for the NDIS Quality and Safeguard Commission for use in service registration and inspection.

Conclusion

Debates about dedifferentiation highlight its benefits and risks for people with intellectual disability (Clegg and Bigby 2017): Benefits such as united advocacy for rights or abandonment of stigmatising labels; and risks such as translating concepts of rights and inclusion into structural adjustments and practices that take little account of cognitive impairments. Advocates and service systems face the conundrum of whether and how to single out people with intellectual disability as different to ensure adjustment of social processes or individual support that meets their needs—while at the same time emphasising their commonality, to reinforce their equal citizenship and avoid stigma, segregation and poor-quality services so common when they are singled out as different (Clegg and Bigby 2017; Bigby and Henderson 2018). A position statement on dedifferentiation captured these tensions, leaving open the question of when and in what circumstances might differentiation be beneficial?

> [Policy and practice should] Treat people with intellectual disability as members of the broad disability group wherever possible, and protect and develop differentiated opportunities, services and research whenever necessary.... Ensure that all services recognise and respond appropriately to the unique needs of people with intellectual disability and staff have the necessary knowledge and skills to do so (Australasian Society for Intellectual Disability 2017).

People with intellectual disability do not necessarily have to be differentiated. It is feasible for the design of policy and practice to embed knowledge and staff skills sufficient to respond appropriately to their needs. There is, however, no strong track record of doing this (Clegg and Bigby 2017); one need only look at the statistics in the health system on avoidable deaths of people with intellectual disability compared to other groups (Heslop et al. 2014). The evidence reviewed in this chapter suggests the relative disadvantage of people with intellectual disability in the NDIS. It will be important to track their progress against that of other impairment groups as the scheme matures. Greater availability of differentiated data through, for example, the quarterly scorecards and NDIA reports to the Council of Australian Governments will be important to doing this. At the time of writing, analysis of available data suggests that differentiated initiatives are necessary to redress the disadvantage of people with intellectual disability by taking more specific account of their group specific needs, particularly in the design and practice of planning, support for decision-making, representation and pricing and regulation.

References

ALRC. 2014. Equality, Capacity and Disability in Commonwealth Laws: Final Report, Australian Law Reform Commission. Australian Government. https://www.alrc.gov.au/wp-content/uploads/2019/08/alrc_124_whole_pdf_file.pdf.

Antaki, Charles, W. Finlay, and Chris Walton. 2009. Choices for People with Intellectual Disabilities: Official Discourse and Everyday Practice. *Journal of Policy and Practice in Intellectual Disabilities* 6: 260–266.

Askheim, Ole Peter. 2003. Personal Assistance for People with Intellectual Impairments: Experiences and Dilemmas. *Disability and Society* 18: 325–339.

Australasian Society for Intellectual Disability. 2017. Dedifferentiation Position Statement. Australasian Society for Intellectual Disability. https://www.asid.asn.au/publications/position-statements.

Bach, Michael. 2017. Inclusive Citizenship: Refusing the Construction of 'Cognitive Foreigners' in Neo-Liberal Times. *Research and Practice in Intellectual and Developmental Disabilities* 4: 4–25.

Baines, Donna, Fiano Macdonald, Jim Stanford, and Jessie Moore. 2019. Precarity and Job Instability on the Frontline of NDIS Support Work. The Centre for Future Work at the Australia Institute. https://agedcare.royalcommission.gov.au/system/files/2020-08/RCD.9999.0460.0008.pdf.

Bigby, Christine, Chris Fyffe, and Elizabeth Ozanne. 2007. *Planning and Support for People with Intellectual Disability. Issues for Case Managers and Other Practitioners*. London: Jessica Kingsley.

Bigby, Christine. 2008. Known Well By No One. Trends of the Informal Social Networks of People with Intellectual Disability Five Years After Moving to the Community. *Journal of Intellectual and Developmental Disabilities* 33: 148–157.

Bigby, Christine, and Frawley. (2010). *Social Work and Intellectual Disability: Working for Change*. London: Palgrave Macmillan.

Bigby, Christine, and Ilan Wiesel. 2015. Mediating Community Participation: Practice of Support Workers in Initiating, Facilitating or Disrupting Encounters Between People With and Without Intellectual Disability. *Journal of Applied Research in Intellectual Disability* 28: 307–318. https://doi.org/10.1111/jar.12140.

Bigby, Christine, Emma Bould, and Julie Beadle-Brown. 2017. Conundrums of Supported Living: The Experiences of People with Intellectual Disability. *Journal of Intellectual and Developmental Disability* 42: 309–319.

Bigby, Christine, Jacinta Douglas, Terry Carney, Shih-Ning. Then, Ilan Wiesel, and Elizabeth Smith. 2017. Delivering Decision-Making Support to People with Cognitive Disability – What Has Been Learned From Pilot Programs in Australia from 2010–2015. *Australian Journal of Social Issues* 52: 222–240.

Bigby, Christine, and David Henderson. 2018. Raising the Voices of People with Intellectual Disabilities and Changing Systems: The Contribution of NSW Council for Intellectual Disability to Social Change. Living with Disability Research Centre, La Trobe University. https://cid.org.au/wp-content/uploads/2018/02/Raising-the-voices-of-people-with-intellectual-disabilities.pdf.

Bigby, Christine, Mary Whiteside, and Jacinta Douglas. 2019. Supporting Decision Making of Adults with Intellectual Disabilities: Perspectives of Family Members and Workers in Disability Support Services. *Journal of Intellectual and Developmental Disabilities* 44: 396–409. https://doi.org/10.3109/13668250.2017.1378873.

Bigby, Christine, Emma Bould, Teresa Iacono, and Julie Beadle-Brown. 2019. Predicting Good Active Support for People with Intellectual Disabilities in Supported Accommodation Services: Key Messages for Providers, Consumers and Regulators. *Journal of Intellectual and Developmental Disability* 44: 279–289.

Bigby, C., & Anderson, S. (2021). Creating Opportunities for Convivial Encounters for People with Intellectual Disabilities: It Looks Like an Accident. *Journal of Intellectual and Developmental Disabilities*. 46, 1: 45–57. https://doi.org/10.3109/13668250.2020.1837606.

Bigby, C. and J. Douglas. 2020. Supported Decision Making. In *Choice, Preference, and Disability: Promoting Self-Determination Across the Lifespan*, ed. R. Stancliffe, P. Wehmeyer and K. Shrogran. New York: Springer.

Carey, Gemma, Eleanor Malbon, Sue Olney, and Daniel Reeders. 2018. The Personalisation Agenda: The Case of the Australian National Disability Insurance Scheme. *International Review of Sociology* 28: 20–34. https://doi.org/10.1080/03906701.2018.1425084.

Carey, Gemma. 2019. What Happened to the NDIS? Centre for Social Impact. https://www.csi.edu.au/news/director-update-what-happened-ndis/.

Carey, Gemma, Adrian Kay, and Ann Nevil. 2019. Institutional Legacies and Sticky Layers: What Happens in the Cases of Transformative Policy Change. *Administration and Society* 51: 491–509. https://doi.org/10.1177/0095399717704682.

Carney, Terry, Shih-Ning Then, Christine Bigby, Ilan Wiesel, and Jacinta Douglas. 2019. National Disability Insurance Scheme Plan Decision-Making: Or When Tailor-Made Case Planning Met Taylorism & the Algorithms? *Melbourne University Law Review* 42: 783–812.

Churchill, Alison, Mindy Sotiri,and Simone Rowe. 2017. Access to the NDIS for people with cognitive disability and complex needs who are in contact with the criminal justice system: Key challenges. The Community Restorative Centre. https://www.crcnsw.org.au/wp-content/uploads/2017/01/CRC_NDIS_BriefingPaper_Jan2017.pdf.

Clegg, Jennifer, and Christine Bigby. 2017. Debates About Dedifferentiation Twenty-First Century Thinking About People with Intellectual Disabilities as Distinct Members of the Disability Group. *Research and Practice in Intellectual and Developmental Disabilities* 4: 80–97. https://doi.org/10.1080/23297018.2017.1309987.

Clift, Kenn. 2014. Access to the National Disability Insurance Scheme for People with Intellectual Disabilities Who are Involved in the Criminal Justice System. *Research and Practice in Intellectual and Developmental Disabilities* 1: 24–33. https://doi.org/10.1080/23297018.2014.910863.

Collings, Susan, Angela Dew, and Leanne Dowse. 2019. "They Need to be Able to have Walked in Our Shoes": What People with Intellectual Disability Say About National Disability Insurance Scheme Planning. *Journal of Intellectual & Developmental Disability* 44: 1–12. https://doi.org/10.3109/13668250.2017.1287887.

Commonwealth Ombudsman. 2018. Administration of reviews under the National Disability Insurance Scheme Act 2013. Report on the National Disability Insurance Agency's Handling of Reviews. http://www.ombudsman.gov.au/__data/assets/pdf_file/0029/83981/NDIS-NDIA-Final-report-on-administration-of-reviews-under-the-Act.pdf.

Cortis, Natasha, Fiona Macdonald, Bob Davidson, and Eleanor Bentham. 2017. Reasonable, Necessary and Valued: Pricing Disability Services for Quality Support and Decent Jobs (SPRC Report 10/17). Social Policy Research Centre, UNSW Sydney. https://www.arts.unsw.edu.au/sites/default/files/documents/NDIS_Pricing_Report.pdf.

Craig, Diane, and Christine Bigby. 2015. "She's Been Involved in Everything as Far as I Can See": Supporting the Active Participation of People with Intellectual Disabilities in Community Groups. *Journal of Intellectual and Developmental Disability* 40: 12–25. https://doi.org/10.3109/13668250.2014.977235.

Crisp, William. 2018. She Proudly Announced She has a Boyfriend from her Day Placement and Wants Him to Sleep Over. The Grounded Theory of the Process of Guiding Self-determination. La Trobe University. http://hdl.handle.net/1959.9/565677.

Douglas, Jacinta, and Christine Bigby. 2018. Development of an Evidence-Based Practice Framework to Guide Support for Decision Making. *Disability and Rehabilitation*. https://doi.org/10.1080/09638288.2018.1498546.

Dunn, Michael, Isabel Clare, and Anthony Holland. 2010. Living "A Life Like Ours": Support Workers' Accounts of Substitute Decision-Making in Residential Care Homes for Adults with Intellectual Disabilities. *Journal of Intellectual Disability Research* 54: 144–160. https://doi.org/10.1111/j.1365-2788.2009.01228.

Fougere, Christine. 2014. Guardianship, Financial Management and the NDIS: NCAT's Experience. Australian Guardianship and Administration Council Heads of Tribunal Meeting, 23 March. https://ncat.nsw.gov.au/documents/speeches/20170323_paper_fougere_agac_hobart.pdf.

Frawley, Patsie, and Christine Bigby. 2011. Inclusion in Political and Public Life: The Experiences of People with Intellectual Disability on Government Disability Advisory Bodies in Australia. *Journal of Intellectual and Developmental Disability* 36: 27–38. https://doi.org/10.3109/13668250.2010.549465.

Grove, Nicola. 2015. Finding the Sparkle: Storytelling in the Lives of People with Learning Disabilities. *Tizard Learning Disability Review* 20: 29–36.

Heslop, Pauline, Peter Blair, Peter Fleming, Matthew Hoghton, Anna Marriott, and Lesley Russ. 2014. The Confidential Inquiry into Premature Deaths of People with Intellectual Disabilities in the UK: A Population-Based Study. *The Lancet* 383: 889–895. https://doi.org/10.1016/S0140-6736(13)62026-7.

Joint Parliamentary Standing Committee on the National Disability Insurance Scheme. 2018. Market Readiness for Provision of Services Under the NDIS. Commonwealth of Australia. https://www.aph.gov.au/Parliamentary_Business/Committees/Joint/National_Disability_Insurance_Scheme/MarketReadiness.

Joint Standing Committee on the National Disability Insurance Scheme. 2019. NDIS Planning Interim Report.Commonwealth of Australia. https://trove.nla.gov.au/work/237625533.

King, Michelle. 2019. Adventures in Becoming a 'Legal' Adult with Severe Intellectual Disabilities: Personal and Research Perspectives. National Conference of the Australasian Society for Intellectual Disability. http://www.asidconference.com.au/2154.

Lloyd, Jan, Karen Moni, Monica Cuskelly, and Anne Jobling. 2019. Engaging with National Disability Insurance Scheme Planning: Perspectives of Parents of an Adult with Intellectual Disability. *Journal of Intellectual & Developmental Disability* 44: 254–263. https://doi.org/10.3109/13668250.2019.1654275.

Lord, John, and Peggy Hutchinson. 2003. Individualised Support and Funding: Building Blocks for Capacity Building and Inclusion. *Disability and Society* 18: 71–86. https://doi.org/10.1080/0968759032000044247.

Lyle O'Brien, Connie, and John O'Brien. 2002. The Origins of Person-Centred Planning: A Community of Practice Perspective. In *Implementing person-centred planning: Voices of experience*, ed. J. O'Brien & C. Lyle O'Brien, 25–57. Toronto, Ontario: Inclusion Press.

Mansell, J.L., and Julie Beadle-Brown. 2012. *Active Support: Enabling and Empowering People with Intellectual Disabilities*. London: Jessica Kingsley Publishers.

Mavromaras, Kostas, Megan Moskos, Stéphane Mahuteau, Linda Isherwood, Alison Goode, Helen Walton, Llainey Smith, Zhang Wei and Joanne Flavel. 2018. Evaluation of the NDIS: Final Report. National Institute of Labour Studies, Flinders University. https://www.dss.gov.au/sites/default/files/documents/04_2018/ndis_evaluation_consolidated_report_april_2018.pdf.

McCarthy, Tess. 2014. Guardianship and National Disability Insurance Scheme. Discussion Paper, Office of the Public Advocate. https://www.publicadvocate.vic.gov.au/resources/research-reports/70-guardianship-and-the-ndis-discussion-paper-2014/file.

Medora, Hectorand, and Ledger. 2005. Implementing and Reviewing Person Centred Planning: Linkes with Care Management, Clinical Support and Commissioning. In *Person Centred Planning and Care Management with People with Learning Disabilities*, ed. Paul Cambridge and Steven Carnaby, 149–171. London: Jessica Kingsley.

Michael, Luke. 2019. Government Vows to Remove Young People with Disability from Aged Care. *Probono*. https://probonoaustralia.com.au/news/2019/11/government-vows-to-remove-young-people-with-disability-from-aged-care/.

NDIS Quality and Safeguards Commission. 2019. Positive Behaviour Support Capability Framework: For NDIS Providers and Behaviour Support Practitioners. NDIS Quality and Safeguards Commission. https://www.ndiscommission.gov.au/pbscapabilityframework.

Needham, Catherine. 2013. The Boundaries of Budgets: Why Should Individuals Make Spending Choices About Their Health and Social Care? Centre for Health and the Public Interest. http://chpi.org.uk/wp-content/uploads/2013/07/Boundaries-of-Budgets-Catherine-Needham-July-31.pdf.

NSW CID. 2015. Position Statement on NDIS Quality and Safeguarding. Council for Intellectual Disability. https://cid.org.au/resource/position-statement-on-the-ndis-quality-and-safeguards-framework/.

NSW CID. 2016. What Should the NDIA Understand About Intellectual Disability. Paper to the Independent Advisory Council to the NDIS. https://static1.squarespace.com/static/5898f042a5790ab2e0e2056c/t/5b19e805f950b7075faba38d/1528424458096/May%2B2016-%2BWhat%2Bshould%2Bthe%2BNDIA%2Bunderstand%2Babout%2Bpeople%2Bwith%2Bintellectual%2Bdisability.pdf.

Ockenden, John, Bev Ashman, and Julie Beadle-Brown. 2014. Active Support – Fundamental to Positive Behaviour Support. *Research and Practice in Intellectual and Developmental Disabilities* 1: 98–107. https://doi.org/10.1080/23297018.2014.961528.

O'Connor, Morrie. 2014. The National Disability Insurance Scheme and people with Mild Intellectual Disability: Potential Pitfalls for Consideration. *Research and Practice in Intellectual and Developmental Disabilities* 1: 17–23. https://doi.org/10.1080/23297018.2014.908815.

Office of the Public Advocate. 2018. The Illusion of 'Choice and Control': The Difficulties for People with Complex and Challenging Support Needs to Obtain Adequate Supports Under the NDIS. Office of the Public Advocate. https://www.publicadvocate.vic.gov.au/resources/research-reports/519-the-illusion-of-choice-and-control?path=.

Office of the Public Advocate. 2019. OPA Annual Report. Documents. https://www.publicadvocate.vic.gov.au/documents/638-opa-annual-report-2018-19?path=.

Perry, Elyse, Rebecca Waters, and Angus Buchanan. 2019. Experiences of National Disability Insurance Scheme Planning from the Perspective of Adults with Intellectual Disability. *Australian Journal of Social Issues* 54: 210–223. https://doi.org/10.1002/ajs4.72.

Pilnick, Alison, Jennifer Clegg, Elizabeth Murphy, and Kathryn Almack. 2010. Questioning the Answer: Questioning Style, Choice and Self-Determination in Interactions with Young People with Intellectual Disabilities. *Sociology of Health & Illness* 32: 415–436. https://doi.org/10.1111/j.1467-9566.2009.01223.x.

Productivity Commission. 2017. National Disability Insurance Scheme Costs: Productivity Commission Study Report. Commonwealth of Australia. https://www.pc.gov.au/inquiries/completed/ndis-costs#report.

Roberts, Stuart. 2019. The NDIS Plan – Speech to the National Press Club, Canberra. Ministers for the Department of Social Services. https://ministers.dss.gov.au/speeches/5266.

Rydzewska, Ewelina, Laura Hughes-McCormack, Christopher Gillberg, Angela Henderson, Cecilia MacIntyre, Julie Rintoul, and Sally-Ann Cooper. 2019. Prevalence of Sensory Impairments, Physical and Intellectual Disabilities, and Mental Health in Children and Young People with Self/Proxy-Reported Autism: Observational Study of a Whole Country Population. *Autism* 23: 1201–1209. https://doi.org/10.1177/1362361318791279.

Sandvin, J., and Soder, M. 1996. Intellectual Disabilities in the Nordic Welfare States. *Policies and Everyday Life,* ed. J. Tossebro, A. Gustavsson, & G. Dyrendhal. Oslo, Norway: Hoyskole Forlaget.

Stancliffe, Roger, Christine Bigby, Susan Balandin, and Nathan Wilson. 2015. Transition to Retirement and Participation in Inclusive Community Groups Using Active Mentoring: An Outcomes Evaluation with a Matched Comparison Group. *Journal of Intellectual Disability Research* 59: 703–718. https://doi.org/10.1111/jir.12174.

Williams, Iestynand, and Dickinson. 2016. Going It Alone or Playing to the Crowd? A Critique of Individual Budgets and the Personalisation of Health

Care in the English National Health Service. *Australian Journal of Public Administration* 75: 149–158. https://doi.org/10.1111/1467-8500.12155.

CHAPTER 15

Inclusion, Work and Wellbeing: Shifting Perceptions of Disability and Employability Through the National Disability Insurance Scheme

Sue Olney

As a signatory to the United Nations *Convention on the Rights of Persons with Disabilities,* Australia recognises the rights of people with disability to "live in the community with choices equal to others" and has pledged to "take effective and appropriate measures to facilitate full enjoyment by persons with disability of this right and their full inclusion and participation in the community" (United Nations 2006a). The case for creating the National Disability Insurance Scheme (NDIS) in 2013 was built on evidence that Australia's disability services system was not up to that task. A public inquiry into the system by the Commonwealth Government's independent economic research and advisory body in 2011 found that disability care and support was underfunded, inflexible, fragmented, and structured around the needs of service funders and providers rather than

S. Olney (✉)
University of Melbourne, Melbourne, Australia

M. Cowden and C. McCullagh (eds.), *The National Disability Insurance Scheme*, https://doi.org/10.1007/978-981-16-2244-1_15

the needs of service users (Productivity Commission 2011). The funding and organisation of services was complex, inequitable and inefficient, with gaps and overlap in state and territory and federal responsibilities, and further complicated by private funding awarded through insurance and public liability claims. Alongside those structural issues, studies revealed persistent poor quality of life for Australians with disability, with high levels of social exclusion and risk of violence, and low levels of income and labour market participation (OECD 2009; Milner et al. 2014; Mithen et al. 2015; Kmjacki et al. 2016).

The first object of the *National Disability Insurance Scheme Act* 2013 is to, "in conjunction with other laws, give effect to Australia's obligations under the Convention" (Australian Government 2013, 4). The NDIS was designed to increase both funding and access to services and support for people with permanent and significant disability, and the control that people with disability have over their lives and the design and delivery of any care and support they need. To drive home the desired paradigm shift, the new approach to funding disability services was framed not as welfare, but as a no-fault social insurance scheme underpinned by actuarial analysis, economic modelling and human rights.

The 2011 Productivity Commission report on the inquiry into Disability Care and Support posed a strong economic case for creating the NDIS, based on calculations that the benefits of the scheme would significantly outweigh its costs in the long term (Productivity Commission 2011, 2). The cost/benefit analysis included assessment of the future fiscal risks of existing arrangements for disability support—the "cost of doing nothing"—and lengthy discussion of work and employment. The Commission argued that people with disability want to work and should be encouraged to work, and estimated that boosting the employment rate of people with mild to profound disabilities would significantly increase GDP and reduce reliance on the welfare system (Productivity Commission 2011, 7, 11, 22, 60, 270, 272, 284, 941, 958–965). The public and private benefits of drawing more people with disability into the labour force were outlined in Sect. 20.5 of the inquiry report, and the proposed way forward reflected Australia's obligations under Article 27 of the *Convention on the Rights of Persons with Disabilities* related to Work and Employment (Productivity Commission 2011, 958–965; United Nations 2006b).

This chapter examines the role envisaged for the NDIS in boosting the workforce participation of people with disability in Australia and how this is playing out in practice. It explores the private and public benefits of employment for people with disability; employment trends for people with and without disability in Australia; the importance of increasing employment for NDIS participants and other people with disability, both as a right and for the scheme's financial sustainability; and internal and external challenges facing the NDIS in providing support to participants to find and keep meaningful employment. It concludes that the NDIS has a clear and important role to play in shifting perceptions of disability and employability to achieve its stated aims. What is less clear, in the wake of the COVID-19 pandemic, is how the NDIS can drive a significant increase in employment for people with disability in a landscape in which it has little control over the policy levers, resources and actors required to achieve that.

The Disability Employment Landscape in Australia

Article 27 of the *Convention on the Rights of Persons with Disabilities* calls on signatories to recognise the right of persons with disabilities to work, on an equal basis with other citizens (United Nations 2006b). It specifies that this right should be actively supported by legislation and other action to prohibit discrimination on the basis of disability in preparing for work, looking for work, recruitment, employment, remuneration, career advancement, working conditions or in starting a business. It also singles out employment in the public sector as a sample strategy for signatories to boost workforce participation and model desired behaviour. The overarching aim of the Article is to ensure that people with disability are encouraged and supported to enter the labour market and to find sustainable and meaningful employment (United Nations 2006b).

Australia's progress towards that aim is important not only on the basis of upholding the right of people with disability to work, but because doing so will build a stronger and more inclusive society and economy (NDIS 2019). The ratio of working-age people to those over 65 is projected to fall from 4.0 to 2.7 by 2060, creating an economic imperative to engage people in the labour market who have historically remained outside it (Commonwealth of Australia 2021, viii). But even without labour shortages, the benefits of making smarter use of Australia's human resources are well-documented (Department of Social Services 2015, 60). Research into employer and worker experiences reveals benefits to businesses of broadening their search for talent, building a diverse and inclusive workforce, and treating diversity and inclusion as a strategic priority and competitive advantage, to varying degrees (Graffam et al. 2002; Instinct and Reason 2014; Australian Human Rights Commission 2017; AND 2020). On a much larger scale, the economic impact of people being excluded from the labour market includes public spending on income support and flow-on pressure on other public services like health, housing and justice; the opportunity cost of that spending; the loss of those citizens' potential contribution to the economy as taxpayers, consumers and producers of goods and services; and deterioration of their talents, skills and motivation to work (OECD 1982, 1988, 2009, 2020). Compounding that, the consequences of income inequality and social exclusion adversely affect people's health and wellbeing and generate social costs that ripple across government and society (Wilkinson and Pickett 2009; OECD 2010, 2020). In 2011, economic modelling by Deloitte Access Economics suggested that closing the gap between labour market participation rates and unemployment rates for people with and without disabilities by one-third would result in a cumulative $43 billion increase in Australia's GDP over the next decade in real dollar terms (Deloitte Access Economics 2011).

There is ample and robust evidence in Australia that boosting employment for people with disability has significant private and public benefits, and that they are willing and able to work (Productivity Commission 2011; Commonwealth of Australia 2011; Deloitte Access Economics 2011; Australian Human Rights Commission 2016). Australia also has legislative and policy frameworks in place to promote and support employment for people with disability (NDIS 2019, 29). Despite this, the labour force participation rate of Australians with disability remains significantly and persistently lower than the rate for Australians without disability (ABS 2018). Internationally, Australia ranks 21 out of 29 among OECD countries on that measure (NDIS 2018, 4), although the OECD has acknowledged that data inconsistencies can skew international comparisons (ILO and OECD 2018, 2). The persistent gap within Australia, however, is indisputable.

A raft of targeted initiatives and investment intended to build better pathways to work for people with disability in Australia—underpinned by both rights-based and economic arguments—have failed to increase their labour force participation rate in a generation. Over the twenty-five years from 1993 to 2018, the rate fluctuated by just two per cent—between 55 per cent and 53 per cent—and ultimately fell from 55 per cent to

53.4 per cent overall (ABS 2003; ABS 2012a; ABS 2015; ABS 2018). This period included a National Inquiry on Employment and Disability by the Australian Human Rights Commission (2005), Australia ratifying the UN *Convention on the Rights of Persons with Disabilities* in 2008; the introduction of Disability Employment Services (DES) in 2010 with the express aim of increasing the participation of people with disability in the labour force; and radical reform of disability services and support under the *National Disability Insurance Scheme Act* in 2013 (Australian Human Rights Commission 2005; Australian Law Reform Commission 2013; Parliament of Australia 2011, 5).

What did change over that time was the environment in which people with disability were seeking work. As the composition of the labour force changed through demographic shifts, economic shifts, changes in employment conditions and the nature of work, and changes to welfare conditionality, the labour force participation rate for people *without* disabilities rose from 76.9 per cent to 84.1 per cent (ABS 2012b) (Fig. 15.1). It is important to note that tightening eligibility criteria for the Disability Support Pension and increasing the qualifying age for the Age Pension moved some people with limited capacity to work into this group over that period (AIHW 2019). Nevertheless, the gap in the participation rate for Australians with disability and Australians without disability widened from 21.9 percentage points in 1993 to 30.7 percentage points in 2018—a period when shifts towards more service-oriented and knowledge work and technological advances should theoretically have improved their relative position. As shown in Fig. 15.2, in 2018, 53.4 per cent of people with disability of working age were participating in the labour force in Australia compared with 84.1 per cent of people of working age without disability; and 47.8 per cent were employed, compared with 80.3 per cent of people without disability (ABS 2018).

The key players funded by the Commonwealth Government to boost participation of people with disability in the workforce are Disability Employment Services (DES), Australian Disability Enterprises (ADEs), the NDIS, and *jobactive*. Approximately 270,000 Australians with disability are receiving assistance to find open employment through DES, at an annual cost of $800 million to the Commonwealth Government (ANAO 2020). The outsourced DES program was reformed in 2018 after extensive consultation, and a mid-term review of the new contract conducted between May and August 2020 recommended further reforms (Department of Social Services 2021a; Department of Social

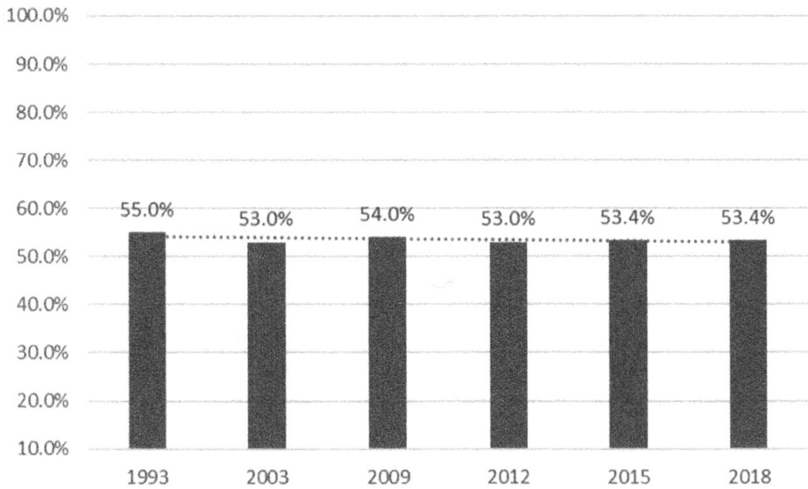

Fig. 15.1 Labour force participation of Australians with disability aged 15–64 1993–2018 (ABS 2003, 2012a, 2015, 2018)

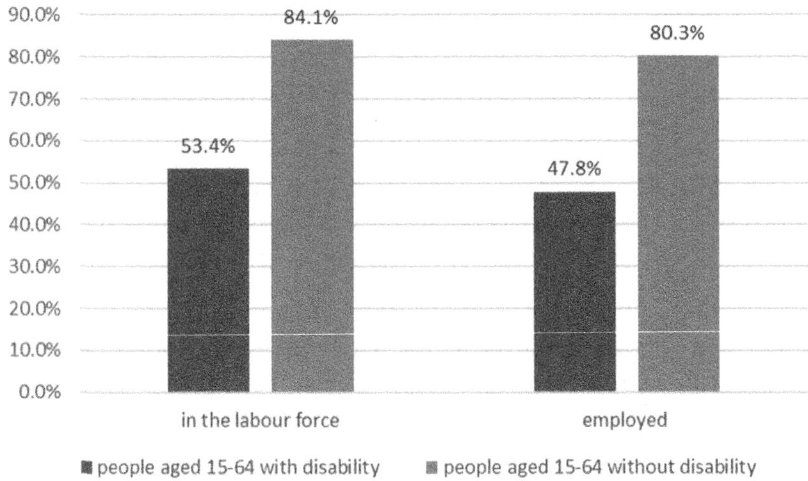

Fig. 15.2 Comparison of labour force participation and employment of Australians aged 15–64 years with and without disability in 2018 (ABS 2018)

Services 2015). There are also 20,000 people with disability employed in ADEs, which are traditionally not-for-profit organisations offering targeted employment opportunities to people with moderate to severe disability. Funding for supported employment in ADEs transitioned from the Disability Employment Assistance program in the Department of Social Services to the NDIS in 2020 (Department of Social Services 2019). Corresponding changes to the pricing model for core funded employment supports may also signal the end of the supported/open employment dichotomy, as NDIS participants can choose to use these supports in a wider range of employment settings (NDIS 2020). More broadly, the NDIS has committed to "enable 30 per cent of participants of working age to be in paid work by 30 June 2023"—150,000 people with permanent and significant disability—by streamlining and broadening pathways to employment with information and interventions (NDIS 2019, 12). Finally, there are now over a quarter of a million jobseekers with disability engaged in Australia's mainstream employment services, *jobactive* (Australian Government 2021). Alongside these key players, a range of targeted programs and initiatives funded by federal, state and territory government departments also focus on increasing employment opportunities for people with disability and other marginalised jobseekers.

Simultaneously, several key intersecting policy components are in a state of flux or review. The *National Disability Agreement* (NDA), which includes a commitment to developing employment opportunities for people with disability (Commonwealth of Australia 2009), was reviewed in 2019 and assessed as ineffective and outdated (Productivity Commission 2019, 2). However, with no response from government forthcoming more than two years after the review report was released, it is unlikely that the Productivity Commission's recommendations for a new NDA and a new overarching structure for disability policy will be implemented (Productivity Commission 2019, 8). The *National Disability Strategy*, which ensures that the needs of people with disability are considered in education and employment policy, public sector employment strategies and infrastructure, expires in 2020 and its next iteration is in development at the time of writing (Department of Social Services 2020). That process includes developing a coordinated ten-year National Disability Employment Strategy (Department of Social Services 2021b). Across jurisdictions, the *Council of Australian Governments* (COAG), which developed principles for interactions between the NDIS and education and employment services in line with the National Disability Strategy, was replaced in May 2020 by a National Federation Reform Council (Council of Australian Governments 2015; Department of the Prime Minister and Cabinet 2020). In addition, the experiences of people with disability in employment are under scrutiny in the Royal Commission into Violence, Abuse, Neglect and Exploitation of People with Disability (DRC 2020).

Structural weaknesses in pathways into and through work for people with disability have contributed to poor outcomes in the past and left Australia under-equipped to address the consequences of COVID-19 for job seekers facing labour market exclusion. As the pandemic disrupts and reshapes the job market, there is a high risk that both the labour force participation rate and the employment rate for Australians with disability will fall. On the demand side of the labour market, the pandemic has had a significant adverse impact on business confidence and recruitment (National Skills Commission 2020). On the supply side, there is fierce competition for available work. In June 2020, there were nearly one million unemployed Australians looking for work, one million underemployed and seeking additional work, and 3.5 million more on time-limited government wage subsidies who may ultimately join the queue for available jobs (ABS 2020; Australian Treasury 2020, 7). As this health and economic crisis plays out, some of these job seekers will be drawn into new industries, different types of employment and new ways of participating in the economy. However, based on lessons from past recessions, it is likely that many will remain on the margins of, or outside, the labour market (Ozkan, Trzeciakiewicz and McManus 2020).

An additional emerging risk is the potential longer-term impact of COVID-19. Medical and scientific studies suggest those who survive severe cases may continue to experience physical, neurological and psychological effects of the illness and treatment for years (Scott, Kent and Timms 2020; Beauchamp et al. 2020; Hendrie 2020; Johnson and Cha 2020). Professor John Fraser, a Brisbane-based intensive care specialist leading a consortium gathering data on COVID-19 patients in 53 countries, noted in a report on ABC's *7.30* in September 2020 that with "20 and 30 million people infected, even if 5 per cent have long-term disability, that's devastating" (ABC 2020). This possibility, combined with further marginalisation of people with disability in the labour market, underpins the warning sounded in the *OECD Employment Outlook 2020: Worker Security and the COVID-19 Crisis* of the risks ahead (OECD 2020, s. 1.4.2):

> In particular, governments should prevent paid sick-leave systems from becoming a pathway into disability benefits for the long-term unemployed, as has happened in many OECD countries in the past after a recession…This is particularly important now, as some workers currently on sick leave or quarantine may not be able to return to their job, as companies may fail to remain in business when job retention schemes phase out. Connecting these workers quickly with occupational rehabilitation or employment services, as appropriate, will be critical to prevent long-term labour market exit of those among them unable to find new jobs.

In the case of people with disability, redressing labour market disadvantage in the wake of COVID-19 calls for new strategies and levers beyond established practice, on both the supply side and the demand side of the labour market. On the supply side of the labour market, it entails ensuring people with disability are equipped, motivated and ready to work in a range of occupations. This pool of workers may include highly skilled health and care workers who survive the virus with lasting debilitating effects. On the demand side—arguably the bigger barrier to employment for people with disability—it calls for evidence-informed policy and practice to address systemic barriers, conscious and unconscious biases, built environment disablers and competition for work affecting employment outcomes and conditions for people with disability. These aims are enshrined in relevant legislation and policy, including the current NDIS Participant Employment Strategy (NDIS 2019, 8–9), but have not gained traction. The key to success is how they are translated into action.

Disability Employment and the NDIS

As noted in the introduction to this chapter, the cost–benefit analysis that underpinned the creation of the NDIS included increasing the number of people with disability in the workforce (Productivity Commission 2011, 960–963). The Productivity Commission estimated that if Australia were to reach the average OECD relative employment rate for people with mild to profound disability, employment would rise by 100,000 people by 2050. This, in turn, would increase Australia's GDP by 0.2 percentage points or $8 billion in 2050. However, the Commission also noted that Australia could "do better than the OECD average in terms of employing people with mild to profound core activity disabilities" based on the strong growth prospects of the economy and the economy's orientation to service and knowledge work seen as suited to people with disability (Productivity Commission 2011, 961). With hindsight, it was a bold call. Nevertheless, it remains that increasing the number of people with disability in employment is fundamental to the financial sustainability of the NDIS, and progress on that front—especially for participants—has been disappointing (Productivity Commission 2017, 138–148; NDIS 2018). In June 2018, the percentage of active NDIS plans with a work-related goal for was 44 per cent for participants aged 15–24 and just 26 per cent for participants aged 25 or over (NDIS 2018, 18). In the same period, there was a 3 per cent increase in the percentage of 15–24-year-old participants who reported that they were in paid work between entry to the scheme and review approximately one year later—from 15 per cent to 18 per cent—but a one per cent drop in the percentage of participants aged 25 and over in paid work—from 25 per cent to 24 per cent (NDIS 2018, 23). History suggests employment could plummet in the fallout of the COVID-19 pandemic, posing significant risks to the scheme.

The NDIS has pledged to have 30 per cent of participants of working age in meaningful employment by 30 June 2023 (NDIS 2019, 12). In June 2019, 24 per cent were in paid work, and 31 per cent had a work-related goal in their NDIS plan (NDIS 2019, 7). As explained elsewhere in this book, the NDIS is administered by the National Disability Insurance Agency (NDIA). The *NDIS Participant Employment Strategy* sets out the NDIA's vision, commitment and action plan to achieve that ambitious goal through five key areas of focus (NDIS 2019, 12):

1. Increasing participant aspiration and employment goals in NDIS plans;
2. Increasing participant choice and control over pathways to employment;
3. Increasing market innovations that improve the path to paid work
4. Improving confidence of employers to employ NDIS participants;
5. Leading by example as an employer.

These are all important steps to shift the dial on disability employment, although not ground-breaking. A fundamental—and welcome—element of the strategy is improving the way the NDIS works with key players and programs that contribute to improving employment outcomes for people with disability in Australia, including participants, government, business, the community sector and other stakeholders (NDIS 2019, 29). While the intent of the NDIS to work with others has always been clearly stated, it has proved difficult to operationalise to date in a policy environment of diffused accountability, competing priorities, service gaps, inconsistent criteria and blurred lines of responsibility across jurisdictions and institutional boundaries (Tune 2019). The strategy acknowledges that challenge, but is light on details of how it will be addressed in practice. The commitment to "enable NDIS participants to achieve their employment goals, by raising the aspiration of NDIS participants, their families and carers, increasing choice of providers and improving the way NDIS works with other systems" is helpful, but increasing employment outcomes in a recession will be a significant challenge (NDIS 2019, 12). There are lingering questions about how the NDIS and DES will work together to help participants prepare for, find and keep a job, for example. Issues already identified in that interface include inconsistent definitions of disability; inconsistent eligibility criteria; inconsistent approaches to collecting and reporting data; inconsistent performance measures; limited knowledge among front-line workers in each service of the respective roles, responsibilities and available resources of each program to support participants in seeking and maintaining work, and limited understanding of the roles and responsibilities of the NDIS and DES in relation to the growing number of government and non-government initiatives aimed at improving employment outcomes for people with disability and other groups of marginalised job seekers across government, industry and the community sector (Devine et al. 2020). These types of issues—jurisdictional ambiguities, information asymmetry, resource asymmetry, problem framing, competing priorities and cost shifting—are common in services working across philosophical and administrative boundaries (Olney and Dickinson 2019; Alford and O'Flynn 2012; Dickinson and Sullivan 2014; Carey et al. 2018; Olney and Gallett 2018).

Research suggests there is no 'one size fits all' approach to increasing the labour force participation rate of people with disability. While most job seekers with disability have faced discrimination entering and navigating the job market to varying degrees—which can and should be universally addressed—they have other diverse motivations and barriers to work that call for nuanced responses. Some barriers may be directly related to their disability, such as the social and built environment in which they live and work, their access to tools and resources to get to and from work and perform work-related tasks, their access to and experiences of education in the past, the extent and duration of their disability, their capacity to work at particular times, modes of communication or chronic or episodic health issues. Some barriers they share with other groups of job seekers struggling to compete in the mainstream labour market, linked to the supply and demand for labour, their socio-economic circumstances, geographic location and the nature and conditions of work available (ABS 2018; NDIS 2019).

The *NDIS Participant Employment Strategy* highlights twelve barriers to work for people with disability that span systems, structures, processes and attitudes (NDIS 2019, 6), set out in Table 15.1. None of these barriers can be addressed by NDIS planners and participants in isolation. Interestingly, barriers flagged by the NDIS do not include the overall supply and demand for labour or competition from people

Table 15.1 Barriers to employment for people with disability flagged by the NDIS (NDIS 2019, 6) and intervention categories

Barrier to work identified by the NDIS	*Intervention category*
Lack of accessible infrastructure, such as buildings and transport	structures
Overly complex legislative and policy frameworks	systems, processes
Perceived disincentives in the income support system	systems, structures, attitudes
Government programs not working well together	systems, structures, processes, attitudes
Lack of suitable transition supports, for example, leaving school or changing jobs	systems, structures, processes, attitudes
Lack of access to high quality employment and disability support services	structures, processes
Poor customisation of jobs to match skills and abilities	processes, attitudes
Sense of isolation in workplaces	structures, attitudes
Disability support needs unable to be met at work	structures, processes, attitudes
Need for assistance from other systems, such as health	systems, structures, processes
Lower education attainment or access to inclusive education	systems, structures, processes, attitudes
Limited opportunities for supported work experience and training	structures, processes, attitudes

without disability for open employment, which arguably reinforces the marginalisation of people with disability in the labour market.

While COVID-19 presents significant challenges to the NDIS in overcoming these barriers to boost the workforce participation of people with disability, it also presents opportunities. The pandemic has disrupted traditional organisational behaviour and customer bases. It offers an opening to reset how work is organised, how productivity is measured, and business hiring and management practices. Developments in technology and remote work have the potential to level the playing field for people with disability in employment. Disability-focused employment targets in the public sector and inclusive procurement and supply chain policies remain crucial in the short term to both boost employment and model desired behaviour (Victorian Government 2018; Victorian Government 2019; Buyability 2020). The NDIS itself is leading by example as an employer. Employers base recruitment decisions on a range of factors, including capability, values, norms and organisational culture. Understanding the value of a diverse labour force, how inclusion and diversity can build creative, resilient and competitive businesses, and what will build employer confidence to tap into more diverse talent pools—underpinned by consultative, coordinated and data-driven effort on a national scale—will be critical to ensure marginalised job seekers, including people with disability, are not sidelined in the workforce of the future.

Conclusions

Widespread marginalisation of Australians with disability in the labour market will generate complex policy problems and costs on multiple fronts. The private benefits of employment for people with disability, and its public benefits in terms of reducing pressure on the welfare, health, disability, housing and justice systems, would be lost. It threatens the sustainability of the NDIS, both because the scheme's financial modelling factored in increased employment for people with disability, their families and carers, and because there may be unanticipated levels of demand for support from people unable to work in future. It presents challenges for Australia in meeting its obligations to citizens with disability as a signatory to the United Nations *Convention on the Rights of Persons with Disabilities*. It also poses a risk that the skills of front-line health and care workers who may have lingering effects from the virus will be lost. Australia stands a better chance of successfully navigating and recovering from the fallout of the COVID-19 pandemic if it harnesses the skills and potential of *all* of its human capital, with strategic investment and support where necessary.

Improving understanding of disability and shifting perceptions of disability and employability is a crucial component of how Australia should respond to COVID-19. Now is the time to focus attention on the implications of the pandemic for Australians with disability and to build necessary resources and principles of equity and human rights into plans to rebuild the economy in the wake of the pandemic. As the front line of government's interaction with people with disability, the NDIS has a critical role to play in that, but it will take concerted and coordinated effort. Key challenges for those who design and deliver disability policy will be ensuring that people with disability can access the health, rehabilitation and social services and support they need for full inclusion and participation in the community, including employment, and to rebuild their trust in government. Failing to do so will have significant, far-reaching and long-lasting social and economic costs.

References

ABC. 2020. Long-term Health Consequences of COVID-19 Becoming Clearer. 7.30, 17 September 2020. Australian Broadcasting Commission. https://www.abc.net.au/7.30/long-term-health-consequences-of-covid-19-becoming/12675810.

ABS. 2003. 4430.0 - Disability, Ageing and Carers, Australia: Summary of Findings 2003. https://www.abs.gov.au/AUSSTATS/abs@.nsf/Lookup/4430.0Main+Features12003?OpenDocument.

ABS. 2012a. 4430.0 - Disability, Ageing and Carers, Australia: Summary of Findings 2012. https://www.abs.gov.au/ausstats/abs@.nsf/Lookup/A813E50F4C45A338CA257C21000E4F36?opendocument.

ABS. 2012b. 4433.0.55.006 - Disability and Labour Force Participation. https://www.abs.gov.au/ausstats/abs@.nsf/mf/4433.0.55.006.

ABS. 2015. 4430.0 - Disability, Ageing and Carers, Australia: Summary of Findings 2015. https://www.abs.gov.au/ausstats/abs@.nsf/Lookup/4430.0main+features202015.

ABS. 2018. 4430.0 - Disability, Ageing and Carers, Australia: Summary of Findings 2018. https://www.abs.gov.au/statistics/health/disability/disability-ageing-and-carers-australia-summary-findings/latest-release.

ABS. 2020. 6202.0 - Labour Force, Australia, June 2020. https://www.abs.gov.au/statistics/labour/employment-and-unemployment/labour-force-australia/jun-2020.

AIHW. 2019. People with Disability in Australia, 3 September 2019. Australian Institute of Health and Welfare. https://www.aihw.gov.au/reports/disability/people-with-disability-in-australia/contents/summary.

Alford, John, and Janine O'Flynn. 2012. *Rethinking Public Service Delivery: Managing with External Providers*. United Kingdom: Palgrave Macmillan.

ANAO. 2020. Management of Agreements for Disability Employment Services: Department of Social Services, Auditor-General Report No. 45 2019–20 Performance Audit. Australian National Audit Office. https://www.anao.gov.au/work/performance-audit/management-contracts-disability-employment-services.

Australian Government. 2013. National Disability Insurance Scheme Act. Federal Register of Legislation. https://www.legislation.gov.au/Details/C2013A00020.

Australian Government. 2021. Labour Market Information Portal: Jobactive Caseload Data - September 2015 to March 2021. https://lmip.gov.au/default.aspx?LMIP/Downloads/EmploymentRegion.

Australian Human Rights Commission. 2005. People with Disability in the Open Workplace: Final Report of the National Inquiry into Employment and Disability. https://humanrights.gov.au/our-work/disability-rights/projects/national-inquiry-employment-and-disability.

Australian Human Rights Commission. 2016. Willing to Work: National Inquiry into Employment Discrimination Against Older Australians and Australians with Disability. AHRC. https://humanrights.gov.au/our-work/disability-rights/publications/willing-work-national-inquiry-employment-discrimination.

Australian Human Rights Commission. 2017. Missing Out: The Business Case for Customer Diversity. AHRC. https://humanrights.gov.au/our-work/rights-and-freedoms/publications/missing-out-business-case-customer-diversity-2017.

Australian Law Reform Commission. 2013. Legislative and Regulatory Framework: United Nations Convention on the Rights of Persons with Disabilities. https://www.alrc.gov.au/publication/equality-capacity-and-disability-in-commonwealth-laws-ip-44/equality-capacity-and-disability-in-commonwealth-laws/legislative-and-regulatory-framework/.

Australian Network on Disability (AND). 2020. Business Benefits of Hiring People with Disability. https://www.and.org.au/pages/business-benefits-of-hiring-people-with-a-disability.html.

Australian Treasury. 2020. The JobKeeper Payment: Three-Month Review. Australian Government. https://treasury.gov.au/sites/default/files/2020-07/jobkeeper-review-2020.pdf.

Beauchamp, Leah C., David Finkelstein, Ashley Bush, Andrew Evans, and Kevin Barnham. 2020. Parkinsonism as a Third Wave of the COVID-19 Pandemic? *Journal of Parkinson's Disease* 10: 1–11.

Buyability. 2020. National Disability Services. https://buyability.org.au/.

Carey, Gemma, Helen Dickinson, Elearnor Malbon, and Daniel Reeders. 2018. The Vexed Question of Market Stewardship in the Public Sector: Examining Equity and the Social Contract through the Australian National Disability Insurance Scheme. *Social Policy and Administration* 52: 387–407. https://doi.org/10.1111/spol.12321.

Commonwealth of Australia. 2009. Council of Australian Governments National Disability Agreement. https://www.dss.gov.au/disability-and-carers/programmes-services/government-international/national-disability-agreement.

Commonwealth of Australia. 2011. 2010–2020 National Disability Strategy: An Initiative of the Council of Australian Governments. Australian Government. https://www.dss.gov.au/sites/default/files/documents/05_2012/national_disability_strategy_2010_2020.pdf.

Commonwealth of Australia. 2021. 2021 Intergenerational Report: Australia over the next 40 years. Australian Government. https://treasury.gov.au/publication/2021-intergenerational-report.

Council of Australian Governments. 2015. Principles to Determine the Responsibilities of the NDIS and Other Service Systems. https://www.coag.gov.au/sites/default/files/communique/NDIS-Principles-to-Determine-Responsibilities-NDIS-and-Other-Service.pdf.

Deloitte Access Economics. 2011. The Economic Benefits of Increasing Employment for People with Disability: Commissioned by the Australian Network on Disability. AND. https://www.and.org.au/data/Conference/DAE_Report_8May.pdf.

Department of Social Services. 2015. A New System for Better Employment and Social Outcomes - Interim Report of the Reference Group on Welfare Reform to the Minister for Social Services. Australian Government. https://www.dss.gov.au/sites/default/files/documents/02_2015/dss001_14_final_report_access_2.pdf.

Department of Social Services. 2019. Supported Employment Under the NDIS: Industry Information and Consultation Paper November 2019. Australian Government.

Department of Social Services. 2020. Developing the New National Disability Strategy. https://www.dss.gov.au/disability-and-carers-a-new-national-disability-strategy/developing-the-new-national-disability-strategy.

Department of Social Services. 2021a. Mid-term Review of the Disability Employment Services (DES) Program. Australian Government. https://www.dss.gov.au/disability-and-carers-programs-services-disability-employ

ment-services/mid-term-review-of-the-disability-employment-services-des-program.

Department of Social Services. 2021b. National Disability Employment Strategy Consultation Paper April 2021. Australian Government.

Department of the Prime Minister and Cabinet. 2020. COAG Becomes National Cabinet. https://www.pmc.gov.au/news-centre/government/coag-becomes-national-cabinet.

Devine Alexandra, Sue Olney, Shelley Mallett, Stefanie Dimov, Georgia Katsikis, and Amber Karanikolas. 2020. Exploring the Interface of the National Disability Insurance Scheme and Disability Employment Services: The Influence on Employment Outcomes for Australians with Disability. Melbourne Disability Institute / Brotherhood of St Laurence, University of Melbourne. https://disability.unimelb.edu.au/__data/assets/pdf_file/0004/3490267/NDIS-DES-Research-Report-3-September-2020.pdf.

Dickinson, Helen, and Helen Sullivan. 2014. Towards A General Theory Of Collaborative Performance. *Public Administration* 92: 161–177. https://doi.org/10.1111/padm.12048.

DRC. 2020. Royal Commission into Violence, Abuse, Neglect and Exploitation of People with Disability Issues Paper: Employment. https://disability.royalcommission.gov.au/publications/employment.

Graffam, Joseph, Alison Shinkfield, Kaye Smith, and Udo Polzin. 2002. Employer Benefits and Costs of Employing a Person with a Disability. *Journal of Vocational Rehabilitation* 17: 251–263.

Hendrie, Doug. 2020. GPs and Hospitals to Tackle 'Long COVID' Together. *News GP.* September 14. https://www1.racgp.org.au/newsgp/clinical/gps-and-hospitals-to-tackle-long-covid-together.

International Labour Organization (ILO) and Organization for Economic Co-operation and Development (OECD). 2018. Labour Market Inclusion of People with Disabilities: Paper Presented at the 1st Meeting of the G20 Employment Working Group. ILO and OECD. http://www.g20.utoronto.ca/2018/g20_paper_persons_with_disabilities_ilo_oecd.pdf.

Instinct and Reason. 2014. Heads Up Initiative: Employer of Choice Study. Beyond Blue. https://www.headsup.org.au/docs/default-source/resources/instinct_and_reason_employer_of_choice.pdf?sfvrsn=4.

Johnson, Carolyn and Ariana Eunjung Cha. 2020. The Dark Side of Ventilators: Those Hooked Up for Long Periods Face Difficult Recoveries. *Washington Post,* April 7. https://www.washingtonpost.com/health/2020/04/03/coronavirus-survivors-recovery/.

Krnjacki, Lauren, Eric Emerson, Gwynnyth Llewellyn, and Anne M. Kavanagh. 2016. Prevalence and Risk of Violence Against People With and Without Disabilities: Findings from an Australian Population-Based Study. *Australian and New Zealand Journal of Public Health* 40:16–21. http://onlinelibrary.wiley.com/doi/https://doi.org/10.1111/1753-6405.12498/abstract.

Milner, A., A.D. LaMontagne, Z. Aitken, R. Bentley, and A.M. Kavanagh. 2014. Employment Status and Mental Health Among Persons With and Without a Disability: Evidence from an Australian Cohort Study. *Journal of Epidemiological Community Health* 68: 1064–1071. http://jech.bmj.com/content/68/11/1064.

Mithen, Johanna, Zoe Aitken, Anna Ziersch, and Anne M. Kavanagh. 2015. Inequalities in Social Capital and Health Between People With and Without Disabilities. *Social Science & Medicine* 126: 26–35. https://doi.org/10.1016/j.socscimed.2014.12.009.

National Skills Commission. 2020. COVID-19 Impacts on Businesses and Recruitment – Survey Results. Labour Market Information Portal. https://lmip.gov.au/default.aspx?LMIP/GainInsights/COVIDInformation/ResearchandInsights.

NDIS. 2018. Employment Outcomes, 30 June 2018. NDIS Participants, Their Families and Carers. National Disability Insurance Agency.

NDIS. 2019. NDIS Participant Employment Strategy 2019–2022. National Disability Insurance Agency. https://www.ndis.gov.au/about-us/strategies/participant-employment-strategy.

NDIS. 2020. Supported Employment. National Disability Insurance Agency. https://www.ndis.gov.au/understanding/supports-funded-ndis/supported-employment.

OECD. 1982. The Challenge of Unemployment: A Report to Labour Ministers. Organisation for Economic Co-operation and Development. https://eric.ed.gov/?q=labour+AND+market+AND+flexibility&pg=4&id=ED227338.

OECD. 1988. Employment Outlook 1988: Steps Towards an Active Society. Organisation for Economic Co-operation and Development. http://www.oecd.org/employment/emp/30%20YEARS%20%20OECD%20EMO%20final.pdf.

OECD. 2009. Sickness, Disability and Work: Keeping on Track in the Economic Downturn. Organization for Economic Co-operation and Development. http://www.oecd.org/employment/emp/42699911.pdf.

OECD. 2010. Sickness, Disability and Work: Breaking the Barriers A Synthesis of Findings across OECD Countries. Organisation for Economic Co-operation and Development. https://www.oecd.org/publications/sickness-disability-and-work-breaking-the-barriers-9789264088856-en.htm.

OECD. 2020. OECD Employment Outlook 2020: Worker Security and the COVID-19 Crisis. Organization for Economic Co-operation and Development. http://www.oecd.org/employment-outlook/.

Olney, Sue, and Helen Dickinson. 2019. Australia's New National Disability Insurance Scheme: Implications for Policy and Practice. *Policy Design and Practice* 2: 275–290. https://doi.org/10.1080/25741292.2019.1586083.

Olney, Sue, and Wilma Gallet. 2018. Markets, Mutual Obligation and Marginalisation: The Evolution of Employment Services in Australia. In *Wrong Way How Privatisation and Economic Reform Backfired*, ed. D. Cahill and P. Toner, 131–146. Melbourne: Black Inc.

Ozkan, Gulcin, Dawid Trzeciakiewicz and Richard McManus. 2020. Economic Recovery Will Come with High Levels of Unemployment: How Should Governments Respond? *The Conversation*, May 5. https://theconversation.com/economic-recovery-will-come-with-high-levels-of-unemployment-how-should-governments-respond-136742.

Parliament of Australia. 2011. Report on the Senate Inquiry into the Administration and Purchasing of Disability Employment Services in Australia. Commonwealth of Australia. https://www.aph.gov.au/Parliamentary_Business/Committees/Senate/Education_Employment_and_Workplace_Relations/Completed%20inquiries/2010-13/disabilityemployment/report/index.

Productivity Commission. 2011. Disability Care and Support Inquiry, Report no. 54. Australian Government. https://www.pc.gov.au/inquiries/completed/disability-support/report.

Productivity Commission. 2017. National Disability Insurance Scheme (NDIS) Costs Study Report. Australian Government. https://www.pc.gov.au/inquiries/completed/ndis-costs/report.

Productivity Commission. 2019. Review of the National Disability Agreement Study Report. Australian Government. https://www.pc.gov.au/inquiries/completed/disability-agreement#report.

Scott, Sophie, Lucy Kent and Penny Timms. 2020. Experts Warn Coronavirus May Cause 'Wave' of Neurological Conditions Including Parkinson's Disease. *ABC News,* September 23. https://www.abc.net.au/news/2020-09-23/covid-19-may-cause-parkinsons-disease-research-finds/12688384.

Tune, David. 2019. NDIS Review of the National Disability Insurance Scheme Act 2013: Removing Red Tape and Implementing the NDIS Participant Service Guarantee. Commonwealth of Australia.

United Nations. 2006a. Convention on the Rights of Persons with Disabilities Article 19: Living Independently and Being Included in the Community. https://www.un.org/development/desa/disabilities/convention-on-the-rights-of-persons-with-disabilities/article-19-living-independently-and-being-included-in-the-community.html.

United Nations. 2006b. Convention on the Rights of Persons with Disabilities Article 27: Work and Employment. https://www.un.org/development/desa/disabilities/convention-on-the-rights-of-persons-with-disabilities/article-27-work-and-employment.html.

Victorian Government. 2018. Getting to Work: Victorian Public Sector Disability Employment Action Plan 2018–2025. Victorian Public Sector Commission. https://vpsc.vic.gov.au/resources/disability-employment-action-plan/.

Victorian Government. 2019. Social Procurement - Victorian Government Approach. Buying for Victoria. https://www.buyingfor.vic.gov.au/social-procurement-victorian-government-approach.

Wilkinson, Richard and Kate Pickett. 2009. *The Spirit Level: Why Equal Societies Almost Always Do Better.* Allen Lane: Penguin Group.

CHAPTER 16

The Role of the Actuary in the National Disability Insurance Scheme

Ash Evans, Alan Greenfield, and Sarah Wood

Introduction—Putting the 'I' in NDIS

Actuaries advise on the financial health of insurers. They provide advice to the insurer's stakeholders and management, to help them define and quantify their financial objectives and to control financial operations to meet these objectives. At a fundamental level, actuaries provide the public financial confidence in an insurance company. In order to understand the role of the actuary in the 'insurance' of the National Disability Insurance Scheme (NDIS), this chapter discusses why the NDIS is considered insurance in the first place.

A New Approach to Funding Disability Support in Australia

In 2010, the Productivity Commission was tasked with undertaking an inquiry into a National Disability Long-term Care and Support Scheme. The Commission found:

A. Evans (✉) · A. Greenfield · S. Wood
Taylor Fry, Sydney, NSW, Australia

M. Cowden and C. McCullagh (eds.), *The National Disability Insurance Scheme*, https://doi.org/10.1007/978-981-16-2244-1_16

> Current disability support arrangements are inequitable, underfunded, fragmented, and inefficient and give people with a disability little choice. (Productivity Commission 2011, 5)
>
> Current funding for disability is subject to the vagaries of governments' budget cycles. People with disabilities have no certainty that they will get reasonable care and support over the long run. Resourcing might be good one year, but insufficient the next, with many people missing out. (Productivity Commission 2011, 3)

In response to the serious shortcomings of the existing disability support arrangements, the Productivity Commission proposed the introduction of an insurance-based approach, noting:

> Some people are uncomfortable with the word 'insurance', but the Commission's use of the word simply reflects the need to ensure that the community pools resources to provide reasonable long-term supports for people acquiring a significant disability. (Productivity Commission 2011, 12)

Indeed, the founding legislation of the NDIS, the National Disability Insurance Scheme Act (2013) codifies the objects of the Act are to be met by governments working together to implement the NDIS, and "adopting an insurance-based approach, informed by actuarial analysis, to the provision and funding of supports for people with disability" (National Disability Insurance Act 2013). This section outlines why the NDIS is considered an insurance scheme, first by explaining what is meant by insurance.

What Makes the NDIS an Insurance Scheme?

What Is Insurance?

Insurance is the business of indemnifying a person or organisation for loss or damage or the liability to compensate for loss or damage arising from specified contingencies (such as fire, injury, death or negligence) in consideration for a payment to the risk involved (Hart 2007, 3–4) In this section, we look at what makes the NDIS an 'insurance scheme'?

An Individual Focus

Insurance is a relationship between the insurer and the insured. The insurer normally considers each individual risk and all its characteristics when deciding whether to accept the risk and in determining a premium to charge. For example, an individual's age, vehicle make and model, usual parking location and kilometres driven affects their car insurance premium.

Similarly, in the NDIS the participant is funded on an individual basis. Participant's support needs are considered based on their individual characteristics during planning and funding. This 'bottom up' individual outlook contrasts with traditional government welfare 'top down' funding which typically considered services rendered rather than the individual's particular needs.

Risk Pooling

The concept of 'risk pooling' is essential to the concept of insurance. One of the earliest forms of insurance involved shipowners, who faced a high risk of losing their cargo and crew at seas. Shipowners pooled their resources, shifting the burden of risk from themselves, to moneylenders, who agreed to cancel the loan if the ship or cargo was lost at sea. Essentially, 'risk pooling' refers to the spreading of financial risks among a large number of contributors to the program. In the NDIS, the contributors are all Australians, and the risk is that they, or a family member, acquire a significant disability.

The Productivity Commission's Report into Disability Care in Support noted:

> A focus on pooled funding to meet [significant care and support needs] is consistent with the fact that risk-pooling through insurance tends to focus on higher-cost, less frequent events, like early death, serious injury and property loss. Many families and individuals have an ability to bear and finance some risks themselves, and this is often a more efficient and flexible way of addressing smaller and more common risks than formal risk pooling through insurance. (Productivity Commission 2011, 13)

Risk Measurement

The individual focus of insurance and the concept of risk pooling lead naturally to insurers needing to measure the amount of risk (or the expected cost) for each insurance contract. This provides the insurer with the ability to charge sufficient premium to meet the cost of claims for the portfolio of business. An insurer measures these expected costs by understanding the characteristics of the risks it insures to calculate the pool of funds required.

Similarly, the NDIS supports participants with different characteristics. The NDIA considers the characteristics of these participants—for example, support needs, disability, age—when estimating the funding pool required to cover the cost of supports.

Peace of Mind

Insurance itself is somewhat of a strange product—the preferred outcome for all parties is that no tangible service is delivered in exchange for the premium paid to the insurer. However, in adverse circumstances, insurance intends to alleviate loss suffered by policyholders. For most policyholders, the intangible service provided by insurance is peace of mind. When describing who the new scheme was for, the Productivity Commission outlined the scheme was for three different groups of people, with the first category (*Tier 1: Everybody*) covering:

> All Australians, since it would provide insurance against the costs of support in the event that they, or a family member, acquire a significant disability. Insurance is valuable even if someone makes no claim. (Many people, for example, insure their houses against loss. Most never make a claim, nor do they expect to, but they willingly pay premiums each year to cover the risk.) The likelihood of someone acquiring a significant disability in any given year is low, but much higher than in many other areas where people want insurance. (Productivity Commission 2011, 10)

The other two tiers are:

- *Tier 2: People with, or affected by, disability* (now referred to as Information, Linkages and Capacity Building by the NDIA) which is used to provide information, link and refer people with disability to available supports, build capacity at the community and individual level, build awareness and provide support for local area coordination. Tier 2 acts as a risk management 'buffer' to limit boundary creep across entry into Tier 3 of the scheme, and also to allow participants to transition out of Tier 3 after early intervention or improvement in functional ability.

- *Tier 3: Access to funded individualised supports*, for the much smaller group of people with significant care and support needs.

Obligation to Pay Legitimate Claims

Insurance is a contract between the insurer and the policyholder: in exchange for a policyholder's premium, the insurer is contractually obliged to pay legitimate claims. Insurers must assess:

- What constitutes a legitimate claim?
- What is required to redress the loss?

What constitutes a legitimate claim is specified in the insurance contract. For a lot of private insurance, this is outlined in detail in the product disclosure statement. What constitutes a legitimate claim needs to be well defined to avoid ambiguity during adverse events. Despite well-drafted policy statements, policy exclusions such as hazards, perils, circumstances or property not covered by the policy can be controversial (e.g. exclusions for flooding for home insurance during the Queensland floods in 2011) (The Australian Government the Treasury 2011). Insurers analyse and refine product disclosure statements: too loose and the insurer may not have collected enough money to satisfy its obligations; too tight and people will not buy insurance or the insurer will not meet the claimant's expectations.

For the NDIS, the equivalent to a product disclosure statement is the definition of eligibility. Under the National Disability Insurance Scheme Act (2013), if a person meets eligibility criteria (discussed later in this chapter), the NDIA must provide support. This presents significant financial risk, especially if the incidence of disability is greater than predicted. The number of eligible Australians was one of the greatest early uncertainties in the roll out of the NDIS. The Productivity Commission's Report in Disability Care and Support estimated 411,000 participants of the NDIS (Productivity Commission 2011, 194). For some types of disability the early estimates have proven accurate. Predictions were easier where significant numbers of participants were already receiving specialist disability services. For other disabilities, such as autism, the prevalence of eligible Australians was underestimated in the lead up to the NDIS (Productivity Commission 2017, 17). In the future, the NDIS may tighten or expand its eligibility criteria, as community expectations of support to Australians with disability change. Small changes in the scope of eligibility can have significant financial ramifications, especially as the scheme in most cases funds support for life.

What is required to redress the loss? Insurance covers loss or damages. It is intended to redress disadvantage caused by an event. The financial, or in-kind, award necessary to redress the loss depends on the specific insurance. For example, for most property insurances there is either an agreed maximum sum insured or a return to the state prior to the insurable event. For personal injury, benefits for economic losses, medical costs and pain and suffering are usually determined through statute or common law.

The NDIS's goal is to redress disadvantage in broadly the same way insurance redresses loss. The amount of funding for an eligible participant is based on what is deemed 'reasonable and necessary' to achieve this goal. The terminology of 'reasonable and necessary' was taken directly from accident compensation insurance.[1] What constitutes reasonable and necessary for any individual's given circumstance is complicated, and is discussed further in this chapter. Similarly, to the eligibility criteria, the amount of funding provided to individual participants poses a significant financial risk to the scheme. Small changes in the amount of support provided to participants can have significant financial ramifications given the large number of participants and the lifetime nature of supports.

Taking a Long-Term View

There are two main reasons insurers take a long-term view:

- They must have adequate funds on hand to cover the cost of claims as they arise.

[1] See, for example, paragraph 6 (1) of the Motor Accident (Lifetime Care and Support) Act 2006 No 16.

- While some insurance lines of business (known as 'short tailed') have claims that are known and can be settled quickly, some lines (known as 'long tailed') have claims that may take years or even decades to become known and ultimately paid.

Long tailed claims, such as those arising from significant injuries at work that need long periods of rehabilitation, require insurers to take a long-term view of claims. This has shifted insurers' focus from a purely financial perspective to one with a greater focus on well-being, especially where reducing claim cost often goes hand-in-hand with improving wellbeing outcomes. For example, investing upfront in relatively costly supports like intensive rehabilitation and home modifications can improve a claimant's wellbeing and make good economic sense since more rapid recovery and better long-term outcomes typically leads to reduced expenses over the claimant's lifetime. Australian workers compensation insurance schemes regularly invest in rehabilitation and treatment upfront to improve return to work outcomes for the worker and claim cost simultaneously (Safe Work Australia 2019).

The design of the NDIS is underpinned by such a long-term view when it comes to decisions about financial management and participant outcomes—perhaps even more so. The scheme's eligibility criteria mean that the majority of participants are likely to have lifetime needs. Investment in the participant's wellbeing through physical modifications and capacity building can satisfy the NDIS's social goals and improve ultimate financial outcomes concurrently.

Prudential Governance and Risk Management

Insurance companies are subject to prudential regulation by government to ensure the financial safety and stability of institutions and the broader financial system. In Australia, the Australian Prudential Regulation Authority (APRA) imposes risk management and governance requirements on insurers, and on their boards, that go beyond regulatory requirements typically required of most other types of companies. This is because they make financial promises to their customers which the community expects will be honoured.

The NDIS Board has also adopted APRA's Prudential Standard for Risk Management which applies to banks and insurers.

What Role Do Actuaries Play in Insurance?

The Risky Business of Insurance

Broadly, the actuary's role is to provide advice to shareholders, potential shareholders and management, to help them define and quantify their corporate financial objectives and to control the company's financial operations to meet these objectives.

Insurance by definition is an uncertain business: insurers cannot know in advance the cost of the claims they will have to pay in the year ahead, let alone further into the future. Instead, they make estimates of short and longer-term future costs, using predictions informed by analysis of past experience, emerging trends in the market and upcoming changes that affect insurance. As outlined above, regardless of the number and size of legitimate claims that emerge, insurers have an obligation to satisfy all of these claims—even if the cost far exceeds their anticipated budget, or the revenue they've collected in premiums falls short. In order to manage their finances, insurers must balance offering competitive premium rates while still generating enough revenue to cover future costs, including higher-than-expected costs. Maintaining this balance is not simple—as a result, insurers carry a high degree of financial risk.

The community has a vested interest in this being well managed, so that insurance companies remain solvent and claims, large and small, can be paid when they occur. This ensures insured individuals are not devastated by random events, such as being severely injured in a motor vehicle accident or losing their house in a fire.

The Role of the Actuary

The actuary has an important role to play in maintaining an insurer's financial sustainability by supporting management to make well-informed, evidence-based financial and operational decisions. To ensure the financial viability of an insurance company the actuary's core role is in:

- Valuing outstanding claims—the actuary determines provisions necessary so the insurer understands the level of funds it needs to have a high probability of being able to meet its obligations to pay claims.

- Managing solvency—the actuary reports on the risks facing the insurer and provides advice to management on capital requirements necessary for the insurer to continue operating unimpeded.
- Premium setting—the actuary analyses experience, patterns and costs to predict the cost of future claims and calculate appropriate premiums for an insurance product.

The responsibilities of the actuary also include operational risk management, strategy and outcomes measurement.

The Role of the NDIS Scheme Actuary

As summarised above, the NDIS is based on insurance principles and shares many characteristics with insurance. As in insurance, the actuary has a key role to play in the financial management of the scheme. The Scheme Actuary's role is to help the NDIA Board make sound, evidence-based decisions to manage the ongoing financial sustainability of the scheme. Specifically, the Scheme Actuary is responsible for advising on the NDIS process:

- Ensuring that decisions about whether applicants meet the NDIS access criteria are made efficiently, consistently and correctly;
- Monitoring, assessing and reporting on consistency and correctness of those decisions;
- Ensuring that decisions about participants' needs, participants' plans and statements of participants' supports are made efficiently, consistently and appropriately;
- Monitoring, assessing and reporting on consistency of resource allocation across regions, planners, disability type and other groupings as appropriate;
- Monitoring, assessing and reporting on consistency in cost and participant outcomes across different providers of support;
- Evaluating and reporting on NDIS outcomes and performance, including against key performance indicators;
- Ongoing research into continuous improvement and best practice;
- The NDIS risk management framework (National Disability Insurance Scheme Act 2013).

This includes making annual cost estimates to assess the scheme's ability to deliver reasonable and necessary supports within the available funding envelope, and to advise the NDIA Board accordingly. The National Disability Insurance Scheme Act 2013 legislates the specific duties of the Scheme Actuary. These are to produce:

- An annual financial sustainability report;
- Quarterly estimates of future expenditure.

The Scheme Actuary is also required to provide information and advice to the NDIA Board on request and report concerns to the Board. The next section outlines how the scheme Actuary considers financial sustainability in the NDIS.

Financial Sustainability in the NDIS

Financial Sustainability in a Traditional Insurance Context Compared with the NDIS

In an insurance context, financial sustainability means an insurer's ability to remain solvent and pay claims as they arise. Insurers are required to have a minimum level of solvency (i.e. for assets to be greater than liabilities, by an amount known as a solvency margin). Essentially, insurers must receive enough income in the form of premium revenue to pay the claims. As some claims are paid over the longer term, there needs to be sufficient funds set aside to pay them in the future. An insurer sets aside money to pay for claims that have not yet been finalised. In actuarial parlance, this is known as 'reserving'.

While the NDIA borrows on insurance principles, the NDIA does not consider financial sustainability exactly as a traditional insurer would. The primary reason is that the NDIS is not required to maintain an asset base to pay support packages for all current participants for all their future needs. If the NDIS did have sufficient assets on hand to pay out all future support costs for all current participants this would be termed a fully-funded scheme. One of the major reasons that the NDIS was not set up in this way is that it would have come at a prohibitively large upfront cost to the taxpayer to set aside funds for the future lifetime support of all people who already had a disability. When recommending the establishment of the NDIS, the Productivity Commission commented on the feasibility of a fully-funded scheme:

> The NDIS will provide supports to hundreds of thousands of people, many of whom receive inadequate resources. A fully-funded scheme would meet the remaining long-term liabilities of these people. In the Commission's proposed design, that would be small for those people approaching the pension age. But for many, such as a five-year-old with cerebral palsy, fully-funding of long-term liabilities would be very high. Given its costs, a fully-funded scheme would only be tenable for new entrants to a scheme — the approach taken in the NSW Lifetime Care and Support Scheme. It would take decades to cover a significant share of people with disability. (Productivity Commission 2011, 672)

Indeed, retrospectively fully funding the NDIS on establishment would have required a prohibitively large upfront contribution of hundreds of billions of dollars. Instead, the NDIS runs as a 'pay as you go' scheme, where the annual contributions from government are intended to meet just this year's expenditure. However, while the NDIS is sometimes described as an 'uncapped scheme', an ultimate cap does exist. This is the willingness of the Australian taxpayer to fund it. This willingness will depend on taxpayers' perception of value for money in terms of:

- People with disability experiencing better lives because of the scheme;
- The scheme making it easier for families and carers to play a supporting role;
- The way the scheme invests in people with disability;
- The confidence taxpayers have that the NDIS will be available to cover their care needs (or those of their loved ones) should disability be acquired in the future;
- The supports that are funded (and the evidence base to support what is funded);
- Efficiency gains and cost savings in the disability support system and other government services.

Cost overruns could lead to pressure to reduce the scope or certainty of care and supports provided, or require governments to provide more funding at the expense of other programs (Productivity Commission 2017, 83).

This means insurance principles for managing financial sustainability are still highly relevant. Forecasts of the long-term costs of the NDIS, which reflect the experience and management response to cost pressures, play an important role in:

- Demonstrating to the Australian public the NDIS represents value for money. (Productivity Commission 2017, 83);
- Providing the Government with cost forecasts so it can plan accordingly.

How Is Financial Sustainability Measured?

The NDIA defines a financially sustainable scheme as a situation where:

- Contributing stakeholders consider the Scheme to represent value for money both now and into the future;
- The Scheme is delivered within agreed funding (National Disability Insurance Agency 2019a, 36).

In practice, this means the Scheme Actuary must be able to forecast and monitor:

- The annual cost of delivering the NDIS;
- The long-term cost of providing reasonable and necessary supports to participants to achieve the required outcomes.

The Scheme Actuary's non-financial roles are discussed later.

The Role of Reference Packages in Financial Sustainability

What are reference packages? The NDIS funds 'reasonable and necessary supports' that help a participant reach their goals, objectives and aspirations, and to undertake activities to enable the participant's social and economic participation. Reasonable and necessary supports are funded by the NDIS in a range of domains, which may include education, employment, social participation, independence and living arrangements. The extent of support coverage directly impacts the costs and benefits of the NDIS—too little will result in lost benefits within the scheme, but too much could create cost pressures and pose a risk to the financial sustainability of the Scheme (Productivity Commission 2017, 24).

The processes and decisions around how much these individual packages of 'reasonable and necessary supports' cost represents the single most important financial risk management tool the scheme has. This is because the application and administration of the rules of the NDIS involve a number of subjective judgements around the level of reasonable and necessary support in any individual case. Without consistent and reasonably objective formulae for determining the amount of support to be provided for any given participant, the level of financial risk associated with individual support package decisions is high. Prior to the start of the NDIS, reference packages were developed to support the planning process. These reference packages are typical or benchmark packages of support based on the age, disability type and level of function of a participant. The aim of the reference packages is to improve the consistency in planners' decisions and therefore reduce the variability in package costs for participants with similar conditions and levels of function.

Participants are allocated a 'reference package', based on their reference group (how this is calculated is discussed below). For each participant, the level of funding is adjusted according to the participant's circumstances. This is done using a questionnaire, which asks the participant about each of the domains, including what supports they already have in place, and whether these are sufficient and sustainable (Productivity Commission 2017, 26).

Estimating these reference packages is a key role of the Scheme Actuary, and is an important tool for providing equitable resource allocation at an individual and subgroup level. Reference packages are intended to play an important role in controlling the cost pressures that have emerged, including:

- Levels of committed support tend to increase as participants move to their second and third plans (over and above the impacts of inflation and ageing);
- Greater than expected variability in package costs for participants with similar conditions and levels of functions, suggesting inconsistencies in planners' decisions (Productivity Commission 2017, 18).

How are reference packages estimated? Reference packages are the expected annual amount of funding for people with similar support needs and characteristics. The Scheme Actuary calculates reference packages by dividing the participant population into homogenous subgroups (known as reference groups) where each person in a subgroup is expected to have a similar 'a priori' (theoretical rather than based on observation of experience) plan cost. The subgroups need to be large enough to have statistical credibility.

The Scheme Actuary estimates reference packages for each reference group based on:

- Age;
- Disability type;
- Severity of disability, as determined by level of functional support needs and diagnostic classification.

The Scheme Actuary measures the level of function using a range of widely accepted and validated tools. Expert groups are convened for each of the main disability types, to provide input into possible indicators, and appropriate amounts of support for each level within the severity indicator. Data is obtained on the distribution of the severity indicators across the relevant disability (i.e. the number of people at each level within the indicator). Recognising the limitations in assessment tools, the effectiveness of the chosen tool is assessed and updated where required. The assessment tool outputs are mapped to a normalised scale across all disability types. This whole process is repeated periodically to continue refining and updating the reference groups and packages.

How Are Future Costs Estimated?

A significant component in the assessment of the financial sustainability of the NDIS is an estimate of the future cost over the near and long term, carried out by the Scheme Actuary. This involves:

- Estimating the future number of participants by cohort (this requires projections of new entrant rates and rates of exits by death and ineligibility);
- Estimating the average payments per plan by participant cohort;
- Estimating the operating costs of the scheme.

The future projections of the scheme's costs provide information for:

- Scheme management to both target and benchmark actual scheme performance;
- Government on ongoing funding requirements.

The assessment of sustainability also includes commentary on the NDIA risk management framework, scheme outcomes, scenario analysis and risks to scheme sustainability.

There are three main criteria for NDIS eligibility:

- Age requirements—the person needs to be under 65 to be accepted into the scheme;
- Residency requirements—the person is required to reside in Australia, and be either an Australian citizen, the holder of a permanent visa, or a special category visa holder who is a protected SCV holder;
- Disability criteria—a person meets the disability requirements if:
  - They have disability that is attributable to one or more intellectual, cognitive, neurological, sensory or physical impairments or to one or more impairments attributable to a psychiatric condition, and
  - The impairment or impairments are, or are likely to be, permanent, and
  - The impairment or impairments result in substantially reduced functional capacity to undertake, or psychosocial function in undertaking, one or more of the following activities: communication, social interaction, learning, mobility, self-care and self-management
  - The impairment or impairments affect the person's capacity for social or economic participation and
  - The person is likely to require support under the NDIS for the person's lifetime.

There are modified criteria to meet early intervention support. The role of early intervention support in managing the financial sustainability of the NDIS is discussed later in the chapter.

These eligibility criteria are effectively the criteria for making assumptions about likely participant numbers, both now and in the future. When initial projections about participant numbers were made in order to project the likely cost of the NDIS, there was no longitudinal database including information on individuals functional support needs, health conditions and use of formal and informal support. Initial NDIS participant numbers were estimated mostly using a combination of the Australian Bureau of Statistics Survey of Disability, Ageing and Caring (SDAC), Australian Institute of Health and Welfare Burden of Disease Study 2003 and existing Australian Government modelling on the number of people with significant and enduring psychiatric disability. Initial estimates suggested about 411,000 (Productivity Commission 2011) or 2.2 per cent of the population under the age of 65 years would qualify. The scheme was progressively rolled out to different states and has grown rapidly. It is projected to continue to grow rapidly and by 30 June 2023, reach about 500,000 participants. By 30 June 2023, it is expected that participant intakes will mainly represent new incidence of disability (National Insurance Disability Agency 2019b, 71).

As the NDIS matures, the Scheme Actuary is able to use actual scheme experience to date as the basis for projecting the number of scheme participants. The relevant information is contained within a person-centred longitudinal database of all NDIS participants. The Scheme Actuary uses this longitudinal database to examine trends in numbers of people with approved NDIS plans receiving support. By comparing the actual numbers with original forecasts and by understanding the differences in speed of enrolment across various regions (some having started earlier than others), the Scheme Actuary is able to continually update the forecasts for the numbers of people supported by the NDIS. Estimating average plan costs involves making projections of payments for supports using actual NDIS experience to date as the basis for assumptions about the future. The plan utilisation rate (i.e. the proportion of annual plan funding that is actually spent by the participant each year) is also analysed.

The Scheme Actuary uses the longitudinal database to analyse and summarise annual plan expenditure. The detail in the database allows the analysis to be carried out for groups of participants at a very granular level. This includes factors such as region and remoteness, disability type, functional needs, age, gender, culturally and linguistically diverse status, and Aboriginal and Torres Strait Islander status. The database also includes the history of participant plans—including key dates (date eligibility determined, dates of plan review) and individual funding payments for supports. The Scheme Actuary uses this data to analyse and forecast the amount of funding utilised by participants with various characteristics.

The Scheme Actuary estimates the projected funding requirements for future periods by combining the projections of numbers of participants, and plan payments for relatively small groupings of participants (e.g. by age, gender, disability type, functional needs and region).

Alongside scheme support costs discussed above, the Scheme Actuary is also required to understand and forecast the scheme's two other major cost categories:

- Agency operating costs—this includes costs such as rent, staff salaries and corporate overheads. Forecasting these costs uses detailed accounting data and trends in operations (particularly trends in participant numbers).
- Community inclusion and capacity development grant costs—this includes the activities that will be supported by the NDIS to promote the social and economic inclusion of people with disability, including people not receiving individualised funded support from the NDIS. The activities include providing information and making linkages and referrals to community or mainstream services, building the capacity of people with disability and their families and carers, building community capacity, building mainstream service provider capacity, and Local Area Coordination. Forecasts of such costs rely on expected expansion of grant payments to meet the Information, Linkages and Capacity Building's Investment Strategy.

Outcomes Measurement

In traditional insurance, a focus on claimant outcomes is typically more associated with 'long tail' insurance products, such as workers compensation or compulsory third-party insurance for those injured in a motor vehicle accident. For 'short tail' insurance (e.g., domestic home contents, or motor vehicle property damage), it typically makes sense for insurers to focus on efficiency and speed of claim settlement in financial terms. 'Long tail' insurance has increasingly focused on claimant outcomes, injury management and psychosocial and vocational rehabilitation. There is a direct financial incentive to do so; by minimising the time these injuries take to recover, the cost to the insurer is reduced.

The NDIS takes a similar view that addressing broader outcomes can also have positive financial benefits for the scheme:

> Monitoring changes in participants' economic and social participation is an important financial sustainability indicator. Better outcomes for people with disability maximise their opportunities for independence as well as reducing their long-term costs of disability support. (National Insurance Disability Agency 2019b, 70)

As discussed above, the ultimate test of the financial sustainability of the scheme is that the Australian public see the value delivered by the scheme. Therefore, in addition to the cost of the scheme, the Scheme Actuary must also measure, monitor and report on participant outcomes. There is a potential tension between financial management and participant outcomes management, particularly when it comes to determining whether supports are 'reasonable or necessary'. The NDIA notes this tension is less likely to emerge where the participant experience is well managed and leads to mutually agreeable outcomes (National Insurance Disability Agency 2016, 12).

Measurement of outcomes in the NDIS encompasses a wide range of areas, from participants' progress towards achievement of their own individual goals, to the broader economic and societal benefits that are expected to emerge from the scheme in the longer term. The NDIS outcomes framework collects information on how participants and their families and carers are progressing in different areas of their lives through questionnaires (National Disability Insurance Agency 2019c). These are used to monitor individual and scheme progress over time, to help uncover the types of support that lead to good outcomes, and to benchmark against the experience of other populations (such as people without disability and other OECD countries). Development of the framework involved a review of existing national and international frameworks, a review of available population data against which to benchmark performance, consultation with a wide range of stakeholders, including the NDIA Independent Advisory Council, and a pilot of the questionnaires. Recognising that different milestones are important for different age groups, the outcomes framework takes a lifespan approach to the measurement of outcomes. Different versions of the outcomes questionnaires are used, for both participants and families/carers, depending on the age of the participant.

The Role of Early Intervention in Financial Sustainability

Unlike traditional disability support systems, and more akin to insurers, the NDIS is required to take a forward view of sustainability. Investments in participants and their social and economic participation and independence will support the long-term sustainability of the NDIS.

In keeping with this requirement, the NDIS is required to invest in activities which will minimise the long-term cost of the scheme. This includes:

- Independence, social and economic participation and choice and control for people with disability;
- The provision of high quality and innovative supports;
- The development and enhancement of the disability sector;
- The development of community awareness of disability and the social contributors to disability;
- Undertaking research into disability, disability supports and social contributors to disability.

As noted earlier, Information, Linkages and Capacity building for the population of people with disability not currently requiring an individual support package also provides an additional risk management approach to protecting the more costly participant individual support packages.

One such early intervention approach has been the introduction of the Early Childhood Early Intervention approach. It was put in place in response to the higher than expected number of children entering the scheme during the trial phase. It targets children aged 0–6 years and aims to ensure that only those children who meet the eligibility criteria become participants of the NDIS. Under the Early Childhood Education Intervention approach, families meet with an early childhood intervention service provider to discuss the needs of their child. The provider then identifies appropriate supports for the child and family, and whether the supports should be provided through the NDIS or through mainstream services (Productivity Commission 2017, 22).

The actuary's role is to assess the value of these early interventions. Typically, new initiatives are run as pilots. Actuaries can compare participants' forecast lifetime costs prior to intervention with their costs post-intervention. A successful intervention is one that both improves participants outcomes and reduces the long-term cost to the scheme.

Reporting

Central to the insurance principles of the NDIS, the Scheme Actuary is required to routinely and regularly test scheme assumptions against emerging experience. It does this quarterly, by reporting to the NDIA Board on:

- Estimates of future expenditure of the NDIS;
- Comparisons of the experience of the NDIS with the projections in the previous annual financial sustainability report or more recent projections, and commenting on any changes in the projections.

  The quarterly monitoring report allows the Scheme Actuary and the Board to monitor the progress of scheme performance. An annual financial sustainability report is required under section 180B of the NDIS Act and provides an assessment of the financial sustainability of the NDIS. A summarised version of this report is included in the NDIA's Annual Report.

Current Risks to the Financial Sustainability of the NDIS

Early identification, monitoring and commentary on risks to scheme financial sustainability is part of the role of the Scheme Actuary. In the annual financial sustainability report, the Scheme Actuary is required to identify the key risks and issues impacting on the financial sustainability of the NDIS, and where the risks have an adverse impact on financial sustainability, the Scheme Actuary is responsible for providing recommendations designed to manage the risks or address the issues. In 2017, a Productivity Commission study into NDIS costs noted scheme costs had been similar to initial estimates, due to several offsetting factors including, higher than expected levels of committed supports, low utilisation of committed supports, slower than expected transition of participants into the scheme and more children than expected entering the scheme (Productivity Commission 2017, 87 and 119). The Scheme Actuary has also reported on several pressures which require management responses (National Insurance Disability Agency 2019b, 71):

- Operational challenges: As the NDIS is in its relative infancy, there have been some operational challenges related to ensuring a timely transition of people with disability into the scheme. These have included eligibility reassessment, recovery of compensation amounts, and the timely provision of assistive technology supports. There have been reports of inconsistency of decision-making for access decisions and plan budget levels.
- Scheme coverage 'scope creep': There are pressures on the NDIS relating to entry, and decisions around what constitutes 'reasonable and necessary' supports. Regarding entry, the original Productivity Commission estimates did not include funding people with a support need solely related to chronic health conditions. The Scheme Actuary has identified management action is required so the scheme does not become a 'funder of last resort', especially when existing funding arrangements (be that mainstream services, community or informal support) may be better suited to providing the required supports.
- Participant cost pressures: The Scheme Actuary notes plan budgets and support payments (e.g. supported living payments) have continued to grow by more than would be expected solely due to normal inflation and ageing.

A Move Towards a Data-Driven Disability Sector

In the early days of the scheme, stakeholders commented on the huge opportunity afforded by the rich dataset that would be created. The Australian Institute of Health and Welfare commented:

> The establishment of the NDIS brings with it the opportunity to capture more comprehensive data, as well as opportunities to enhance data access in line with the Australian Government's public data agenda. Indeed, for the first time in Australia, data on scheme participants will enable a joined-up view of their disability support needs, the services provided in response to those needs, and the social and economic outcomes of those services. (Productivity Commission 2017, 473)

Now, several years in, the Scheme Actuary has been able to use this data to play an important role in disseminating data on the NDIS. This gives the public a picture of the needs, successes and challenges for Australians who live with disability, those who support them and those who work within the sector. To date this has included 'deep dives' on topics of interest, such as outcomes for participants with Autism Spectrum Disorder and people with psychosocial disability in the NDIS.

Over time, the longitudinal dataset will of course continue to become richer and richer, as the number of participants grows, and the longitudinal history of participants extends. This will give the Scheme Actuary even greater opportunity to comment on which aspects of the scheme add to or detract from its financial sustainability.

References

Australian Government. 2013. National Disability Insurance Act 2013. Federal Register of Legislation. https://www.legislation.gov.au/Details/C2018C00276.

Hart, David. 2007. *The actuarial practice of general insurance*, 7th ed. Sydney: The Institute of Actuaries of Australia.

National Disability Insurance Agency. 2016. Version 5, Insurance Principles and Financial Sustainability Manual. Canberra: Commonwealth of Australia. https://www.ndis.gov.au/about-us/publications.

National Disability Insurance Agency. 2019a. 2019–23 Corporate Plan. Canberra: Commonwealth of Australia. https://www.ndis.gov.au/about-us/publications/corporate-plan.

National Disability Insurance Agency. 2019b. Annual Report 2018–19. Canberra: Commonwealth of Australia. https://www.ndis.gov.au/news/3816-2018-2019-ndia-annual-report-now-available.

National Disability Insurance Agency. 2019c. NDIS Participant Outcomes 30 June 2018. Canberra: Commonwealth of Australia.

Productivity Commission. 2011. Disability Care and Support, Report no. 54. Canberra: Commonwealth of Australia. https://www.pc.gov.au/inquiries/completed/disability-support/report.

Productivity Commission. 2017. National Disability Insurance Scheme (NDIS) Costs, Study Report. Canberra: Commonwealth of Australia. https://www.pc.gov.au/inquiries/completed/ndis-costs#report.

Safe work Australia. 2019. National Return to Work Strategy 2020–2030. Canberra: Commonwealth of Australia. https://www.safeworkaustralia.gov.au/doc/national-return-work-strategy-2020-2030.

The Australian Government the Treasury. 2011. National Disaster Insurance Review: Inquiry into flood Insurance and Related Matters. Canberra: Commonwealth of Australia. https://treasury.gov.au/sites/default/files/2019-03/p2011-ndir-fr-NDIR_final.pdf.

CHAPTER 17

The National Disability Insurance Scheme and the Not-for-Profit Sector

Penny Knight

Introduction

Not-for-profit organisations are an essential part of community service delivery in Australia. Prior to the introduction of the NDIS, they were contracted by Australian State and Territory Governments to deliver disability services, mainly through large block funded contracts. Although this funding model presented little choice for people with disability, it did provide the not-for-profit sector with certain amount of stability. The introduction of the National Disability Insurance Scheme (NDIS) shifted the funding model from block funding to individualised services. This represents a significant change for the sector.

This chapter provides an overview of the not-for-profit organisations in Australia, their role in delivering disability services and the disruption that the introduction of the NDIS has created. It examines four key assumptions that help explain what has gone wrong for the relationship between the not-for-profit sector and the NDIS: the market assumption; the inefficiency and low-quality assumption; the assumption that human needs can

P. Knight (✉)
BaxterLawley, Nedlands, WA, Australia

M. Cowden and C. McCullagh (eds.), *The National Disability Insurance Scheme*, https://doi.org/10.1007/978-981-16-2244-1_17

be defined as a package of transactions that can be administered from a central agency; and the assumption that the NDIS is or can be the whole system.

Not-for-Profits in Australia

Not-for-profit organisations play a huge role in our lives and in our economy but receive little recognition (Knight and Gilchrist 2014). Australian Not-for-profits (NFPs) support improvements in maternal and infant health, so you were born healthier than previous generations (e.g. Telethon Kids Institute 2020). As a child you probably attended community playgroup or kindergarten and more than a third of us attended NFP schools (ABS 2019). If you went to a university it was probably a NFP and if you play a sport with a club or are involved in the arts, most likely these are also NFP organisations. Your health and your car could be insured by NFP providers and your superannuation could be with an industry super fund. Most trade or professional bodies are NFPs (ABS 2013). NFP organisations run half of all aged care services and the majority of palliative care in Australia (ACFA 2020). NFP organisations support us from birth to death and it is hard to imagine our lives without them.

It is estimated that there are approximately 600,000 NFPs in Australia, of which about 70,000 are charities (Knight and Gilchrist 2014). Most of these organisations are very small, but others are household names, such as The Red Cross, Vinnies, AustralianSuper, Health Insurance Fund of Australia (HIF) and the Sanitarium Health Food Company.

On the surface, the larger and more commercial NFPs can appear identical to a For- profit organisation, but they are unique in important ways. The primary purpose of For- profit businesses is to make a profit for investors. In contrast, NFP organisations are established to achieve a specified purpose and any profit generated must be retained by the entity and directed to pursing its purpose (ATO 2020).

Both For-profit and NFP organisations own resources, such as buildings, vehicles and brand names and both have staff, management and boards, but NFPs do not have shareholders. Instead, the NFP is 'owned' by the members who have control over the direction of the entity, but are precluded under its constitution from receiving financial benefit either while the entity is operating or in the event that it is wound up

(ATO 2017b).[1,2] NFP organisations can have a number of different legal structures, but most are either an Incorporated Association (incorporated under their State/Territory legislation) or a Company Limited by Guarantee (incorporated under the Corporations Act (Cth), 2001).

Because NFP organisations do not exist to achieve a profit and cannot distribute any profit they generate, they do not pay income tax and are considered by the Australian Taxation Office (ATO) as tax exempt. They are also exempt from some other forms of State/Territory taxes and fees and these vary a little across the jurisdictions (ATO 2017a).

Charities are a sub-category of NFPs. That is, all charities are NFPs, but not all NFPs are charities (ATO 2017b). For example, sports club or health insurance companies can be NFPs but generally they cannot be registered charities. In Australia, for an organisation to have charity status it must be both a Not-for-profit and it must also work exclusively for specified public benefits, which is defined by the Charities Act 2013 (Cth).

Prior to the introduction of the NDIS, nearly all organisations providing disability services were charities (Gilchrist and Knight, Results: Disability Markets Survey 2016). This is relevant in understanding the historic costs of supply of services as these service providers are not just tax exempt, they can apply to the ATO to have Deductible Gift Recipient (DGR) status and for exemption from paying Fringe Benefits Tax. Being a DGR helps to attract donations and exemption from Fringe Benefits Tax enables them to offer employees 'salary packaging' thereby reducing overall staff costs (ATO 2017a). Although most organisations providing disability services are charities, for this discussion, the term NFP is used as it includes a slightly broader group of organisations.

[1] This can be confusing as NFP organisations must also pay salaries for staff and in some cases directors for the services they perform on behalf of the NFP, otherwise they could not function. However, financial remuneration must be in keeping with market levels.

[2] The law relating to NFPs and Charities and their taxation is complex and these paragraphs provide a simplified overview. Readers interested in these topics should not rely on this information and seek further information.

Why Do NFPs Exist?

The reasons NFP organisations emerge and grow in our communities have been well discussed and debated in literature.[3] Simply put, For-profit organisations tend to emerge where there is demand, consumers have money and are willing to buy goods or services to fulfil these demands, and commercial organisations can profit from offering these. However, there are many products and services that people need but that cannot be supplied economically on a user pays basis, that consumers will not pay for at market prices, or for which there is no commercial supply. Governments raise taxes to provide many of these services, such as defence, transport, social infrastructure, utilities, public hospitals, education and human services such as aged care, housing and disability services. When there is community demand that is not supplied by either a commercial entity or government, NFP organisations can emerge to fill the need.

Prior to the introduction of the NDIS, the majority of non-government providers of disability services in Australia were NFPs established to meet the otherwise unmet needs of people living with disability (Productivity Commission 2011). Thenumber and range of providers of disability services also grew in response to shifts in government policy. Under various Acts and regulations, the responsibility for providing and funding disability services rested with the States and Territories and for most of the twentieth century the sub-national governments were also the main provider of services. However, from the 1970s and 1980s, State and Territory Governments began actively exiting direct service provision and instead contracting out the supply of disability services to non-government providers, almost exclusively to NFP organisations (Productivity Commission 2011).

The pace and extent of this change varied across the jurisdictions. Governments retained overall responsibility and controlled budgets, access and quality (Productivity Commission 2011). Inresponse, NFP providers grew in size and complexity, but they also became highly dependent on government funding and policy. NFP organisations are separate, independent legal entities with their own governance structures, but when they receive over 95 per cent of their funding from government, often a single government agency, in practice they can become de facto controlled

[3] For example, see (Ben-ner and Van Hoomissen 1991) and (Powell and Bromley 2020).

by government, while retaining the risks and responsivities of being a non-government body (Gilchrist and Knight, Australia's Disability Services Sector 2019b). It would be fair to say that the quality of the relationships between NFP providers and their respective State and Territory Governments varied. In some jurisdictions, governments actively and regularly sought input from the sector in regard to disability services policy and service delivery. In others, relationships were more arm's length (Gilchrist and Knight, Results: Disability Markets Survey 2016).

The 'Before' Story

As other contributors have noted, prior to the NDIS, many people with disability received minimal or no support from either governments or Not-for-profit organisations and were (and many still are) almost entirely self-supported or supported by their family and community.

For those that did seek support, just prior to the introduction of the NDIS, many were receiving services from one or more NFP organisation under contract with their State or Territory government.

The Australian Institute for Health and Welfare (AIHW) collects and publishes the Disability Services National Minimum Data Set which records services provided under the National Disability Agreement. In the Productivity Commission's report of 2011 which gave rise to the NDIS, the AIHW (2012) was quoted as reported the following.

- In total, 314,252 people in Australia received specialist disability supports in the 12-month period.
- Expenditure on disability services was $6.2bn, of which $5.8bn was allocated for service delivery and the remainder spent on administration and capital grants. The amount spent by service type was as follows:
    - 45.1 per cent Accommodation support (100 per cent funded by States/Territories);
    - 15.5 per cent Community support (95 per cent funded by States/Territories);
    - 10.8 per cent Community access (99.6 per cent funded by States/Territories);
    - 6.0 per cent Respite (98 per cent funded by States/Territories);

- 11.0 per cent Employment (100 per cent funded fully by Commonwealth Government);
- 1.0 per cent Advocacy, information, communication o 3.0 per cent Other supports;
- 7.6 per cent Administration;
- 0.2 per cent Capital grants.

- In total, 2,283 agencies provided services from 13,883 'outlets'. (An agency can have many outlets.) Of the agencies, 82 per cent (1,872) were non-government organisations and of these 1,610 or 86 per cent were charities. Others were NFPs and there were some For-profit providers, most of which were very small.
- Approximately 27 per cent of service users accessed services from two or more providers.

In addition to the services captured in this data, the Productivity Commission noted people with disability also received services through other government programs, such as the Commonwealth Government funded Home and Community Care Program and often these services were provided by NFP organisations.

This brief amount of data illustrates the size, maturity and complexity of the disability services industry prior to the introduction of the NDIS. It also highlights the limited knowledge and experience of the Commonwealth Government in the sector, particularly in regard to the complexity of provision and costs of services.

At this time, National Disability Services, Australia's peak industry body for disability services providers had approximately 2,000 organisation members across Australia, nearly all of which were NFP organisations (Gilchrist and Knight, Results: Disability Markets Survey 2016).

These NFP providers consisted of specialist organisations that only provided services to people with disability as well as those that provide other services, such as aged care, child protection or mental health. In the metropolitan areas, it is often the larger organisations that provide a wider range of human services. In regional and remote areas, it was not unusual to find quite small organisations serving a diverse client base (Gilchrist and Knight, Disability Services Market Report 2018a).

Where Were the For-Profit Providers?

When seeking supply of disability services, State and Territory Governments almost exclusively contracted with NFP rather than For-profit organisations. It is unclear whether this was an explicit policy at the outset, a preference that emerged over time, or the result of pricing and terms being insufficient to attract For-profits (Gilchrist and Knight, Results: Disability Markets Survey 2016). However, by the time the NDIS was introduced, many State/Territory Governments had developed explicit policies that either excluded For-profits from bidding or was strongly biased towards NFP providers (Butcher and Gilchrist 2017). In addition, by 2010 the terms of many human services funding agreements also contained provisions not generally found in other government contracts. For example, providers could not include depreciation in the costing of services, were limited on the amount of funds that could be attributed to overheads and if they made a 'surplus', they had to return the surplus to government. Further, the State/Territory Auditors General had powers to inspect the books of service providers. Even if permitted to bid for work, these conditions and the low (or no) returns on investment were very unattractive for most For-profit providers (Butcher and Gilchrist 2017).

Despite the apparent size and diversity of the sector, by 2010 many NFP organisations were receiving 90 per cent or more of their disability services funds from the State/Territory governments on contracts as short as three years, in some cases for only one year. At an individual level, the only choices available to providers were to stop the provision of services or agree to these terms. In effect, the State/Territory Governments had monopolistic power and had used this to limit resources available to the sector. This is often described by academics and industry commentators as the 'starvation cycle' (Goggins Gregory and Howard 2009). In each jurisdiction, NDS (the peak body for service providers) lobbied hard for a more mature approach to service design and funding, but the results varied. Furthermore, NDS was itself partially funded by governments (National Disability Services 2020a).

How Good Were the NFP Providers?

Across Australia the provision of funding for disability services was subject to economic and political forces that often bore no relationship to the needs of people with disability or the rising cost of service provision (Productivity Commission 2011).Providers were subject to ever-growing demand for services, along with steadily rising salary and other costs, but funding usually grew at a slower pace. Short contracts meant they could not offer permanent positions to employees. They often described themselves as 'living hand to mouth' and had little funds available for investment in efficiency improvement, IT, staff training or improvement in facilities. NFPs raised whatever resources they could from the public and became adept at overt and covert lobbying of government agencies and ministers. They also became adept at using every dollar well (Gilchrist and Knight, Results: Disability Markets Survey 2016). The quality and efficiency of services varied across jurisdiction and from provider to provider, but most were as good as they could be (Productivity Commission 2011).

Disability Services Funding: The Old Way and the NDIS Way

Before the introduction of the NDIS, funding of NFPs to provide disability services was based on a 'block funding model'. Under this model, governments contracted and paid providers directly (usually via quarterly payments in advance) to deliver a specified amount of service—often measured in units (e.g. hours, bed nights, equipment). The provider would then work with eligible people with disability and their families as required and specified by the contract (Productivity Commission 2011).

Prior to the introduction of the NDIS, disability services varied across jurisdictions and in many cases, there were major problems with access to and quality of services. The Productivity Commission described the provision of disability services as "underfunded, unfair, fragmented, and inefficient, and gives people with disability little choice and no certainty of access to appropriate supports" (Productivity Commission 2011).

Of the stakeholders, NFP service providers had had a front-row seat to the problems with service provision and funding and when the proposal to implement the NDIS was announced it received their overwhelming support. NFP organisations exist to serve, not to make a profit, and the NDIS was a promise of being able to do this significantly better and for more people with disability. People with disability, disability advocates, State and Territory Governments, both sides of federal politics and the broader community were also united in their support of the NDIS and recent research has found that this support remains strong, despite the implementation challenges (National Disability Services 2020b).

As other authors have described, one of the key selling points of the NDIS is that it would work on market principles. People with disability (called participants) would receive an allocation of funding themselves and be able to 'shop around' and chose what they wanted and who they wanted to provide it. For the mostly NFP providers, the NDIS would free them from the constraints of block funding, from term contracts and from having to provide services according to uniform scripts defined by governments. Further, their income would no longer be constrained; they would have the opportunity to pay staff reasonable wages and the potential to create a profit that they could invest in efficiency improvements and innovation.

So What's the Problem?

More than seven years into the NDIS roll out and many problems have emerged. Some are 'teething' problems associated with transition into the scheme, but others are structural problems that will place critical limits on the capacity of the NDIS to deliver on its promise (National Disability Services 2020a; Tune 2019).

To date, the focus of the roll out has been on registering and allocating funding packages to as many eligible participants as quickly as possible and the amount of funding flowing into the sector has grown substantially in a very short period. Many people now have access to disability support for the first time and some existing service users are receiving more support. However, others who were promised that they would get at least the same level of support as they had under the old system found themselves with less. Of those receiving funding, many are not spending all the funds they are allocated and the NDIS is running significantly under budget. In some cases, participants cannot spend their funding as there are no suppliers for the services they want. Other participants are 'saving them for later' or find it difficult to pace their consumption (Productivity Commission 2017).

Scope creep is also affecting roll out. It was initially estimated that about 420,000 people would be eligible for NDIS and total funding would be approximately $14bn when fully rolled-out (Productivity Commission 2011). Current estimates are that at least 475,000 people will be eligible (an increase of 13 per cent) and the total costs will be more approximately $22bn or 1.1 per cent of GDP (Productivity Commission 2017). There are on-going disputes about the eligibility of those with mental illness and other disabilities. One of the most significant areas of scope creep concerns children with autism. In response to the significant increase in availability of funding and support, the number of children diagnosed with autism has increased rapidly resulting in the need for the NDIA to restate and try to enforce the definition of disability intended under the NDIS act (Tune 2019). There are previous examples of the impact of policy changes on rates of diagnosis and therefore these pressures on the scheme were predictable.

The supply side has also experienced major problems. For the scheme to deliver on its promise, there must be a strong, capable and efficient portfolio of suppliers willing and able to provide service at the prices offered. The nearly 2,000 experienced NFP providers with existing resources and relationships with participants were clearly the best positioned to meet this demand. However, these organisations have been underfunded for decades and many have insufficient resources to invest in transition (Gilchrist and Knight, Disability Services Market Report 2018a).

Furthermore, the prices the NDIA is allowing providers to charge for some services are low, often at or below break-even. While they have promised that prices will eventually reflect the true cost of service, there is little appeal for existing providers to invest heavily to transition to the NDIS only to find that the provision of services that may not be financially sustainable (Gilchrist and Knight, Australia's Disability Services Sector 2019b). The NDIA has focused on enrolling participants in the scheme as quickly as possible, resulting in significant growth in the demand for services. However, suppliers report that they are not keeping up with demand and many do not intend to do so. At this stage sector leaders are being asked to introduce large scale, fundamental changes to their organisations in situations of uncertain policies and pricing, tough general economic conditions, staff shortages and with no guarantee that things will get better. The outcome is a lack of supply and competition (Gilchrist and Knight, Australia's Disability Sector 2018: Report 3 Financial Performance Summary of Key Findings 2019a).

Importantly, although the NDIA has been consulting with the sector, its tone towards suppliers, particularly existing NFP suppliers, has often been dismissive and in some cases, condescending and disrespectful. While the NDIS is in theory based on market principles, in practice, the NDIA is the new monopsonistic buyer and when this buyer is not listening, this creates fear and uncertainty (Gilchrist and Knight, Disability Services Market Report 2018a).

Where Did It Go Wrong?

The NDIS is working for some participants and some providers, but there are four key assumptions that underpin the design of the NDIS that will limit its capacity to achieve the promises made or do so in way that is cost efficient and financially sustainable. Identifying and understanding these are key to improving the effectiveness of the NDIS.

1. The market assumption.

The NDIS policy is explicitly built on market principles. That is, the intention is to create a demand for disability services will result in an efficient market for supply, similar to those existing for other consumer services. Proponents of the NDIS have stated that once participants have choice and control and there are no constraints oversupply, then this market will be self-correcting as the forces of negotiation between the buyer and seller about attributes of the service and the price, create market efficiency (National Disability Insurance Agency 2020a).

However, the NDIS is not a real market and can never be one. Unlike normal markets, the price and many of the attributes of disability services funded by NDIS are not determined through negotiation between buyers and sellers, but instead are decided centrally by the NDIA in advance of the transaction (National Disability Insurance Agency 2020b).

The NDIA would like to believe that this is an interim problem, but in reality, there is no practical alternative to the NDIA controlling the market. The NDIS does not give everyone unlimited choice and control nor unlimited funds to pay for what they want. Before they can begin a conversation about reasonable and necessary support, the NDIA must make assumptions and decisions about the quantity, quality and price of the services at a specific time and place. Even simple decisions about how services are unitised for sale and purchase (e.g. deciding if service time is measured in hours or half hours, or travel is measured in miles or minutes) control the way buyers and sellers interact. If, over time, some of these basic factors can be determined, the NDIA can never accurately determine true market price for each transaction, which is one of the most critical market variables. For example, to accurately determine the amount of funding required to get a participant to work in Frankston, Victoria, the NDIA needs to know the usual cost of taxi services for that journey and travel costs by alternative means, such as public transport or even the cost of a private driver who might also be able to provide other services. The actual costs on any given day can even be determined by the traffic or the weather and the total cost might be impacted if the participant is off sick or on leave. For funding fulltime, in-home care, the NDIA needs to know the cost per hour every hour of the week, weekends and public holidays of suitably qualified carers of the preferred gender, and possibly age or cultural background, in that location.

In reality, the NDIA determines the price and package of funding based on its best estimates of the average cost of production or market prices for the average service. In some cases, it can adjust prices and package allocation in response to indirect indicators of market response, such as provider or participant feedback (National Disability Insurance Agency 2020a). It then applies these nationally, whether or not they represent consumer choice or are realistic in all situations. Some allowances are made for the additional costs of unique services and costs in regional and remote services, but by any measure, the determination of prices and funding package is not being negotiated between the user and sell of the service. Instead, it is a very blunt-edged tool defined by administrators in the NDIA head office and updated once or twice per year. The NDIA is the new monopolistic buyer and price setter. Participants and providers are price takers, with very little market power.

As such, the NDIA manages both demand (i.e. participant access) and costs, and it must keep downward pressure on both, potentially to the point where some participants are not receiving services. The other alternative is for the NDIA to pay above efficient market prices to ensure supply, which would encourage supply-side inefficiency or create large profits for providers and waste taxpayer's funds. Neither of these are how efficient markets work. Furthermore, unlike normal markets, many buyers and sellers do not have the option of delaying or choosing not to supply or take services. Vulnerable people and/or those with critical needs must have certainty of supply and we cannot leave people without nursing care or meals and wait for the market to respond (Gilchrist et al., Six Years and

Counting: The NDIS and the Australian Disability Services System—A White Paper 2019).

The other variable critical to the existence of an efficient market is the capacity to exercise choice over quality. In real markets consumers and suppliers trade-off quality and price across a wide spectrum of quality or prices (consider the range of quality available and prices paid for clothing, hotels and housing). However, under the NDIS the minimum quality of service will be specified by the standards and the maximum quality of service will be determined by the price, which is capped (NDIS Quality and Safeguards Commission 2020). There is no incentive for a provider to offer services above the specified minimum quality level. The NDIA says participants can choose the services that offer the best value for money, but in practice there be little to no alternatives to choose from. Instead, the quality will be determined by the supplier based on their business model and choices.

Finally, there is also little to no flexibility for either the buyer or seller to make decisions about packaging and service design. In real markets, suppliers constantly adapt not just what they provide, but how it is packaged, priced and delivered. For example, airlines, banks, supermarkets and mobile phone providers frequently change how and what they offer us, using such things as discounting, loss leaders, multibuy discounts, customer loyalty discounts as incentives. Providers and users of disability services have very limited flexibility in product offerings (National Disability Insurance Agency 2020a).

The only real choice within the control of the participant is to substitute one service or service provider for another. That is, they can choose transport over in-home support or employment services over community engagement, and they can decide who provides these services, but no more. For service providers, the only real choice they have is whether to supply a service or not at the quality and volume level specified (Gilchrist and Knight, Disability Services Market Report 2018a).

What does this mean for the long run success of the NDIS? The NDIA has been examining the risk and impact of 'thin markets' which will address some issues but not the basic problem that exists in this quasi-market (Cary et al. 2020). They have also been investing in the collection and analysis of market intelligence to enable better service specification and pricing (Gilchrist et al., Green Paper 1: Data Assets, Efficiency and the NDIS 2020). While digital technology has made huge strides, realistically, this will only ever produce estimates of the costs of services and these could be out of date before being published. It is simply not possible for single, central body to accurately determine prices for hundreds of potential services across the breath of Australia. The result is that some services are well overpriced and others well under-priced, which creates a different form of market distortion (Gilchrist and Knight, Disability Services Market Report 2018a).

Many participants have quickly recognised that the degree of choice and control they were promised in this free market is not really available. For those with previous experience 'in the system', disappointment is not new, and any additional choice is an improvement. Participants that know how to 'work the new system' will get better funding and better services (Tune 2019). However, those with little experience or skills in self-advocacy or those who have simply not got the time or support will be vulnerable to exploitation and under-supply. Even where they are able to voice concern, in the absence of alternatives, participants may have no option but to accept a poor service or risk going without service altogether.

Existing and potential service providers have also had to adjust to the reality that they have little choice or control, and this has dampened confidence and impacted investment. They have also realised that the market has not replaced their need to advocate for proper funding and good service design. Indeed, lobbying has become harder for most. Previously they could approach local elected officials and State or Territory government agencies; now they have to deal with the much larger, more distant Commonwealth Government agency (Gilchrist and Knight, Disability Services Market Report 2018a).

Despite the fact that they must now sell into a highly controlled quasi-market, providers are still operating in real markets when it comes to buying resources for production. They have to compete in real markets and with other sectors to attract staff and deal with rising compliance obligations and continual cost increases, particularly in workforce, property, insurance, marketing and information technology (Gilchrist and Knight, Australia's Disability Services Sector 2019b).

Real market forces are also evident in the number of exits, mergers and closures of disability services by existing providers in recent years and these are likely to continue for the next three to five years as the supply side adjust to the realities of operating in a NDIS world (Gilchrist and Knight, Findings from Investigation of Mergers of Disability Services Providers 2018b).

Finally, providers must meet continuously increasing community expectations of the standards of care provided. In an environment where prices are low and quantity is controlled, there will be continual downward pressure on quality. Minimum quality standards and inspections of providers will reduce the overall risk to participants but increase the costs and risks for providers. Boards and CEOs will need to constantly juggle quality and cost within a very small range and there is a high potential for services to fall below standard. Mission-driven NFP organisations will increasingly be called on to make very difficult choices between turning clients away, providing services that they feel fall below their own standards or running services at a loss (Gilchrist et al., Six Years and Counting: The NDIS and the Australian Disability Services System—A White Paper 2019).

The idea of choice and control in a free market is hugely appealing to all stakeholders, which is perhaps why this assumption is so enduring. But in reality, the NDIS will never operate that way and trying to make it fit the ideology is not helpful. Instead, if we accept and work with the quasi-markets we have, we will be in a much stronger position to design effective policy that will attract and support an efficient supply of services (Gilchrist et al., Six Years and Counting: The NDIS and the Australian Disability Services System—A White Paper 2019).

2. The NFP Inefficiency and Low-Quality Assumption

Unlike the market assumption, the NFP inefficiency and low-quality assumption is not explicit in NDIS policy, but is instead evident in the language and actions of the NDIA and other key stakeholders.

In 2010, prior to the publication of their report giving rise to the NDIS, the Productivity Commission (2010) published a report on the Contribution of the Not-for-profit Sector. In this formative study, the Commission praised the contribution of NFP organisations but also stated that there are too many NFP organisations and that the sector is inefficient and, in some cases, ineffective. This opinion is not unique. In Australia and internationally and over many decades economists and others have prosecuted the view that without a profit motive, there are insufficient personal drivers to ensure that services provided by NFP organisation are provided in a cost-effective or high-quality manner. Supporters of this theory believe that For-profits will be inherently more efficient and provide better service than NFPs (Australian Charities and Not-for-profits Commission; Knight 2016).

The view that 'NFPs are inherently inefficient' and 'not very good' is strongly held across government, commerce, the public and even by those leading NFP organisations themselves. There is no evidence that supports this theory and indeed there is an opposing argument that by the nature of their drive for purpose and their ability to attract volunteers and donations, NFP organisations are in fact more efficient than For-profits (Knight 2016). Further, as NFPs do not need to distribute profits to shareholders, all value is retained in the organisation and can be leveraged for social purpose, thereby achieving a greater return on investment (Australian Charities and Not-for-profits Commission n.d.). Nonetheless, the negative perceptions of NFP organisations persist and in the absence of any supporting data can be likened to the hegemonic biases that perpetuated sexist and racist beliefs. Importantly, because these beliefs are implicit rather than explicit, they are not open to debate and the result is poor decisions and unexpected outcomes.

This assumption was applied specifically to the disability sector by the Productivity Commission in their 2011 report, which paid little attention to the existing supply side. Only 55 of the nearly 1,000 pages of report addressed the existing service provision and there was almost no discussion of the size and structure of services provided by NFPs and the contribution they make. In many ways, the existing services providers were presented as part of the problem, even blamed for the poor services for people with disability. The tone of the rhetoric was 'out with the old and in with the new' and the Productivity Commission and later NDIA policymakers were confident that when the NDIS was introduced a more efficient and better-quality suppliers would emerge and meet supply (Productivity Commission 2011).

Unfortunately, the Commission's initial calculation of the cost of the NDIS and the NDIA's pricing of supports was based on this inefficiency assumption. They assumed that for the prices offered, many For-profit providers would enter the market and not only would the cost of service fall over time, but also that the quality would increase (Productivity Commission 2011). They were wrong. We are now more than seven years into the roll out of the NDIS and prices have risen not fallen. And despite widely repeated comments that the large corporate providers, such as BUPA, Serco and Ramsey Health, would come into and dominate the market, this has not eventuated (Gilchrist and Knight, Australia's

Disability Sector 2018: Report 3 Financial Performance Summary of Key Findings 2019a). We can only assume that the major For-profit providers did their calculations and decided the returns on investment were not attractive.

Instead, thousands of sole practitioners and micro-businesses have registered as providers, most of which provide allied health services (e.g. physiotherapy), in home support and transport. These small businesses are typically providing a salary to the owner or partners and have none of the overheads of larger specialist organisations required to support those with complex needs. Many are attracted by the low barriers to entry and high prices paid under the NDIS for these services (about $200 per hour for physiotherapy) which is higher than the standard private rate (Gilchrist and Knight, Disability Services Market Report 2018a).

These small businesses are a valuable contribution to the sector, but they can only meet certain needs. At this stage, the specialised services, those in regional and remote areas or those that require capital investment such as residential accommodation, continue to be provided by the larger existing NFP operators. However, because these organisations are losing their profitable add-on services (e.g. therapy) to small For-profit businesses this places further pressure on the sustainability of their other services (Gilchrist and Knight, Disability Services Market Report 2018a).

Highlighting the weakness of the 'NFP inefficiency' assumption is not intended to suggest that NFPs should necessarily be treated differently to other sellers of disability services. There are many very high-quality, person-centred For-profit providers of health and other services that are well placed to meet market needs. However, it is clear that prior to the introduction of the NDIS there were thousands of NFP providers with billions of dollars of assets, experienced staff and a strong motivation to support people with disability. The loss of good NFP providers due to poor policy design would be a waste of resource to the sector and the Australian community (Gilchrist and Knight, Australia's Disability Sector 2018: Report 3 Financial Performance Summary of Key Findings 2019a). Further, given that NFP providers must reinvest profits into service delivery rather than pay dividends to investors, it makes sense to consider them an important and efficient contributor to supply.

3. The assumption that human needs can be defined as a package of transactions that can be administered from a central agency

Humans are complex and changeable. The intent of the NDIS was to build a system that provided each individual receiving services to create a bespoke group of supports that catered to their unique needs and that could be adjusted over time. As an insurance scheme, the NDIS was also designed to provide these supports at the best possible time to improve long-term outcomes and reduce costs.

The outcome of the scheme and the focus on markets rhetoric has instead resulted in people being defined as a set of needs that can be met through the provision of package of specified and costed transactions (Gilchrist et al., Six Years and Counting: The NDIS and the Australian Disability Services System—A White Paper 2019). These needs and packages are defined by an assessor (Local Area Coordinator) who may have little if any understanding of the person or disability and in some cases only speaks to them or a representative over the phone. As evident from the AIHW data above, the Commonwealth Government had little experience in the provision of disability services and limited experience they have in administering provision of other Human Services comes mostly from aged care, which appears similar, but differs in several key aspects.

For example, aged care services are accessed by a much larger percentage of the population but usually for a relatively short period of their life. The needs of the aged more homogeneous and many people will have experience of caring and supporting an elderly relative before they themselves need help. People receiving aged care support will interact with health and to a degree with housing services, but typically will not have much interaction with education, judicial and other services provided by the State and Territory Governments. In contrast, people living with disability represent a relatively small portion of our population, but they need and access a very broad range of services sometimes for their entire life, or at least for many decades. Their needs can encompass everything from early intervention services, schooling, tertiary educations, employment, housing, supported accommodation and health. Families with a person with disability are often profoundly impacted by their caring responsibilities. For many people with disability or carers, accessing disability services for the first time can be a difficult, confusing and highly emotional experience. Parents and siblings of a child born with disability may spend nearly their entire life caring and supporting their relative, putting great stress on the family and resulting in much higher rates of unemployment, poverty, poor health, divorce and substance abuse (Productivity Commission 2011).

The Commonwealth Government has limited capacity to work closely with the highly complex, diverse population of people with disability, their families and communities. For people living with disability who have relatively simple, stable needs and advocate for themselves, the NDIS model works. However, for others with more complex needs, intellectual or psychosocial disability or whose needs can change rapidly due to such things as illness or death of parent, the centralised transaction model will either not work and/or be very costly to run (Tune 2019).

4. The assumption that the NDIS is or can be the whole solution

In Australia, states and territories have responsibilities for health, education, training, transport, mental health, policing, judicial, corrections, housing and other services. Under the National Disability Agreement, other legislation and regulations, the states and territories are responsible for ensuring that people with disability can access these public services and are not discriminated against. Local governments have also had responsibilities for in-home support and enforcement of codes that ensure buildings are accessible (Productivity Commission 2011).

In addition, many NFP and For-profit organisations, individual volunteers and others have provided a wide range of support for people with disability. This includes everything from holding telethons to raise funds for research to the services of Make a Wish Australia and volunteer drivers.

When recommending the introduction of the NDIS, the Productivity Commission noted that while more needs to be done, there is support for people with disability that is embedded into day-to-day operations of other organisations and activities, and that the NDIS was to supplement not replace these.

However, as the NDIS is rolled out and the states/territory governments wind-down direct disability funding and support, disputes are arising about the responsibilities of sub-national governments. For example, in some cases it is not clear which agency is responsible for funding such services as education support assistants, some types of housing and even health services. The consequences can be significant. In the past, people with complex disability may have been funded by state governments for 24-hour carer support if they were admitted to hospital. Hospitals are not well equipped to serve people with complex disability and by providing support workers, patients often made faster and better recovery. This is not just better for people with disability, it reduced overall costs associated with longer hospital stays. These services are rarely included in NDIS packages and have been either removed or provided without charge by the NFP service provider or self-funded (Gilchrist, Person Centred Planning within the NDIS. Current Limitations and Prosective Opportunties 2017).

The introduction of the NDIS has also impacted donations, fundraising and volunteering. Organisations that raise funds for research and equipment are now expecting that these resources will be provided under the NDIS and shifting their focus to other areas of need (Gilchrist and Knight, Results: Disability Markets Survey 2016).

The NDIA rightly needed to present the NDIS as the big, bold solution to encourage sector support and participant engagement. However, when combined with its arm's length approach towards the providers, state/territory governments and others with decades of experience, presenting itself as the disability support expert and the NDIS as the whole solution is not just overconfident, it is also unrealistic. Importantly, it risks creating greater segregation rather than integration of people with disability. Acts, including the Disability Discrimination Acts, other discrimination laws, industrial relations, consumer and other legal requirements that compel organisations and communities to incorporate the consideration of needs of people with disability in everyday service provision must continue to be enforced. If the NDIS is seen as the whole solution, the result may be specialist services that, for example, see children with disability encouraged to attend 'special' rather than mainstream schools, and the development of disability specific housing, employment and health services. Of course, where needed, specialist supports must be provided, but the goals of people with disability will only be achieved with integration, not segregation (Productivity Commission 2019). Further, if the NDIS is presented at the whole solution, the costs will centralise, escalate and risk being unsustainable.

The Way Ahead

We all want the best possible care and support for Australian's living with disability, and there is overwhelming support from all quarters to get this right. When there is so much at stake, large amounts of funding and conflicting opinions, it is not unusual for emotions to run high. It is also to be expected that the introduction of reform of the size and complexity of the NDIS will have teething problems and we will learn from our mistakes. But what Australians with disability and the wider population will not tolerate is investing heavily and seeing on-going hardship, complaints of inequity or a system bogged down in bureaucracy and with fundamental flaws that result in a divisive approach and significant funds being diverted to running the system, rather than supporting those in need.

To deliver on the promises made to people living with disability, their families and supporters and to the Australian public, politicians, leaders of the NDIS and others need to objectively dissect and test the assumptions that underpin the NDIS. Persisting with trying to force the NDIS to fit into structures and systems that do not exist will be costly and frustrating to all stakeholders. Eventually, the real structural forces described above are likely to encourage the system to adapt to the real world anyway, but the time, resources and opportunity costs of waiting for, rather than leading these changes will be enormous and will be felt acutely by those for whom the system is supposed to be supporting.

For those of us who have been observing or involved in the day-to-day roll out of the NDIS, the following changes are self-evident.

1. Acknowledge that the NDIS and the NDIA can only ever be part of the solution. Pressure must be kept on all levels of government, and the private and NFP sectors until inclusion is second nature.

To provide equity and achieve efficiency, we must work with, not against the existing system. Our three tiers of government and federated structure has many problems, but it is the system we have, and it is not likely to be changed soon. It is better to acknowledge and work with this system rather than bypass or forget it.

The relevant Commonwealth and state/territory agencies will need to ensure their own and other government entities provide people with disability with full access to mainstream public and private sector services and provide specialist support if necessary. They will also need to fund and support advocacy organisations and those that promote awareness and inclusion of people with disability in community. This is not only necessary to ensure the costs of disability-related services are shared and managed throughout government and the community, but also to underpin the core principles of social inclusion that many disability organisations have worked so hard to achieve over the last fifty years (Productivity Commission 2019).

2. Understand the whole person, the whole family and the whole community.

Australia's disability services policy is built on the fundamental principles outlined in the Convention on the Rights of Persons with Disabilities, ratified by Australia in 2008 and the Disability Discrimination Act (United Nations 2007; Disability Discrimination Act (Cth) 1992). These include respect, equality, equality of opportunity, dignity, autonomy and participation.

However, the NDIS approach to discussing support for people with disability can lead us into 'deficit' thinking and 'fixing', rather than simply working out how we can better integrate and organise our resources to create a good life for all. While some disability services can readily be defined and supplied using the transactional approach of the NDIS, many cannot. For example, the quality of the relationship between a service recipient and a specialist support worker, employer, nurse or teacher fundamentally effects the impact and outcome achieved (Government of Victoria 2006). Similarly, how a person with disability and their family feel when they visit a local swimming pool or cinema can have a deep impact on their overall quality of life. These things cannot be codified, costed and then delivered by a service provider (Government of Western Australia 2013). To achieve the outcomes we all want, we must build policy and services that take a systems perspective, and that does not just recognise, but respects and mobilises the capacity of the family, community, social and government eco-systems in which we all live. We want people with disability to be fully integrated into our communities and their support to be an unconscious part of what we do (Inclusion Australia n.d.).

This is not news to the organisations with experience in providing complex human services, which include some of the state/territory and local government agencies and the many NFP organisations that work for the public benefit. While these organisations have not always got it right, they recognise that if they want to provide human services that genuinely impact quality of life, they must first understand and build a relationship with the person they seek to serve and engage with other organisations and individuals who can support their goals. This is particularly important when supporting people with disability as their needs are so highly diverse and changeable (Gilchrist et al., Six Years and Counting: The NDIS and the Australian Disability Services System—A White Paper 2019).

3. Structure control and accountability of the NDIS so that decisions can be made by the people with the best information

Related to the need to keep people with disability in the driving seat, we must recognise that 'big data' has its limits, and nothing will replace the power of 'little data' in the hands of the decision-makers on the ground to ensure the successful and efficient delivery of human services (Gilchrist et al., Green Paper 1: Data Assets, Efficiency and the NDIS 2020).

When a trained and caring social worker or carer has a good relationship with a client, they can sense when things are well and not well, from tiny changes in someone's activities, appearance or even tone of voice. No amount of central databases, information systems, inspections or predictive data can replace the unique information, care and decision-making capacity of someone who genuinely knows and cares about you. When that person works as part of a team of carers, that may include family and others, the quality of care is even better (Gilchrist et al., Green Paper 1: Data Assets, Efficiency and the NDIS 2020).

Big data is essential in supporting policy decisions, in detecting population change, measuring program efficiency and other decisions made by back office management, but it will never replace the importance of humans in the delivery of human services (Gilchrist et al., Green Paper 1: Data Assets, Efficiency and the NDIS 2020).

Prior to the introduction of the NDIS, Western Australia's disability services front-line workers were Local Area Coordinators (LACs) who had the primary responsibility for supporting people with disability and their families in their local area. Under the old WA system, the LACs were familiar with the whole family and were skilled in advocating for their client with local services, including schools, support providers, transport, therapists, mental health services and others. Importantly, they had a local budget and the capacity to shift some resources between their clients quickly and on an ad hoc basis when needed (Disability Services Commission 2013).

To be effective, the NDIS should really put LACs at the core of their structure as was outlined in the Productivity Commission's initial recommendations (Productivity Commission 2011).

Following the model used in WA, LAC's would be organised into local teams to provide greater opportunity to match the person with disability with someone that they feel best understands their needs and with whom they can develop a caring relationship (e.g. a young man with disability might prefer a young male LAC). Teams would also allow continuity of service when a LACs is on leave and the capacity to share knowledge and experience.

In addition to facilitating the provision of NDIS funding, the LAC would connect participants with other government and not government services and assist with advocacy when needed. As they also know the organisation or individuals providing services in their area and get regular feedback from participants, they are best placed to have daily oversight of quality of services and advise participants on best value for money. The LACs would also be allocated a pool of funds to be used in special circumstances so they can quickly and effectively respond to changes in needs. For example, should a participant need to be hospitalised or their family carer need urgent respite, the LAC could draw from locally held funds to support this. Overtime the LACs will be able to predict the times of the year additional services might be needed or types of clients most likely to need additional support. With appropriate accountability and reporting systems in place, the LAC or LAC teams can be given the autonomy to manage their own budgets, which would likely reduce not increase spending.

Again, this idea of embedding semi-autonomous teams of skilled workers into communities to provide human services is well established and there is evidence of its effectiveness (Productivity Commission 2011).

4. Value the enormous capacity of existing NFP providers to lead and support service delivery

The success of the NDIS is dependent on the availability of good quality, well-priced services that meet participants' needs. The leaders in Australia's disability services sector have decades of experience and a wealth of knowledge in providing front-line services. Across the country, they run NFP organisations that exist for the sole purpose of serving people with disability and with billions of dollars in resources. It makes sense to value and leverage these assets and ensure that they form the foundations on which the supply of Australia's future disability services are built (Gilchrist and Knight, Australia's Disability Services Sector 2019b).

The NDIA has provided many opportunities for existing disability services providers to discuss their concerns and make suggestions on how the NDIS can be better designed and implemented, but these have failed to create a culture of partnership across the sector. Many providers feel disempowered and ignored, and are worried that their organisations will not be financially sustainable because the people in the NDIA have no idea of what it is really like to run a business, let alone a disability service business. This will not change until the NDIA can fully appreciate this, stops assuming it knows better and begins to genuinely listen to providers (Gilchrist and Knight 2018c).

Conclusion

Now we have got this far, it is timely for disability services policymakers and the NDIA to stop, step back and look at the assumptions that underpin the design and implementation of the NDIS. It is important that the overwhelming support for the aims of the NDIS and the huge investment of resources is not interpreted as a sign that all will be well.

Realistically, the NDIS will never be able to provide the free choice and control that was promised and that exists in real markets. To get as close as possible will require the NDIA to devolve many of its responsibilities in leadership, decision-making and budgets to the front-line users and providers of services. The NDIA can then do what central agencies do best—set nationally consistent policy, strategic direction and overall budgets, and then monitor access, equity and compliance with minimum quality standards.

References

ABS. 2013. Australian National Accounts: Non-Profit Institutions Satellite Accounts. Cat. No. 52560, Australian Bureau of Statistics, Canberra.

ABS. 2019. Schools Australia. Australian Bureau of Statistics, Canberra.

ACFA. 2020. *Eighth Report on the Funding and Financing of the Aged Care Industry*. Aged Care Financing Authority.

ATO. 2017a. *What Tax Concessions Are Available?* Australian Taxation Office. 19 June. Accessed September 2020. https://www.ato.gov.au/Non-profit/Getting-started/What-tax-concessions-are-available.

ATO. 2017b. *What Type of NFP Is Your Organisation?* 19 June. Accessed September 2020. https://www.ato.gov.au/Non-profit/Getting-started/What-type-of-NFP-is-your-organisation.

ATO. 2020. *Not-for-Profit Organisations.* Australian Taxation Office. 4 September. Accessed September 2020. https://www.ato.gov.au/general/aboriginal-and-torres-strait-islander-people/not-for-profit-organisations.

Australian Charities and Not-for-Profits Commission. n.d. *Are There Too Many Charities in Australia?* Accessed December 2019. https://www.acnc.gov.au/for-public/understanding-charities/are-there-too-many-charities-australia.

Ben-ner, Avner, and Theresa Van Hoomissen. 1991. Nonprofit Organisations in the Mixed Economy: A Demand and Supply Analysis. *Annual of Public & Cooperative Economics* 62 (4): 519.

Butcher, John, and David Gilchrist. 2017. *The Three Sector Solution. Delivering Public Policy in Collaboration with Not-for-Profits and Business.* Edited by John Butcher and David Gilchrist. Canberra, ACT: ANU Press. Accessed September 2019. https://theconversation.com/not-for-profits-must-adapt-as-one-arm-of-governments-three-sector-solutions-72971.

Cary, Gemma, Eleanor Malbon, David Gilchrist, Satish Chand, Anne Kavanagh, and Damon Alexander. 2020. Not-for-Profits UWA NDIS and Disability Services. March. Accessed March 2020. https://www.research.uwa.edu.au/not-for-profits-uwa#ndis-disability-services.

Charities Act (Cth) 2013.

Disability Discrimination Act (Cth) 1992.

Disability Services Commission. 2013. *Local Area Coordination Supporting People with Disabilities in Their Communities.* Disability Services Commission, Perth: Government of Western Australia.

Gilchrist, David. 2017. *Person Centred Planning within the NDIS. Current Limitations and Prospective Opportunities.* Perth: The Independent Centre for Applied Not-for-Profit Research.

Gilchrist, David, and Penny Knight. 2016. *Results: Disability Markets Survey 2016.* Canberra: National Disability Services.

Gilchrist, David, and Penny Knight. 2018a. *Disability Services Market Report 2018: A Report for National Disability Services.* Canberra: National Disability Services.

Gilchrist, David, and Penny Knight. 2018b. *Research Report: Market Design and Evolution for Better Outcomes. Findings from Investigation of Mergers of Disability Services Providers.* Crawley: University of Western Australia. Accessed June 2018.

Gilchrist, David, and Penny Knight. 2018c. 2017 Joint Standing Committee on the NDIS. *Not-for-Profits UWA*. University of Western Australia. Accessed May 2020. https://www.research.uwa.edu.au/__data/assets/pdf_file/0009/3395529/2018-Joint-Standing-Committee-on-the-NDIS.pdf.

Gilchrist, David, and Penny Knight. 2019a. *Australia's Disability Sector 2018: Report 3 Financial Performance Summary of Key Findings*. Sydney: University of Western Australia and National Disability Services.

Gilchrist, David, and Penny Knight. 2019b. *Australia's Disability Services Sector 2019. The National Performance Benchmark Project Report 3: Summary of Key findings*. Canberra: National Disability Services.

Gilchrist, David, Penny Knight, Craig Edmonds, and Thomas Emery. 2020. *Green Paper 1: Data Assets, Efficiency and the NDIS*. Crawely: University of Western Australia.

Gilchrist, David, Penny Knight, Craig Edmonds, and Tom Emery. 2019. *Six Years and Counting: The NDIS and the Australian Disability Services System—A White Paper*. Crawley: University of Western Australia.

Goggins Gregory, Ann, and Don Howard. 2009. The Nonprofit Starvation Cycle. *Stanford Social Innovation Review*, 49 to 53.

Government of Victoria. 2006. Recognising and Supporting Care Relationships. A Department of Human Services Policy Framework. Department of Human Services, Melbourne.

Government of Western Australia. 2013. Count Me In. A Better Future for Everyone. Disability Services Commission, Perth.

Inclusion Australia. n.d. *About Us*. Accessed May 15, 2019. https://www.inclusionaustralia.org.au/about-us-2.

Knight, Penny. 2016. *2016 NFP Governance and Performance Report*. Sydney: Australian Institute of Company Directors.

Knight, Penny, and David Gilchrist. 2014. *Australian Charities 2013: The First Report on Charities Registered with the Australian Charities and Not-for-Profits Commission*. Melbourne: Australian Charities and Not-for-Profits Commission.

National Disability Insurance Agency. 2020a. *Market Position Statements*. 9 September. Accessed September 2020. https://www.ndis.gov.au/providers/working-provider/market-information/market-position-statements.

National Disability Insurance Agency. 2020b. *Prices Guides and Pricing*. 4 October. Accessed November 2020. https://www.ndis.gov.au/providers/price-guides-and-pricing.

National Disability Services. 2020a. *NDS Annual Report*. Canberra: National Disability Services.

National Disability Services. 2020b. State of the Disability Sector Report 2020. *nds.or.au*. Accessed October 2020. https://www.nds.org.au/images/State_of_the_Disability_Sector_Reports/SoTDS_2020.pdf.

NDIS Quality and Safeguards Commission. 2020. *Home*. July. Accessed November 2020. https://www.ndiscommission.gov.au/.
Powell, Walter W., and Patricia Bromley, . 2020. *The Nonprofit Sector: A Research Handbook, Third Edition*. Stanford University Press.
Productivity Commission. 2010. *Contribution of the Not-for-Profit Sector, Research Report*. Canberra.
Productivity Commission. 2011. *Disability Care and Support, Report no. 54*. Canberra: Commonwealth of Australia.
Productivity Commission. 2017. *National Disability Insurance Scheme (NDIS) Costs, Study Report*. Canberra.
Productivity Commission. 2019. Review of the National Disability Agreement. Study Report. Canberra.
Reeders, Daniel, Gemma Carey, Eleanor Malbon, Helen Dickinson, David Gilchrist, Gordon Duff, Satish Cand, Anne Kavanagh, and Damon Alexander. 2019. *Market Capacity Framework: An Approach for Identifying Thin Markets*. Sydney: Centre for Social Impact.
Telethon Kids Institute. 2020. Accessed September 30, 2020. https://www.telethonkids.org.au.
Tune, David. 2019. *Review of the National Disability Insurance Scheme Act 2013. Removing Red Tape and Implementing the NDIS Participant Service Guarantee*. Canberra: Department of Social Services.
United Nations. 2007. Convention on the Rights of Persons with Disabilities—Articles. March. Accessed November 2, 2019. https://www.un.org/development/desa/disabilities/convention-on-the-rights-of-persons-with-disabilities/convention-on-the-rights-of-persons-with-disabilities-2.html.

CHAPTER 18

"Who Can Tell Us We Have Got It Right?" Advocacy and the NDIS

Samantha Jenkinson

Introduction

This chapter looks at the campaign, development and ongoing implementation and improvement of the National Disability Insurance Scheme (NDIS) from the perspective of people with disability and advocates with disability. "Nothing about us without us" has been the catchcry of the disability movement in the UK, USA, and Australia since the 1960s and 1970s. How that is put in practice and what role advocacy and the peer movement play in reality are not always a given. The NDIS has the promise of a fundamental power shift in the way disability support is done, but it takes conscious work to keep the shift moving in the right direction, from those within the scheme as decision-makers, and those advocating.

On 31 July 2011, when the Productivity Commission released their Inquiry Report Disability Care and Support with the following statement as the second key point, there was a collective sigh of relief from people with disability and their families across Australia.

S. Jenkinson (✉)
Perth, WA, Australia

M. Cowden and C. McCullagh (eds.), *The National Disability Insurance Scheme*, https://doi.org/10.1007/978-981-16-2244-1_18

> The current disability support system is underfunded, unfair, fragmented, and inefficient, and gives people with a disability little choice and no certainty of access to appropriate supports. The stresses on the system are growing, with rising costs for all governments. (Productivity Commission 2011, 5)

In the weeks following the Productivity Commission's report release, the four words "underfunded, unfair, fragmented, and inefficient" were quoted in newspapers, in Parliament and in speeches. They were the same words used by the National Disability and Carer Alliance the year prior in their advocacy for a scheme. People with disability, their families and carers felt as if they had finally been heard after decades of campaigns on unmet need. Stella Young in her blog on the ABC website 'Ramp Up' said "I actually teared up with joy when I read that" (Young 2011).

What was most refreshing was that the Productivity Commission report was putting people with disability front and centre in the system design.

> The central message of this report is that a coherent and certain system for people with a disability is required — with much more and better-directed resourcing, a national approach, and **a shift in decision-making to people with a disability and their carers**. (Productivity Commission 2011, 5) (*emphasis added*)

This quote summed up the thrust of the advocacy campaign and calls for change needed that had been ongoing for decades. Knowing that the Productivity Commission had really heard what people with disability were saying was a watershed moment. We had the pre-eminent organisation that was all about economics and money agreeing with us that drastic change was needed, and we (people with disability) needed to have the choice and control to make that change. I remember meeting Patricia Scott, the head Commissioner of the feasibility study into an NDIS after providing evidence at a public hearing and feeling such relief that she 'got it'. She had heard our frustration, our anger and our need for a system that would support and raise up people with disability out of our second class citizen status.

People with disability and advocates were not saying anything new in their submissions to the Productivity Commission in terms of what needed to change. The push for individualised funding and direct payments to people with disability and their families had been building over decades with some states like Western Australia further ahead than others. Every state, though, had seen campaigns on the unmet need and none of that need was unknown to government (Ohlin 2009).

What was different this time was the coordinated groundswell nationally. The effort started in 2009 calling people to give evidence to the Productivity Commission inquiry and culminated in the Every Australian Counts Campaign through 2011 and onwards. The campaigning for the NDIS was bringing people with disability, carers and service providers together after years of division over limited resources, and in-fighting over who was speaking for who (Manne 2011). The campaign recognised that advocacy for a scheme that put people with disability at the centre needed a campaign that also put people with disability at the centre.

The Campaign

In campaigning for an NDIS, people with disability and advocates wanted:

- People with disability at the centre, with personalised approaches, choice and control of their lives and supports;
- Certainty, sustainability and sufficient funding, which had national consistency.

These two elements are reflected in the key findings from the 'Shut Out' report of 2009, which was the catalyst for the National Disability Strategy (National People with Disability Carer Council 2009).

A perfect storm of people in the right places at the right time through 2008 to 2012 brought together all the elements for major reform of disability support systems in Australia, and people with disability and their families were at the centre. Rhonda Galbally OAM as chair of the National People with Disability and Carer Council was essential in bringing the voice of people to the table through the 'Shut Out' report and bringing people with disability and carers together on the issue of the NDIS. In the same year, Bruce Bonahady, an economist and father of two sons with Cerebral Palsy, was on the Disability Investment Group along with John Walsh, an actuary and quadriplegic who later became one of the commissioners for the Productivity Commissions inquiry into disability care and support. People with disability and families were in positions of influence, and the government had politicians who could see the issue and were listening (Dodd 2016).

The disability rights movement had also gained momentum in Australia, and for people with disability and advocates, it was extremely important that the changes often talked about in principle—the involvement of people with disability in all levels of discussion and decision-making, including policy development—were put into practice. In April 2010, when the inquiry into an NDIS was just starting, Bruce Bonahady was lined up to be the keynote speaker at the Second National Disability Summit, yet another event where people with disability were playing a limited role relegated to a panel session at the end of the conference. He gave his keynote spot to me (Samantha Jenkinson), a disability advocate, to put that principle into action. As an advocate and a person with disability, I brought the day-to-day experience of people with disability to the conference and explained what reform needed to look like for people on the ground.

> When speaking with, and listening to, a range of people with disability in preparation for this presentation, I basically heard that a lot of services are pretty shitty, support workers get paid inadequate amounts, response and feedback to a person's needs is often minimal, and people with disability are scared shitless to complain because they might get even crappier service, or they are totally apathetic about complaining because 'nothing ever changes', or they simply don't have the energy or skills to complain and advocates are few and far between. So don't think just because you get no complaints that you provide a good service.... Policy is not meeting practice, partly because practice is skewed by assumptions and expectations. So we talk in policy about individual needs, but in practice, we look for the label to tell us what to do ... or the pro-forma to fill in...
>
> I am hearing that people with disability want a dedicated funding stream they know will be there for when they need it. We want our rights, the rights we have enshrined in the CRPD which Australia has signed, to become a reality in our lives. And we need cultural change – participation, control, community inclusion. - to be reflected in policy and practice and made sustainable by the continuous involvement of the huge diversity of people with disability in meaningful, deep, intent, purposeful dialogue and action. (Jenkinson 2010)

The same Disability Summit in 2010 had the Honourable Bill Shorten speaking in his role as Parliamentary Secretary of Disability and Carers. In his opening speech for the conference, he called for a united campaign for the NDIS and gave advice to the sector based on his experience as a Union campaigner (Shorten 2010). Many advocates and campaigners saw the call to arms from Bill Shorten as essential in bringing the three groups together to campaign on common ground.

People with disability and advocates knew that real involvement meant more than just someone fronting up to give a speech, but rather that there were people with disability being decision-makers in the campaign. This was part of the fundamental shift that was being asked for in the campaign. That united stance happened with the formation of the National Disability and Carer Alliance in 2009. This brought together the Australian Federation of Disability Organisations—representing people with disability; Carers Australia—representing families and carers; and National Disability Services (NDS)—representing disability service providers (Australian Federation of Disability Organisations 2019). The hurdle to forming the Alliance was getting key representatives together from a sector that had been at war.

> The sector was in complete disarray... the media was characterised by burden... you'd come out of it feeling like cutting your throat as a person with a disability because there you were, you'd ruined everyone's lives and the families were in tragedy, and so people with disabilities organisations didn't get on at all with carers' organisations, and both were united – probably quite rightly – in being highly critical of the services that hadn't changed in about the last 50 years—Rhonda Galbally OAM. (Dodd 2016)

The campaign steering committee had the CEOs of the three peak bodies of the Alliance as well as one extra representative from each sector. In 2010, the planning work included discussion on the greatest risks for the campaign and 'holding the various parts of the sector together' was considered a key risk alongside getting bipartisan political support (National Disability and Carer Alliance 2010). Disability advocates saw a big risk that a campaign driven by the service sector would be focused on ensuring sustainability and consistency of funding, but not the power shift of people with disability having real choice and control of decision-making in their lives. There was also the risk that too strong an emphasis on families and carers did not represent the diversity of disability and would present a paternalistic view that again would not bring the power shift required. The service provider sector virtually funded the entire campaign and so these risk factors were highly relevant and a key part of early discussions in shaping the campaign.

The complexity behind the interactions of people with disability, families and carers, and the service sector is still evident in the scheme now with sometimes contradictory and conflicting positions causing issues as discussed further in this chapter. The unified approach to the campaign for the NDIS was what gave it strength, and the commitment from all parties that this reform was about people with disability having the support to be included socially and economically in their communities (Deane 2020).

The NDIS was complicated, expensive to implement and had never been seen before in the world. As a member of the steering committee for the campaign, I was acutely aware of how careful a line we were treading with asking people to share their experiences. There was a risk that in our effort to tell the truth of a broken system, we would get a pity response from the community, and a heavy emphasis on the 'burden' that carers and families experienced.

People with disability, their families and carers were given the platforms and tools to be the advocates for the campaign and tell their stories. Limited resources meant it had to be a grassroots campaign to have an impact. People with disability, families and carers rose to the occasion (Deane 2020). "Every Australian Counts" became the name of the NDIS campaign to capture the feeling of a fair go for everyone with disability.

Kirsten Deane was a key part of the campaign team, whose personal experience as a family member of a child with Down syndrome brought her into the sector.

> It was people with disabilities and their families who were centre stage… and I genuinely believe the reason that the campaign was successful was that it belongs to people with disabilities and their families. It is all those thousands, hundreds of thousands of people all around the country who letterboxed their communities, and held community events, and went to rallies, and pestered their family to sign the petition, and pestered their friends to sign the petition, and shared the material. The campaign success is entirely up to them. (Deane 2020)

The Every Australian Counts champions were people with disability and families who showed how the messaging could be done. The champions were on postcards, posters and YouTube clips calling for change and action. The message was simple—that as people, we counted, and we should have the support needed to live full lives.

Every state was represented, and campaign workers were employed in the biggest states forming a national team under John Della Bosca, former NSW politician. Although the three partners in the Alliance were working together, advocates and people with disability were disappointed that none of the campaign staff were people with disability, although some, such as Kirsten, were family members. Occasionally, the underlying tension of people with disability not seeing themselves represented in the campaign team would come to the fore, for example Todd Winther on Ramp Up commenting on the Queensland Campaign Committee:

> The most disappointing thing about the whole experience was the committee members themselves. Every single member represents a service provider or advocacy group. That's right; once again there is a committee for and about people with disabilities and not one of them is independent of service providers or advocacy groups. (Winther 2011)

There were also local champions, many connected to advocacy organisations, peer and carer groups, or service providers who spoke at local events to encourage others to campaign. Between the Productivity Commission report release in July 2011 and the NDIS Act in March 2013, there was an exhilarating frenzy of activity for the campaign where people with disability were engaged to a degree not seen before. Thousands of people with disability attended rallies and events with hope for change and sent messages to politicians asking them to make the NDIS real (National Disability and Carer Alliance 2016) (Table 18.1).

Table 18.1 Claire's story

Claire Anderson. Local councillor, author, life coach and mother, Claire was one of our early Every Australian Counts supporters campaigning to make the NDIS a reality for so many Australians
Claire has FSH Muscular Dystrophy and had been using a wheelchair for ten years when she shared her story
With her condition deteriorating, her movement became more limited and she found herself unable to lift her arm to put the key in the lock of her front door
In Claire's words:
"If we had the NDIS, as a family we would have been able to plan, to put these supports in place before we get to a time where I can't get out of bed any more, and my nine year old is trying to help me up and we're in a crisis"

The Development of the NDIS

There was a lot of activity between the Productivity Commission report being released and the legislation being read into Parliament that was driven by the government. The Labour Federal government set up a select Council with expert groups on key areas of policy and invited stakeholders from across the sector to be involved in these groups. These expert groups ranged in size from eight to 14 people with representatives from the service system, people with disability, carers and policymakers, and in some areas, such as workforce, there was also union representation. At the same time the expert groups were meeting, there was further consultation being done on more of the detail that would go into the NDIS.

A media release from the Hon. Jenny Macklin MP, then Minister for Human Services and Senator Jan McLucas, Parliamentary Secretary for Disability, at the time focused on the need for people with disability their families and carers to participate in the consultations that would shape what the scheme looked like. There was a very strong recognition by the 'Every Australian Counts' campaign that people with disability needed to be heard in the consultations and on the expert groups. However, the campaign also needed to keep the bipartisan political pressure on to ensure that legislation and funding would be in place.

I was a member of the expert group on choice and control. There were 10 members in the group, three with disability, two family members, two representing service providers and a union representative, and two with disability policy and program development backgrounds. Myself and another member of the workforce expert group, Samantha Connor, felt it was important that we could reach further out to other people with disability to get their views on the types of issues we were talking about for the detail of the NDIS.

Some initial online group discussions became the NDIS Grassroots Discussion Facebook page. The page was established on 27 June 2012 and now has over 45,000 members. From the 'about' section:

> To quote Samantha Jenkinson, who started the inbox conversation that prompted this group, we need to work on "bringing the lived experience of disability to the table and being very clear about what choice and control means to those who often don't have it in their lives, and the support required".

The initial purpose of the page was to explore the ideas around how the NDIS could work in practice.

Although the concepts being explored in these expert working groups were not new to many of us, how to put those into practice in ways that would work for people with disability had only been done on a very small scale previously. Reflecting back, there are still many of the same issues that were raised in those early expert groups which have still not been properly addressed in the scheme. The very nature of planning in the scheme and the issues around the expertise of planners as well as who has ownership of the plan process and product are still not in line with people with disability being in control and being the decision-makers in their own lives at that fundamental level.

From the grassroots discussion page, there were many great ideas, discussions and examples shared, which still happens to this day. Parents shared unique accommodation and support they had set up with direct funding trials, examples of circles of support and creative problem solving. At the same time, there was this overwhelming frustration with the bureaucratic levels of government which needed to put things in a format of legislation that had to be in a certain way and had to have certain rules around what could be in and out. It felt like although we were bringing the great ideas and examples of how this scheme could be put into practice, we had to fit into a government bureaucratic framework. We had to build an evidence base, there had to be forms and processes that would need to be validated, and there had to be permissions given at different levels.

Part of what we were confronting in the 'expert groups' was that this was something new and there wasn't a big evidence base to draw from. We had the evidence of direct payment systems and individualised funding from the UK, from Western Australia, and the bits and pieces of good but small scale work that was happening all over Australia. There's never been a great amount of data about how people with disability were being supported at a qualitative level as well as a quantitative level. The Productivity Commission had done some of that research but it wasn't enough, and our lived experience narrative that we brought to the table didn't provide a robust evidence base.

The development of the reasonable and necessary criteria is a good example of how the interaction of government systems and people's lived experience played out. The expert group talked about people with disability being supported if necessary, to develop their own plans and goals, and have ownership of the funding to spend on the things that a person would need to meet their goals. When looking at the criteria of reasonable and necessary, there was a lot of discussion about whether there was a requirement for a value for money criteria. I argued that if a person was meeting all of the other criteria of reasonable and necessary, then the value is surely established without needing it to be a specific criterion. From a government perspective, there was a tension between trusting people with disability and their families to use the money as they said, and the need for accountability of public (taxpayer) monies.

The findings of the Select Council and their work with the expert groups became the foundation of the legislation. The principles in the NDIS Act are something that the advocates and campaigners are proud of, as they clearly came from people with disability and a human rights perspective. The principles put people with disability front and centre and the role of advocacy is clearly stated, with recognition of families and carers. The United Nations Convention on the rights of people with disability is there in the principles as the foundation for the NDIS.

It is because the principles in the act are so clearly in line with what people with disability want from the NDIS that keeps the hope and promise of the NDIS alive even when there are significant issues still occurring for many people.

Competing Forces

In the many ways I have been involved in the NDIS, it often feels like there are at least two or three competing forces that drive the agenda at different levels. You hear people talk over and over about choice and control but it seems to mean so many different things to different people depending on the perspective that they come from. Add to that, there is a huge diversity of disability and socio-economic status within the NDIS and it often feels that people are talking at cross purposes, particularly when trying to decide on what the best way forward will be for policy.

The framing of the NDIS in market terminology has often butted up against these ideas of expanding opportunities for a group who have been powerless in shaping the choices that they have. People with disability and family members, in many of the submissions they have made about the NDIS, talk about how difficult it is to get services and supports when they are in a crisis, and to know that those supports are going to be there if they need them. A competitive market is not going to provide a lot of choice in providers of last resort for those people and families who have not been able to get support from anywhere else because of complex circumstances and behaviour. Things like the development of complex pathways and providers of support for crisis coordination are really only becoming fully developed now, six years into the scheme.

Of course, providers need to be sustainable and available to provide support in times of crisis, but do some need core support funding? Who chooses which ones? Assumptions are rife in the disability sector with different groups all vying for their piece of power in the NDIS space. When it comes to support, a growing number of people want to self-manage their funding or have a plan manager rather than leaving the agency or a provider in control. The strong emphasis on self-management and plan management in the scheme is one of those areas where there is a benefit to people with disability and families in having more self-direction, choice and control. It can also be a tool that gets around fixed service systems and allows people to do things more innovatively in their community with their informal supports. It can be seen as one of the tools in driving changing demand in the market. However, it works best when people with disability and families are feeling empowered and able to make decisions and not be in crisis mode. Self-management works well when there are strong peer networks of people with disability and/or their families and both formal and informal advocacy to give a power boost when needed.

In a system where self-management of funding also means people with disability and their families employing their own staff, the workforce starts to look different. People with disability want a flexible workforce that will support them when and where they need. Advocates have often been coming from a different perspective to the unions and some providers on issues like workforce training, flexibility of use of funding, continued options of group housing and supported employment under the ADE model. Having a minimum level of training such as a certificate four in disability for all disability support workers simply doesn't work given the diversity of disability and needs that are in the community. Unions are worried that the workforce is not well paid or protected and becoming more casualised. People with disability will often say that when they have a good worker, they are very happy to pay higher rates and provide good conditions, but a good worker is not necessarily somebody with a certificate qualification.

The emphasis on an insurance model and understanding what that means has also added to the tension of these different forces shaping the NDIS. Insurance models are supposed to focus on early intervention and rehabilitation yet people with permanent disability may actually need increased support over time not less. Many people with disability and advocates choose to view the insurance aspects as more of a social insurance model—that there is support there for anyone that needs it without needing to take out a private insurance.

I don't believe that any of these factors are necessarily mutually exclusive. It is more about how those different elements are brought into the system and designed to allow for the diversity of responses, in line with what people with disability need and want. People with disability who are advocates are there to push the boundaries and make sure that our voice is heard in all of these discussions. The most fundamental change that people with disability have wanted is to be supported and able to make the decisions about their own lives. Although this fits in with person-centred ideology, for people with intellectual disability there has not been a strong emphasis on supported decision-making in the scheme or from the service sector. It often feels like change is happening very slowly with a lot of pushback from large service providers.

Advocacy Through Transition

An important recognition made by the Productivity Commission and the expert groups was that the diversity of disability and the power imbalance inherently felt and experienced by many people with disability meant there was a need for formal advocacy to be in place.

Throughout the transition period of the NDIS, there has been some divergence in the advocacy and campaigning about what needs to be fixed. Service providers, people with disability and families have agreed on many things such as the need for better training of planners about disability, flexibility in plans and quicker processes regarding things like reviews of plans. The biggest difference has been in the emphasis that the service system has had on advocating and lobbying for higher prices to cover their costs. This lobbying has particularly come from National Disability Services and the large service providers that are well established and had been very entrenched in the system with influencing government policy on disability in the past. The Every Australian Counts campaign moved from being based with National Disability Services to being based with AFDO which is a clear outward sign of that divergence.

The views and experiences of people with disability have always been heard through informal and formal advocates as well as activists. They have been vital in developing policy on disability services and expert advice on the implementation of the NDIS through advocacy organisations and through the Every Australian Counts campaign. Although there are still campaigns where work is done with the service sector, that strength of alliance that came with the NDIS campaign is no longer there.

Advocates are often people with disability themselves or very closely connected through family and friendship. Most of the formal advocacy agencies, whether peak systemic advocacy agencies or individual advocacy organisations have played an important role in being a conduit for the issues experienced by people with disability in the transition to the NDIS.

Advocacy is specifically recognised in the NDIS Act, and it is important to note that advocates wanted to keep funding for advocacy separate from the NDIS so that independence could be maintained. Having it recognised in the legislation shows its importance:

> Quote from NDIS Act 2013, Part 2, 4
>
> (13) The role of advocacy in representing the interests of people with disability is to be acknowledged and respected, recognising that advocacy supports people with disability by:
>
> > a). Promoting their independence and social and economic participation, and promoting choice and control in the pursuit of their goals and the planning and delivery of their supports; and
> >
> > b). Maximising independent lifestyles of people with disability and their full inclusion in the community.

Advocacy organisations have been key in doing the analysis of the NDIS from the perspective of people with disability. People with Disability Australia undertook a citizen's jury process over 2014–2015 with a diverse group of people with disability looking at the implementation of the NDIS (People with Disabilities 2015). People with Disabilities Western Australia also did large-scale surveys and focus groups of the Western Australian trials in both 2015 and 2016. If you look at the submissions to Senate enquiries and other consultations on the NDIS you will find many submissions from advocacy organisations that provide direct experience of people with disability when things are not working well.

The citizen jury process that was done by People with Disability Australia relayed their scorecard to the NDIA. Their findings are highlighted in a report with the key points being:

- Planners need to be well resourced and have the right skills.
- There is a need to ensure collaboration between planners and Local Area Coordinators (LAC).
- The LAC role is vital to locate the supports people need.
- There is also an opportunity to develop the skills and capacity among participants as well as a need to accelerate information, linkages and capacity building (ILC) supports.
- A number of the recommendations confirm the benefits of independent advocacy and advice to support people throughout the planning process (People with Disabilities Australia 2015).

In Western Australia (WA), the last state to sign up for the NDIS, there were conflicting views from people with disability and families about the two trials of the scheme. People that had a very good experience with the state-based Local Area Coordination scheme were arguing strongly that the NDIS should be controlled and delivered locally which was being trialled through the Western Australian (WA) NDIS. People who had previously had a bad experience with the local system or not gotten services from the state system were advocating for WA to be in the national scheme. This was occurring at the same time as transition was happening in other states where there was a mixture of stories of lives that were transformed, as well as those coming up against bureaucracy and inflexibility. The findings from the two surveys that were done in Western Australia show many of the same issues with inflexibility and bureaucratic systems that are still aiming to be resolved now (People with Disabilities Western Australia Inc 2016).

The same issues about plan flexibility, seeing a draft of a plan, and the skills and knowledge of the NDIA planner and Local Area Coordinators that were highlighted in all of these reviews of the scheme by people with disability and advocates have continued to be the same issues raised by the Every Australian Counts campaign. What is most frustrating is that these are the same issues that were seen as being a potential problem by the expert groups.

At an individual level, the role of advocates has been essential in assisting those people who have been most powerless. Funded individual advocates have quickly become experts in the NDIS processes and requirements of the system. National Disability Advocacy Program-funded agencies spent about 35 per cent of advocacy time on NDIS issues in 2018–2019 (Mallet 2019). Mary Mallet from Disability Advocacy Network Australia spoke at the 2019 Victorian Advocacy conference about the massive increase in advocacy required by people with disability due to the NDIS and the very real issue of burnout of advocacy staff in organisations across the whole of Australia.

A small amount of funding is provided for advocates to assist people with appeals to the AAT. These only account for about 8 per cent of advocacy time with the majority of advocates time spent playing a vital role in assisting people to evidence access requests and review their funding plans. Advocates are filling the gaps where people have had had no supports to gain evidence and documentation, or pointing out where the planner has simply not listened or read the evidence provided. Those that go to appeal show how the bureaucratic nature of the scheme puts barriers constantly in the way of people being able to get the support they need. Many of the appeals which are overturned with the support of advocates are related to decisions and guidelines that are not in line with the principles in the legislation. Over a 12-month period, People with Disabilities Western Australia (PWDWA), just one small advocacy organisation, assisted with 76 plan reviews relating to inadequate funding for reasonable and necessary supports. This included:

- Lack of core support funding;
- Lack of therapy funding;
- Assistive Technology not being approved or included in plans.

Advocacy Case Studies

Case Study One

A family with a daughter who has profound and significant physical disability reported that in the second plan, they went to the planner with everything documented about their daughter's supports. This included all equipment, consumables, personal care, community and civic participation and demonstrated conclusively the last 12-month plan had been successful in meeting their daughter's needs, no increase required. The planner commended them on how well prepared they were and said they had made her job easy. The plan came back rewritten with half the supports missing and requiring an internal review.

Case Study Two

A primary carer had advised NDIA, through a change of circumstances/s48 request, that they would not be able to care for their spouse (who required 24-hour care) due to upcoming surgery. The carer provided NDIA with 3 months' notice, requesting that the participant's plan have an unscheduled review to ensure reasonable and necessary supports were available. Two weeks before the surgery, NDIA had still not responded to the change of circumstances/s48 request. The carer was concerned that his spouse would be at real risk of harm if adequate supports were not implemented. With the support of an advocate escalating the matter through a specific escalation pathway, the change of circumstances was finally actioned, but not before the delay had caused significant distress to the carer (People with Disabilities WA Inc 2019).

The experiences that are being documented by individual advocates is informing the systemic work of many of the advocacy organisations. This systemic work includes providing advice to reference groups of the NDIS such as the intellectual disability reference group having representation from advocacy organisations that specifically support people with intellectual disability. In Western Australia, the funded advocacy organisations worked together to support the NDIS experiences report and have since tried to ensure regular meetings with the NDIA at the local level to feedback issues.

Advocates have been able to get the introduction of urgent criteria for reviews and specific escalation pathways so that people in crisis get the support they need. At a local level, advocates have influenced the way that Local Area Coordinators work. In Western Australia, some have taken on the direct feedback from advocates to provide more information and drop-in support at their offices.

In my prior role as the CEO at PWDWA, we hear that the same issues arising for advocacy organisations in every state. We thought that in WA, because the transition happened later that some of these issues would be ironed out. Unfortunately, that has not been the case with issues like the length of time people are waiting for reviews and appeals, the consent forms of advocates not being recognised and plans not reflecting what people have detailed as their needs, being the same in Western Australia as in other states.

Advocacy has been vital particularly for those with complex situations. Advocacy has not just been from formal funded advocates but also family members' friends and peer groups. With every advocacy organisation at capacity, the role of peers and family in supporting each other in advocating within the NDIS has been vital.

Peer Support

One of the issues that have continued to be raised by the NDIA and advocates is that a market approach can't work if you don't have empowered and informed consumers. This was always going to be a big ask given people with disability were often used to being in a system where they were grateful for any support that they could get. Building the capacity of individuals and families to wield their decision-making power in an NDIS world has been a key component of the Information, Linkages and Capacity Building programs of the NDIA.

The increase in the number of peer support groups and online groups is slowly starting to change what the system looks like. In the old system, the service providers were negotiating directly with government. The NDIS world is a negotiation between the service provider and people with disability.

While service providers and unions talk about pricing and the need for more money to do the work that they need to do, online peer support groups have people with disability and families comparing costs and noting how much is being done for what they are being charged. Previously, these costs were all hidden and people often felt grateful for getting a service in a rationed system. Now that the pricing is open and available people question what value for money looks like. However, while there is still a limited number of services for particular groups of people or areas of support, there remain limitations in choice and control.

The building of peer-led groups has increased significantly because of work done by the NDIA on a project to build peer support groups from 2015 to 2018. Some states had strong peer associations already that had been supported by their state-funded systems. For others, the Peer

Connect project provided a fantastic opportunity to build the capacity of individuals and families. Over 50 peer networks were supported through this project that are still current (JFA Purple Orange 2016).

The Peer Connect website is still in place; however, the funding to provide that national community of practice for peer support stopped at the end of the project. Many of the peer groups have stayed in place and developed their own networks; however, others have fallen to the wayside without a concerted effort to support them. A lot of the online groups have continued to be very strong such as the NDIS grassroots discussion page. This page as an online presence has come to be one of the pre-eminent spaces for peer support and sharing of information by peers on the NDIS. It does this by having dedicated moderators who are very clear that the space is for people with disability. If you have a look at these pages, they are really valuable for peer support where people are asking questions of each other about how they've managed funding, what they can use funding for, and getting into debates about what good practice looks like.

Interestingly at the end of the Peer Connect project was when I found out that there had also been a self-advocacy project occurring funded by the NDIA. The self-advocacy project was also trying to build networks of self-advocacy across Australia and also build a website with the self-advocacy groups that were being supported (Self Advocacy Resource Unit 2019).

Both of these projects developed masses of resources on planning, pre-planning, self-management and many other aspects of life with disability. The resources were developed by people with disability and their families, for people with disability and families. It is such a pity to see these projects supported and then left hanging. The newest rounds of individual capacity building funding from the Information, Linkages and Capacity Building grant rounds do seem to be trying to build on this work with their disabled people's and family organisations' focus. At least, these projects are three years long which allows for some continuity and capacity to be built. There still doesn't seem to be an understanding that some level of funding will always be required when you are trying to support a network of people to come together to share information and resources.

Peer Support is vital given the underfunding of formal advocacy. There are many examples of how access to formal advocacy also supports Peer Support. On both the NDIS grassroots page and the NDIS in WA peer support page, people share advice and help they have been given by advocates. A person supported by advocacy sharing with others that service providers can't demand a copy of your plan from the NDIS for example, pointing out that a person has a right to appeal a decision and that there are advocates who could help. Often using an advocate to can give people confidence to support others.

Involvement of People with Disability at a Policy Level

Where the NDIS currently sits on 'nothing about us without us' seems to be getting less and less. At governance and policy level, the numbers of people with disability on the board of the NDIA are decreasing. The Independent Advisory Council has a good number of people with disability involved and also has reference groups and other external members engaged to get a wider perspective but they also do not seem to have a large influence or any decision-making powers.

Early on in the development of the NDIS, there seemed to be a lot more engagement with people with disability in specific reference and design groups. Now, the NDIA has an autism reference group and a mental health reference group while the Independent Advisory Council has an intellectual disability reference group and some topic-specific reference groups (National Disability Insurance Agency 2020).

It's also important to note that although the proportion of people with disability employed by the agency is quite high for a public sector agency, there are still not many people with disability who are actually in decision-making positions. This is a real gap particularly as people like myself get called on over and over to provide advice and sit on reference groups. It is through peer groups and advocacy organisation that disability leaders are coming up but not finding spaces in the NDIS where they can lead.

Advocates and advocacy groups will keep raising up this issue of people with disability being in the governance and leadership positions of the NDIA. Sometimes there is a real feeling that by supporting and funding peer groups and user-led organisations, the agency is saying "look we want you to be building leadership capacity and building your capacity to have a good life", while at the same time they are not bringing in new people with disability to be the decision-makers at the Board and executive levels and so maintaining the 'them and us' paternalistic attitude.

Christina Ryan, a disabled activist who founded the Disability Leadership Institute, noted in an interview on the broken systems in Australia in February 2020 that "The main policy department that looks after disability in this country, there's not one single disabled person in their executive level staff" (Ryan 2020). This was in reference to the Department of Social Services, but she also goes on to talk about people with disability not being in decision-making positions when it comes to the design of services for people with disability.

Who Tells You if You've Got Things Right?

People with disability are the end user of this scheme. If it's not working, it is us who feel its effects. This means there is a bigger onus on people with disability and advocacy to keep raising these issues. The NDIS has deliberately been promoted as a system that's around people with disability having choice and control. However, that choice seems to be around the small things not the large decisions or the ownership of our person-centred plans.

From the very beginning of campaigning for an NDIS, people with disability have been fighting to be the voice that is driving the system. Now that we are into full scheme, people with disability are still fighting to be the voice that is driving the system.

There has definitely been an increase in peer support both because of and despite the NDIS as well as increased national advocacy and campaigning for the rights of people with disability to have a system that works for them. There are also many examples of people having more individual control in their own lives.

The role of peer support and advocacy is key to making the NDIS Quality & Safeguards Commission successful, because it is through our peer support and advocacy that people will feel confident to make complaints about service providers and to share their stories of what is good practice. There is still a long way to go through in bringing people with disability to the decision-making table both within the NDIA, the NDIS Quality and Safeguards Commission and the sector.

It is advocacy and peer-led organisations that can provide the feedback for continuous improvement of the NDIS at policy and practice level. It is vital that government and the NDIA recognise and fund advocacy and peer support so they can provide the real stories and critical analysis that the system needs for its improvement. For the real change that is still needed to make this scheme "nothing about us without us", it is going to take change at the governance and the executive levels. The first change would be finding the leaders with disability that are out there and bringing them into the scheme in decision-making roles.

References

Australian Federation of Disability Organisations. 2019. The Alliance. https://www.afdo.org.au/our-work/alliance/. Accessed 10 January 2020.

Deane, Kirsten, and Samantha Jenkinson. 2020. NDIS Campaign Reflections (13 January).

Dodd, Andrew. 2016. Change Agents: Rhonda Galbally and Bruce Bonyhady on the Birth of the NDIS. *The Conversation*. August 10. https://theconversation.com/change-agents-rhonda-galbally-and-bruce-bonyhady-on-the-birth-of-the-ndis-63662. Accessed 9 January 2020.

Jenkinson, Samantha. 2010. Funding, Rights, and Sustainable Change. National Disability Summit 2010.

JFA Purple Orange. 2016. Peer Connect. https://www.peerconnect.org.au/. Accessed 27 February 2020.

Mallet, Mary. 2019. State of Play: Disability Advocacy Sector 2019, Strengthening Disability Advocacy conference 2019: Advocacy Under Pressure. Disability Advocacy Resource Unit. https://www.daru.org.au/conference-session/opening-address-3.

Manne, Anne. 2011. Essay: Two Nations; the Case for a National Disability Insurance Scheme. *The Monthly*. August.

National Disability and Carer Alliance. 2016. Every Australian Counts—News hub. https://everyaustraliancounts.com.au/friday-flashback-claires-story/. Accessed 14 January 2020.

N/A. 2010. NDIS Campaign Steering Committee Strategic Planning Meeting.

Every Australian Counts. 2018. Review of NDIS Prices—What Does it Mean for People with Disability? https://everyaustraliancounts.com.au/review-ndis-prices-mean-people-disability/. Accessed 12 December 2019.

Every Australian Counts. 2019. Yep, it NDIS Groundhog Day… Again. https://everyaustraliancounts.com.au/yep-its-ndis-groundhog-day-again/. Accessed 12 December 2019.

National Disability Insurance Agency. 2020. Independent Advisory Council. https://www.ndis.gov.au/about-us/governance/iac. Accessed 10 May 2020.

National People with Disability and Carer Council. 2009. Shut Out: The Experience of People with Disabilities and Their Families in Australia: Consultation Report. Commonwealth of Australia. https://www.dss.gov.au/sites/default/files/documents/05_2012/nds_report.pdf.

Ohlin, Jackie. 2009. Unmet Need in Disability Services: Shortfall or Systemic Failure? Current Issues Brief 1999–2000. Parliament of Australia, Social Policy Group. https://www.aph.gov.au/About_Parliament/Parliamentary_Departments/Parliamentary_Library/Publications_Archive/CIB/cib9900/2000cib06.

People with Disabilities Australia. 2015. NDIS Scorecard Published: Citizens' Jury Delivers Its Verdict. https://pwd.org.au/ndis-scorecard-published-citizens-jury-delivers-its-verdict/. Accessed 10 October 2019.

People with Disabilities WA Inc. 2019. *Submission NDIS Act Review and Participant Service Guarantee (Tune Review)*. Perth: Submission.

People with Disabilities Western Australia Inc. 2016. NDIS Experiences 2016: Evaluation, Perth. WA. https://www.pwdwa.org/documents/submissions/NDIS_Experiences_Report_2016.pdf.

Pierpoint, Jack. n.d. Inclusion Press. https://inclusion.com/inclusion-resources/change-makers/john-obrien-books-videos/. Accessed 1 May 2020.

Productivity Commission. 2011. Disability Care and Support Vols 1 & 2. Commonwealth of Australia. https://www.pc.gov.au/inquiries/completed/disability-support/report, https://www.pc.gov.au/inquiries/completed/disability-support/report/disability-support-volume2.pdf.

Ryan, Christina. 2020. Interview by ABC The Drum. https://www.abc.net.au/news/programs/the-drum/.

Self Advocacy Resource Unit. 2019. Voices Together. https://www.voicestogether.com.au/self-advocates/toolkits-resources-how-to/resources/. Accessed 27 February 2020.

Shorten, Bill. 2010. Opening of the National Disability Summit, Melbourne. Former Ministers. https://formerministers.dss.gov.au/3248/opening-of-the-national-disability-summit-melbourne/. Accessed 10 January 2020.

Winther, Todd. 2011. The NDIS; All Style and No Substance? Ramp Up: Disability. Discussion. Debate. 22 February. https://www.abc.net.au/rampup/articles/2011/02/22/3145273.htm#comments. Accessed January 2020.

Young, Stella. 2011. Ready for a National Disability Insurance Scheme, Ramp Up: Disability. Discussion. Debate. Australian Broadcasting Corporation. https://www.abc.net.au/rampup/articles/2011/03/01/3152192.htm. Accessed 14 January 2020.

Part III

CHAPTER 19

Stories from the Wild West Frontier: The National Disability Insurance Scheme Experiences of People with Severe and Profound Intellectual Disability

David Henderson and Christine Bigby

One afternoon in February 2019, the father of a person with intellectual disability spoke at a training session about the challenges he had faced over the years in supporting his daughter to make decisions. At one point during the session, he spoke about the National Disability Insurance Scheme (NDIS) and likened his own experience of navigating the scheme to living on the American frontier during the westward wave of expansion and settlement that began in 1865, shortly after the end of the American Civil War. "My mind always goes to the Wild West", he explained of his feelings about the NDIS and of "everything as being fairly lawless, but also a place of great opportunity". The father acknowledged that not everything about the NDIS was perfect and also that the NDIA often promised more than it could deliver. But, he said that it was

D. Henderson (✉) · C. Bigby
La Trobe University, Melbourne, VIC, Australia

M. Cowden and C. McCullagh (eds.), *The National Disability Insurance Scheme*, https://doi.org/10.1007/978-981-16-2244-1_19

"worth ignoring all of that, and just pushing ahead and taking advantage … of how the regulatory framework is still evolving".

This chapter seeks to understand something of the lives of people living on that 'Wild West frontier' of the NDIS. More specifically, it explores personal stories of people with severe and profound intellectual disability and the issues they have encountered in their dealings with the scheme since it began being implemented across Australia in 2016.

The NDIS defines a new era in disability service delivery. As a universal, rights-based scheme, it represents a historical shift in allocation principles in disability policy and is expected to favourably influence the health and wellbeing of many people with disability in Australia (Bonyhady 2014; Mavromaras et al. 2018). The actuarial model and the principle of "reasonable and necessary" disability support that underpins the scheme's objective to provide lifelong, individualised support to people with disability should be celebrated (Kendrick et al. 2017; Lakhani et al. 2018). By exploring the personal stories of two participants who have accessed and navigated the NDIS, this chapter asks if the scheme is living up to those celebrated ideals.

An aim of the NDIS is to shift authority over disability service design and direction from service provider to service user. By prioritizing the stories of NDIS participants with severe and profound intellectual disability, this chapter seeks to emulate something of this shift in authority and in doing so, insert people with severe and profound intellectual disability into public narratives about the NDIS. Most commonly people with physical or sensory disability are the public voice of disability advocacy (Bigby 2020a). Even when advocacy is more nuanced, there is a tendency for people with mild intellectual disability to act as proxies for all people with intellectual disability (Burton and Kagan 2006). But unless others represent people with severe and profound intellectual disability in public arenas of advocacy and in private transactions with the NDIS, their stories are liable to go unnoticed and ignored. To this end, what follows is an in-depth exploration of two individual stories of the NDIS experiences of people with severe and profound intellectual disability.

Yet the question of how, or even if, we can garner the perspectives of a "voiceless" and marginalised population is not so easily resolved. There is little more seductive, as John Arnold (1998, 380) notes, "than the promise of access to the 'voices' of those normally absent from the historical record". But communicating the views of such groups is not a straightforward process, made more difficult when the cohort whose experiences one is trying to represent do not use words to communicate. Our own approach was to use life review interviews with parents of children with severe and profound intellectual disability, a methodology that draws on the overlapping methods of oral history and life story interviews (Atkinson 2004; Frisch 1990; Henderson and Bigby 2017a, b). For this chapter, we conducted two such interviews with one participant and one with another. Each interview was recorded and then transcribed, and a general inductive approach was used to analyse the data (Thomas 2006). Perhaps working against current convention, both informants chose to use their own names, though each was given the option of using a pseudonym. Approval to conduct this study was obtained from the La Trobe University Human Research Ethics Committee and this chapter was reviewed by each participant (HEC19244). One of the aims of the interviews was to facilitate participants of the study to talk, in as much detail as possible, about their own—and by extension their child's—experiences of the NDIS, but also about the routines of their daily lives and how these have changed over time (Atkinson and Walmsely 2010; Thomson 2003). As such, the interviews focused on an individual's experiences prior to, during and after the implementation of the NDIS. By taking such an approach, this chapter seeks to excavate the experiences of people with severe and profound intellectual disability.

Bethany Palmer

Bethany Palmer is 20 years old and has a condition called Dravet syndrome, which is a rare and catastrophic form of intractable epilepsy that begins in infancy. It is a debilitating, lifelong condition that can severely impede a person's quality of life. People with Dravet syndrome experience frequent seizures, poor seizure control and developmental delays, including intellectual disability. Bethany's intellectual disability is at the profound end of the scale. Dravet syndrome, explained Damian Palmer, Bethany's father, is something that you are born with although usually it does not show immediately after birth. Often, Dravet syndrome manifests about six months after birth and it was exactly at six months old that Bethany "had her first seizure" although it was another two years before the Palmers had a clear diagnosis. For the first two years, "we thought she had epilepsy, and that any developmental delay that she was having was caused by the epileptic seizures".

It wasn't until she was two years old that the Palmers realised the "seizures were a component or a symptom of something bigger". Even then, Damian explained, the "actual diagnosis of Dravet… wasn't all that significant a moment". For Damian, that moment was when Bethany's intellectual disability was confirmed. "I think it was before her second birthday, before she turned two", Damian recalled. He and his wife Christine were living in Canberra at the time and had travelled to Sydney so that Bethany could undergo some tests at the Children's Hospital in Westmead. The tests were ostensibly concerned with locating where Bethany's seizures "started in her brain" but the outcome of those tests were readings that indicated Bethany had an intellectual disability. "I can remember my response to that", Damian recalled, 'because not long before that I'd eaten a big bowl of potato wedges and I just walked straight into the bathroom of Bethany's hospital room and deposited the full bowl of wedges, vomited the whole lot into the toilet'.

In the early days, the Palmers spent more time navigating the health system rather than the disability services system and it was not until Bethany was 11 years old that they began accessing disability specific services. At the time, the Palmers were looking for some form of afternoon/evening support, after Bethany returned home from school. There was "no easy way of doing it", Damian recalled, other than "to go hunting, go looking, contact disability service providers" to see what sort of services were available. Working within this framework, the Palmers managed to cobble together some services for their daughter although the quality of those services was "mixed". Some of the service providers were better than others but usually the "people who were actually coming to the house" did a pretty good job. He recalled how he and his wife probably felt like they needed more support for Bethany than they could arrange but he also explained that he never really thought about services in terms of what we thought "we should have". Certainly, no one was talking about what Bethany had "a right to expect", Damian said, nor about access to services in terms of "what was reasonable or fair".

Today, Damian Palmer can recite the pertinent dates around the introduction and rollout of the NDIS in Australia. He knows, for instance, that the Productivity Commission handed down its first major report in July 2011. And he knows that the report recommended the introduction of an insurance scheme, having concluded that disability support arrangements in Australia were "inequitable, underfunded, fragmented, and inefficient" (Productivity Commission 2011, 5). Palmer knows that the National Disability Insurance Scheme Act was passed into legislation in March 2013. He also knows that on 1 July 2016, full implementation of the scheme commenced in all Australian states and territories except Western Australia. In the period leading up to the passage of the NDIS Act through parliament however, Damian was vague about what was happening with the NDIS and what it would actually mean for Bethany. "I follow federal politics reasonably closely", Damian said, but "I don't have a clear memory of the NDIS and the steps that it went through" at the time. "I remember thinking it was there and… that this could be really good… in terms of decent funding for disability services and a more coherent overall service provision".

It is not surprising that Damian was not "entirely on top of what was going on" with the NDIS because it was during that time that Bethany had a feeding PEG put in. A PEG, or percutaneous endoscopic gastrostomy, is a procedure in which a flexible feeding tube is placed through the abdominal wall and into the stomach. It allows nutrition, fluids and medications to be put directly into the stomach, bypassing the mouth and oesophagus. The Palmers had made the decision to insert the PEG after Bethany went "through a period where she simply stopped eating". It was a difficult time for the whole family. No one knew why Bethany stopped eating but it got to a point where "we were down to syringing fluid into her mouth". Bethany "ended up having to be hospitalised and fed through a nasal tube for a while, and they basically had to build her back up". For "a whole year there we were living …with her really fading away", Damian recalled. After the PEG was put in "things picked up", said Damian, "and by that stage the NDIS had been legislated and it was some point after that that I started paying a bit more attention".

In 2016, Damian made it his responsibility to "get a handle" on what the NDIS was about. He wanted to know how it was "supposed to work" and what it was "going to mean for Bethany". And although "we didn't know when Bethany would actually get contacted and transitioned into the scheme", Damian explained, "we knew we lived in an area that was starting full rollout from 1 July 2016". In early 2016, Damian went to "a couple" of information sessions "to get a sense of what was going to be involved". Then, as Damian is wont to do "when something catches my interest", he explored the "bigger picture side of things". He read the Productivity Commission Report, he looked at the legislation, delved even further into some disability related literature. Damian got "quite immersed", as he put it, "in the practicalities of what it [the NDIS] was going to look like, what it was going to involve". By now he was optimistic about the scheme. He had "a reasonable understanding" of how it should work. The "next step", said Damian, was to wait for the "call from the NDIA and off we'll go".

In the meantime, Damian and Christine Palmer began to think about the preparation of Bethany's first NDIS plan. The preparation of an NDIS plan is obliged to conform to certain principles including that "so far as reasonably practicable" a plan should be "individualised" and "be directed by the participant" (NDIS Act, S.31). A crucial part of this process is, of course, that a participant's plan includes a statement, prepared by the participant, "that specifies … the goals, objectives and aspirations of the participant" (NDIS Act, S.33). This statement covers both the goals and aspirations of the participant as well as the environmental and personal context of that participant's life, such as living arrangements, family and community supports, and the extent of their social and economic participation. During this planning process, potential NDIS participants are asked to think "about your needs and goals" and about how they would like their life to be in a few years. To assist with the process, a planning workbook asks participants to think about their goals as they relate to various aspects of their lives, which might include employment, education, social participation or living arrangements.

Bigby (2020b) has pointed out in the previous chapter that individualised funding schemes that elevate the importance of market models of service delivery rely on participants in such schemes to be discerning consumers—consumers who can exercise choice and control and consumers who can make important decisions about how they would like to live their lives. These embedded assumptions about self-direction and decision-making capacity at the heart of the scheme are already problematic for most people with intellectual disability. They are even more so for people with severe and profound intellectual disability. And they can be summed up in a question like the one Damian Palmer has asked himself on many occasions. How do you set goals if you cannot articulate them? The Productivity Commission acknowledged this particular issue when it noted that "some people with disability are not able to make all of their own decisions (as is the case with profound intellectual disability)" (Productivity Commission 2011, 356). In such cases, the Productivity Commission suggested that decisions "will often be made jointly with or by primary carers", who are usually familiar with "the strengths, goals and other preferences of the person with a disability". Yet as Bigby (2014, 93) has argued elsewhere, there are "lingering concerns" that the complexities of "supporting people with intellectual disabilities to exercise choice and control over their lives" have yet to be fully articulated.

Drawing on his own experience, Damian Palmer would agree. How best to support Bethany to exercise choice and control over her life is a challenge that he has grappled with since he filled in the statement of goals on her behalf in latter half of 2016, a process he found particularly unpleasant. Damian believed that on some level, the NDIS' insistence that Bethany's plan contain a statement of goals represented a failure of the scheme to accept her for who she is: that is to say someone who is unable to conceive of, nor articulate such goals. On another level, it can be understood as a flaw in a scheme that is resolutely committed to regarding all participants as members of a homogenous group—people with disability—without taking into account the specific impairment group to which they also belong (Clegg and Bigby 2017). Whenever Damian raised this issue at NDIS information sessions, the advice he received was almost always the same. As Bethany's informal carers, he and Christine would have to complete the planning process for Bethany but that they would have to do it in a way that made it appear as if Bethany had completed it herself.

For Damian Palmer, it was an incongruous experience to think of his daughter's needs and goals and answer the question how you would like your "life to be in a few years". The assumption at the heart of the process is that the participant has an experience of time and the experience of acting for a purpose. As Damian explained, his view is that such suppositions, "are not true for people with severe and profound intellectual disability like Bethany". He explained how Bethany could, to a certain extent, communicate certain preferences: she will choose chocolate cake over a peanut butter sandwich, and she does have interests to the extent that she likes dogs and trees. Even so, according to Damian, it is difficult to perceive of Bethany as having goals, at least of the kind intended in the NDIS planning process. What Damian tried to articulate is that the NDIS had failed to take into account people with intellectual disability in general, and people with severe and profound intellectual disability in particular. "I see the embrace of goals in this case as an act of exclusion", he has written elsewhere. An exclusion "of both Bethany as a person with a profound intellectual disability, and of myself as one of her informal carers" (Palmer 2016, 7).

Damian Palmer did, of course, fill in the forms. He had no choice. "In Bethany's current plan", he explained, "there are six goals that are all written from Bethany's perspective because that is what is required". Damian was "just working within the system", as he put it, in order "to get the best results we can for Bethany and for us":

> So, her goals are all in there – supposedly from her perspective. But again, I have this question about is that actually fully respecting the person that she is, or is that still expecting her to be a particular way, or pretend that she is and should be? Just kind of how – almost whether it's a denial of the reality that Christine and I live with, that we have to pretend, play some kind of pretend game or voice it or word it in a way, present it in a way that's not actually a true representation of Bethany and our life together as a family.

The problems associated with preparing Bethany's first NDIS plan were compounded, to some extent, by the delay between Bethany's acceptance as an NDIS participant and her first planning meeting. However, the Palmer family was not alone in such experiences. In 2016 and 2017, the sheer volume of applications, combined with staffing difficulties at the NDIA, meant that substantial time could elapse between becoming a participant and attending a first planning meeting (Carney et al. 2019). Damian recalled the time of waiting for Bethany to get onto the scheme as an important part of the story because of the way it all played out. "I've got very little in the way of positive things to say about the way the NDIS has actually been implemented", Damian said, "and particularly the way the agency, the NDIA, actually operates". Damian then went on to describe what he called "a series of appalling interactions" with the NDIA "from the point of first contact onwards".

Damian's first experience of dealing with the NDIA was in the latter half of 2016, when he visited the Local Area Coordinator (LAC) in his neighbourhood. "I walked into the first meeting with our first LAC with a whole framework of thinking I understood what was happening", recalled Damian. His expectations of the meeting were underpinned by his understanding of the LAC role, which was to "be on the ground in communities connecting people with disabilities with mainstream services". He thought he was meeting "a LAC who was going to be supporting us through the planning process". In fact, he was already in his first planning meeting.

In the early days of the roll out of the scheme, most initial plans were formulated on the basis of telephone conversations, rather than in face-to-face meetings with planners as is now the practice, so in one respect, Palmer could count himself lucky to have been able to sit down with someone and go over Bethany's plan together. But he bemoaned the lack of transparency that was such a feature of Bethany's planning meetings with the NDIA. Every time he attended a planning meeting for Bethany, it went differently, and it was never clear when the LAC collected certain information what they intended to do with that information. "They do particular kinds of assessments of the participant", Damian explained, but "they don't necessarily tell you what assessment they are doing". Damian said of that first meeting that "we had this conversation" and the LAC "collected this information or whatever, and next thing we had a plan". "I just said, 'what's going on'", Damian recalled, "this is not the way I understood this to be working". He was shocked and distressed, not least because the plan was littered with a number of glaring errors and inappropriate omissions. He was also disappointed that he never saw a draft of Bethany's plan before it was approved, but the NDIA had abandoned the practice of sharing a draft of the plan with participants in the middle of 2016, only to reinstitute it again in early 2020. "As far as I am concerned that's just entirely inconsistent with the notion of choice and control", said Damian, because "you can be slapped with a plan that has all kinds of mistakes and doesn't represent the things you said".

The mistakes in Bethany's plan ranged from comical to pretty serious. For one thing, the NDIA could not get the names of Bethany's parents right—Christine Palmer, Bethany's mother was named as Samantha Palmer on that first plan—a mistake that would only be corrected after the Palmers requested a scheduled review. Other omissions were more serious. Damian and Christine Palmer had put an extraordinary amount of time into thinking about Bethany's statement of supports. They had written lists of everything Bethany needed, calculated the costs of each item and tallied up totals in spreadsheets. But the plan reflected nothing of all that work at all. There was "no funding for any of Bethany's tube feeding whatsoever", even though Damian had made it clear in his meeting with the LAC that Bethany required tube feeding. But "none of that basic information" collected during the planning meeting "would have flagged the fact that Bethany was tube fed" so it never made it into the package. And the Palmers only got funding for about half as many nappies as Bethany required for the year. When he asked the LAC for clarification, she explained that "that is the maximum" amount of funding allowed for person with Bethany's disability.

The glaring omissions and mistakes in Bethany's first plan forced Damian Palmer to reassess his understanding of the NDIS and how it was operating at the time. And drawing on his own experience, Damian would have been unsurprised by the 2018 Productivity Commission report that concluded that "planning processes were not operating well" (Productivity Commission 2017, 181). Of particular concern to Damian were two of the three main issues the Productivity Commission report also identified as "the main sources of complaint" by many participants attempting to navigate the scheme at that time: the lack of transparency around the planning process and the lack of sufficiently skilled planners. "I was still working on the assumption that the scheme" would ask what you needed, Damian explained, and you would say "we need this and that" and they would say "is this reasonable or necessary? Yes, fair enough, okay, so there you go". Damian had not yet realised that what was actually happening was quite different and that the NDIA was "spitting out these generic packages", which ultimately meant that there were things in Bethany's plan "that just didn't match anything that we had actually said about her" at the time.

When Damian reflected on those early interactions with the NDIA, he said that it was "easy in hindsight to see what assumptions I should and should not have made all along the way". But he assumed that the NDIA staff, the LACs and others tasked with implementing the scheme would "have at least the level of understanding that I had of the basic principles of the scheme ... but it was perfectly clear they did not". The lack of sufficiently skilled planners meant that someone like Damian—who had a nuanced understanding of the principles underpinning the NDIS and how it might work—could become quickly deflated by the way it was operating in practice. "You could mention the Convention on the Rights of Persons with Disability", said Damian, and they had "no idea. You could talk about choice and control, reasonable and necessary, the basic philosophy of the scheme; no idea whatsoever". The staff at the NDIA had "just been on boarded very, very quickly", he said, and the NDIS was operating poorly as result.

In spite of the serious deficiencies in Bethany's plan, there were some positive outcomes once her plan had been approved by the NDIA and come into effect. And Damian pointed out that his approach to the scheme remained "a positive one". For one thing, he considered the shift of "having the resources allocated to Bethany" a fundamental development that allowed him and his wife to make "decisions about where we spend those resources". This development had allowed them to get a feel for assisting Bethany to exercise "choice and control", said Damian, particularly in terms of the services Bethany could now access. As an example, Damian described a typical Wednesday in Bethany's life which, Damian explained, would have been impossible to implement prior to the NDIS. "We've got an amount of core funding we can spend for Bethany", Damian said, and "we've chosen that on a Wednesday what that looks like is having Sally [a support worker] here for the day with her, taking her to her hydrotherapy session". The hydrotherapy sessions are funded as part of the capacity building element of Bethany's funding. Bethany "loves going for drive", so after hydrotherapy another element they built into her Wednesday was a trip, with the support worker, to McDonald's where they eat cheeseburgers, one of Bethany's favourite foods. "All of that would not have been possible", said Damian, "or it would've been a lot harder to do previously".

Another "more positive side" of the NDIS for Bethany was the "insurance element of the scheme", especially in regard to the area of early intervention and assistive technology. Damian explained how this was "probably one area where my interaction with the agency on the issue of planning has worked well", because it had worked "exactly how it should work". All of Bethany's requests for funding of ankle supports, hydrotherapy and other capacity building measures had "been properly funded" and Damian acknowledged that these measures were essential because they contributed to Bethany "maintaining the ability to walk". For Damian, the funding of Bethany's capacity building measures represented "an example" of the NDIS functioning properly, because if "it properly funds her needs in that area through hydrotherapy and her Ankle Foot Orthosis, well then longer term that does have a financial payoff for the scheme".

Yet Damian also acknowledged there were other things that had not dramatically changed in terms of Bethany's support network. For instance, two support workers who worked with Bethany regularly before the NDIS continued to do so after it was rolled out in their area in 2016. These support workers had left their previous employer and joined Hireup: an NDIS registered online platform for people with disability to find, hire and manage support workers who fit their needs. And Damian had been happy enough to cut ties with those service providers anyway, because their administration had become difficult to navigate. But he had retained the services of "the support workers themselves" because "they were so good at what they did and so good with Bethany".

Taking a step back, Damian still hopes that the NDIS can work. "When you think about people's interaction with... the NDIS", he said, there are "at least two very clear aspects to it". First, there is the experience of facing and engaging with the NDIA. Second, there is the experience of facing and engaging with service providers. "Most of my interactions with the agency itself have been ... way, way below what it should be", said Damian. And while "engaging with the service providers hasn't been all smooth sailing" either, Damian believed that everyone was doing their best to make things work. "We're working it out, they're working it out", he said, "and it's going to take time for a new system like this to work it all out". So, after four years of navigating the scheme, Damian remains optimistic, even if there is still "a lot of work" to do. The system is "better than it was previously", he said, and better than it "would have been if the scheme hadn't been introduced".

Nick

When Jane Tracy spoke about her son, Nick, in our interview, she did so with obvious love and compassion. And, during our interview at least, she started by describing his character and then moved on to describing some aspects of his disability. Nick is Jane's oldest child. He is 34 years old and, as Jane put it, he is "a really fun bloke to be around". Nick's exuberant character gives Jane "lots of joy in the moment" and helps her "stay focused on being present". He also has a cheeky side which gives him and his family "tremendous fun". When I visited Jane in her home to talk about Nick, she had just returned from visiting him and his physiotherapist in order for him to try out a new walker. She recounted how Nick, while testing out his walker, could not help but play a few jokes on her and the physiotherapist. He would head "off down the road" when we wanted him to go in the other direction, Jane explained, and soon he had "everybody laughing".

Nick has an intellectual disability, cerebral palsy and epilepsy. As indicated above, he uses a walking aide to assist him with his mobility. Jane explained how Nick "can walk a few steps around the house without an aide" but for "longer distances we use a wheelchair". Though he "doesn't use speech to communicate", Nick is a very resourceful communicator and uses a communication App called Proloquo2Go on his iPad. Proloquo2Go is "a multi-layered sort of program", Jane explained, so Nick can "select a symbol – for instance, eat or drink or activities or people that he wants to talk about – and then that takes him to the next layer down". From there, he can get increasingly specific options, but the program requires Jane to fill in these options under each broad category or symbol. Thus, to some extent, Jane explained, Nick communicates through symbols and images based on what "I imagine that he would want to say". There are, of course, other ways for Nick to communicate and these days he "communicates through his facial expressions, as well as his body language, his behaviour and his gestures". Over the years, Jane has become something of an expert in understanding all of Nick's forms of communication.

Jane was a GP working in family general practice when Nick was born, and when Nick started attending primary school, she returned to part-time work. By this time, she was more interested in disability than she had been in the past and she started looking for jobs in that field. I started to think "how can I combine what I feel I've learnt on this journey with him [Nick] so far with my medical qualification?" Jane recalled. She took a job "working in paediatrics developmental disability" and later, when an adult unit was opened at Monash University, she started working there. Later still, she joined the Centre for Developmental Disability Health and rose to become the education lead, and then eventually the director of the Centre. "I've felt very privileged to work in the area", Jane said, and "being able to bring the experience and understanding that I had through being a parent over that 34 years so far, as well as my medical qualifications".

It was probably Jane's extensive experience in the field of intellectual disability that appealed to the Hon. Mary Woolbridge MP, Minister for Community Services Victoria, when she asked Jane to be on the Victorian NDIS taskforce. The taskforce—which later became the NDIS Implementation Committee—was formed shortly after the Productivity Commission tabled its report in 2011. By her own account, Jane "was very involved" in the NDIS from that point on. She thought that the NDIS was "a fantastic idea" and recalled thinking broadly at the time about what the NDIS might achieve. One of her main hopes was that the NDIS might address what she referred to as the "inequity around how you got your disability". She was distressed that "when somebody had their brain injury from a car accident then they had money that went to them" through the Transport Accident Commission, but "for somebody like Nick there was nothing except Medicare". Another big issue, as far as Jane was concerned, was the commitment of the NDIS to building capacity in community services. Jane was "excited about the opportunities" that might emerge in services for people with disability if the NDIS focused on capacity building, and she hoped that this might ultimately contribute to building a "more inclusive community overall".

A lot of these issues crystallised in her own mind during the months leading up to Nick's first NDIS planning interview. Given that Nick was living in supported accommodation at the time, there were no issues around the establishment of eligibility. But that did not mean the process went smoothly. First, the planning interview kept on being put off, and by the time she did get the call, Jane had "spent a long time preparing for it, thinking about what I wanted for him, and one of the really nice things that's come out of this, for me, has been I spent a lot of time thinking, documenting and developing a vision for the kind of life he could have". All of which was, of course, based on her knowledge and understanding—developed over the 34 years of a shared life journey—of what is important to him and what is important for him.

Jane Tracy did not have the same concerns as Damian Palmer about filling in Nick's statement of goals. She thought about what "would be good for him, in terms of friends, in terms of communication, in terms of independent mobility, in terms of what kinds of things I wanted for him in the place that he lived". Then, she filled in the goals accordingly. She also thought about "ways of getting him choice, how to make choices, how to feel more in control of his life, the importance of having something to look forward to". Jane explained how the planning process helped "me crystallise my knowledge of Nick, and my vision of his life based on what is important to him, into a written document". It also provided her with a sense that Nick might be provided for in future. "I kind of felt 'well, I can die now'", said Jane, "I've put all this stuff down, my vision for Nick is now written down, and other people could take it and run with it … so that was really helpful".

It is worth considering what the different approaches to planning adopted by Jane Tracy and Damian Palmer suggest more broadly about of role of advocacy for people with severe and profound intellectual disability within the framework of the NDIS. Bigby (2020b) has noted elsewhere that by accepting that some participants would need support in their engagement with the NDIA, and by stressing that participants' plans would be self-directed "so far as reasonably practicable", the NDIS acknowledged the important role that support mechanisms would play to ensure equitable access to the scheme. Yet the NDIA never clearly stipulated what types of support mechanisms would be made available to those less capable of self-directing the planning process. This absence of formal requirements for supported decision-making means that participants have to rely on their own network—usually family members or service providers—for planning assistance (Bigby 2020b; Carney et al. 2019). The problems sometimes associated with the heavy reliance on parental advocacy for adult children with intellectual disability, such as paternalism, risk aversion or reduced participation in decisions about one's own life, have been explored in detail in the literature about planning and decision-making support for people with intellectual disability (Antaki et al. 2009; Bigby et al. 2019; Lloyd et al. 2019). And service providers are similarly, if not more, conflicted (Carney et al. 2019). All of which suggests that people with intellectual disability are liable to be disadvantaged in an individualised funding system that makes no clear provisions for structured, intensive and ongoing planning and decision support.

This is not to suggest that either Damian or Jane did not have the interests of their children at heart or attempt to stand in their shoes as best they could when they completed the planning process. On the contrary, both are strong and willing advocates. But with no strict guidelines about how to support a person with severe intellectual disability during the planning phase, each was left to navigate their own quite different path through the process. Despite adopting different approaches, each achieved relatively good outcomes, which begs a second, no less important question: what occurs when there is no strong parent to act on behalf of a participant seeking to gain access to the NDIS? If good outcomes for people with intellectual disability in individualised funding systems are dependent on strong advocacy, as Mavromaras et al. (2018) have shown, then it suggests a more systemic problem that could ultimately lead to poorer outcomes for people without strong advocates. Damian Palmer and Jane Tracy both acknowledged this issue in their own way. Damian explained that by being "a persistent advocate" some people he interacted with in the NDIA tended to see him "as a troublemaker", but he also expressed concern for those who, for "various reasons", could not or would not advocate strongly for their children. Jane also acknowledged her own "privileged position" gave her an advantage in a system that rewarded strong advocates: "English is my first language", she said, "I've got education, I can advocate… people who don't have any of that are much worse off".

In any event, Jane was optimistic after Nick's first NDIS planning meeting. She had a good understanding of the actuarial principle of the NDIS in terms of "front-loading" the plan to offset future expenses. To this end, an important part of Nick's plan included funding for "an intensive block of effort" around communication that was aimed at helping the staff at his home "learn about how to use his communication device". Jane no longer wanted to be "programming it all the time" because if "staff can do it, both at the day program and at the house", Nick's needs would be better met by those involved in providing his daily support. Jane also "wanted some one-to-one work to help his health and fitness". Jane believed that there was "a bit too much sitting around at the house" and that it was important to get him to "go for a walk, to go to a friend's house". She explained that Nick lives on the site of the now demolished Kew Residential Services, about twelve kilometres from the Melbourne CBD. She hoped it would be possible for Nick to "develop friendships with young people in the local area with similar interests in, for instance, movies", if there was someone who could help facilitate such actions. While Jane hadn't been able to get any of the staff in the Nick's house to identify and nurture such relationships she knew "in theory" that Nick "would love to have the opportunity to walk to a friend's house, that sort of thing, and they could watch a movie together".

It is possible that in outlining her vision for Nick, Jane was seeking to challenge the culture in his group home, which she explained, "is not right yet". She said that the staff at the house did not approach their work as facilitating the engagement of the residents in their own lives. The culture at house, Jane explained, is still "the house is our workplace, and gee we're so busy doing the laundry and cooking the meals and mopping the floor that … we don't have any time for this other stuff". Yet Jane imagined how "it might be for Nick to go and see a friend, to go to a movie with a friend, to learn how to play some role in doing his washing, and to explore new interests and activities as an individual, you know, active support". So, it appears that Jane saw the NDIS planning process as a chance to implement some of those changes. She worked out the costings. And she calculated the hours of one-to-one support Nick would need during the week. "I'd operationalised it … all according to the price guide", Jane explained, "and we got a good package. That was fine, they said "that's great, yes, that all sounds entirely reasonable"'.

Except Jane could not get Nick's plan to work, she "couldn't bring the vision to life and make it Nicks reality". "We grossly underspent", Jane explained, "because I couldn't get the one-to-one" support. For most people with severe and profound intellectual disability, the NDIS planning process had been achieved with minimal fuss, because bilateral agreements between the Commonwealth and the states around "in-kind" supports had generally resulted in a rollover of existing supports into the NDIS (Carey et al. 2019). But it appears that Nick's more tailored, individualised plan represented a challenge the market could not rise to meet. Essentially, what Jane wanted was a support worker—who was part of his staffing team, both at the house and at his day activities—to work regularly with Nick and learn about his methods of communication. This would involve getting to know Nick and also getting to know how to use and program his communication App Prologquo2Go. Jane's reasoning for such an approach was pretty clear: "you can't support Nick without communicating with him". And even though there were provisions in his NDIS plan for such support, the Department of Human and Social Services—which managed Nick's house at the time—could not work out a way to employ staff at the house "to do some of the one-to-one stuff" around communication. Jane believed that it was probably "a systems thing", which is true enough. But it is also another example of what Lloyd et al. (2019) have identified as the problems many people with intellectual disability have experienced in translating their plans into action.

That the NDIA didn't cut Nick's package (due to underspending) at his second planning meeting a year later is probably a testament to Jane's advocacy. Jane said that:

> ...we haven't spent the money, and it's not because he doesn't need it, it's not because we asked for too much, it's because I can't spend it; I can't, because there was difficulty getting that one-to-one work happening ...because everybody's trying to learn this...They were having trouble with the staffing...I guess it's like turning around a big ocean liner, when you're talking about big organisations.

By this time, Nick's house had been taken over by a non-government service provider, and when Nick received the same funding for his second package, they did eventually manage to spend it on what it had been designed for. Jane explained how the new service provider was "now doing lots of one-to-one with him".

Like many NDIS participants, Jane's experience of NDIS planning process has been fraught with errors, missteps and many frustrating moments. "We had some problems", Jane said, and she went on to recount an excruciating story about making about 30 phone calls to have Nick's in-shoe orthotics replaced. And she spoke eloquently about the general exhaustion of having to jump through so many hoops. "I feel like I'm not doing a good enough job for Nick", she said. Jane was convinced that the people on the NDIS who were doing OK were those who "have a parent working fulltime on the NDIS", because ultimately the system is so "hard to manage". It is good, she said, that there are more opportunities:

> If I push hard enough and put enough time into it, I can get a workshop happening with a speech therapist… If I keep on their case and hound them, I can get the assistance and the one-to-one time and the speech pathology assistance to get them to learn more about his communication, and that will be good.

But what concerned Jane is that she was still the one driving everything. "That's the tiring, exhausting bit", she said, "I'm tired of that". Jane explained that the only way she could properly manage Nick's NDIS plan was to step back from her own work. 'I am stepping down from my position', she said, "to reduce my hours at work so I can work out the NDIS".

Jane is intelligent enough to see the irony of her situation. "It's the driving that's the exhausting bit, the staying on top of it all", she said, "which comes back to one of the reasons we all wanted the NDIS in the first place". Jane, like many parents, is concerned about what will happen to her child after she dies and still has hope that the NDIS will be operating well enough to give him the "reasonable and necessary sort of supports" he needs to live a decent life. She believes that in five- or ten-year's time that "things will improve", and like Damian, she is convinced of the importance of NDIS. She appreciated how the NDIS was founded on notions of individual rights rather than welfare and the way that the insurance model focused so much on optimising people's "participation, contribution and inclusion".

Conclusion

On 29 November 2012, the then Prime Minister, the Hon. Julia Gillard MP, moved a second reading of the National Disability Insurance Bill in the House of Representatives. In her speech that day, Gillard declared that the NDIS represented "a transformational approach" to the provision of disability services in Australia (Parliamentary Debates 2012, 13878). "We will build a new system from the ground up", she said, and it 'will respond to each individual's goals and aspirations for their lifetime, affording certainty and peace of mind for people with disability and their carers alike'. More than seven years have passed since Gillard made her speech and this chapter seeks to assess whether the scheme is living up to some of those ideals. Of course, the chapter explores the experiences of just two NDIS participants, but it remains a worthy exercise because it is through the accumulation of such stories that we can begin to understand the complexity and variety of a collective, though ultimately fractured experience of the NDIS in Australia.

Scholars and advocates have argued that the NDIS is failing to take into account some of the unique needs associated with having an intellectual disability (Bigby 2020a; Crofts, personal communication; NSW CID 2014; O'Connor 2014). The experiences recounted here of Damian Palmer and Jane Tracy in navigating the NDIS for their adult children with severe and profound intellectual disability suggest that they are correct in their assertions. While Palmer and Tracy recounted quite different stories, each, in their own way, acknowledged that a more nuanced understanding of people with severe and profound intellectual disability and what the exercise of rights looks like for them is integral if the NDIS is to properly accommodate them in the scheme. For one thing, use of the first-person voice is, as Palmer pointed out, more problematic for people with severe and profound intellectual disability because it ultimately renders such people unable to complete the planning process as stipulated by the NDIA. While Palmer and Tracy recognised the benefits their adult child had derived from the NDIS, both were concerned about equity—about what happens for those people with severe and profound intellectual disability whose parents are not around, or not well educated, or not particularly articulate advocates. Moreover, that Jane has recently reduced her hours of work in order to better manage the NDIS for her son is an awkward indictment of the scheme. If the NDIS is not yet working as some might have hoped, one of the reasons for this is that it places such a great administrative burden on parents who want nothing but a good outcome for their children.

Despite such reservations, the optimism of Julia Gilliard's 2012 speech can still be discerned in the way that Damian Palmer and Jane Tracy speak about the NDIS today. Each tended to view the NDIS as an ongoing process and both thought it a better system than the one it replaced. They also both acknowledged that building a new system from the ground up is a fraught process that can take some time. After all, the transformation—if we may call it that—of the Wild West in the USA took more than thirty years.

References

Antaki, Charles, W.L. Finlay, and Chris Walton. 2009. Choices for People with Intellectual Disabilities: Official Discourse and Everyday Practice. *Journal of Policy and Practice in Intellectual Disabilities* 6: 260–266.

Atkinson, Dorothy. 2004. Research and Empowerment: Involving People with Learning Difficulties in Oral and Life History Research. *Disability & Society* 19: 691–702.

Atkinson, Dorothy, and Jan Walmsely. 2010. History from the Inside: Towards and Inclusive History of Intellectual Disability. *Scandinavian Journal of Disability Research* 12: 273–286.

Arnold, John. 1998. The Historian as Inquisitor: The Ethics of Interrogating Subaltern Voices. *Rethinking History* 2: 379–386.

Bigby, Christine. 2014. Is the National Disability Insurance Scheme Taking Account of People with Intellectual Disabilities? *Research and Practice in Intellectual and Developmental Disabilities* 1: 93–94.

Bigby, Christine, Mary Whiteside, and Jactinta Douglas. 2019. Supporting Decision Making of Adults with Intellectual Disabilities: Perspectives of Family Members and Workers in Disability Supported Services. *Journal of Intellectual and Developmental Disabilities* 44: 396–409.

Bigby, Christine. 2020a. "Glossing Over Issues in the Rush to Have Everybody Under the Disability Banner": Dedifferentiation and People with Intellectual Disabilities in Australian National Disability Insurance Scheme. *Journal of Intellectual and Developmental Disabilities*.

Bigby, Christine. 2020b. 'The Scheme Was Designed with a Very Different Idea in Mind of Who a Disabled Person Is': The NDIS and People with Intellectual Disabilities. In *The National Disability Insurance Scheme: A Public Policy Experiment in Australia*, ed. Mhairi Cowden and Claire McCullagh. Melbourne: Palgrave Macmillan.

Bonyhady, Bruce. 2014. Tides of Change: The NDIS and Its Journey to Transform Disability Support. *Australian Journal of Psychosocial Rehabilitation* 7: 7–9.

Burton, Mark, and Carolyn Kagan. 2006. Decoding Valuing People. *Disability & Society* 21: 299–313.

Carey, Gemma, Adrian Kay, and Ann Nevil. 2019. Institutional Legacies and Sticky Layers: What Happens in the Cases of Transformative Policy Change. *Administration and Society* 51: 491–509.

Carney, Terry, Shih-Ning. Then, Christine Bigby, Ilan Wiesel, and Jacinta Douglas. 2019. National Disability Insurance Scheme Plan Decision-Making: Or When Tailor-Made Case Planning Me Taylorism & the Algorithms? *Melbourne University Law Review* 42: 783–812.

Clegg, Jennifer, and Christine Bigby. 2017. Debates About Dedifferentiation: Twenty-First Century Thinking About People with Intellectual Disabilities as Distinct Members of the Disability Group. *Research and Practice in Intellectual and Developmental Disabilities* 4: 80–97.

Frisch, Michael. 1990. *A shared Authority: Essays on the Craft and Meaning of Oral and Public History*. Albany, New York: State University of New York Press.

Henderson, David, and Christine Bigby. 2017a. Whose Lie Story Is It? Self-Reflexive Life Story Research with People with Intellectual Disabilities. *Oral History Review* 44: 39–55.

Henderson, David, and Christine Bigby. 2017b. 'We Were More Radical Back Then': Victoria's First Self-Advocacy Organisation for People with Intellectual Disability. *Health and History* 18: 42–66.

Kendrick, Michael, Margaret Ward, and Lesley Chenoweth. 2017. Australia's National Disability Insurance Scheme: Looking Back to Shape the Future. *Disability & Society* 32: 1333–1350.

Lakhani, Ali, Donna McDonald, and Heidi Zeeman. 2018. Perspectives of the National Disability Insurance Scheme: Participants' Knowledge and Expectations of Scheme. *Disability & Society* 33: 783–803.

Lloyd, Jan, Karen Moni, Monica Cuskelly, and Anne Jobling. 2019. Engaging with National Disability Insurance Scheme planning: Perspectives of Parents of an Adult with Intellectual Disability. *Journal of Intellectual & Developmental Disability* 44: 254–263.

Mavromaras, Kostas, Megan Moskos, Stéphane Mahuteau, and Linda Isherwood. 2018. Evaluation of the NDIS: Final Report. National Institute of Labour Studies, Flinders University. https://www.dss.gov.au/sites/default/files/documents/04_2018/ndis_evaluation_consolidated_report_april_2018.pdf.

NSW CID. 2014. Conference Report Getting the Best from the NDIS Making It Work for People with Intellectual Disability. https://cid.org.au/.

O'Connor, Morrie. 2014. The National Disability Insurance Scheme and People with Mild Intellectual Disability: Potential Pitfalls for Consideration. *Research and Practice in Intellectual and Developmental Disabilities* 1: 17–23.

Palmer, Damian. 2016. 'Can't I Just Be Me?' When the Embrace of Goals Is an Act of Exclusion. Exclusion and Embrace: Disability, Justice and Spirituality Conference. https://exclusionandembrace.melbourne/.

Parliamentary Debates. 2012. *House of Representatives*. Commonwealth of Australia. https://www.aph.gov.au/parliamentary_business/hansard/hansreps_2011.

Productivity Commission. 2011. Disability Care and Support: Productivity Commission Inquiry Report—Volume 1. Commonwealth of Australia. https://www.pc.gov.au/inquiries/completed/disability-support/report/disability-support-volume1.pdf.

Productivity Commission. 2017. National Disability Insurance Scheme Costs: Productivity Commission Study Report. Commonwealth of Australia. https://www.pc.gov.au/inquiries/completed/disability-support/report.

Thomas, David. 2006. A General Inductive Approach to Analysing Qualitative Evaluation Data. *American Journal of Evaluation* 27: 237–246.

Thomson, Alistair. 2003. Sharing Authority: Oral History and the Collaborative Process. *Oral History Review* 30: 23–26.

CHAPTER 20

Individual Stories of the National Disability Insurance Scheme

Samantha Jenkinson

Introduction

This chapter collates the personal stories of seven people who have accessed the National Disability Insurance Scheme (NDIS) since it was introduced: Andrew F, Joseph G, Georgie H, Peter Darch, Sally M, Lynne F and Melinda Smith. Each story, told in the person's own words or by their families and carers, describes a different experience of the individualised planning process and with NDIS staff and service providers including Planners (employed by the NDIA and responsible for approving participant plans), Local Area Coordinators (LAC) (who work with participants to develop and implement their plans) and Support Coordinators (who support those needing extra help implementing their plans). Some participants are self-managing their NDIS plans, while others have plan-managed funding (where the NDIA provides funding to a 'Plan Manager' to pay service providers on a participant's behalf) or NDIA-managed funding (where the NDIA pays providers on the participant's

S. Jenkinson (✉)
Perth, WA, Australia

M. Cowden and C. McCullagh (eds.), *The National Disability Insurance Scheme*, https://doi.org/10.1007/978-981-16-2244-1_20

behalf). All stories include some positive reflections on the NDIS, as well as criticisms of the scheme.

Andrew F

Andrew is a peer leader in the amputee community known as 'the One-Legged Sax Player'. This is his NDIS Journey (so far).

"I had my first planning meeting with a delegate from the NDIS in January 2019. The meeting was held at the NDIS Office in Joondalup WA, in a very inaccessible building and with no accessible carparks anywhere close to the office.

The delegate had never done a plan for an amputee, so I spent quite a lot of time explaining to him why I had asked for things such as socks and the difference between a day leg, a sports prosthetic and a water limb. The planning meeting went for well over three hours. Way too long.

I was pleasantly surprised at the plan that was given to me. It had all that I had asked for in it. I had asked for a new socket for my day leg, a complete water leg and a new wheelchair. I didn't ask for any Core Supports [supports to complete activities of daily living such as transport and assistance with household tasks] as I wouldn't use them. He didn't question this either. I had all my funds agency managed, especially the Capital Supports [higher-cost pieces of equipment, assistive technology, home or vehicle modifications and funding for one-off purchases], which were all "quote required supports" [supports which require a quote before funding can be made available].

Here is where the fun began. It took 3 months from the time the quote for a new socket for my day leg was put in to the NDIS. In that 3 months I had to go back into my old wheelchair as I couldn't walk using my old socket. After much backwards and forwards with the NDIA it was finally approved. My prosthetic provider started the new socket build and I suggested that it would be good to get the quote in for the water leg as it would take about six to nine months minimum to get it approved.

We put the Assistive Technology request together, submitted it to the Assistive Technology Team and six days later got an email saying it had been approved 100 per cent. Exactly as I wanted. Two weeks later I had a brand-new water leg.

My wheelchair was similar. My Occupational Therapist (OT) got me an appointment at Motum [a mobility solutions company]. We went there and tried out a bunch of chairs. My OT wrote up an Assistive Technology assessment and request for the agency, including a second set of off-road wheels and a Free Wheel. These were put in as separate Assistive Technology requests just so if they knocked them back, we would still get the new chair. Now, being as though I am not a fulltime chair user, and the NDIS had just funded me $13,000 for a new water leg, we were not confident that they would approve what we had requested. A week later my OT had an email from the Independent Living Centre [an allied health and assistive technology provider] Assistive Technology Assessment Team, asking her if I still needed the chair. She replied yes, he does. A week after that we get an email from the Assistive Technology Team at NDIS saying the fund for the chair, the second set of wheels and the Free Wheel, will be in my account tomorrow. So, the whole process was done and dusted in about four weeks. The new chair is awesome.

First plan complete. Second plan: January 2020. I attended my planning meeting in Warwick. The Local Area Coordinator had never worked with an amputee. The planning meeting went on for about 3.5 hours. I felt I was listened to and validated.

Predominantly my plan was about maintenance of my current Assistive Technology and the ability to have repairs and minor rebuilds done as required. I also asked for home modifications to be placed in the plan so I could start the process of having my house made accessible. With this in mind, I gave my Local Area Coordinator the Functional Capacity Assessment that my OT had completed. This Functional Capacity Assessment had all the photos and requirements we wanted for the home modifications.

The plan was approved on the 19 January 2020 and on 20 January 2020 went to be reviewed. The NDIA delegate decided that the home modifications were not reasonable and necessary.

Two and a half months later I get a call from the Assistive Technology Review Team wanting to know why I hadn't put any quotes or building designs in for the home modifications. I had to explain to him the process, being: they open the line item in my plan, fund me to get the quotes and designs, I send it back, they review and say yes or no. This seemed a very hard concept for him to grasp.

Two weeks later, end of April, I get a letter from the NDIS stating that they are going to stick to their original decision of my home modifications not being reasonable and necessary, but they will give me fifteen…hours to get another OT report and to complete the Complex Home Modification Form, $500 to engage a builder to do some plans and an extra $5,000 in my Assistive Technology budget.

At the end of this process, they have asked me to put in for another plan review for them to look at. As I write this, I have engaged a specialist OT who only does home modifications, and she has completed the Complex Home Modifications Form for the NDIA. I am waiting to hear from the builder she has recommended, and I haven't spent any more of the Assistive Technology funds.

So that brings us up to date. As I write this, I have an issue with my socket and am in my really nice NDIA-funded chair. The issue is though, I cannot get said chair out of the house, due to steps at the front and the back and I can neither shower, nor use the toilet, as the chair doesn't fit into those rooms. So much for my home modification not being reasonable and necessary and being told, in writing, that the home modification request was not effective".

Joseph G

Joseph is a young man with a supportive family, who previously had support from State Government funding. He is on his third plan. His family and Support Coordinator have shared his experience and that of his family through their transition to NDIS.

"Joseph loves people, outdoors, and entertaining at home. He is currently 22 years of age, and lives in an accessible rental home with 24/7 supports and his pet dog Crystal. Joseph has occasional employment participating in making training and community materials about people with complex communication needs. His goals are to increase his lifestyle choices and have enhanced communication opportunities and relationships.

Joseph's first plan was for six months. We asked for funding to move from our partially self-managed state funding arrangement pre-NDIS to being managed by the agency. We had been self-managing to get the dollars to stretch to meet Joseph's needs in his own home as he had been in group living previously. That first plan had insufficient funding to meet Joseph's needs. The family were forced to continue self-management, which meant we were doing all of the organising and administration of his 24/7 support. There was inadequate allocation for support or therapy. There seemed to be adequate funding for equipment.

We requested a review by the NDIA, and the family were supported by an advocacy agency. The family voice was not clearly communicated to the NDIA via the advocacy agency representative which left us feeling unheard, dismissed and further stressed. Joseph's second plan was also for six months following the review. There were some improvements to supports for daily living, such as having Joseph's need for two-person transfers acknowledged. However, there was still inadequate funding for agency managed supports, and insufficient therapy allocation.

Joseph then went a few months without a plan, with insufficient support. We put in a change of circumstances request to NDIA with support from our Specialist Support Coordinator and another advocacy agency. We enlisted the support of our local federal MP this time. This was a very stressful, time-consuming process. Joseph and us – his parents – were in desperation, so we visited the NDIA office in person to attempt to expedite the process and be listened to. This had a positive impact.

Joseph is now on his third plan, which is for 12 months. This third plan has funding allocated through Supported Independent Living (SIL) [help and/or supervision of daily tasks to help participants live as independently as possible while building skills] for agency-managed supports, but there is still insufficient funding for therapy. Nursing support and dietetics support has been included and is welcomed.

This year, six months into the third plan, we have needed to put in for change of circumstances as there has been significant changes in Joseph's abilities. He has reduced swallowing skills and his risk has increased, and he has a significant increase in consumable needs (RIG, caecostomy syringes, pads, uridome etc.), plus increased nursing coordination required.

As a family we are hopeful that the current planner seems to understand well Joseph's needs and was very disappointed, distressed even, to learn of current struggles to have basic hygiene needs met. The planner wrote to the SIL provider with detailed, pertinent questions which resulted in immediate improvement in the staffing level to accommodate two more changes a day to address incontinence. The new planner has also re-opened dialogue between Joseph and his SIL provider. The planner has helped us, Joseph's parents, to understand that the provider needed to be accountable to Joseph directly, not just to NDIA, in how they allocated the SIL funds.

Overall, as the NDIA gets to know Joseph better, and provides staff with better knowledge and skills, the plans Joseph receives are getting better at meeting his needs. We are hopeful that the current change of circumstances with increased need for consumables and therapy will be met. Although the plans are slowly moving closer to what Joseph needs, we are not there yet. This change of circumstances request is the first to be dealt with in a reasonable timeframe and without us contacting the NDIA repeatedly. This is a big improvement. We have confidence that the planner will advocate fairly for Joseph and that we will be listened to. We have provided detailed reports, and lots of information to the NDIA before, but it feels like this is the first time that we can tell they've been read and paid attention to. This is a big improvement.

Prior to this current planner there were problems with having frequent requests for new reports from therapists because [Joseph's] plan was so short. There was an unwillingness of planners to 'accept' first reports (e.g. that Joseph needs two-person transfers, despite 12-page documents citing all examples and the therapy report). Current planner seems to accept what his therapists are saying.

Having found a very good Specialist Support Coordinator has made a big difference in plan funds being utilised and Joseph being supported in meeting his goals. Joseph's Support Coordinator has many years' experience in NDIS engagement, terminology, and processes which has helped us immensely.

We chose a service provider that we knew well to [manage] the support as we have several years working together and felt they knew Joseph and his family's values well. Unfortunately, we are finding that as managers they have so many rules that choice and control feels limited, although they try. We may opt to move to a smaller agency in the future.... or even go to self-managing if we must to get flexibility, choice and control. Joseph has a large team of workers and managing them is a huge job. This is why we wanted agency management...but we are finding significant loss of flexibility and support workers now having less commitment to Joseph because they perceive they work for the service provider and not Joseph. This change in attitude wasn't anticipated, and we're working on improving it.

Having SIL is limiting, as we have to ask the provider for permission to allocate hours to training for staff on new equipment etc. and we lose flexibility. We have to convince the provider of things we know from our previous self-management experience work for Joseph and his team.

Joseph has also had significant problems getting approvals for equipment, with several month delays in getting pressure and postural equipment approved. This has resulted in further permanent postural deterioration in Joseph's body as well as associated pain.

This has felt like an epic journey with wins and losses. Battles have been had with disability providers, the NDIS, as well as with mainstream health. The journey is far from over as we are into another change of circumstances.

The emotional rollercoaster has been up and down, waiting for an NDIA response when timelines were getting close to funding running out and the feeling of frustration and helplessness at the system. When Joseph got funded for a large amount of SIL we thought most problems would resolve. But here we are, still looking at issues with SIL and agency management and getting Joseph's needs met".

Georgie H

> Georgie is on her second NDIS plan and about to go for review. She is deaf and Auslan is her first language.

"When I went to my first planning meeting, they did have an interpreter, but it was not an interpreter of my choice. I didn't have a choice of which agency they used for their interpreters and they [the LAC] told me they could only use the one agency.

I couldn't be sure that what I was saying was being interpreted and heard by the planner. The interpreter knew who I was, because the deaf community is small, but was not someone who knew me and was not someone I felt I could trust to understand my personal circumstances and relay that well. I couldn't hear the words she said, so I had to trust she was interpreting what I had signed. I really didn't have a very good vibe at that first meeting with the LAC and the interpreter they provided.

They really should ask me if I am happy with the interpreter. The same thing happened with my second planning meeting where they didn't even ask me who I wanted to use or let me book the interpreter. Because they refused to let me book the interpreter that I wanted, I had a Support Coordinator who was also an interpreter that came along to the meeting and provided interpretation for me. As my Support Coordinator she was fighting for me to be able to choose who I had as interpreter, but we kept getting told that they had to use the one agency that provides interpreters. They kept refusing me from having a choice. My Support Coordinator could come as my Support Coordinator and was also able to be an interpreter for me because that was her background.

When I did my first plan there were no Support Coordinators who were fluent in Auslan. It felt like just me against the world and I had nowhere to go. I didn't know what to ask for or what to say, and everywhere I would go, like to the organisations that normally help deaf people, they didn't know either. Now they know, but then they didn't, and they couldn't help. I also didn't want to use those organisations because the deaf community is small and things are not always as confidential as you want them to be. It's really important to find people who have all the deaf awareness and can speak Auslan but are independent.

In my first plan I got funding for interpreters but not enough. I managed, but that's the problem, I really had to manage! So sometimes I had to choose which day I would have an interpreter and which day I wouldn't because the money was quite limited. I have to make a choice when really, I want to be able to use interpreters ongoing and I feel like I am stopped from being able to do things. I'm being held back in doing what I want to do in my life because I can't have an interpreter all the times I need.

In my first plan they also refused to give me funding for equipment. In my second plan, I got more funding for interpreters and funding for equipment. I am using lots of Internet and needing my devices to connect with people. I can use interpreters that don't have to be with me when I have good equipment, and things like Zoom, so I can have a meeting with someone and get the interpreter on my phone. This is fantastic, it's great giving me more choice, but I have to get my head around the technology and all the equipment. It's not just the technology but also the data and the Wi-Fi. Sometimes it's really great but sometimes it's really slow and that can affect the interpreter if their connection isn't good.

It's still very new for me. I prefer having meetings face-to-face with an interpreter there. Unless the technology improves a lot, which might take some time, I don't think they are there yet.

I got funding for support coordination in my second plan and I was really hoping it would make a difference. I was hoping that they would be able to find and give me the information that I would need about how the NDIS works, how to use the funding and what all the things in the plan mean when they keep changing them all the time. They keep changing the way it's set out and I can hardly keep up. I get quite easily overwhelmed with all the things happening in my personal life, and then dealing with NDIS as well.

I was really disappointed. The Support Coordinator was planning things behind my back without telling me, and so I ended up paying double for things. It's really about trust, and I don't feel that I can trust right now. It felt like someone trying to control me and using the money without my consent.

Then because I was getting overwhelmed, I delayed putting in some payments and some requests for payments. The second year really didn't go very well. I am self-managing my funding but I'm thinking about changing my mind now. I can talk about it and understand it, but when it comes to doing all of the actions like making bookings and doing the payments, then putting in the requests, that's when it becomes overwhelming.

I'm talking to a bookkeeper to see if they might be able to help. They seem very nice and they can help with paying the bills but they can't do following up on things with the NDIS. They can only do this one small part though and I'd rather have one person who is able to do the managing of everything for me. They are also hearing so I need an interpreter when talking with them.

The NDIS has made a difference because now I can have an interpreter on those important days which before, through all my life it was a barrier to be able to get an interpreter when I needed. The door is opening, and it is an improvement. So yes, things are better but there are not enough interpreters. So, I have the funding now to pay for interpreters more of the times that I need them, but because there are not enough qualified interpreters it's hard to always get the ones that I want and who I know work well for me.

I can read and write in English but I know that there are people in the deaf community who don't have that same level of education and it worries me that they are not going to be able to get the right support and be heard. For understanding concepts like 'reasonable and necessary' in the NDIS I really need to have an example because they are new ideas.

The NDIS doesn't seem to understand how important having the right interpreter is for me. I need to feel I've got the right vibe with the interpreter, that we are going to understand each other, so then I know they are going to interpret correctly. Both the NDIA and the LAC are really not very good at communicating. I have told them to communicate with me via email and text and they still will call. There is a big sign on my information that says 'DEAF' and they still call me all the time.

I use the portal to pay the invoices and get the funding. I find the portal can get really confusing with all of the different groups and categories to put against the funding. I'm worried that I'm not putting the things in the right groups and I just wish that there was the one group and that was just my funding and my plan. I wish the NDIA would just work out behind-the-scenes the right categories that they can check with me then at the review. I am worried because I have heard that other deaf people have done it wrong on the portal and then had to pay the money back, and I don't want that to happen.

Interpreting is the one category that I definitely know where to put the invoice, but all the others like the occupational therapist and the equipment I'm never sure which category is the right one.

I have my review coming up and I'm a little bit worried because I won't have the Support Coordinator with me this time. I want to be able to choose and book the interpreter myself, but I am worried that they will pick the interpreter for me. Right now, I am just keeping moving forward with using the NDIS, but I feel like I don't know where to go next because I don't have the same choice of providers. It has meant that I can do more of the things that I want to do because I can access funding for interpreters and equipment, but it is also overwhelming, and I do need help".

Peter Darch

Peter Darch is an Every Australian Counts Campaign Champion on the NDIS. Here he shares his experience with the scheme since he became a participant in 2017.

"I was stuck between the state funding system, which provided my funding for personal care and in-home support, and the lack of support I could get to do my job, to be employed, because that was a federal issue and not provided".

When he was a teenager, Peter broke his neck in a swimming accident and became quadriplegic. After completing studies as a Youth Worker, Peter had support from a Disability Employment Service (DES) to find work with the City of Mandurah. As a work placement, the DES was able to provide the physical support Peter needed while in the workplace, but once he was employed that support stopped.

"It was just ridiculous because I got funding from the state to get support at home, I could apply to get funding from the state to get support to go out and into the community for recreation, but if I have a job, I can't get the support I need in the workplace".

As a way to raise awareness of how the system was failing people with disability in employment when they were doing a great job, Peter's colleagues nominated him for a WA Youth Worker of the Year Award. Peter won the Award, and was also awarded the 2011 WA Young Person of the year. The Every Australian Counts campaign and the promise of the NDIS seemed like the perfect vehicle to continue his own campaign and was highlighting the same issues of a system that was disconnected from people's lives.

Peter has been receiving NDIS for over two years. "I really thought that DES would be absorbed into NDIS, so you weren't dealing with two different systems. I think that is still a problem that needs to get sorted".

"I expected the system would work with every year you say: 'this is where I am at, this is what I need'. It has taken a little while to get the support I need, but I can honestly say the support I get at home is good, the staff are getting paid properly, the Assistive Technology is perfect. The separation of employment support with DES is still a problem. I just need more physical support at work, particularly when you first start a job - getting your desk set up, paperwork, getting lunch out for me – things like that. My next NDIS plan will have that employment support in the plan which is great".

"I have had a little frustration with planners and I know others have too. There has to be trust that we [people with disability] know our lives and time to build confidence in us. People who haven't got a disability don't get it. They can't understand it's not the big things, but the little things like needing to ask someone to get your lunch out for you and put the fork in your hand".

"We really need more people with disability in planner and LAC roles. Just saying 'lived experience of disability' is a cop out as its too broad. Advocates and peer workers should also be working alongside planners and LACs to help them understand the diversity of people".

"I get worried public servants might resent working in NDIS and supporting people with disability if we are not working alongside them at every level. The involvement of people with disability feels more limited now than at the beginning. Advocacy is really needed to keep them [the NDIA and governments] honest and we have managed to get some good policy change through advocacy, but we also need people with disability working alongside, doing the training, being planners and LACs".

Sally M

Sally all is a young woman with Elhers Danlos Syndrome. This is her account of the NDIS six months into her first plan in February 2020.

"NDIS is both a blessing and a curse. I am grateful for the funding to access much needed supports, equipment and services. It is, however, a giant maze.

I am quite a well-educated, intelligent person, but I find the whole process really hard to navigate. The waiting times for some things are super inconsistent, unpredictable and long. It was so hard to get everything together to get onto the NDIS. The information on the NDIS website is not accessible nor is it easy to read. I have provided feedback on multiple occasions to NDIS. Still nothing has changed. Everything seems to be PDF and I cannot access PDF documents. I only have a basic phone, no computer or ipad or other device for internet access. PDF is not screen reader compatible. Half the time I can't print them either. All their information is written like a politician's document.

I get concerned that as a person who is university educated, if I don't understand the process and relay of the information, then how can someone with an intellectual disability or no support system access this?

It took a couple years and two attempts to get my NDIS application accepted, even with an OT report and lots of documents. I had to pay to get the OT reports which cost over $500 and I have since helped others that have paid over $1000 in getting reports for their NDIS application and planning. I was also referred to Mission Australia for help with my second application, because I couldn't afford more appointments and reports, only to be told they didn't help with access requests. I had some help from a friend who played a big part in getting my second application over the line. It's impossible to get access to NDIS without additional help: none of which I knew about the first time. All this was after waiting two years for NDIS to be in my area (I was told ages later that technically I could have applied earlier).

Then, once my access was approved, I had a planning meeting with Mission Australia, waited, then got pushed to an NDIA planner, where I was told that my plan should have been approved a year before. Meanwhile all this waiting caused huge amounts of stress and put my health at risk as I could not access some necessary equipment that the hospital no longer supplied, as they said it should have been done by NDIS. My application was processed under the highest priority, but it still took about six months, which was too long.

Once on it, the maze gets bigger and more tangled. I still can't access all of what I need as I don't know how to navigate the system. On one hand I am told that with NDIS I have independence, choice and control, but in reality, I don't. There is so much assumed knowledge, and with such long waitlists with the therapists who would be best suited to my care, it's really hard. So, I go without.

For example, ages ago we spoke about beds, I was told by my OT to go look at beds that would be better for me. I did. I found one that would make it easier for me to get in and out of, has an IV pole, and pressure care mattress and I told the OT. I am yet to see the OT report.

Similarly, at the time we had spoken about beds I was also told to look at Assistive Technology, recliners and any other equipment I needed. I looked and got quotes then sent them to the OT months ago, and I have only just seen the Assistive Technology form by the OT. It did not match the conversation I had with the OT about what I need and shouldn't be sent to NDIS as it misses out all of my goals and is just rubbish.

But I don't know who else I can see. Not all OTs know how to write Assistive Technology forms. So again, I go without. Again, I have lost independence, choice and control. Again, I am isolated because of a lack of supports.

There doesn't seem to be recourse for what happens if OTs or service providers charge a service but don't deliver. There seems to be a massive lack of accountability. To my knowledge there is no service directory. There is no accessible cheat sheet to know what is and isn't covered.

However, on a positive with NDIS I have a choice in my support workers which has been a massive game changer. I was under Home and Community Care previously and stuck with an awful support service where I had to support the support workers, which was not ok.

I can fairly easily access the supplies I need for my feeding tube. When I know where to go for low-risk Assistive Technology and for my wound care, I can get the supplies needed instead of putting myself at risk like I was pre-NDIS.

Once the right things are in place, it's amazing. I am grateful for being able to choose my support worker and get some low cost/low risk Assistive Technology stuff that I have been waiting years for. I have been lucky with my planners, but it was super intense having to go through it twice.

With NDIA, the plan I have now was only meant to be six months so all the figures they told me were based on six months. When they implemented my plan, they put 12 months, so now there's an issue with bed, power chair, recliner, vehicle mods and IT as although they're included in my plan, it looks like there won't be enough funding. It's frustrating...

It is easy knowing what I need to be funded, but hard to know how to access the funding to get what I need. Trying to navigate through it all is really bloody hard".

Lynne F

Lynne lives in Geelong and was in the first group of NDIS participants in 2013.

"Before the NDIS came in, lots of people just took it for granted. I had an Individual Support Plan (ISP) from the State Government. An organisation in Geelong cobbled together some funding so I could get some Personal Support as I was never in the system.

I was a campaigner to get the NDIS started in 2011, so finally seeing a major reform come in 2013, which was such a short time, was incredible. I had attended all the workshops and conferences on the NDIS you could think of, learning everything about how it was going to work. However, the day you go into your first planning meeting, you forget all you learnt, but it is all still there in you, just pushed to the back of your brain.

I guess we were lucky as Geelong is the National Office, so we were the first to roll out. I started jotting down the things I needed, I didn't have much anyway, so it was easy to think of what I needed. I knew from day one I wanted to have a Plan Management Agency, as I was traveling and living in the only state that had the agency at that time, I wouldn't be able to use my funding out of Geelong if it was Agency Managed. I wanted a Support Coordinator, as its someone to go to if you're having issues, and I find it's great to have a second opinion.

My first plan was amazing, in fact they gave me too much I thought at the time (back then you never saw the dollar figures). Naturally, I needed a new power wheelchair and a manual wheelchair. I think I really felt overwhelmed, because I didn't have enough hours before and suddenly I had more. There were things I really wanted and made sure they were in the plan, like going surfing twice a year with the Disabled Surfers Association. That falls on a Sunday which I couldn't do prior to NDIS as my provider said they could only provide essential services on Sundays.

I know when my first NDIS plan rolled over the budget had blown out, as they had forgotten that the Assistive Technology equipment was worn out or just too old to use, and I had to get new ones.

We all learn as we go along. What works for us and what does not. I have had 13 plans since I started and coming up to my 14th in August 2020. Every plan the Agency kept on forgetting things. Yes, I have had a few issues with my plans. Simple things like they put down Agency Managed instead of Plan Managed, but in those two or so weeks before they can change it back no one gets paid. Instead of just tweaking the plan, they have to send you a completely new plan with different start and end dates.

At one stage my power wheelchair was a write off, so I was hiring one though my plan. I ended up hiring one for four months or so and that was only last year, while I was waiting for my new one to come through. I do know a few people from the agency, but I don't like to take advantage of that. However, they heard my plea on ABC radio, so they acted quickly to get my new chair on the go.

I guess I have been lucky with my planners (I've had mostly good ones). The chair issue last year would have been the worst thing that has happened to me, as the hire chair also wasn't adapted for me and it did take longer that it should have, but also that was the supplier".

Melinda Smith

Melinda Smith is on her second NDIS plan. Melinda has Cerebral Palsy and was previously receiving support through the Victorian State Government system.

"NDIS... A Success? My first plan was implemented in July 2018. I was reasonably happy with it, particularly after all my effort to write my personal plan, highlighting my goals and needs. I had spent months preparing and researching, what plans should look like and what I could ask for.

My first plan meeting was pretty stressful, and I ended up with a planner who was 18 years old, a male with cerebral palsy. I obviously was there to educate him, so perhaps this went in my favour, simply, I could at least argue my rights, because I knew more than him.

My first plan gave me the basis of what I thought I needed at the time, which was not great. I had enough to do the minimum in my day, week and knew I could get through it by budgeting really well.

My second plan, which fell into place 12 months later, was a completely different situation. I knew more about what to ask for, as well as a much more definite grip on my goals, and work-life balance desires. My confidence had developed as had my knowledge and trust in the NDIS. My second plan has been amazing in terms of helping to maintain the supports I need in my day-to-day life.

I have been able to achieve some incredibly simple goals in my life, things like going for walks in my walking frame, constructing my own vegie garden and having more meals each day, which has improved my health and energy level. I can also assist with cooking, and I have more support with my employment which means my jobs have increased so much more.

My second plan has given me more time to do the things I'm passionate about. I don't need to think twice about saving my hours for an activity I want to do. If I want to spend six hours exploring my camera and have someone around to help me change the SD card or battery, adjust my tripod etc. I can do this comfortably.

The only thing that has not worked very well through NDIS is the equipment and Assistive Technology funds. I'm self-managed and this is the one area of my plan that is absolutely crap! It took over 12 months to get my new communication device despite my self-advocating, and now I go through the same with my new manual wheelchair – 6 months have gone by since my physio submitted an application and quote... and nothing has been said since...".

Conclusion

The individual stories of Andrew, Joseph, Georgie, Peter, Sally, Lynne and Melinda touch on many of the broader challenges and experiences that have emerged since the NDIS was introduced. The next chapter—the final of this book—synthesises some of the wider themes and lessons that have begun to emerge as the NDIS in implemented across Australia. It also identifies some of the challenges and opportunities for the NDIS as it moves into full operation across the country.

CHAPTER 21

Conclusion: The Challenges and Opportunities for the NDIS

Mhairi Cowden and Claire McCullagh

Introduction

In the previous chapter, on the experience of people with disability with the National Disability Insurance Scheme (NDIS), Sally M describes the scheme as a 'blessing and a curse'. When she used this phrase, she was speaking about the impact of the NDIS on her own life. For Sally, the blessing is the funding, services and equipment that the NDIS provides. The curse is the giant maze of the scheme itself. This maze is unpredictable, inconsistent, and takes time and effort to navigate effectively.

Describing the NDIS as a 'blessing and a curse' is not only true at an individual level. It also works to describe the scheme as a whole. The NDIS has brought much-needed support to many people with disability. It has cemented an entitlement to support in legislation and put front and centre the concept of choice and control. Making the bold decision to introduce the NDIS has brought with it praise for governments across Australia. Implementing this vision, however, has been a curse

M. Cowden (✉) · C. McCullagh
Nous Group, Perth, WA, Australia

M. Cowden and C. McCullagh (eds.), *The National Disability Insurance Scheme*, https://doi.org/10.1007/978-981-16-2244-1_21

for many. Things have not gone so well for vulnerable people with disability trying to access the scheme. It has been difficult for Australian politicians and policymakers to lock down long-term funding for the scheme: a challenge which appears even more pressing given Australia's first recession in 30 years following the COVID-19 pandemic. The transition out of a state-based disability system into a centrally managed one, while designing and introducing a new statutory agency—the National Disability Insurance Agency (NDIA)—has also been challenging.

The chapters of this book have touched on the 'blessing' and 'curse' that is the NDIS through many different lenses. In this final chapter, we draw together the key themes and lessons learned from the implementation of the NDIS so far. We begin by identifying the headline challenges for the NDIS as it moves into full scheme operation. We then offer comment on what has worked well during the transition and the opportunities that the NDIS represents. The NDIS offers hope to many, and we hope these reflections will help ensure the scheme is implemented in a way that lives up to these expectations.

Challenges

The first part of this book has provided an overview of what the NDIS is, the history of disability services and the different journeys each Australian state and territory has taken. Through these chapters, we have argued that the NDIS is a unique piece of public policy as it marries together several key objectives:

- It creates an entitlement to reasonable and necessary supports for people with disability.
- It puts people with disability at the centre of decision-making regarding their own services, including managing their own funds where appropriate.
- It introduces a national scheme where there had previously only been varied state and territory systems, leading to inconsistency and a 'postcode lottery' of services.
- It is based on insurance principles. It takes a lifetime approach to cost and risk, and invests in early intervention to improve outcomes and reduce the need for expensive interventions later in life.
- It dismantles block funding (where funding is allocated to organisations or agencies, not individuals) and builds a new market for

disability services, where people with disability are consumers with buying power.

However, the NDIS has not been the wholesale policy reform that was originally envisioned. According to the blueprint set out by the Productivity Commission's 2011 Disability Care and Support report, the NDIS was intended to do away with old ways of working and set out a completely new approach. What has instead been adopted in legislation, policy and practice is a system with new features, but which also retains many of the old ones too. In Chapter Eight, on implementation of the NDIS, Gemma Carey and Eleanor Malbon show us that there is no such thing as a blank canvas for the introduction of new policy initiatives. They argue that 'path dependency' and 'policy layering' mean that we take with us where we have come from and build on old systems. As a result, what citizens end up with is often very different from what was initially 'designed'.

Carey and Malbon's theory of path dependency provides important context to the following six challenges we have identified for the NDIS:

1. Outcomes for people with disability are varied in the NDIS.
2. National consistency must be balanced with flexibility.
3. The disability services market is still developing.
4. The true opportunity of service 'personalisation' has not yet been realised.
5. Difficulties remain with the interface between the NDIS and other service systems.
6. A sustainable funding model is essential for the NDIS to continue.

Each of these challenges is discussed below.

Outcomes for people with disability are varied in the NDIS

The first theme that is clear throughout almost all chapters in this book is that people with disability who have entered the NDIS have varied outcomes and experiences. For some people with disability, the NDIS has allowed them to access services or equipment that they previously had to fight for, or to have choice over their service providers for the first time in their lives. Some people with disability have found the NDIS empowering and enabling.

For others, the NDIS is not working. The 2018 Evaluation of the NDIS report found that the NDIS is working well for the majority of the people that it touches which is a major achievement. However, the NDIS also leaves a large minority (around one-third) about as well of as they were before, and it makes a small minority (between 10 and 20%) feel worse off (Mavromaras et al. 2018, xxiv–xxv). For some, initially negative encounters with the NDIS have improved with time. The individual stories in Part Three of this book show that it can take a while for the NDIS to get to know people's needs and to develop a meaningful support plan with them. However, an improved experience often seems to vary depending on the capability of the particular NDIA staff working with a participant.

This book has shown that there are a few cohorts of people for whom the NDIS presents particular challenges. In their chapter, Theresa Williams and Geoff Smith explore the challenges of the NDIS for people with psychosocial disability. The 2018 Evaluation of the NDIS found that people with psychosocial disability were less satisfied with the quality of their supports than other participants, reported less choice and control and lower levels of wellbeing and social connections than other types of disability (Mavromaras et al. 2018). Williams and Smith argue that the NDIS was largely designed with limited reference to the needs of people with a psychosocial disability. They assert that the NDIS represents the philosophical underpinning of the disability sector's advocacy cohort—focused on person-centred and self-directed care, independence, community inclusion and participation. They also argue that one of the eligibility requirements for the NDIS—to demonstrate that a disability is permanent—appears at odds with the philosophy of the mental health sector and its focus on recovery: that is, living a meaningful life, with or without symptoms.

In her chapter, Christine Bigby paints a similarly disappointing picture of the experiences of people with intellectual disability. Bigby argues that the NDIS is not working for people with intellectual disability in the same way that it is working for other cohorts. She argues that 'while other groups, such as people with psychosocial disability or rural dwellers, were also relatively disadvantaged in the scheme, data available showed that people with intellectual disability generally fared the worse'. Bigby claims that the 'de-differentiated' approach of the NDIS—the focus on individuals with no specific reference to the disability or impairment type—may not be working, and that differentiated responses could be needed for adults with intellectual disability.

The NDIS is not always living up to its promise of personalisation, choice and control for Indigenous Australians. In her chapter, Jody Barney discusses how Indigenous ways of knowing are often determined by the experience, sharing and telling of stories. Her own chapter embodies this approach, highlighting issues with the NDIS through the stories of Indigenous people with disabilities and their interactions with thin service markets (markets too small to support the competitive provision of services). The stories that Barney tells in her chapter—of Dave, Naomi, Sally, Bill and Kath—demonstrate again that the NDIS does not work for everyone. It presents Dave, with the only option of moving away from his home, his family and his country, Naomi, whose services are not tailored to her needs, and Sally, Bill and Kath, whose rights to self-determination are forgotten during a process that disengages, disempowers and causes unnecessary angst. These stories demonstrate that many of the issues with Australia's previous disability system still exist within the NDIS.

Participant experiences of the NDIS have also often been found to vary with age. In her chapter, Mhairi Cowden highlights that the NDIS has not had the desired impact for children who are participants, and has negatively affected the wellbeing of those caring for children with disability. Cowden argues that better outcomes for children and their families in the NDIS can only be achieved through investing in supported decision-making—that is, where formal support is provided to a person with disability to help them make choices and decisions.

The chapters of this book have demonstrated that we can't take for granted that the NDIS will work the same for everyone. This presents a new challenge that is discussed in more detail in the next section: how to continue to deliver on the promise of national consistency while also responding to a diversity of needs and experiences.

National consistency must be balanced with flexible responses

The federated system of government in Australia – where responsibility for public services is split between different levels of government—was always going to be a challenge for the delivery of a public policy reform the size and scale of the NDIS. The scheme was introduced in part to address the 'postcode lottery' of the previous state-based disability services system. This previous system meant there was significant inconsistency and inequality across Australia in how disability services were delivered. However, the geography of Australia means that the delivery of services in inner-city Sydney, and in the remote parts of the Northern Territory (NT), is going to require different approaches.

The nationally consistent design of the NDIS is a strength, but can also prevent the scheme from adapting to different local and individual conditions. In his chapter on the NDIS and the healthcare system, Ian Thompson identifies that a lack of flexibility has meant the scheme has struggled to function appropriately in regional and remote areas. In her chapter on the NDIS and its impact on the not-for-profit sector, Penny Knight calls for a balance between centralised consistency and the ability of the scheme to respond to local markets.

Balancing national consistency with flexibility is also a challenge when catering for the diverse needs of participants accessing the scheme. In his chapter, Thompson identifies that the NDIS does not have the flexibility to respond appropriately to Indigenous people, Culturally and Linguistically Diverse (CaLD) people and people with complex needs. Thompson points out that the flexibility that was previously available to health providers to broker local solutions to service gaps with state and territory governments is not available through the centrally administered NDIS.

Similarly, in their chapter, Williams and Smith argue that if the eligibility permanence requirement is not changed for people with psychosocial disability (and it seems unlikely that it will), then the NDIS needs to be delivered in a more flexible way in order to work for people with psychosocial disability. This conclusion is reached in the Productivity Commission's review into scheme costs, which recommends that a specialised entry gateway for people with psychosocial disability be established (Productivity Commission 2017, 51). On this front, the Commonwealth Government has announced that a psychosocial disability stream will be introduced progressively from June 2020 (Fletcher and Henderson 2018). This demonstrates that the NDIS is evolving in the light of feedback and experiences.

In response to geographic differences and diverse participant needs, it appears that the original hardline 'de-differentiated' approach of the NDIS, which Bigby discusses in her chapter, has softened to a more tailored approach for some groups. This includes through the introduction of new pathways into the scheme and empowering state-level directors of the agency to make decisions and respond appropriately to the context in which they are working. However, these changes have occurred in a somewhat ad hoc manner. As Bigby argues, there is a risk that the NDIS will respond to groups capable of assertive advocacy and will potentially leave behind those who do not have strong political or social capital.

The disability services market is still developing

Choice and control for people with disability can only be achieved when there is a robust market of disability service providers for participants to choose from. In their chapter, Carey and Malbon discuss that the early years of the NDIS have been characterised by higher numbers of participants and higher average package costs compared to what was expected. Despite this, the NDIS has remained within its funding envelope. This is because participants have not been spending what is in their plan, due in part to the lack of a mature market of services for them to make purchases from.

Although thin markets are not new to disability systems, they have emerged as a significant challenge in the context of the NDIS. The issue of thin markets is particularly prominent in the NT, which has a dispersed population, the highest proportion of people living in remote and very remote areas (40.4% of the population) and the highest proportion of Indigenous people (30.3% of the population) in Australia (NT Department of Treasury and Finance 2016). Thin markets have been described by the NT Government (2017, 2) as "the biggest policy challenge for the implementation of the NDIS in the [NT]".

Thin markets are not just affecting regional and remote areas. The 2018 Joint Standing Committee inquiry into the NDIS transition identified that market failure is happening where people with complex needs cannot access appropriate services (Parliament of Australia 2018, 66–67). The Productivity Commission (2017, 36) similarly identified those with complex, specialised or high intensity needs, Indigenous people, people from CaLD backgrounds and those with acute and immediate needs as being most at risk of thin market effects. As Thompson points out in his chapter, thin markets are also appearing where services are highly specialised, and in some cases, this unmet demand is being picked up through other systems, such as the health system.

For Barney, thin markets are also not just defined by location, but also for people with complex needs, including cultural needs. Indigenous people with disability therefore experience a doubling effect of thin markets when their cultural needs are combined with living in regional areas. Barney argues that addressing the problem of thin markets for Indigenous people with disability is not a case of simply introducing the 'right' mode of communication or engagement. Rather, there are deeper flaws in the structure of the NDIS, because it assesses services as 'rigorous' when viewed as such from a mainstream Western lens, although when viewed from a cultural lens, are not rigorous at all. Barney argues that there is an urgent need to strengthen capacity and upskill Indigenous people to be support workers and deliver culturally appropriate services through the NDIS.

A functioning disability services market in Australia will rely on disability service providers adapting to new ways of working under the NDIS. However, adapting to the scheme has proven challenging for not-for-profit organisations, which are major contributors to the disability service delivery market in Australia. In her chapter, Penny Knight provides an overview of how the not-for-profit sector has fared with the introduction of the NDIS. She finds that the move to an individualised funding model under the NDIS—where funding is allocated against individual participants rather than directly to organisations as 'block funding'—has led to mixed outcomes for the sector. She explains that many not-for-profit organisations did not have the capital they needed to invest in transitioning their business to the NDIS and have found the scheme's new pricing structures challenging. This suggests the not-for-profit sector may be limited in its capacity to contribute to a robust service market under the NDIS.

Some of the key assumptions regarding the NDIS service market have not transpired. Not-for-profits have not been able to achieve 'efficiencies' by delivering more services at a larger scale, and the cost of service delivery has risen, not fallen. Big for-profit providers have not entered the market, indicating that they too believe the return on investment may not be worth it. Instead, there has been an increase in sole practitioners and small businesses in the allied health space arising as a result of the scheme.

In their chapter, Carey and Malbon identify that the retention of 'in-kind' services—where the Commonwealth Government, and State and Territory Governments continue to directly fund some disability services—partly explains why the NDIS looks so different to the scheme originally designed by the Productivity Commission. Continuing the existing contracts that governments had with service providers before the NDIS has, on the one hand, provided organisations with some stability in terms of revenue. On the other hand, it has removed elements of choice for parts of participant plans. The continuation of in-kind services also arguably provides a disincentive for service providers to adjust to the new world of individualised funding, as existing block-funding arrangements for some services are allowed to continue.

Market stewardship—that is, efforts to address market deficiencies, such as thin markets, market gaps or other market failures—will be a critical part of the success of the NDIS. With the Commonwealth Government assuming control of the administration of disability services, State and Territory Governments have begun to step out of this space. It will be difficult for the Commonwealth Government to execute market stewardship alone, as stewardship requires an intimate understanding of the market and operating context of different geographic locations and services. This knowledge has been traditionally held by State and Territory Governments. In reality, market stewardship will require both levels of government to work together. The challenge will be getting them to do so.

The true opportunity of service 'personalisation' has not yet been realised

The NDIS envisioned by the Productivity Commissioned was to provide more personalised care—where individuals can directly commission, co-design and co-produce services—for people with disability (Leadbeater 2004). However, personalised care is about more than having an individual budget to spend on supports. In her chapter, Bigby describes the person-centred planning which arose in the 1980s, designed specifically for people with a diverse range of intellectual capabilities. She argues that the person-centred planning models emerging at this time focused on: "...listening in all its guises, to build a shared picture of who the person is, their talents and gifts, their visions for their life, what matters most, what support they need to move toward that future, who will help them". Person-centred planning conducted in this way is relational, unhurried, based on trust and informed by multiple sources.

The nuanced and intentional process of supporting person-centred planning, described by Bigby, is not yet a consistent feature of how the NDIS operates. In their chapter, Carey and Malbon argue that the NDIS is not providing truly personalised care: where service responses are tailored to each individual participant, and choice and control is central. Instead, they argue, the scheme offers individualised budgets with which to purchase services, without the other elements critical to good person-centred planning. While NDIA Planners and Local Area Coordinators are employed to support personalised planning processes, the limitations of their capability to support meaningful planning have been raised by multiple contributors to this book.

This book has highlighted some of the challenges associated with undertaking personalised planning with people who have limited capacity to make independent choices. Bigby identifies the challenges of realising choice and control for people with intellectual disability, where allowing choice can result in poor outcomes. She argues that, without proper support, individualised funding schemes and market models "rely on people with disability being good consumers who can exercise choice and control", which will not deliver good outcomes for everyone. Bigby asserts that, by not taking seriously the communication and decision-making difficulties of adults with intellectual disability, the NDIS has failed to put the person at the centre of their care. In the absence of proper facilitation and advocacy, these participants must rely solely on the support of family and friends throughout the planning process, which works for some, but can be inappropriate or insufficient for others.

Supported decision-making will be a critical part of personalised care, and having choice and control, for some children with disability. In her chapter on the NDIS and children, Cowden identifies the challenges associated with properly supporting a right to choose for those still developing that capacity. She describes how people with disability under the age of 18 are automatically assigned a child representative to act for them throughout their NDIS journey. This reversal of the assumption of competence means that many children with disability who are capable of making their own decisions are denied this opportunity. Cowden argues that, for choice and control to be respected for children with disability, properly resourced and delivered supported decision-making is needed.

The stories of Indigenous people with disability, told in Barney's chapter, also highlight that parts of the system are not yet working to meet the needs of individuals are instead being driven by the needs or service organisations and government workers. For Indigenous people, personalisation means delivering services in a culturally appropriate way, engaging on the right terms and understanding cultural obligations. This can only be achieved by appropriate training, knowledge and the investment of time in developing relationships. Transactional care will only exacerbate inequalities.

One of the issues raised by both critics and supporters of the NDIS is that giving participants greater choice and control won't be helpful unless they feel empowered and informed to make use of these entitlements. It is the power of consumer choice that is supposed to drive the development of a diverse and high-quality disability services market, and more personalised care. Yet not everyone enters this market on an equal footing and some people have more capacity, resources and experience in making informed choices than others. In her chapter, Samantha Jenkinson argues that choice and control works best for people with disability and their families when they feel empowered, and able to make decisions, rather than being in 'crisis mode'. She contends that the self-management of funds works best when people with disability have access to strong peer networks and both formal and informal advocacy.

Exercising choice and control in the context of the NDIS will also be contingent on there being a market of services to choose from. The issue of underdeveloped and thin markets, explored earlier in this chapter, clearly undermines many people with disability's ability to personalise their services. Supporting individual choice and control as part of the NDIS will therefore depend critically on the successful promotion and facilitation of a diverse market of services for participants to choose from.

Difficulties remain with the interface between the NDIS and other service systems

The NDIS has not been designed to function as 'the whole system' for people with disability. It was not intended to be a one stop shop for all of the services that people with disability need in their lives. As discussed throughout this book, people with disability accessing the NDIS will continue to use a range of other 'mainstream' services including health, mental health, education and housing services.

The relationship between the NDIS and other services continues to pose challenges for all levels of government. In his chapter, Thompson reflects on some of the interface challenges between the NDIS and the health system. He describes how an underdeveloped disability services market has left the health system to pick up responsibility for some services that have fallen through the gaps. Williams and Smith describe similar difficulties in the mental health system, and Cowden identifies continued issues in delineating between the disability services children with disability receive from the NDIS versus state education systems. These challenges reflect that the boundaries of what constitutes a 'disability service', compared to a 'mainstream service', are still being worked through. While these difficulties are not wholly the fault of the NDIS (many pre-date its introduction), getting this interface right will be crucial to ensuring people with disability don't miss out on essential services.

Of all the mainstream system interfaces, that between the NDIS and the housing system is especially complex. Access to appropriate and affordable housing is something that can be particularly difficult for people with disability, and the housing system itself—which includes a mix of public, affordable and private housing—is complicated. In his chapter, Ilan Weisel points out that, while people with disability seeking housing must overcome affordability issues, discrimination and shortages of social housing options suited to their needs, NDIS funding for Specialist Disability Accommodation (SDA) is only available to a small number of participants with very high support needs. Wiesel argues that the lack of emphasis on social and affordable housing in the NDIS is intentional, as the Productivity Commission did not want to remove the incentive for state governments to properly fund social and affordable housing. Wiesel asserts, however, that the idea that funding from the NDIS would discourage investment from the state governments is hard to defend, and there are many examples of the NDIS funding that which is arguably a state government responsibility (e.g. taxis and specialist transport). Wiesel concludes that the NDIS should fund housing for all those excluded from mainstream housing systems and should work with governments and the private sector to promote new housing supply and ensure existing housing meets the needs of people with disability.

The intersection between the NDIS and the aged care system is also contentious. Issues here relate to the inequity experienced by people with disability who can only access the aged care system (such as those who acquire their disability after the age of 65 and are therefore not eligible for the NDIS). A number of submitters to the 2018 Joint Standing Committee inquiry highlighted concerns about the ability of the aged care sector to adequately support people over 65 years of age with disabilities. Many considered aged care services unsuitable and inappropriate for people with a significant disability. Another issue raised was that, unlike the NDIS, aged care program funding is capped in that it limits the amount of government funding which people can access (Parliament of Australia 2018, 21–22). While the NDIS provides people with disability access to care based on what is “reasonable and necessary”, those with disability who rely on the aged care system have their government contribution capped at around $50,000 (Commonwealth of Australia 2020). This creates inequity between the aged care and disability systems which will need to be addressed.

The challenging interface between the NDIS and other service systems will hopefully be improved with time, but it is unlikely to ever be completely clear. Australia’s federated political system means that ongoing cooperation between governments will always be a feature of ensuring positive outcomes for people with disability.

A sustainable funding model is essential for the NDIS to continue

Long-term funding for the NDIS is a critical part of ensuring its ongoing position in the Australian policy landscape. Yet, despite lots of political rhetoric about the NDIS being ‘fully funded’ from both sides of politics, the scheme is not in fact ‘fully funded’ according to the correct insurance terminology. If the NDIS were a fully-funded scheme, each participant’s estimated lifetime care costs would be paid into the scheme at the point at which they entered it, and thus, there would always be enough funding in the scheme to pay for the lifetime care costs of all its current participants. This ‘fully-funded’ model was considered unrealistic by the Productivity Commission in its 2011 report, given the up-front expense. Instead, the Commission recommended that the NDIS be set up as a ‘pay as you go’ arrangement where funding would be allocated each year based on the estimated cost of running the scheme in that year. To ensure enough funds were set aside each year, the Commission (2011, 85; 672) recommended that an annual amount to be paid from Commonwealth Government consolidated revenue into the NDIS, based on a prescribed formula written into legislation.

Contrary to these recommended arrangements, the NDIS is currently funded through a mix of Commonwealth Government, and State and

Territory Government funding arrangements outlined in multiple intergovernmental agreements reviewed every few years. There is currently no legislated formula which guarantees the sustained provision of government funding to cover the full cost of the scheme. While the NDIS is currently within its budget, this is largely due to participants not spending the full allocation of services budgeted within their plans. These 'low utilisation' rates have, at various points throughout this book, been seen as the result of the complexity of navigating the scheme, thin markets and inaccurate plans being developed. If these implementation issues are addressed, and plan utilisation rates rise, identifying a clear and enduring funding source for the scheme will become even more important.

The sustainability of the NDIS will be critically connected to the amount of 'reasonable and necessary' supports the scheme funds. In their chapter, Alan Greenfield, Ash Evans and Sarah Wood argue that the single most important financial risk management tool the scheme has is the processes and decisions that go into determining the 'reasonable and necessary' supports each participant receives. As the NDIA cannot control the number of people entering the scheme, financial sustainability must be managed through the amount of supports each participant receives. Greenfield, Evans and Wood argue that, although the scheme is formally 'uncapped' in terms of what it can pay out to participants, the amount of support it can provide is effectively capped by the amount of money Australian taxpayers are willing to contribute to the scheme. The NDIS must therefore continue to provide value for money for taxpayers to ensure their continued willingness to pay for the scheme.

Increasing the number of people with disability in employment will also be fundamental to the financial sustainability of the NDIS. In her chapter, Sue Olney argues that progress on this front—especially for participants—has been disappointing. Despite multiple targeted initiatives intended to build better pathways to work for people with disability in Australia, Olney points out that labour force participation rates for people with disability have remained mostly static over the past two decades. In June 2018, there was an increase in the percentage of 15- to 24-year-old NDIS participants who reported that they were in paid work between entry to the scheme and review approximately one year later, and a one per cent drop in the percentage of participants aged 25 and over in paid work (NDIS 2018, 23). Olney argues that, in the case of people with disability, redressing labour market disadvantage in the wake of COVID-19 calls for new strategies and levers beyond established practice: on the supply, it will involve ensuring people with disability are equipped, motivated and ready to work in a range of occupations. On the demand side, it calls for evidence-informed policy and practice to address systemic, attitudinal and physical environment barriers which continue to affect employment outcomes for people with disability.

A final note on scheme challenges

The six challenges outlined above will not be simple to solve. Addressing them calls for an intimate knowledge of how the disability services sector works, the needs of people with disability and the political realities at play. It is no surprise that the NDIS has been difficult to implement: the scheme is grand, ambitious and, as Jenkinson highlights in her chapter, completely new. There is no blueprint for the NDIS, which identifies the potential pitfalls, challenges and issues which will need to be overcome as part of its implementation. Governments, the NDIA and people with disability and their families are all in unchartered waters, participating in a public policy experiment on a large scale.

Hope and Opportunity

The story of the NDIS is also not just about its challenges. With the scheme now operational in all Australian jurisdictions, the positive changes which it has brought about have also become apparent. To end this book, we reflect on the positive impact which the NDIS has had on the lives of some people with disability and their families, and the opportunities it represents for the future. In particular, we argue that the NDIS has meant:

1. A renewed public focus on the experiences of people with disability;
2. An unprecedented entitlement to services;
3. Good experiences for many participants;
4. New insights on choice and control;
5. National consistency, with some emerging flexibility;
6. Better data to inform decision-making and innovation.

While the NDIS has not achieved everything that was originally envisioned, we think it is important to acknowledge and reflect on these benefits in the hope that they will continue to define and shape how the scheme is implemented in future.

A renewed public focus on the experiences of people with disability

The NDIS has brought the lives and experiences of people with disability to the forefront of political agendas and public consciousness. The advocacy campaign leading up to the introduction of the NDIS: 'Every Australian Counts' was effective at cementing the stories and experiences of people with disability within the minds of the Australian public. So much so that providing disability services through a national scheme, that all Australians financially contribute to, is something that is now broadly accepted by the Australian population and is supported by both major political parties. The hard-fought campaign for the NDIS has brought into focus the lives and experiences of people with disability, their families and carers. This renewed focus means the experiences of people with disability have become more visible to other Australians, so much so that de-funding or reducing the scope of the scheme would be extremely challenging for any political party.

An unprecedented entitlement to services

The NDIS has created a new level of entitlement to services for those who are eligible for the scheme. The significance of this achievement should not be understated. Once a participant has met the eligibility requirements for the scheme, they do not have to continue to provide evidence of, or arguments for, their need for care and support. They can continue to access NDIS supports up to the age of 65, and beyond if they choose. This entitlement, enshrined in legislation, is a powerful change when compared to previous state-based approaches where entitlements varied by jurisdiction and often depended on how a person's disability was acquired. Before the NDIS, in some states, only those who most urgently needed care were able to access services or equipment, while those who would benefit from early intervention support were de-prioritised.

Through its new approach to determining eligibility for supports, the NDIS has provided many people who likely would not have received services with access. As of 30 September 2020, of the 412,543 NDIS participants with an approved plan, 193,977 (47%) were receiving support for the first time (NDIA 2020, 20). The fact that the NDIS has successfully reached so many people who were not previously accessing supports, within less than a decade, is an accomplishment that should be celebrated.

Good experiences for many participants

For its issues, the NDIS does appear to be working well for most people that it touches. As previously outlined in this and other chapters, the 2018 Evaluation of the NDIS trials showed that the NDIS has, overall, improved satisfaction with the quality of supports for people with disability and their family and carers (Mavromaras et al. 2018, 21). Recent NDIA data of NDIS planning processes tells a similar story. In the September 2020 quarter, 86% of NDIS participants surveyed rated the plan review process as either good or very good, 84% rated the access process as either good or very good, 83% rated the pre-planning process as either good or very good and 85% rated the planning process as either good or very good (NDIA 2020, 34). These reported satisfaction rates have improved steadily over the eight quarters reported (NDIA 2020, 35).

Clearly, not everyone has had a good experience of the NDIS. Chapters throughout this book have emphasised the variation in experiences of the scheme, with some groups experiencing significantly worse outcomes than others. There is plenty of room for improvement, especially in how the scheme works for people without the capacity to advocate for themselves, for those with psychosocial or intellectual disability, for Indigenous Australians and for families of children with disability. However, the benefits which the scheme has brought about for others should not be forgotten.

New insights on choice and control

Throughout this book, we have discussed the challenges facing the NDIS in realising the potential of personalisation, and in enabling true choice and control for people with disability. The NDIS provides policymakers with an opportunity to consider what independence, choice and capacity look like within service systems, and how these qualities can best be designed for and facilitated at a system level. Lessons from the implementation of the NDIS show that providing choice and control is complex, and that people's capacity to make informed choices is not always consistent. The scheme experience so far also illustrates some common enablers of choice and control, including the prevention of thin markets, training of skilled and informed staff, establishment of responsive systems and the provision of supported decision-making for some.

If the NDIS continues to explore and improve upon the way in which it provides choice and control to participants—which has certainly been a focus of key changes to the scheme to date, such as the introduction of the new NDIS pathway in 2017—its implementation will have important implications for other public policy areas where governments have struggled to meaningfully support choice and control. This will be especially important for systems where service users have traditionally been seen as lacking the capacity to make decisions for themselves.

National consistency, with some emerging flexibility

One of the original goals of NDIS was to achieve a nationally consistent approach to the provision of disability services across Australia. This has in many ways been achieved, with the *National Disability Insurance Scheme Act 2013* (the Act) and the intergovernmental agreements for full scheme describing an NDIS that is delivered by a single agency—the NDIA—and is broadly consistent across Australia,

However, as has become apparent through early implementation experiences, allowing flexibility in the way the NDIS is operationalised can be a good thing. The experience in the Barkley trial site, where choice and control was initially 'an almost theoretical concept' due to the absence of a viable disability support market, illustrates the need for flexible approaches in regional and remote areas (Mavromaras et al. 2018, xxiii). Furthermore, as Bigby points to in her chapter, the NDIS has begun to tailor operations more carefully to specific groups of people with disability. This includes creating separate access pathways for some cohorts, recognising the need for specialist knowledge about impairment types, establishing impairment specific advisory or reference groups, the appointment of senior strategic advisers for autism and psychosocial disability, and, through the Information, Linkages and Capacity Building (ILC) program, funding for impairment specific information projects and self-advocacy groups.

There is an opportunity to build even more flexibility into the way the NDIS operates, including by allowing devolved decision-making where it makes sense to do so. This could include empowering and building the capacity of local NDIA offices to make decisions about some operational matters and Local Area Coordinators playing a greater role in building community infrastructure and mainstream capacity (as they were originally intended to do). This flexibility could (provided costs are appropriately benchmarked) allow the NDIS to stay responsive to differences in local markets and participant cohorts without jeopardising the financial sustainability of the scheme.

Better data to inform decision-making and innovation

In their chapter, Greenfield, Evans and Wood discuss how the NDIS has created an unprecedented joined-up data set about people with disability, their families and carers. When initial projections about NDIS participant numbers were made, there was no longitudinal database including information on the functional support needs, health conditions and use of supports by people with disability. Now, the Scheme Actuary is able to use data collected to build a picture of the needs, successes and challenges for people living with disability, their families and carers and those who work within the sector. Over time, this longitudinal dataset will continue to build as the number of NDIS participants grows, enabling an even more detailed picture of the support needs of people with disability, the services provided in response to those needs and the social and economic outcomes enabled by those services (Productivity Commission 2017, 473).

The dataset created by the NDIS has long been recognised as an enormous opportunity for policymakers within and outside of the scheme. As Greenfield, Evans and Wood point out, it allows analysis to be carried out for groups of participants at a very granular level, including by region and remoteness, disability type, functional needs, age, gender, and CALD and Indigenous status. This paves the way for data-driven decision-making about key aspects of the scheme and provides a powerful demonstration of the value of such datasets for other areas of public policy.

There are good stories about how the NDIS is driving innovations, and the new dataset created by the scheme allows the effectiveness of new approaches to be assessed. Examples of innovations in service delivery include projects targeting those who were receiving relatively little support prior to the introduction of the scheme and early intervention support for young children with autism and developmental delay.

The newness of the NDIS, coupled with the datasets it enables, creates an opportunity to engage in continual innovation and improvement. The national nature of the scheme also forces lessons to be shared across jurisdictions in a more open and transparent way.

Conclusion

In this book, we have sought to provide our readers with an understanding what the NDIS is, where it has come from and where it is headed. We have considered how people with disability have been treated historically, and traced the various influences that have shaped the scheme design, including insurance and personalised care models. We have considered some of the key policy and legislative instruments which underpin the NDIS, including the Productivity Commission's 2011 Disability Care and Support report, the *National Disability Insurance Scheme Act 2013* and the various intergovernmental agreements negotiated for the NDIS trial, transition and full scheme operations. Chapter authors have explained how the NDIS intersects with various groups and sectors, and participants in the scheme and their families and carers have told of their individual triumphs and frustrations with the scheme. We don't pretend to have captured everything there is to know about the NDIS. What we have aimed to provide, with the help of our contributors, is a foundational understanding of the scheme.

The NDIS continues to grow and change. The driving force behind this continual evolution is people with disability. As Jenkinson states in her chapter: "from the very beginning of campaigning for an NDIS, people with disability have been fighting to be the voice that is driving the system. Now that we are into full scheme, people with disability are still fighting to be the voice that is driving the system". It remains to be seen whether the NDIS will deliver consistently better outcomes for people with disability over the long term. We believe that there is hope it will do so.

References

Australian Bureau of Statistics. 2016. 3238.0.55.001—Estimates of Aboriginal and Torres Strait Islander Australians. https://www.abs.gov.au/ausstats/abs@.nsf/mf/3238.0.55.001.

Commonwealth of Australia. 2020. Home Care Package Costs and Fees. My Aged Care website. https://www.myagedcare.gov.au/home-care-package-costs-and-fees.

Fletcher, Paul, and Sarah Henderson. 2018. Government Announced Improved NDIS Mental Health Support. NDIA. https://www.ndis.gov.au/news/400-government-announces-improved-ndis-mental-health-support.

Leadbeater, Charles. 2004. *Personalisation Through Participation: A New Script for Public Services*. London: Demos.

Mavromaras, Kostas, Megan Moskos, Stéphane Mahuteau, and Linda Isherwood. 2018. Evaluation of the NDIS: Final Report, National Institute of Labour Studies. National Institute of Labour Studies Flinders University. https://www.dss.gov.au/sites/default/files/documents/04_2018/ndis_evaluation_consolidated_report_april_2018.pdf.

NDIS. 2018. Employment Outcomes 30 June 2018 NDIS Participants, Their Families and Carers. NDIA.

NDIA. 2020. NDIS Quarterly Report to Disability Ministers, 30 September. NDIA. https://www.ndis.gov.au/about-us/publications/quarterly-reports.

NT Department of Treasury and Finance. 2016. Population. Northern Territory Economy. https://nteconomy.nt.gov.au/population.

NT Government. 2017. NT Government Submission to the Productivity Commission Review—Position Paper NDIS. https://www.pc.gov.au/__data/assets/pdf_file/0007/220597/subpp0359-ndis-costs.pdf.

Parliament of Australia. Joint Standing Committee on the NDIS. 2018. Transition Arrangements for the NDIS. https://www.aph.gov.au/Parliamentary_Business/Committees/Joint/National_Disability_Insurance_Scheme/Transition/Report.

Parliament of Australia. Joint Standing Committee on the NDIS. 2019. Progress Report 2019: General Issues Around the Implementation and Performance of the NDIS. https://www.aph.gov.au/Parliamentary_Business/Committees/Joint/National_Disability_Insurance_Scheme/General_NDIS/Report.

Productivity Commission. 2011. Disability Care and Support. https://www.pc.gov.au/inquiries/completed/disability-support/report.

Productivity Commission. 2017. National Disability Insurance Scheme (NDIS) Costs. https://www.pc.gov.au/inquiries/completed/ndis-costs#report.

Index

M. Cowden and C. McCullagh (eds.), *The National Disability Insurance Scheme*, https://doi.org/10.1007/978-981-16-2244-1

D

E

F

G

Q

R

W

Y

The manufacturer's authorised representative in the EU is Springer Nature Customer Service Centre GmbH, Europaplatz 3, 69115 Heidelberg, Germany. If you have any concerns regarding our products, please contact ProductSafety@springernature.com

Printed and bound by CPI Group (UK) Ltd, Croydon, CR0 4YY

30/09/2026

02225326-0020